HEAVY-WEIGHT

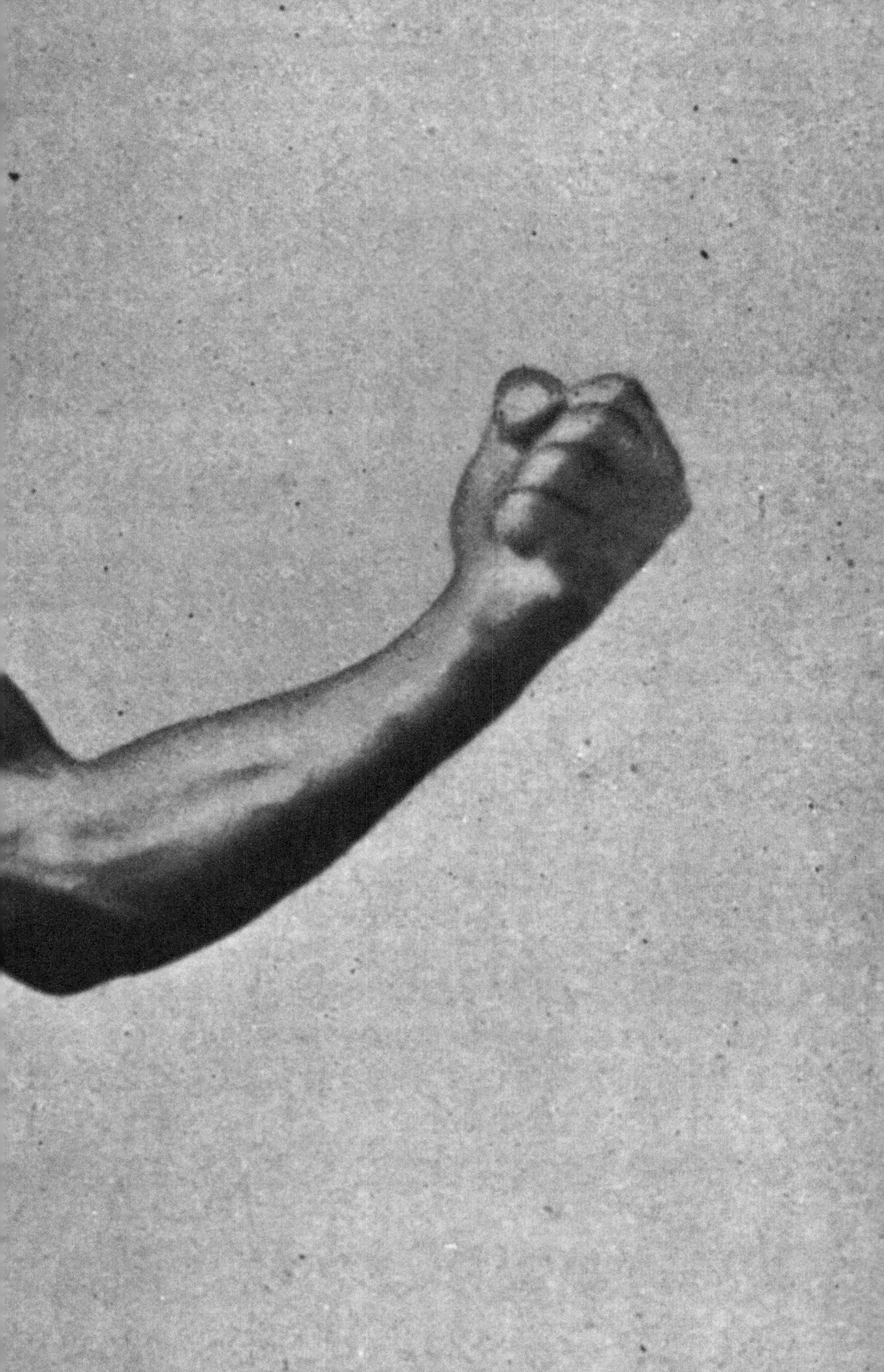

HEAVY-WEIGHT

BLACK BOXERS AND THE
FIGHT FOR REPRESENTATION

Jordana Moore Saggese

Duke University Press   *Durham and London*   2024

© 2024 DUKE UNIVERSITY PRESS. All rights reserved.
Printed in the United States of America on acid-free paper ∞
Project Editor: Ihsan Taylor
Designed by Courtney Leigh Richardson
Typeset in Knockout and Garamond Premier Pro by
Copperline Book Services

Library of Congress Cataloging-in-Publication Data
Names: Saggese, Jordana Moore, [date] author.
Title: Heavyweight : Black boxers and the fight for
representation / Jordana Moore Saggese.
Description: Durham : Duke University Press, 2024. |
Includes bibliographical references and index.
Identifiers: LCCN 2023040702 (print)
LCCN 2023040703 (ebook)
ISBN 9781478030638 (paperback)
ISBN 9781478026402 (hardcover)
ISBN 9781478059646 (ebook)
Subjects: LCSH: African American men in art. | African
American boxers. | Boxing in art. | Racism in art. | Masculinity
in art. | Racism in sports—United States. | Masculinity in
sports—United States. | BISAC: ART / History / Contemporary
(1945–) | SPORTS & RECREATION / Boxing
Classification: LCC NX652.A37 S24 2024 (print) | LCC NX652.A37
(ebook) | DDC 796.83089/96073—dc23/eng/20240505
LC record available at https://lccn.loc.gov/2023040702
LC ebook record available at https://lccn.loc.gov/2023040703

Cover art: "Peter Jackson: Champion of Australia," 1894. Albumen
print. From Billy Edwards, *Portrait Gallery of Pugilists of America and
Their Contemporaries* (Philadelphia: Pugilistic Publishing Co., 1894).

FOR

L,

R,

AND

V

Contents

I came to this book project from a very personal place. In the spring and summer of 2012, I followed the coverage of two intersecting incidents of racial violence—one in Europe and the other in the United States. The first was the murder of seventeen-year-old Trayvon Martin by George Zimmerman in Sanford, Florida. Martin, a Black boy wearing a black hooded sweatshirt, was followed by Zimmerman on the night of February 26 as he walked from a nearby convenience store to the Twin Lakes townhome community, where the boy's father was living at the time. On a phone call to the Sanford Police dispatch, Zimmerman was instructed to stay in his vehicle and avoid approaching the boy. Instead, Zimmerman (a former neighborhood watch captain) got into a violent encounter with Martin that ended with a fatal gunshot. Trayvon died just seventy yards from the rear door of the townhouse where he was staying.

What struck me, and many others, about this incident was the immediate perceived threat Zimmerman described upon encountering the boy. In police reports Zimmerman identified Martin as "a real suspicious guy." Was he "suspicious" because he was a Black kid in a predominantly white neighborhood? Because he was wearing a hoodie? Because he was, at more than a decade younger, four inches taller than Zimmerman? In fact, although Martin's autopsy showed that the boy was five feet eleven and weighed 158 pounds at the time of his death, a popular rumor spread on social media that summer alleging that the media-circulated image of Trayvon was an outdated image. These critics claimed that Martin was six feet two and had a muscular build of 175 pounds.[1] When Zimmerman was acquitted of second-degree murder the next year, I began to wonder about the perceived physical threat of an unarmed Black boy.

Just a few months after Martin's murder I found myself engulfed by the press coverage surrounding the 2012 UEFA European Football Championship, which began in early June and coincided with my family's annual trip to Italy. While not a regular spectator of this sport (or of any sport, for that matter) I became fascinated by the presence of a Black player on the Italian team, Mario Balotelli. Coming into the competition, Balotelli had already been the subject of racial slurs and abuse. In April 2009, fans of the Juventus team in Italy famously sang "There are no Black Italians" during a match against Inter Milan, Balotelli's team at the time. In later matches, fans from opposing teams were known to throw bananas onto the pitch when Balotelli played. In media coverage leading up to the 2012 Euros, Balotelli warned: "I will not accept racism at all. It's unacceptable. If someone throws a banana at me in the street, I will go to jail, because I will kill them."[2] Nevertheless, a few weeks later, an image began to circulate of a match steward holding a banana, which was thrown onto the pitch while Balotelli played for Italy in a June 14 match against Croatia. The photographer who captured the shot reported hearing monkey noises directed at Balotelli from the stands.

While not explicitly related to one another, these acts nevertheless coalesced in my mind that summer for their bold assertions of Black subjection.[3] Somehow all this was happening—in the United States and in Europe—in public view; we were all experiencing anti-Blackness in real time. I began to ask myself then, and I still ask myself now, how does this happen? How do Black men become dehumanized, positioned as threats? How is it that Black men are so hyper-visible in popular culture, yet remain disempowered in political culture? And where does this genealogy begin?

Examples of the Black athlete (and of the Black athlete's body in particular) as a problem for mainstream Americans have proliferated in the twenty-first century. Take, for example, the April 2008 cover of *Vogue* magazine, which featured Brazilian model Gisele Bündchen alongside the twenty-one-year-old NBA player LeBron James for an issue on the "best bodies."[4] Dressed in a green, shimmering, strapless gown, Bündchen appears on the right of the composition in a running pose. She lunges forward on her right leg while her opposite arm bends at her side; an industrial fan blows her hair back, visually emphasizing her efforts to move toward the viewer (and presumably escape James). And as we look closer, we see that Bündchen, although giggling for the camera, is being held back. The basketball forward's left hand holds the model at the waist and constricts her movement.

In contrast to the supposedly lighthearted appearance—in both costume and pose—of his companion, James appears in dark clothing, squatting downward, and with a grimace. The sections of his body that are revealed to us outside his black athletic shorts and tank top appear contracted and taut, like James's face, which has opened widely to reveal what seems to be a scream. It took me only a moment to recognize that this image—printed on the cover of a magazine with 1.1 million monthly readers and shot by the renowned photographer Annie Leibovitz—intentionally positions James as an oversexualized brute, with Bündchen as the damsel in distress.[5] The blogger Rogers Cadenhead discovered a potential source for Leibovitz's composition—a 1917 World War I recruitment poster entitled "Destroy This Mad Brute," which translated the threat of a German invasion into a racist and sexually charged scene. Perhaps intended as a clever take on James's nickname (i.e., King James as King Kong) and despite the forced smile that may have been intended to camouflage Liebowitz's leveraging of racist history, the image nevertheless rehearses a catalog of stereotypes assigned to Black men. Here we see James as the savage, oversexualized Black brute, perfectly poised as a threat to the white woman in his grasp.

Also consider the images of kneeling Black football players that dominated the global press in the fall of 2016, during the run-up to the US presidential election. Initially started by San Francisco 49ers quarterback Colin Kaepernick, kneeling during the national anthem was a protest against the murders of unarmed Black men by police. This was just a few months after the murder of thirty-two-year-old Philando Castile, who was shot seven times during a traffic stop in a suburb of Saint Paul, Minnesota, on July 6, 2016. Castile's death, which was recorded and livestreamed on Facebook by his girlfriend in the passenger seat, ignited a fresh wave of protest. Kaepernick's version began on August 26, when he refused to stand up from his seat on the player's bench for the anthem preceding a home game against the Green Bay Packers. After the game, he explained his decision in an exclusive interview with NFL media: "I am not going to stand up to show pride in a flag for a country that oppresses Black people and people of color. . . . To me, this is bigger than football and it would be selfish on my part to look the other way. There are bodies in the street and people [are] getting paid leave and getting away with murder."[6] The backlash, however, was immediate. Within forty-eight hours, on September 3, Kaepernick was replaced as a starting quarterback; national attention to the controversy increased when President Obama defended Kaepernick's actions as a "constitutional right" during a press conference for the G20 summit in China on September 5. The next day the NFL commissioner, Roger Goodell, issued his own statement, which intimated Kaepernick's actions as unpatriotic.

On September 8, the first Sunday of the 2016 NFL season, it became clear that the predominantly Black players were on Kaepernick's side. Players for the Indiana Colts wore warm-up shirts that read "Black Lives Matter," and the New England Patriots' new quarterback Cam Newton wore cleats that read "7 shots" (a reference to Castile) and "No Justice, No Peace." Players on other teams, such as the Detroit Lions, the Miami Dolphins and even the 49ers, locked arms with one another along the sideline during the anthem—a gesture most frequently used by protestors as a mode of protection (i.e., a way to defend against the removal of a single individual) and as a visualization of solidarity.[7] The protests endured throughout the first years of Donald J. Trump's presidency and continued even after Kaepernick left the 49ers. At a rally in Alabama in 2017 Trump told the crowd that NFL owners should eject kneeling players from the game: "Wouldn't you love to see one of these NFL owners, when somebody disrespects our flag, to say, 'Get that son of a bitch off the field right now. Out! He's fired. He's fired!'"[8]

From my vantage point as an art historian, I was compelled by the number of images that came out of this debate. Each week there were dozens upon dozens of photographs of Black men kneeling on the sidelines every Sunday, deploying whatever cultural capital they had as successful athletes in the most lucrative professional sporting league in the United States. And then there was the image of Kaepernick on the cover of *Time* magazine on October 3, 2016, under the headline "The Perilous Fight." Situated on a black ground—that is, removed completely from the context of an NFL game—he appears alone. We notice that even the bold red letters of the masthead have been transformed into a medium gray. Kaepernick, in his full 49ers uniform, kneels so that his right knee touches the ground at the center of a glowing circle created by a single light source projected downward onto the figure, suggesting an ethereal glow. Kaepernick's face is turned slightly upward as his eyes rest on something outside the frame, as if caught in a moment of quiet contemplation. Through the devices of composition, pose, gesture, and light, Kaepernick is transformed here into a martyr.

Just over a year after this saintly appearance—and following several unsuccessful attempts to secure a contract with an NFL team for the 2017 season— Kaepernick appeared once again on the cover of a mainstream magazine. However, the November 2017 issue of *GQ*, a men's magazine that advertises itself as a guide to men's fashion, fitness, and health, shows a very different Colin Kaepernick. This figure appears in a closely cropped frame and he gazes directly into the lens of the camera. He has substituted an NFL uniform for an all-black ensemble of turtleneck and leather blazer; a gold pendant hangs from his neck. And instead of the neat cornrows that we saw a year earlier, Kaepernick has styled his hair as a picked-out Afro that radiates outward and takes up the entire top-third of the composition. No longer the martyr, this version of Kaepernick explicitly relies on the visual iconography of the Black Power movement to assert his alignment with their cause. He appeared in the interior of the magazine with a single fist raised above his head.

Contemporary Black athletes undoubtedly occupy a dual function within white mainstream media—as a body that is both criminalized and commodified simultaneously.[9] This is territory well-tread by contemporary sociologists and historians, who have taken up the relationship between sports and cultural formation in the last three decades. And in many ways, this book is built on the foundation of that scholarship. But what I am most interested in is the ways these bodies and their images function within the white cultural imagination and rehearse a genealogy of Blackness rooted in violence, abjection, and even desire.

This book is organized around the constitutive power of images, as theorized by Stuart Hall in the early 1990s. In his lecture "Representation and the Media" from 1997 Hall clarifies the difference between a common understanding of representation (i.e., as representing a meaning that is somehow already there) and his own understanding of representation as "enter[ing] into the constitution of the object that we are talking about. It is part of the object itself; it is constitutive of it. It is one of its conditions of existence, and therefore representation is not outside the event, not after the event, but within the event itself."[10] These images function not only as art objects but also as cultural artifacts. They illustrate how Black bodies are viewed by white audiences (regardless of gender or sexual orientation), connecting back even to Reconstruction-era expressions of white, mainstream anxieties and fantasies about the Black body.

Heavyweight is about the place of athletes within a visual history of Blackness with an equal investment in the production and the reception of these images. It explores representations of Black boxers and considers the ways in which these images have transformed our understanding of Black masculinity. I argue that we can find lurking in these images the blueprint for our conceptions of the Black male body as existing somewhere between fear and fantasy, simultaneously an object of desire and an instrument of brutal violence. This historical tension between the violent and the erotic dimensions of the boxer lays bare our societal ambivalence toward Blackness, and the increasingly ambiguous role of

Black men in American culture. There is a politics to this work, to exploring the past to navigate our present. *Heavyweight* looks back in order to move forward.

And finally, I would like to note that some of the images and ideas discussed in the pages that follow are racist and problematic. They have been included here because we must better understand the past in order to build a more inclusive future.

Acknowledgments

It has been a unique privilege to carry out the research that has culminated in this book, but I would not have been able to do so without the generous support of many individuals and institutions. And so, let me use this opportunity to express my gratitude. First, to the Center for Advanced Study in the Visual Arts at the National Gallery of Art, Washington, DC, which provided me an opportunity to think deeply about the nineteenth century in a way that transformed the trajectory of this book. I benefited greatly from the many informal and formal conversations with my colleagues there, from the ingenuity of the librarians, and from the patience of the guard staff who allowed me to sit on the first floor with George Bellows's painting *Both Members of This Club* for many, many hours. Thank you also to the Department of Art History and Archaeology at the University of Maryland, and specifically to department chairs Meredith Gill and Steven Mansbach, as well as the graduate students in my fall 2019 graduate seminar "The Athletic Turn," who rigorously and enthusiastically explored the world of sports representation with me. The University of Maryland's Independent Scholarship, Research, and Creativity Award allowed me to take time off from teaching to finish this manuscript. And it has been a joy to work with the students Talia Desai, Claire Rasmussen, JooHee Kim, and Nan Zhong, all of whom performed research on my behalf and humored my often-ambiguous requests for information.

In the decade or so that I have been invested in this topic I have had the opportunity to present portions of my research in several venues, including conferences of the College Art Association and the American Studies Association, and lectures at Vanderbilt University, the University of California, Santa Barbara, the University of Pittsburgh, and New York University. I am grateful to the audiences in each of these places, who provided generous commentary and feedback throughout the development of the book. Anyone who knows me will also know that I am forever indebted to the writers who have shared collaborative and critical space with me (in person and virtually) for the last fifteen years. Thank you to my East Bay Writers Group—Kim Anno, Paula Birnbaum, Irene Cheng, Tirza Latimer, Rachel Schreiber, Jenny Shaw—for their patience with me and their guidance as this project found its footing in its earliest days. And thank you to Valerie Heffernan and Shatha Almuwatha for their constant accountability. Nicole Archer, Nijah Cunningham, and Jessica Ingram offered support throughout a most challenging time (not only for writing but also for just living in general) and demonstrated a considerably high tolerance of my cheesy gifs. I am also grateful to Ken Wissoker, whose last-minute meeting with me in Chicago in February 2020 allowed the manuscript to come into closer view.

I finally sat down to start this manuscript—after many years of scattered research—in March 2020 just days before a global lockdown. With three kids at home, I did not know if I was going to make it. And I surely would not have without the support of my husband, Giampaolo, as well as the understanding of my children—especially the oldest two. I hope that they will all one day recognize the gift that they have given me in allowing me the time and space to pursue my own projects while also being their mother.

The 1965 photograph of boxer Muhammad Ali (1942–2016) standing victorious in the center of the ring after securing (for the second time) the world heavyweight title remains one of the most recognizable images of the twentieth century (fig. I.1).[1] Ali appears in the center of the frame, standing upright inside the ropes while his opponent Sonny Liston (1932?–70) lays prone on the canvas after a surprise knockout in the first round. Positioned as the aggressor, Ali glares directly downward at Liston, teeth gnashed. Ali's right arm is bent, acting as a frame for the developed musculature of the arm and torso—the physical origin of the punch that has created this dramatic scene. The image, captured ringside by Associated Press photographer John Rooney, appeared on dozens of sports pages across the United States the next morning and received first prize for a single sports photograph in the World Press Photo contest of 1965.[2] It was also the lead image for Ali's obituary, which appeared upon his death in June 2016. When I type "Muhammad Ali" into my browser's search bar, it is the second image that appears on the screen. This photograph is what many of us see, in our mind's eye, when we think of Muhammad Ali.

To understand the weight of this image within the story of Ali, within the history of boxing, or even within US culture, we might turn to the word "iconic." An "iconic" image exists outside history; it is a type of representation that makes us forget we are looking at an image at all.[3] Art historians may be

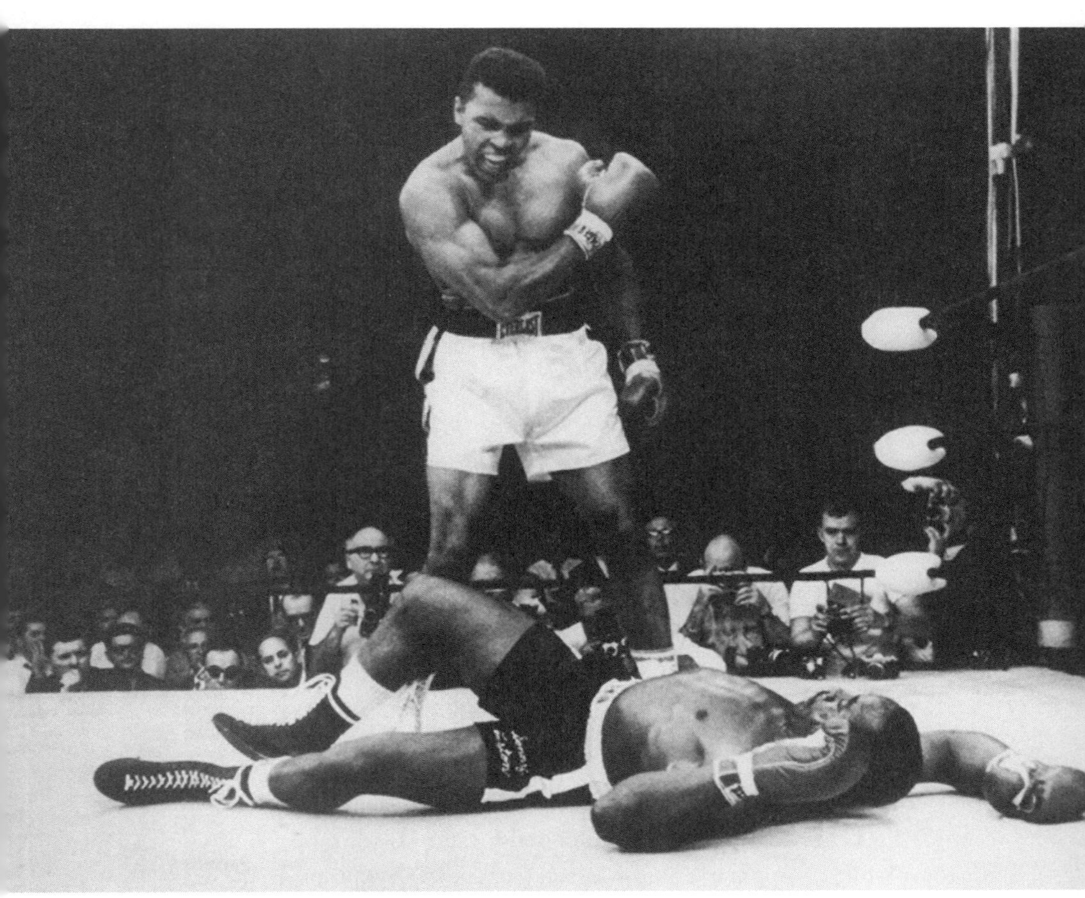

I.1

—

"Muhammad Ali Stands over Fallen Challenger Sonny Liston," 1965.
Photograph by John Rooney, 13.5 × 18 inches. David C. Driskell Center,
University of Maryland, College Park. Gift of Sandra and Lloyd Baccus.

tempted to overlook such images, passively accepting them as true and perhaps even as representative of a set of universal values. Such images are victim to the enduring Hegelian unconscious within the discipline. That is, on the one hand a work of art embodies the specific values of the culture or society that produced it, but on the other hand the discipline puts more emphasis on those images that exceed their specific time and place or that express (in Hegel's term) an "absolute idea." Such impulses force us to focus on the classical composition of Rooney's photograph, which echoes in part the stage-like space and clear narratives of the neoclassical style.[4] We immediately fixate on the dramatic action of the subject, the binary of the victor and the vanquished—all at the expense of historical specificity.

On its face, this image communicates victory. We see an illustration of an American hero. This is the narrative of Ali that we have brought into our present: Ali as a champion, as the "titan of the twentieth century," as the proud recipient of a Presidential Medal of Freedom in 2005. Memorialized in his obituary for the *New York Times*, Ali "became something of a secular saint, a legend in soft focus. He was respected for having sacrificed more than three years of his boxing prime and untold millions of dollars for his antiwar principles after being banished from the ring; he was extolled for his un-self-conscious gallantry in the face of incurable illness, and he was beloved for his accommodating sweetness in public."[5] And while we may at first accept this image as nothing more than a portrait of a great boxer in the prime of his career, what might happen if we reoriented ourselves to a historical reading of this image? What if we were to dislodge it from its status as icon and consider instead its place within a wider visual and cultural history—of boxing and of Blackness? What if we used Rooney's photograph as an opportunity to think through the historical legacies of Black heavyweight boxers and their role in shaping a visual economy of Black masculinity?

Heavyweight questions the gap between popular culture and critical culture, looking at the sport of boxing specifically as a performance of cultural values. I am working from the example of contemporary sports scholars, who have argued quite convincingly that the study of sports is intrinsic to any account of the American past.[6] The intersections of sports with issues of labor, capitalism, and urban studies underscore its importance as a cultural practice. Its role in constructing identities based on gender, sexuality, ethnicity, and nationality highlight the political dimension of something we might at first think of as "just a game." And for the Black athlete specifically, sports hold even more critical significance. In a 2011 special issue of the *Journal of African American History*, Scott Brooks and Dexter Blackman acknowledged "African Americans' use of sports as a mechanism for demonstrating their humanity, equality, or superiority to whites on the playing fields; and as a source of racial pride and a means to upward social mobility."[7] However, it would be another ten years before the specific subfield of African American sports history would be acknowledged.[8] This was possible, in part, due to the emergence of a class of sports historians invested in a methodology informed by Black studies. These historians acknowledge the ways that African American sports connect to larger conversations in African American history. In 2021, Amira Rose Davis wrote that this "new direction" in sports history—exemplified by the work of Amy Bass, Adrian Burgos Jr., Theresa Runstedtler, Maureen Smith, Louis Moore, Derrick E. White, and Davis herself—"asks how sport and the critical scholarship on it change our understandings of African American sports history."[9] These scholars have all shown that the study of sports and its athletes provides a unique way into thinking about Blackness writ large. *Heavyweight* attempts to brings these frameworks into the visual realm.[10] More specifically, I am interested in the ways that images of athletes (boxers, in particular) have been a means to produce difference.[11]

While often overlooked as topics of study within art history, or outright dismissed on account of their connections to popular culture, these athletes and their representations produce specific knowledges about Black male subjectivity. I read images like that of Ali from 1965 not as "iconic" but as historical, and embedded within a web of political and social debates about race and masculinity that begin in the Reconstruction period. I am writing a visual history of boxing and of Blackness because we cannot separate one from the other; both involve a fight for recognition. *Heavyweight* argues for the history of sports as a critical part of the visual history of Black men in the United States. The representations studied in this book (and to some extent the sport of boxing itself) play a critical role within an ecology of white violence.

Looking again at this 1965 representation of Muhammad Ali from the perspective of sports history, for example, introduces a layer of complexity that we do not immediately see in the photograph. Despite the construction of the image as a moment of athletic triumph, the events surrounding it are much more ambivalent. Controversy surrounded this particular fight, even before the opening bell. Ali entered this challenge for the heavyweight title amid a public fall from grace. As a member of the Nation of Islam, an organization viewed both by the federal government and the white public as a hate group, Ali had recently become a more vocal supporter of racial segregation. His opponent Sonny Liston was in a similarly precarious position, having been recently charged and arrested for speeding, reckless driving, and carrying a concealed weapon.[12] In fact, just before this match, the WBA stripped Ali of his title and dropped him from its rankings, along with Liston.

But just a few years before this photograph Ali had been an American hero, an ideal athlete embraced equally by both white and Black fans. This had been the case for most of Ali's professional career, starting in 1960 when the eighteen-year-old from Louisville, Kentucky, captured the attention of the world through his unconventional approach to the sport and a tendency to speak almost exclusively in verse. Ali's fighting style was more rhythmic than other boxers and included an unparalleled footwork that allowed him to evade other fighters in the ring. His superior head movement made it difficult for opponents to connect their punches. Ali coined the term "dancing jab" to describe the way he bounced (often on tiptoes) around the ring while delivering unexpected, flicking jabs to the head that produced a whiplash effect. Still a teenager, Ali traveled to Rome to represent the United States in the 1960 Olympics.[13]

While there, he functioned as a surrogate for democracy. When asked by a Soviet reporter after the award ceremony to express his feelings about winning gold for a country that would not allow him to eat at a lunch counter in his hometown, Ali promptly responded: "To me, the USA is still the best country in the world, counting yours."[14] Proclaiming him a national hero, dozens of newspapers printed this incendiary statement, which the boxer would later deny. Ali soaked it up, announcing in his trademark poetic style:

To make America the greatest is my goal
So I beat the Russian and I beat the Pole
And for the USA won the medal of Gold.[15]

After returning from Rome, Ali made the decision to turn professional, and an increasingly exuberant and braggadocious presence in the media soon followed.[16] He openly goaded and mocked opponents, and in media appearances he continuously bragged equally about his fighting skills and his physical beauty. "It's hard to be humble," he purportedly said, "when you're as great as I am."[17] Such proclamations made many audiences uncomfortable; Black athletes were expected to quietly succeed and openly conform to the expectations of white audiences.

Ali was in every way the opposite of his predecessor Joe Louis (1914–81)—the Black heavyweight champion who held the title from 1937 to 1949. Working in the shadow of Jack Johnson, whose boxing career (discussed further in chapter 4) ended subsumed by controversy and even a criminal conviction, Louis's managers were quick to set down some ground rules for the fighter. According to his biographer, Randy Roberts, "Louis was instructed never to humiliate an opponent, gloat over a victory, or visit a nightclub alone." Because Johnson had been shunned for his public relationships with white women, "Louis was forbidden from ever having his photograph taken alone with a white female." He also almost never smiled in photographs, preferring a deadpan expression—again to contrast with Johnson's "golden smile." According to Roberts: "Everything Louis did, every image he projected, carried the same message: '*I am not Jack Johnson.*' No verbal boasts, no flashy smiles, no public sexual exploits—just machinelike fighting and Bible-reading innocence."[18] The public image of Louis, known as "the Black Clark Gable," was consciously and continuously shaped in response to white expectations. Ali by contrast seemed boastful, arrogant, and eager to insert himself into American politics and the Civil Rights movement. His open challenge to expectations of the white public engendered public disapproval, and in his early professional career crowds frequently booed when he came into the arena.

The rhetorical structure of boxing requires that the men competing inside the ring be ideologically positioned as opposites—one dominant, one submissive, and both competing for total control. In the early twentieth century, when title fights included both Black and white opponents, the antagonism was explicitly racist. The Black heavyweight Jack Johnson was billed in his 1910 match against James J. Jeffries (1875–1953) as "the Black Peril," with Jeffries as the "Great White Hope." But as the twentieth century progressed and more and more title fights occurred between two Black fighters, the racial antagonism at the heart of boxing persisted in a new form.[19] And the unfixed nature of Black male subjectivity was further exposed. For the matches between Ali and Liston, for example, the two men oscillated between the roles of "hero" and "villain."

In the lead-up to Ali's first heavyweight title fight against Liston, who was at the time the reigning champion, in February 1964, few believed that the young fighter from Kentucky stood a chance. Two days before the fight, the sportswriter Arthur Daley wrote under the headline "Boy on a Man's Errand" that "the loudmouth from Louisville is likely to have a lot of vainglorious boasts jammed down his throat by a ham-like fist belonging to Sonny Liston."[20] Liston, thirty-one years old at the time, was an ex-convict with rumored associations with the New York mafia; his reputation as a "bad Negro" was already well worn. Many feared Liston's long reach and formidable power; in the previous two title fights, Liston famously knocked out his opponent, Floyd Patterson, in the very first round. But his reputation nevertheless eclipsed his athletic talents, and the media's attention emphasized associations with Black stereotypes. Journalists often described him as a "gorilla" or "jungle beast." Even after winning the heavyweight title in 1962, the harassment continued. One writer for the *Philadelphia Daily*

News wrote: "A celebration for Philadelphia's first heavyweight champ is now in order... Emily Post would probably recommend a ticker-tape parade. For confetti we can use torn-up arrest warrants."[21] Liston did in fact have multiple runins with the police, even as a professional boxer. In 1961 he was arrested by a patrolman for loitering, despite Liston's claims that he had merely been signing autographs and chatting with fans. Throughout his professional career and afterward, Liston was haunted by the specter of stereotyping, where Black men are framed as intrinsically aggressive brutes—all brawn and no brains.

When Ali emerged victorious in that 1964 match, defeating Liston in the seventh round to the surprise and adulation of a roaring crowd, he became the David to Liston's Goliath, suddenly and enthusiastically embraced by the media.[22] But fewer than forty-eight hours passed before Ali's celebrity became clouded by politics. The morning after his ceremonious defeat of Liston in Miami, he confirmed his membership in the Nation of Islam at a press conference after a reporter abruptly asked if he was a "card-carrying member of the Black Muslims"—a phrasing that carried with it echoes of McCarthyism.[23] In fact, a majority of the white American public misinterpreted Ali's public alignment with the Nation of Islam as communist sympathy. Two weeks later, the new champion announced he had taken the name Muhammad Ali, granted to him by Elijah Muhammad. And eight months later, when Ali fought Floyd Patterson (1935–2006) right before Thanksgiving for the WBC world heavyweight title, he was suddenly repositioned as the renegade with Patterson as the more respectable figure.

The match between Ali and Patterson was well publicized, alongside several carefully orchestrated media events leading up to the fight. For example, after Ali nicknamed Patterson "the Rabbit" (playing up the idea that the challenger was terrified of taking on the heavyweight champion), he showed up at one of Patterson's training sessions with a bag of carrots. Ali also reportedly called Patterson an "Uncle Tom" for refusing to call him "Muhammad Ali."[24] The media encouraged their (mostly theatrical) rivalry with several carefully orchestrated events leading up to the fight. The fight, according to the art historian Kobena Mercer, was "an anchoring point for opposing positions in racial discourse."[25] Ali's position was becoming untenable; his position as a Black sports hero was increasingly shaky, not only caught in the middle of Black-white relations but in the middle of Black-Black relations as well. At this moment, we see how the spectacle of boxing exists inseparable from its history. The media continuously deployed Ali's image to construct and to contend with the political power of the Black body.

Ali's controversial affiliation with the Nation of Islam produced a rupture in the entanglements of racial discourse, sports, and politics. For the white audiences that had embraced him, Ali's new affiliations led to a sudden disavowal. Referencing boxing's relationship with Cold War politics in the early twentieth century, the sportswriter Jimmy Cannon claimed that Ali's association with the Nation of Islam was a "more pernicious hate symbol than Schmeling and Nazism."[26] At the same time, Black writers and other public commentators expressed initial anxieties about the heavyweight champion's new affiliation, and, by extension, his repeated public confrontations with mainstream America. Although sports (and particularly Black athletes) had long been involved in a narrative of social progress, Ali was uniquely willing to speak forthrightly on both political and religious issues. Such candor was surprising given the precarious nature of national politics during the Cold War; under the shadow of the House Un-American Activities Committee, almost any public engagement in protest or any traces of ideological debate drew swift charges of communism and treason along with them. According to one biographer, Ali's boxing career suffered as he proved unable to secure a fight; he was barred from several cities, including his hometown of Louisville, by politicians desperate to prove their patriotism as the US presence in South Vietnam began to increase rapidly."[27] Even before his controversial refusal of induction into the US armed services, the champion found himself adrift in the American public, occupying an ambivalent position within a culture continually constructing and contending with the Black body.[28]

John Rooney's iconic photograph that opened this chapter was taken during Ali's second title fight against Liston, when he entered the ring under very different circumstances than the first match. No longer the David to Liston's Goliath, he was loudly booed by the audience when he entered the arena. Even his victory over Liston (which we appear to witness in this scene) was immediately contested. According to reports, Liston fell onto the canvas after a "phantom punch"—a controversial right hook delivered by Ali that purportedly never connected with his opponent. Some historians have even written that this image shows us Ali shouting down through his clenched teeth at Liston to get up. At this moment the binary of "good" versus "evil" on which the narrative of boxing (and of this "iconic" image) so deeply depends is breaking down. Sonny Liston, the deviant, stereotypical Black brute suddenly becomes a passive victim, forced to the ground by a newly aggressive Ali. If we only consider this image as "iconic," we misremember the controversies surrounding Ali in this fight, and we exclude the racial politics at play in this moment. Instead, to account for this image's complex context of race, sports, and geopolitics is also to account for the complications of Blackness—wherein Ali is (in the terms of curator Hamza Walker) "renigged."[29] This cycle of negation and acceptance is one that most Black athletes, including Ali, must endure.

Reading this image historically we can discern the increasingly ambivalent position of Ali (and other Black men) within the cultural imagination. We begin to recognize the ways athletic competition produces, rehearses, and regulates Blackness. The photograph captures Ali in a moment of transformation. For white audiences Ali is simultaneously an object of adulation and one of fear, while for Black audiences he becomes a symbol of the power of Black masculinity. With his exposed torso, flexed musculature, and tight grimace he takes up macho signifiers of masculinity—being tough, in control, independently minded—to compensate for a lack of political capital in the era of Jim Crow.[30] Ali was both celebrated and vilified. *Heavyweight* argues that within the context of the United States, the production and the reception of these images are deeply connected to the politics of slavery and Jim Crow. I focus here on the shifting terrain of Black masculinity, wherein Black boxers alternately serve as examples of heroic, ideal manhood and (especially when they defeat white boxers) of the subhuman nature of Blackness. But this is not only about Blackness. *Heavyweight* explores the ambivalent narratives that make up this so-called moment of Blackness as well as their explicit connections to the instability of whiteness.[31]

Art historians have previously studied the links between athletics and aesthetics, looking specifically at how these discourses of masculinity converged with artistic expression in the late nineteenth and early twentieth centuries. Martin Berger's work on the presence of athletes in works by Thomas Eakins, for example, considers the artist's paintings "as both a material expression of, *and* site for, gendering beliefs and practices."[32] In other words, Eakins's paintings played a key role in building, modifying, and even naturalizing constructs of gender for Gilded Age audiences. Marianne Doezema takes up a similar tack in her examination of the early twentieth-century boxing paintings of George Bellows (1882–1925).[33] But in both these cases, the knowledge we gain on the formation of masculine identity is always specifically white, middle class, and heterosexual. And we scarcely move outside the realm of the fine arts. In looking closely at a contemporary image like this photograph of Ali, however, we can see its meaning exceeds the athlete himself. Reading the image against its larger visual, political, and cultural context challenges the dominance of such simple, teleological narratives of Ali specifically, and of Black boxers more generally. But what would happen if we considered this image within the wider history of boxing, where in the earliest days of the sport Black athletes were caught up within narratives around the Black body and Black sexuality? Could we think about how Ali's aggressive image (coupled with those open challenges to white authority) engages visual codes of Blackness that have circulated since the time of slavery in the United States and have been consistently reinforced over time to shore up the ideology of white supremacy? In other words, while we may be tempted to think of this image as solely a visual record of an athletic event or a record of Ali's triumph, what if we saw it instead as primary evidence of how the narrative of the Black man as eternally violent and dangerous comes to be constructed and repeated?

Academic literature on the image of Black men in visual culture has recognized the impact of athletes (and their representation) on the formation of Black subjectivity. In the 1992 essay entitled "Endangered Species" Kobena Mercer addressed the paradox of Black men in the American psyche—at once both invisible and overdetermined. Black men remain overrepresented in grim statistics, while misrepresented in the popular media via invented associations with crime, disease, and illicit drugs. Black masculinity, in Mercer's terms, is a "key site of ideological representation, a site upon which the nation's crisis comes to be dramatized, demonized, and dealt with, wherein we see not the truth of Blackness but a reaffirmation of the apparatus of white supremacy."[34] As bell hooks has similarly argued, "the Black body has always received attention within the framework of white supremacy, as racist/sexist iconography has been deployed to perpetuate notions of innate biological inferiority."[35] These are representations that have historical roots in the antebellum period in the United States, when Black bodies were marked a threat in the era leading up to and immediately following major political controversies. In the 1830s, for example, the prevalence of minstrelsy—white performers in blackface delivering songs, group performances, narrative skits, and jokes—was simultaneously rooted in the reality of white racist anxiety and in the political development of a national identity, always within and against the idea of Blackness. More than passive entertainment, these shows circulated ideologies of a primitive and pathological blackness that must be kept in check by white authority. Most important for a study of boxers, minstrelsy reaffirmed the "Black buck" stereotype of a violent, rude, even lecherous Black man who refuses to submit to white authority and has a violent attraction to white women. This trope rested on the presumption of both the extreme physical power of the Black body (uniquely suited to the demands of agricultural labor) and a deviant sexual appetite.

The overrepresentation of Black men does not provide them agency (or even individuality) but instead relies on oversimplification—a catalog of stereotypes—that directly informs whiteness in turn. We must remember that the formation of white, middle-class masculinity was always already constructed in a dialectical relationship to Blackness. At the turn of the twentieth century, W. E. B. Du Bois attempted to conceptualize the construction and the experience of race for Black Americans. In his essay "The Souls of Black Folk," Du Bois introduced the concept of the veil—a mechanism used to shut out the Black person from the mainstream while simultaneously allowing for a view to what lies just beyond reach. The veil was a metaphor for the experience of seeing (and knowing) oneself only through the apparatus of a majority culture—in Du Bois's terms, "always looking at oneself through the eyes of others."[36] Here, Blackness takes place both within and outside the individual simultaneously. The experience of being Black, Du Bois argues, takes shape on a personal as well as a social level. This is what he terms, "double consciousness," an experience of self-awareness that all Black people must negotiate.[37]

While we might be tempted to read this duality, or this twoness, as a binary, considering the veil as dialectical may in fact be more productive. As W. J. T. Mitchell argues in his lecture "The Moment of Blackness":

> The veil was not only a medium of opacity and blockage but, like the medium of photography, an instrument of "second sight" and the revelation of what would otherwise have remained invisible and concealed; or like the medium of cinema, a screen on which both realistic and fantastic images could be projected.[38]

Du Bois's veil, then, is not only a barrier but a point of connection. In the frame of the dialectic, therefore, the space between Black and white is not one of opposition but of interdependence. So, while this book traces a visual history of Blackness it does so in connection to whiteness. In focusing on Black boxers, we can discern a relationship between the Black men at the center of Rooney's photograph and the exclusively white men in the audience.

To understand boxing, we must consider not only the athletes, but the spectators as well.[39] In Rooney's photograph of the 1965 match between Muhammad Ali and Sonny Liston, we cannot help noticing the emphasis on looking. Reorienting our focus to the margins of the photograph, we see a sea of spectators surrounds the central scene and recedes upward and out of view, enveloped by darkness. Of course, when two boxers meet in the ring, they are also simultaneously on stage, under a spotlight and elevated above the audience that looks on. In this photograph we see the surrounding faces rapt with attention; a cadre of photographers in the lower right of the image stand at attention with their lenses focused on the scene before them. The forearms of one photographer, whose twin-lens camera appears just beside the left ankle of Ali, rest on the canvas itself alongside two other cameras to the left. Here we see that the sporting event and its image are inseparable, co-constituted in the ring of the match. The spectacle of the fight itself does not only affect the athletes in the ring but transforms the viewer as well.

I am particularly interested in the ideas of expertise proposed by Walter Benjamin in direct relationship to sports and the spectacle of its performance. In "The Work of Art in the Age of Mechanical Reproduction," he writes:

> It is inherent in the technology of film, as of sports, that everyone who witnesses these performances does so as a quasi-expert. Anyone who has listened to a group of newspaper boys leaning on their bicycles and discussing the outcome of a bicycle race will have an inkling of this.[40]

Benjamin argues that sports are a unique way for us to render ourselves as experts. In this vein, *Heavyweight* explores how images of Black heavyweight boxers provide an opportunity for white spectators to render themselves as experts on Blackness and Black masculinity.

As a sport that is both visual and corporeal, boxing and its place within visual history seems particularly worthy of our reexamination. After all, in most other major spectator sports (e.g., baseball, football, basketball, hockey, soccer) we have a field, a team, a ball, a hoop, a goal. Boxing has none of these. What we have in boxing are two figures wearing thin, silk boxing trunks and leather boxing gloves, and a square, elevated platform surrounded by ropes. The emphasis remains on these two bodies and their physicality alone. The specifically corporal nature of the sport is reaffirmed by both the standard boxing uniform, which leaves most of the athlete's body exposed, and by the sheer quantity of images devoted to reproducing that body for our visual consumption. Unlike other sports, where images of athletes are primarily taken of the body in the direct pursuit of an athletic feat, the sport of boxing produces a landscape of images before, during, and after the match—a collection of images in excess of the action of the match itself. This is perhaps due to the unique nature of the sport, wherein athletes rely on promoters and agents to arrange matches and are paid most directly by ticket sales. We see boxers fighting, but we also see them training; we find them posing for the camera for promotional photographs and performing for the audience during a match. The body of the professional boxer is continuously exposed to our gaze.

While we might more typically think of the boxer's body as the site of physical, corporeal power, we also find elements of sexual desire and pleasure. In the words of Joyce Carol Oates, "one might wonder if the boxing match leads irresistibly to this moment: the public embrace of two men who otherwise, in public or in private, could never approach each other with such passion."[41] As the boxers carefully negotiate which parts of the exposed body are open to or restricted from blows, the action of the match and the pleasure we derive from watching it center on the boxer's ability to escape or endure pain. For the viewer of a boxing match the physical sensation of pleasure is superseded by spectatorship; we cannot touch these fighters, but we consume them instead visually. The boxing match transforms the viewer into voyeur. As we will see in chapter 3 of this book, the visual culture of pornography and that of boxers existed in parallel in the nineteenth-century United States. The composition of many promotional photographs that circulated in this period and after, which show a nearly nude boxer alone in the frame, allows for the viewer to create a one-to-one fantasy with the photographic subject. The sexual dimension of the sport positions these Black men as objects of both fear and fantasy. The body of the heavyweight boxer is of interest—on the one hand an object of perfect symmetry, an expression of the aesthetic ideal, and on the other hand an instrument of extreme violence. As viewers, we oscillate between the admiration and the explicit fear of this body's brutal power.

When I began writing this book, I set out with the intention of considering the present. However, in looking at press photographs of Muhammad Ali, we realize that these images were embedded within a history of representation that began long ago. Before Muhammad Ali there was Jack Johnson (1878–1946)—another sensational Black boxer who rose to prominence in the early twentieth century as the first Black world heavyweight champion and suffered a very public downfall shortly afterward, a victim of his own success. But before Johnson we also have a history of Black boxers that stretches back to the last quarter of the nineteenth century, men who were denied the opportunity to fight for a world title but who nevertheless played a formative role in the public perception of Blackness. As many cultural critics have argued that one cannot understand the current state of anti-Blackness without going back to the formative moment of slavery and the failures of Reconstruction, *Heavyweight* similarly takes up the late nineteenth century—a transformative period in both the reconstruction of the nation and in the sport of boxing.

Looking back to the earliest visual histories of Black boxers in the United States also shows that these men were more than athletes; they were celebrities, the imago of Blackness. Contemporary newspapers reported on their travel habits, their diets and training regimens, their sartorial choices, and even their romantic lives. These Black men were among the most reproduced in a thriving media culture, and as such should be considered as part of the visual record of Blackness. Images of Black boxers circulated widely and internationally in the nineteenth century—in news media, in cabinet cards, in films, even on tobacco tins. Alongside the circulation of these images, we also find the circulation of ideas about Blackness—many of which persist into our present. Ideas of the Black man as inherently violent and dangerous, as lacking in subjectivity, and as a sexual predator are all represented in the figure of the Black heavyweight boxer. As we will see in the following chapters, these were stereotypes explicitly cultivated in visual representation. Once slavery ended, images of Black boxers in popular newspapers and magazines were one of the primary means for the white public to reinforce the linkage between Blackness and depravity, insolence, and savagery. Throughout this book we will examine the connections between white racial dominance and manhood that preoccupied middle-class America in this period, a moment in which we find the origins for what the historian Gail Bederman has called "a racially based ideology of male power" that has very real consequences today.[42]

This study of boxing, race, and masculinity begins in the nineteenth century because we cannot understand Muhammad Ali without taking a closer look at the visual and cultural history of the period that preceded him. *Heavyweight* attends to this forgotten genealogy to expose the operative white supremacy that has always already been in play with Black men in American culture. While we may more easily connect other types of Black representation and performance— lynching or minstrelsy—from the Reconstruction period within a schema of anti-Blackness, the images of Black boxers are more complicated. Looking closely at these earlier images allows us to think more carefully about the politics of our practice, to explore the unconscious structures that produce our knowledge about Blackness, and to intervene in an art history that privileges the image over the cultural event. We find here not only origins for corporeal stereotypes about Black masculinity but also expose the roots of anti-Black violence in the United States. In this way I am not only interested in the images themselves but in the conditions of possibility they produce for Black men.

A HALF CENTURY BEFORE the Ali-Liston fight, on December 26, 1908, or more appropriately "Boxing Day," the Black heavyweight fighter Jack Johnson finally met Canadian Tommy Burns (1881–1955) in Sydney, Australia, for a world championship battle (fig. I.2).[43] At this point Johnson had been chasing Burns for more than a year, trying to lure the white champion into the ring, and the public anticipation became palpable. Spectators began to line up outside ticket windows at 2:30 a.m. (i.e., more than eight hours before the scheduled start of the match), and thousands were waiting outside the stadium gates when the 250 police officers arrived to open the venue.[44] According to reporters on the scene, the sky that day "was threatening, and in the dark clouds, the

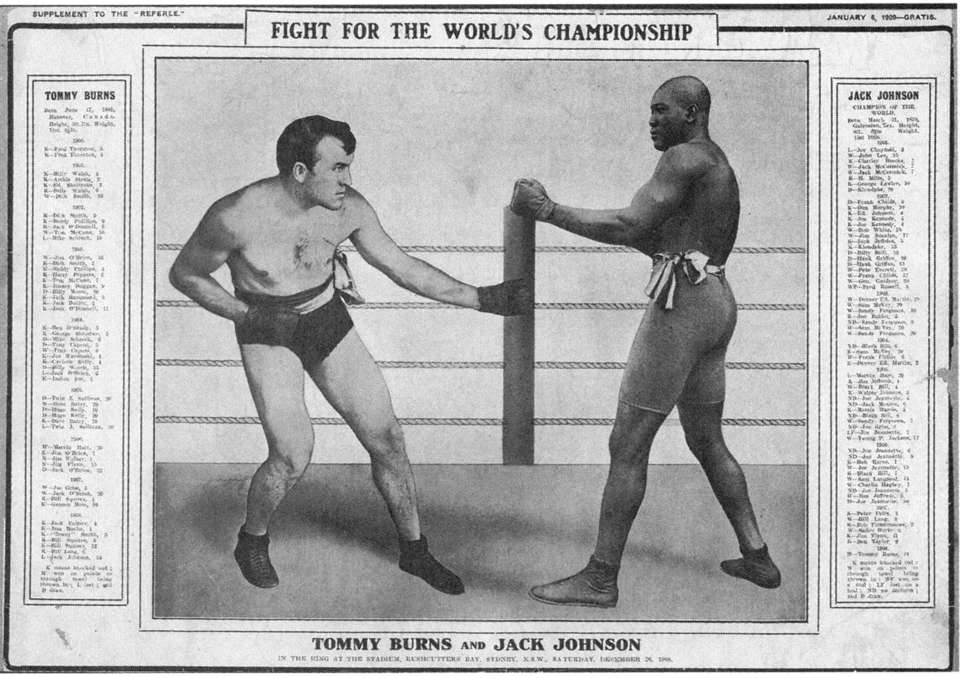

I.2

Illustration marking the Burns-Johnson fight,
Sydney, December 26, 1908. Charles Kerry Collection,
National Library of Australia.

augurs read an omen of disaster, for that huge crowd was aggressively white in its sympathy."[45]

In the months preceding the fight, Burns and Johnson had endured a prolonged debate through a variety of media outlets; the fighters went back and forth in challenges filled with taunting and blatant racism. But it seemed that Burns, despite his professed willingness to fight, was wary of entering the ring with the Black fighter. According to Johnson, his search for an opponent during this period was exhausting: "It was fatiguing to listen to [Burns's] miles & miles of excuses. For the last few years, I have been half round the world trying to secure boxing matches but on the whole it seemed to me that I had not been successful. Like Micawber, I had changed my place of abode time after time in expectation of something turning up but it never came to pass."[46] Burns turned the media's attention to his own exorbitant payment demands ($30,000 for a single fight—win, lose, or draw) in a strategy to avoid facing Johnson in the ring. While on tour in Australia, Burns met with questions from reporters about his willingness to fight Johnson. According to Johnson's biographer, Geoffrey C. Ward, Burns "claimed that Johnson had been dodging *him*, that if Johnson—who suffered from the 'yellow streak' to which all black people were prone—wouldn't fight him, he planned to retire. 'All niggers are alike to me' he told another 'but I'll fight him even though he is a nigger,' and he would 'make it tough for Mr. Coon' when he did so."[47] In the weeks leading up to the match, press coverage dramatically increased. The *Bulletin*, an Australian national weekly paper, summarized the stakes in its post-fight coverage, claiming that the majority white spectatorship "had not come to see the fight so much as to witness a black aspirant for the championship of the world beaten to his knees and counted out."[48]

The match eventually took place, at the arrangement of the promoter Hugh McIntosh, who managed to meet Burns's demand for $30,000 and persuade Johnson to fight for one-sixth of that price. But, in his earlier proclamation, Burns clarified how consequential racial bias had been for this matchup. This was underscored by the shouts of "coon" and "nigger" that issued from the crowd of twenty-thousand spectators, as Johnson eventually entered the ring.[49] Those who had expressed a desire to see Johnson beaten, however, were disappointed after he was declared the winner in the fourteenth round by promoter-turned-referee McIntosh. While Johnson waved his hands in victory, the predominantly white crowd remained silent and stunned. The *Bulletin* struggled to spin Burns's unceremonious defeat, writing of the "heroism with which Burns took his smashing, and gamely came again and again." Nevertheless, for the first time in the history of boxing there was a Black world heavyweight champion.

The Johnson-Burns fight was certainly one of the most dramatic moments in early twentieth-century sports, but this was not the first public defeat of a white fighter by a Black opponent. Twenty-two years before that fight in Sydney, the Saint Croix–born Peter Jackson (1861–1901) won the Australian heavyweight title by knocking out Tom Lees (1858–1947) in the thirtieth round.[50] In May 1891, Jackson fought for sixty-one rounds against the American boxer James "Gentleman Jim" Corbett (1866–1933) before the referee declared a draw. These matches were almost immediately followed by Jackson's challenge of the then heavyweight champion John L. Sullivan (1858–1918). An American fighter born in Boston to Irish parents, Sullivan became the nation's first sports celebrity. He was also racist. He interrupted a theater performance in San Francisco (Peter Jackson's adopted hometown), standing up from the audience to proclaim to the room:

> Ladies and gentlemen, I wonner [*sic*] say a nigger's no good. If God wonned [*sic*] a nigger ter [*sic*] fight, why did'ne [*sic*] make him white? Nigger's no good. I'kn [*sic*] lick'im—lick any nigger.... A nigger can't fight. He ain't no good. Ain't as good as a white man, anyhow. No nigger is; if he was he'd be white.[51]

Incendiary statements like these were quite common for Sullivan, who possessed a predilection for self-promotion, even taking out advertisements in the sporting newspaper *National Police Gazette* to challenge members of the public to fight for prize money.[52] But in the end he never fought Jackson or any other Black fighter. When asked in 1905 by the *San Francisco Sunday Call* about his unwillingness to fight Jackson, Sullivan replied, "A white man has nothing to gain by swapping punches with a negro."[53]

Although Jackson had won the Australian heavyweight championship in 1886 and in 1892 defeated the British title holder, the closest he ever got to a world heavyweight title was his sixty-one-round draw with Corbett, who would later win the world title from John L. Sullivan in 1892. Sullivan's refusal to fight denied Jackson the opportunity to claim the American (and by default the world) heavyweight title. When reporters asked Sam Fitzpatrick, a trainer who worked closely with Jackson as well as later with welterweight Joe Walcott (1873–1935) and Jack Johnson, who was the best of the three Black pugilists, he replied, "Peter Jackson was the best man in the world and would have beaten Johnson."[54] Jackson's only limitation in the American context was his ability to secure matches with white fighters—a problem that Johnson would later face as well. We can imagine that the public reaction surrounding the Johnson-Burns fight in 1908 was necessarily connected to this late nineteenth-century history of boxing, in which issues of race were deeply intertwined.

The cases of both Peter Jackson and Jack Johnson demonstrate the many social and political conflicts that are allowed to "play out" within the boxing arena. Both fighters struggled to define themselves as champions within a system that resisted interracial matches, as evidenced by the widespread racial violence that their interracial matches provoked. In the US context of the Reconstruction, Black boxers like Jackson and Johnson functioned as early models for Black resistance to white, patriarchal authority. They were also subject to the mythologies of brutality and savagery that helped to support a widespread ideology of white supremacy. Most important for this book, the integration of boxing in the last decades of the nineteenth century in the United States coincided with a rise in the representation of Black athletes, including Jackson and Johnson, across all media. We see the bodies of these athletes across the fine arts, in the photographs of Eadweard Muybridge (1830–1904) and the paintings of George Bellows. Boxers appear on postcards, tobacco advertisements, and on the covers of newspapers.

A major question for this study is how images of Black boxers in this period shape the social position of Black men in contemporary American culture at large via their simultaneous articulation and critique of stereotypes, and in specific relation to white masculinity. But to do this we must go back to the nineteenth century—a moment of profound transformation for masculine identities. According to the historian E. Anthony Rotundo, in this era: "Bourgeois manhood embraced new virtues and new obsessions. The male body moved to the center of men's gender concerns; manly passions were revalued in a favorable light; men began to look at the 'primitive' sources of manhood with new regard; the martial values attracted admiration; and competitive impulses were transformed into male virtues."[55] In answering these questions, we must first consider the role that athleticism played in defining a hegemonic masculine ideal that was unapologetically white.

IN THE LATE VICTORIAN ERA, participation in sports activities, particularly blood and gambling sports, were a mark of manliness in an era of sharp divisions along gender lines (in work, in family, and in leisure activities). The closing of the Western frontier in 1890—a stalwart symbol of freedom and possibility—and the subsequent turn toward industrialization led to a transformation of the relationship between men and labor.[56] The restless pioneer declined at the same time as the small farmer and other self-employed workers, meaning that men were no longer as autonomous as they once were. In 1883 the American economist Henry George wrote that machines rendered the working man dependent, "depriving him of skills and of opportunities . . . ; lessening his control over his own condition and his hope of improving it; cramping his mind, and in many cases distorting and enervating his body."[57] Citing the preponderance of linguistic references to labor in descriptions of the ring, cultural historian Elliott J. Gorn has even gone so far as to argue that boxing provided a type of surrogate workplace for both fighters and spectators. "Boxing," he writes, "was 'a profession,' and pugilists were 'trained' in various 'schools' of fighting. Newspaper reports regularly used such phrases as 'they went to work,' or 'he did good work,' in their round-by-round coverage."[58] Despite the rapid erosion of skilled labor that followed industrialization, prize fighters were able to retain a sense of craftsmanship as well as their autonomy. We might consider the training regimens, the regulations, and even the vocabulary associated with boxing as indicators of its role in reviving the culture and language of skilled artisans.

The growth of bureaucratized corporate capitalism and consumer culture during the industrial age also provided working men with unstructured free time. As shifting labor conditions transformed the old apprenticeship system into one based on wage workers, individuals experienced a sharp distinction between work and leisure hours. Moreover, as the professional opportunities for middle-class men narrowed, the opportunities for commercial leisure increased. This was a change from earlier in the century, when work and family formed the center of middle-class identity. Rising industrialization produced fear among those who believed a move to the factory would undoubtedly produce lazy, even slothful, citizens. Social critics at the time pointed to an increase in cases of neurasthenia, a new psychological disorder first identified as early as 1829 but made famous by the neurologist George Miller Beard, who reintroduced the concept in 1869.[59] Neurasthenia, an affliction to which both men and women were thought to be vulnerable, caused a mechanical weakness of the nerves that could also lead to symptoms such as dizziness, faintness, headaches, and heart palpitations. Beard located the cause in the stresses of modern civilization: "steam power, the periodical press, the telegraph, the sciences, and the mental activity of women" were all to blame.[60] Many believed Americans to be particularly prone to the condition. Beard and his contemporaries specifically recommended that male, urban professionals afflicted by neurasthenia turn to sports—running, weightlifting, and boxing—to combat its effects. The frequency with which one finds advertisements for neurasthenic treatments alongside reports of boxing matches in periodicals such as the *National Police Gazette* attests to the explicit connections late nineteenth-century audiences made between the sport and health. To counteract the threat of these new urban pathologies, many turned to physical exercise.[61]

Class issues in the Gilded Age had a deep impact on men's bodies, their identities, and their access to power in this period. Manhood was crucial to middle-class identity—a way to assert authority over women as well as over the lower classes in a paternalistic fashion. With the influx of lower-class and immigrant labor—both in the workplace and in the political arena with increasingly violent labor movements—middle-class men suffered from a sudden loss of authority and agency. "Middle-class men," historian Gail Bederman writes, "worried that they were losing control of the country. The power of manhood, as the middle class understood it, encompassed the power to wield civic authority, to control strife and unrest, and to shape the future of the nation."[62] The protests of working-class and immigrant men, which threatened the authority of US-born, Anglo middle-class men, led to an increased focus on white manhood as a site of power. More specifically, new immigrant populations feeding into the United States, starting in the nineteenth century, created a need for the construction of whiteness as a distinct racial identity. White men sought to develop further justification for their authority and power within public culture through the conscious association of immigrant bodies with depravity, stupidity, and sloth.[63]

Free Blacks in these urban centers presented another problem, further requiring white working-class men to assert some privilege or distinction from emancipated Black men. As I will discuss in chapter 4 of this book, the sport of boxing was from its origin immersed within these debates around immigrants, Black men, and their status within the newly urban cultures of places like New York, Boston, and Philadelphia in this period. Although initially burdened with negative associations due to its popularity within immigrant populations, boxing transformed in the latter decades of the nineteenth century into a white, middle-class, gentlemanly pursuit.[64] Boxing and prizefighting, too—long associated with the working class—fascinated middle- and upper-class men. Amateur sparring became popular and respectable enough for even YMCAs to offer instruction. By the time Jack Johnson emerged as the world heavyweight champion in 1910, many middle-class men had come to accept athletes like Jim Jeffries (his opponent) as embodiments of their own sense of manhood.[65]

The popularity of boxing in this period immediately connected to wider concerns around the conditions of manhood. Sport and exercise were broadly touted as the ideal way to promote good health and good morals among the new white middle classes. Athleticism was promoted in the mid-nineteenth century as a way to teach young people values (including respect for authority) and to "toughen up" a populace unfamiliar with hard labor.[66] As historian Michael Kimmel has claimed in his study of masculinity in the American context, in the late nineteenth century, middle-class men relied on boxing—long associated with the lower classes—to express masculine prowess and to define a hegemonic notion of masculinity in a time of turmoil. In this moment, manhood (previously thought to be an inner experience) was refocused outward, in the physical formation of a sturdy and muscular frame. "By the 1870s," Kimmel argues, "the idea of 'inner strength' [popularized in previous decades] was replaced by a doctrine of physicality and the body."[67] To combat perceived increases in "weakness," men worked overtime to masculinize society—recruiting male teachers, ridiculing women's suffrage, and even adopting a new vocabulary (i.e., "sissy," "pussy foot"). Some men began to appropriate activities previously assigned to the lower classes—a "rough, working-class masculinity" that "celebrated institutions and values antithetical to middle-class Victorian manliness—institutions like saloons, music halls, and prizefights; values like physical prowess, pugnacity, and sexuality."[68] In the American context, then, sport and athleticism were directly linked to the white (masculine) body politic. Bare-knuckle prizefighting emerged in a context wherein masculine identity was still under construction.

Sports began to take on political value as well. For example, in 1893 Theodore Roosevelt proclaimed that "manly out-of-door sports" would be instrumental in the revitalization of commercial America, as well as in the formation of an Anglo-Saxon super race. He prescribed outdoor sports and exercise (e.g., game hunting, boxing, and football) as the remedy to the effeminate and luxurious lifestyle that had left many men unfit and unprepared for war.[69] In this period, athletics were both sanctioned and financed by the federal government. Experts in recreational sports convinced the nation that exercising, boxing, and playing football and baseball would ensure the continued virility of young American men.[70] Many of these men, the first in recent memory to lack experience in direct combat, questioned their own military fitness compared with the generation that preceded them. Participation in sports provided a method to prove one's readiness to defend and protect the new, increasingly imperialistic nation.

Boxing gave meaning, and perhaps even order, to the daily violence experienced by those living in urban America at the turn of the twentieth century. Residents in overcrowded cities without modern sanitation faced staggering levels of disease, violence, death, and overall despair. "Boxers," writes the sports historian Elliot Gorn, "like fighting cocks and trained bulldogs, made bloodshed comprehensible and thus offered models of honorable conduct. They taught men to face danger with courage, to be impervious to pain, and to return violence rather than passively accept it."[71] Fighters responded to a violent world with violence. Within this new context of industrial wealth, men obsessed over their own "over-civilization." Away from the workplace, where their power and authority seemed to diminish at an alarming rate, these men found alternative sources of esteem. Many viewed pronounced physical strength as symbolic of power in the larger social sphere. Violent sports provided the possibility for men of the elite classes to enjoy the material comforts of their success while simultaneously demonstrating that they did not lack any of the masculine attributes of the pioneers or soldiers who had come before them.[72] Prizefighting allowed for the expression of brutal force and masculine power that many explicitly valued. It provided the opportunity for men to indulge their taste for violence.[73] By the end of the nineteenth century, white middle-class American men were obsessed with health and athletics, as they sought to form muscled physiques that would communicate their inner virility and hopefully reclaim some of the social or personal power lost through an increase in sheer physical strength.

The shaping of masculinity was a critical project in the nineteenth century, one rooted in social experience but with tangible political and personal effects. Outward, physical markers of masculinity (e.g., a highly muscled body) were promoted as the antidote to fears of feminization. The gym became a place for men to transform their listless, feminized bodies into manly physiques, to display their physical strength as evidence of their masculine power. A precursor to what we may recognize now as bodybuilding, physical culture explicitly responded to a pressing need to express masculine power (and thus reestablish hegemonic masculinity). Suddenly, according to Kimmel, "the body did not *contain* the man within; that body *was* the man."[74]

Wrestling and "strongman acts" grew in popularity during this period, the latter moving from the circus to the music hall.[75] The rising physical culture stars—George Hackenschmidt (1877–1968), Bernarr Macfadden (1868–1955), Eugen Sandow (1867–1925), and Charles Atlas (1892–1972)—promoted the benefits of repeated, sustained isometric exercise through books, magazines, and other, more theatrical, means such as vaudeville performances and staged wrestling matches. These men used their own bodies as primary examples of "fitness," promoting a specific regimen of diet and exercise that they argued could shape the male body into an ideal representation of masculine authority and control. Most active in the last decade of the nineteenth century, Sandow, for example, reportedly modeled his body on Greek statuary and created a series of photographs and performances well into the twentieth century that demonstrated the perfection of his own body.[76] These men were living examples of the masculine ideal, repeating and reiterating gender norms for wide audiences in text, image, and performance.

A renowned wrestler in Europe, the Estonian-born Hackenschmidt published his book *The Way to Live in Health and Physical Fitness* in 1908. Divided into two sections, the book includes a training manual, followed by Hackenschmidt's autobiography. In the text he argues for physical culture as the antidote to industrialization and urbanization: "It is a well-known fact that the majority of men today are relatively weak, whereas the struggle for existence demands now more than any previous epoch that we should all be strong!"[77] Throughout the book, Hackenschmidt uses his own body as the example of physical achievement. In one plate (fig. I.3) he stands in dark wrestling trunks that seem to dissolve into the dark background and highlight the contours of his white, muscled physique. He appears in a pose that current bodybuilding competitors would recognize as the "front relaxed pose." His feet press firmly against the floor to emphasize the upper-quadricep muscles of the leg, while flexing of the latissimus dorsi (or lats) of the upper body causes the arms to lift slightly upward. Here we are meant to marvel at the body that Hackenschmidt has achieved, noting every flexion and contour. In a radical departure from the ideal physique of the 1860s (a thin, wiry frame), by the end of the nineteenth century bulk and prominent muscles defined the ideal body. The explicit message here focuses on the ideal physical form of the masculine body—a body actively under construction. The visual rhetoric of the boxer in this period was imbricated in the discourses of corporeal masculinity and its intersections with the ideals of whiteness.

This new emphasis on the appearance of the male body carried consequences for thinking about masculinity—that is, as something constructed via representation or outward physical qualities, rather than generated from within. This new physical obsession included specific recommendations about diet, hydration strategies, bloodletting, and even sexual behavior.[78] As with the physical culture athletes, images of boxers appeared in newspapers, magazines, and books; they circulated on cabinet cards, postcards, and tobacco cards collected by fans.

Race played a key role in the fashioning of manhood in this period, as many of these ideas about social authority operated by drawing correspondences between male power and white supremacy.[79] Like manhood, these ideas about race drew on established ideological links between the body, individual identity, and power. To some extent, manhood had long been associated with white

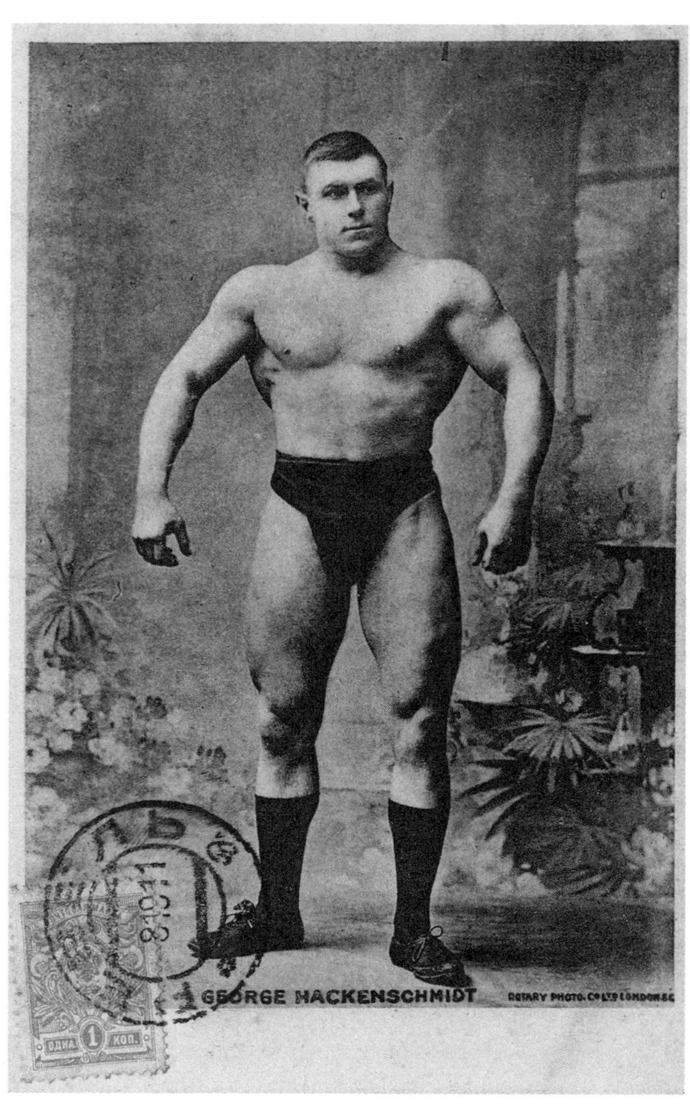

I.3

George Hackenschmidt, ca. 1905. Rotary
Photographic Co. LTD., London

supremacy. For example, the architects of state constitutions in more than a dozen northern and western US states placed Black men in the same category as women, as "dependents." The widely accepted notion that Black men, unlike their white counterparts, were not quite men helped to justify their exclusion from political and social life. Images of heroic white men among the "savage" tribes of Africa in popular magazines such as *National Geographic* visualized the attendant discourse of civilization.[80]

The 1893 World's Columbian Exposition serves as yet another example of the impulse to connect white supremacy to a sense of manhood. The fair itself was divided into two racially specific areas: the White City—a collection of seven white beaux-arts buildings—symbolized all the progress of white civilization, while the Midway Plaisance represented the undeveloped primitive nature of the dark races. Each of the seven buildings in the White City focused on a single aspect of the masculine world of commerce—manufacturing, agriculture, and so on—and, by extension, to the celebration of the power of white manhood. This explicit connection between whiteness and manhood was apparent to contemporary viewers; in one edition of the *Chicago Daily Inter-Ocean,* poets described it as "A Vision of Strong Manhood and Perfection of Society."[81] Such explicit efforts to confirm the supremacy of whiteness connected to the politics of Jim Crow. The subordination of Black bodies during the period after slavery was integral to the maintenance of a national order that privileged whiteness, and this included the transformation of Blackness from a racial designation based on status (e.g., as slave versus free) to one based on accepted notions of cultural and/or biological difference. As Black bodies and white bodies came into closer contact in the late nineteenth century, a need to further underscore the superiority of whiteness and to do so by further separating it from Blackness also emerged. The heavyweight boxer, whose physical form had already been identified in the earlier Victorian period as the perfect example of manhood, was a particular point of fascination.

Any history of boxing in the United States must also by pure definition be a history of Blackness as well. The first boxers in the United States were slaves, who fought one another (sometimes while wearing iron collars) for the amusement of their plantation owners. After Emancipation, boxing had a unique status among other sports because it was desegregated. In the boxing ring, the widespread racial tensions during Reconstruction often played out between white and Black opponents. For Black men, sports provided one of the few available paths toward financial (and thereby social and political) autonomy within this context. Excluded from the wider labor markets in the urban North, many Black men turned to boxing, for example, to generate income. As the historian Paul R. D. Lawrie explains, "boxing—despite its brutality, meager purses, and illegality—provided a rare chance for working men across the color line to acquire a modicum of financial autonomy outside traditional labor markets."[82] Promoters of these integrated matches capitalized on the racism in American society, with audiences ready to witness the brutality of the sport. The Black body, once again, was placed in a precarious position for limited financial gains. But these early audiences also got something they did not bargain for—a victory for a Black fighter would also signify a challenge to white supremacy.

Perhaps recognizing the threat of a Black fighter's victory, the white heavyweight champion of the 1880s, John L. Sullivan, discussed above, famously refused to fight Black opponents, arguing that he did not want to "sully the white race."[83] A decade later, when the Black featherweight champion George Dixon fought the white amateur champion Jack Skelly in New Orleans in 1892, the crowd was disturbed by what it saw. Dixon controlled the fight from the start, even breaking Skelly's nose before knocking him out completely in the eighth round. According to one report, "white fans winced every time Dixon landed on Skelly. The sight was repugnant to some men from the South. A darky is alright in his place here, but the idea of sitting quietly by and seeing a colored boy pommel a white lad grates on southerners."[84] To appease the irritated white audience, the fight's venue, the Olympia Club, banned any further mixed-race matches. The anxiety around Black fighters in the ring with white opponents is perhaps best expressed by Charles A. Dana, the editor of the *New York Sun*, who wrote an impassioned plea in 1895:

> We are in the midst of a growing menace. The black man is rapidly forging to the front ranks of athletics, especially in the field of fisticuffs. We are in the midst of a black rise against white supremacy. . . . If the negro is capable of developing such prowess in those divisions of boxing, what is going to stop him from making the same progress in the heavier ranks?[85]

The threat of a Black boxer in the ring exceeded that of his opponent; this was an open challenge to the social order.

The menace of the Black boxer was perhaps most evident in the match between Jim Jeffries and Jack Johnson in Reno, Nevada, in 1910—a match that concludes this volume and the first public, mixed-race, heavyweight title fight in the United States. Promoters and the media advertised the fight as the "Battle of the Century." Popular illustrations from the era consistently portrayed Johnson in the visual trope of the Sambo—a caricature of the uneducated rural slave made popular in minstrel performances. Take, for example, a cartoon from the *San Francisco Chronicle* in 1910, titled "Chicken versus the Championship,"

I.4

LeRoy Robert Ripley, "Chicken versus the Championship,"
San Francisco Chronicle, June 14, 1910.

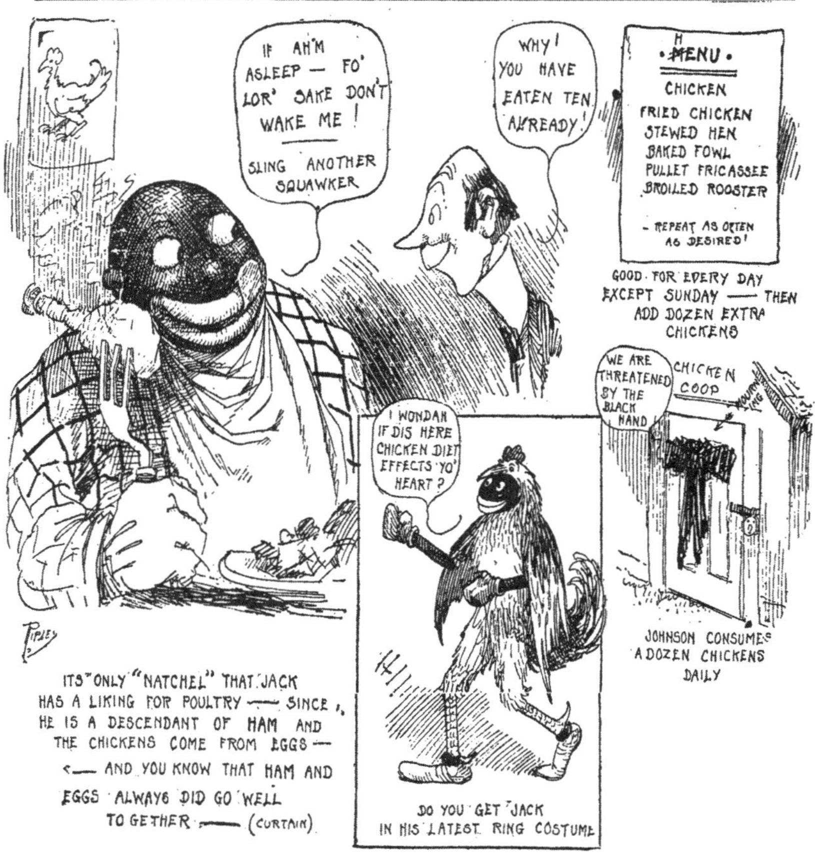

which extrapolates and exaggerates the well-worn stereotype of Black people's love for fried chicken (fig. I.4). Johnson appears twice in the multi-paneled cartoon. In the left of the composition, he is shown seated at a table; a plate in front of him holds a towering pile of food. He wears a checkered coat with a large napkin tied around his neck as a bib, and in his right, white-gloved hand he holds a fork on which a large drumstick is impaled. Johnson's head has been depicted with his forehead flattened and his cheeks exaggerated to appear rounder. The dark crosshatching of the skin appears even blacker when viewed in contrast to the sharp white of Johnson's bulging eyes and the distorted, wide mouth with bulging lips that stretches impossibly across his face. A tongue protrudes from the mouth, and as we follow the arc of its curvature upward to the left cheek we read a speech bubble containing Johnson's warning to the waiter who appears directly opposite his figure: "If Ah'm asleep—fo' lor' sake don't wake me! Sling another squawker." In addition to the racism in both image (the Sambo) and text (via the exaggerated diction) we have the insinuation of Johnson's insatiable appetite. In this image, Johnson's athletic prowess—in the five years before his match against Jeffries in July 1910 Johnson had lost only one of twenty-nine bouts—is diminished as he is transformed into a caricature. As he smiles and licks his lips, his perceived threat to white supremacy is reduced, and the audience presumably laughs along with this ridiculous scene.

Heavyweight considers the presence of these men across media and, more specifically, how visual culture reinforced the corporeal and patriarchal definitions of white masculinity that persist into our present moment. We will see throughout this book how representation—in both fine art and popular media—expressed and managed the threat of Blackness. While race, as an ideological construction rather than a biological reality, organizes nearly every aspect of our social lives, it depends almost entirely on visual perception. *Heavyweight* relies on scholarship from within visual culture studies, which has in recent decades turned its attention toward the dialectical relationship between representation and Blackness. Photography, in particular, has been a ripe subject for scholars in this vein as the history of the medium is so closely connected to the regulation of difference (often under the guise of empiricism). As the artist and cultural critic Coco Fusco, explains, "Rather than *recording* the existence of race, photography *produced* race as a visualizable fact."[86] This happened through the direct manipulation of bodies within the frame (pose, gesture) as well as through the persistent rhetoric of photography as a scientific medium. The photograph itself was a mode of information and, in the words of Leigh Raiford, "a way of seeing, a visual means of relaying fact and imposing order."[87] While the assertion (and the consequences) of the photograph as an index of reality will be further explored in chapter 2, I want to highlight here the work that scholars like Raiford, alongside Tina Campt, Saidiya Hartman, Eric Lott, Shawn Michelle Smith, Deborah Willis and many others have done to investigate the "truth claims" of these images as well as their role in histories that marginalize Black life. They have asked us to look again at family portraits, news photographs, and even mug shots to find humanity and joy, where previously we saw only tragedy and horror, to consider the historical roots of the stereotypes of Blackness that circulate in our contemporary world, and to chart the visual dimension of race and its intersections with the photographic medium.[88] All this research argues for a closer consideration of vernacular culture, of work that typically escapes the archive, as a way to explore the violence, the terror, and the pleasure of Black life in nineteenth-century America. *Heavyweight* builds on the work of these scholars and is similarly invested in unpacking the role of the image in constructions of Blackness, both historically and contemporarily. But while the scholars noted above have produced landmark studies of lynching, portraiture, minstrelsy, and even the fine arts of the late nineteenth century, they have also largely ignored popular representations of the Black boxer. I am invested throughout this book in the concept of the "shadow archive," first theorized by Allan Sekula. According to Sekula, it is not enough to consider a single, perhaps well-known photograph or image; we must also consider that image in relation to all others to find meaning. The shadow archive includes the entire social field of representation—both fine art and vernacular, public and private.[89] With this book I argue that images of these men, circulated in both fine art and popular media, are critical to our understanding of the ways Black masculinity has been shaped, policed, fetishized, and even made abject over the last 150 years.

HEAVYWEIGHT FOCUSES ON images made in the United States between 1880 and 1910—dates chosen for their significance within the history of Jim Crow, the rise of print culture, and the history of interracial boxing. Each chapter centers on a single Black boxer in order to explore the visual rhetoric of Black masculinity across a range of media that includes print illustration, photography, and painting. The first chapter provides an overview of the sport of boxing in the United States, its place within the critical project of white manhood in the nineteenth century, and its intersections with an increased focus on the physical body as the site of masculinity. I deal here with the circulation of images in popular illustrated print media, including the sporting paper the *National*

Police Gazette—a model for the monetization of visual culture and the cult of celebrity that still operates today.

The second chapter looks closely at the photographs taken by Eadweard Muybridge of the mixed-race boxer Ben Bailey in 1885 as a historically situated racial project wherein the social categorization of Black people played out. I argue that these pictures of Bailey must be read within the larger context of nineteenth-century photography, in which the bourgeois classes were excessively preoccupied with the classification of difference, and looked to the medium, with its strong associations of "truth," for evidence to support a general drive to regulate, even criminalize, the presence of an unwanted underclass in the new urban environment. I am particularly interested here in the introduction of the anthropometric grid in these photographs, which uniquely pathologizes Bailey. Muybridge's presentation of this body, and its translation of Bailey's dynamic movement into a series of discrete and identifiable poses, rehearses an attempt to fix and constrain the Black body within the photographic frame. I further explore how these photographs gave visual form to these fantasies (and fears) about Black bodies in the public sphere, looking both to fine art and vernacular photography for comparative treatments of the Black body as both a scientific and an aesthetic object.

Chapter 3 centers on the Australian heavyweight boxer Peter Jackson, known as "the Black Prince," and a series of nude photographs taken of him in San Francisco in 1889. Unlike chapter 2, which investigates a unique photographic project with a limited audience, my concern here is how Jackson's body features as part of a much wider and international visual program that classicized, sexualized, and eroticized the Black body in order to manage its threat to the white public after the Civil War. I will also explore the connections between Jackson's body and the fin de siècle development of a new "physical culture," which promoted the development (and strengthening) of the physical body, through comparisons with the nude photographs taken in 1889 with images of bodybuilder Eugen Sandow from the same period. A major aim of this chapter is to explore how the body of the Black heavyweight boxer—perhaps the most threatening of them all—was consciously and consistently shaped by discourses of sexuality, and how the erotic and the violent became entangled through representation.

The fourth chapter centers on the painting *Both Members of This Club* (1909) by the Ashcan School artist George Bellows. While this image has been explicitly discussed in terms of its interactions with rhetorics of manhood (or even Bellows's progressive idealism), such analyses remain largely white, middle-class, and heterosexual. The integration of boxing in the first decade of the twentieth century certainly brought issues of race into the public arena, and my goal here is to do the same for Bellows's work. In this chapter see how the widespread racial tensions following Emancipation and Reconstruction played out between white and Black opponents, and within the fine arts, exploring how the visual culture of this period (including the work of Bellows) played a critical role in fomenting and even justifying racial violence.

Although most histories of boxing tend to emphasize the physical violence of the encounter between two bodies, this book instead tells a visual history of the sport, framing it as an ideological apparatus through which whiteness establishes the violent mythology of its supremacy. I argue that boxing in the nineteenth century normalized a culture of anti-Black violence that persists in our present moment. *Heavyweight* locates a new origin of anti-Blackness stereotypes, reclaiming a history of Black heavyweight fighters whose images circulated widely and internationally. In the reconstruction period and after, these images exceeded reportage and became the primary means by which the white public positioned Black men as opponents. I argue that we can find lurking in these images the blueprint for our conceptions of the Black male body as existing somewhere between fear and fantasy, simultaneously an object of desire and an instrument of brutal violence.

THE BARE-KNUCKLE BREED

On April 17, 1860, the San Francisco-born prizefighter John C. Heenan faced Tom Sayers of England for the very first international "world title" fight.[1] The match alone lasted an excruciating two hours and twenty-seven minutes, but the buildup to this decisive fight was months in the making. The nationalist tenor of the fight—a contest between the American and English champions—provided a welcome distraction from the explosive racial politics of the burgeoning Civil War. In the latter half of the nineteenth century, the more specific ethnic identities of immigrant boxers (e.g., Irish) in the United States had shifted toward a generalized whiteness. Such a transformation allowed for Heenan and Sayers to perform metonymically for the white, middle-class audience as national representatives for American and British audiences respectively. American middle-class men in particular regarded the fighters' struggles in the ring as representative of their own battles for political and economic independence from Britain.

As is true today, most fighters in the sport earn their income from box-office sales. Each fighter benefits from a manager, whose primary job is to secure matches and oversee a promotional campaign that stokes public interest in the weeks leading up to the match. For the Heenan-Sayers match this included several prefight sparring exhibitions and even drinking mugs.[2] In the nineteenth century, the rise of illustrated (and later photographic) media introduced yet another source of revenue. Visual ephemera—medals, *cartes de visite*, figurines, trading cards, and broadsides—circulated on a mass scale, as the fighters amounted to celebrities and heroes for both the working and middle classes.[3] In anticipation of the Heenan-Sayers match, a full-page etching appeared in *Harper's Weekly*, while *Vanity Fair* published a satirical engraving titled "The Two Champions," showing George Washington on one side leading his troops into battle, and on the other side Heenan gripping Sayers in a headlock. After the match, the printmaking firm Currier & Ives released a commemorative print—their first documenting a match rather than an individual fighter (fig. 1.1). Produced in New York City, the print (a lithograph) would have been consigned to pushcart vendors and book stores in nearly every major American city, as well as sold via mail for under $3.00 (roughly $105.00 today) to middle-class buyers.

The Great Fight Championship between John C. Heenan and Tom Sayers of England (1860) shows the fighters and the figures surrounding them in exceedingly static poses. Heenan and Sayers appear in the center of the boxing ring, the ropes of which echo the boundaries of the rectangular composition. We can see the full face of Heenan, who raises his fists toward his opponent, although his gaze seems to land somewhere outside the ring. In each of the four corners of the ring we see referees—standing, kneeling, perched on a stool—observing the action of the fight. Just outside the ropes two men crouch in opposite corners, each holding a water bottle for their fighter. A row of reporters observe the fight with pens poised above their notepads as they watch the action unfold before them. Just behind the ring, rows of spectators line the top of the composition, seeming to recede into an infinite distance. These men are all smartly dressed, each wearing the stovepipe hat popular among middle- and upper-class white men of the era. They sit at a considerable distance from the action; they do not crowd around the ring as we might expect at a saloon, for instance. Instead, the composition emphasizes the separation of the audience from the scene before

1.1

"The Great Fight for the Championship (Heenan v. Sayers)," 1860.
Photographic print, 9.75 × 6 inches (2.54 × 15.24 cm). Published by
Currier & Ives, New York. Courtesy of the Museum of History,
Benicia, California.

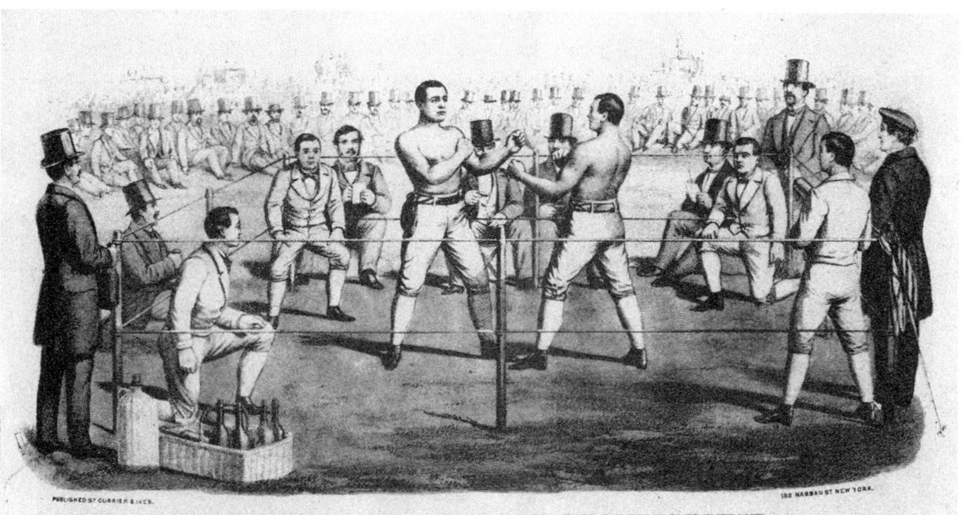

them. The distance maintained compositionally may in fact reinforce the social divide between this lower-class activity and other, more gentlemanly, pursuits. But despite this distance (physically and perhaps ideologically), we notice that everyone in this image appears to be white.

In the United States, prizefighting (and later boxing) existed as a critical component of the larger project of white, middle-class masculinity. In the late nineteenth century specifically, the transformation of the sport from bare-knuckle prizefighting to boxing ran parallel to the rise of the new, white middle-class. In a moment of extensive social, economic, and cultural changes, manhood was under negotiation. For the purposes of this book, I am most interested in how this negotiation took place within a visual field suddenly transforming with the rise of print media. That is, how did images of boxers and prizefighters participate in the formation of white, middle-class identity? How did this sport create specific links between the individual body (its power and strength) and wider social authority? And how did the affirmation of white manhood intrinsically rely on visualizing Blackness? In this chapter I explore the century-long rise of boxing in the United States—from the late eighteenth through the late nineteenth centuries and the parallel developments of both whiteness and the mass media.

More specifically, I hope to show how the image of the boxer explicitly connected from the very start to what the historian Gail Bederman has called the "metonymic facets of manhood—body, identity, and authority"—and how Black fighters figured within the visual rhetorics of white manhood.[4] While the sport of boxing (or prizefighting) has long been a source of inspiration for artists in the US context, the general lack of scholarly attention granted to sports in the field of art history has left a considerable gap in the field. This book in large part aims to fill that gap, looking specifically at the appearance of Black boxers in American paintings, prints, and photographs from the Gilded Age. These images, I argue, were instrumental in giving visual form to fears (and fantasies) about Black bodies in the public sphere. This will require that we consider a history of the sport entangled with aesthetics, and that we recognize the role of the visual in the alignment of boxing with whiteness. Because boxing in the US context has always been about race, this chapter explores how boxing initially accrued and aligned itself with whiteness—historically, culturally, formally, and ideologically. Of particular importance will be the intrinsic instability of whiteness in the nineteenth century, constantly challenged and reshaped in the face of immigration, as well as threatened by the influx of Black bodies after Emancipation.

In *Playing America's Game*, the sports historian Adrian Burgos argues that understanding the operations of race (and racial exclusion) in professional baseball requires an analysis of who remains *included*, namely Latinos. The terms of their inclusion, in Burgos's view, provides a frame by which to study the "dynamics of the color line" within the sport, as it oscillates between inclusion and exclusion.[5] He contends that "the process of incorporating Latinos illustrates the participation of league and team officials in the production of racial categories to accommodate the limited inclusion of nonwhite Others."[6] Most important for my own research, Burgos looks specifically at the cases of individual players. He considers "how specific actors sought to alter, negotiate, and transform *terms of inclusion*" within a sporting institution that manifested difference across its economic, cultural, and even social policies.[7] This methodology is one I bring forward in *Heavyweight*. I am interested in studying the individual, and extremely limited, examples of Black boxers who somehow managed to make their way into the world of professional heavyweight fighting in the Jim Crow era. What can these men and the specific terms of their inclusion tell us about the economic, social, and cultural politics of Black men more broadly? And how can the production and circulation of their images across a wide range of media shift our understanding of Blackness in this period?

We simply cannot argue that the presence of Black heavyweight boxers in the ring, in the theater, or in the newspaper are evidence of the embracing of these men. Rather, we must consider the ways that these bodies (and their images) further complicated the conflicting impulses of a white, middle-class public. As Burgos describes this phenomenon in baseball, "their desire to expand their consumer base to include Blacks was counterbalanced by concerns that white consumers preferred racial exclusivity."[8] In other words, looking at Black heavyweight boxers reveals not only the perceptions of Blackness, but the terms of whiteness as well. These boundaries were not only policed by specific rules and regulations provided within the sport, but also constructed and reaffirmed through representation. Images played a powerful role in the production of racial knowledge and in the construction of transhistorical difference.

Throughout this chapter, I rely on representations in the mass media, using these popular images to think through the entanglements of race and aesthetics. This runs counter to a history of art that privileges objects along a hierarchy of "high" and "low." I am also working against histories of photography and media that ignore the critical capacity of popular (or even iconic) sporting images. In *No Caption Needed: Iconic Photographs, Public Culture, and Liberal Democracy* Robert Hariman and John Louis Lucaites argue that these images are of little interest to media studies because of their perceived limited function within "specific subcultures." They write:

> Many devoted baseball fans will be familiar with several of the most re-vered images from the history of baseball, including "the swing" taken by Joe DiMaggio, "the slide" by Jackie Robinson, and Babe Ruth's farewell as he leaned on his bat while looking up at the stands. Each photo is sold as a commemorative object, referenced in verbal remembrance, and often re-produced more widely. They could be called icons within the subculture and they are salient without, but they don't do the same work for public life as they do for baseball.[9]

Hariman and Lucaites argue that iconic images have no power; their frame-work does not provide the possibility for this type of representation to produce wider ideology. However, I argue that in the context of the nineteenth century these images exceed the specifics of the sport itself to manifest definitions of masculinity and of race for a public grappling with profound political, social, and economic changes.

The historian David R. Roediger has written that the formation and mainte-nance of racial categories exceeds a legal process. "Race and the value of white-ness," he writes, "is learned in schools, churches, neighborhoods, factories, and families."[10] Throughout *Heavyweight* I argue that the value of whiteness is learned through images of sports as well. As spectators surround a boxing ring, watching the brutal play before them, they are also learning about Blackness and whiteness in real time.[11] Looking at the performative and representational aspects of boxing and prizefighting, we can begin to understand how the sym-bolic expressions of power taking place inside the ring are an attempt to fix the inherent instability of whiteness, and how the eventual emergence of promi-nent Black fighters, their images, and their performances, threatens to subvert established hierarchies of gender and of race.

Early Boxing in the United States and Britain

The earliest reports of prizefights in the United States appear in the eighteenth century.[12] The French emigre, Médéric Louis Élie Moreau de St. Méry, who had fled the French Revolution in 1794 for Philadelphia, described a match he wit-nessed in such riveting detail that it merits extended quotation:

> Boxing has its rules and regulations. The two athletes settle on a site for the fight. They strip to their shirts, and roll up their sleeves to the elbows.

Then at a given signal they run at each other and swing on chest, head, face and bellies, blows whose noise can only be realized by those who have been present at such spectacles.

At each new clash, they draw back, and start again from the mark. If one of the two has fallen in one of these attacks, his adversary cannot touch him as long as he is on the ground; but if he makes the slightest movement to get up, the other has the right to hit him again and force him to remain on the ground. Nobody interferes to separate the combatants: a ring is made around them, and the spectators urge on their favorites.... At the end of the fight the boxers are bruised, disfigured, and covered with blood, which they spit out, vomit out, or drip from the nose. Teeth are broken, eyes are swollen shut, and sometimes sight is completely obliterated.[13]

These matches would have taken place at night, shielded from both legislative authority and the public rules of decorum. Reading Moreau de St. Méry's description, we notice immediately the strange balance between control and chaos that the sport requires. The ring here serves not only a framing device for the fight, but also a space around which moral and social imperatives may be suspended. The fight proceeds according to a loose series of agreements—between the fighters in the ring, but also between the spectators who surround them—that makes violence not only possible but palatable.

The history of boxing in the United States is by very definition also a history of race. In the eighteenth century, immigrants in the newly urbanizing North and Black slaves in the rural South—that is, those struggling for recognition in the public sphere—were the main competitors. Boxing in colonial North America was much more violent than versions of the sport practiced in large urban centers in Britain during the same period. One North Carolina governor in 1746 described the sport as "barbarous and inhumane"; others frequently referenced it as "gouging"—a connection, no doubt, to the popular combat style, which emphasized the maiming of one's opponent by either gouging out an eye or biting off a nose or ear.[14] The brutality of the sport and its explicit emphasis on physicality also found a home in the United States, which at that point reflected those same values.[15] It would be several decades before bare-knuckle prizefighting transformed into gloved boxing, and it would transition from an immigrant (or plantation) blood sport to a middle-class pursuit.

As we have seen in the 1860 print of the Heenan-Sayers fight that opened this chapter, the boxing match provided a meeting place for the upper and lower classes; the space of the arena was one of ambiguity. While certainly not the most popular sport practiced in the United States during this period, boxing's facilitation of class mixing (within audiences) and interracial dynamics (inside the ring) was particularly unique. Initially a sport for immigrant underclasses, boxing was predominantly practiced among the Irish who streamed into New York, Boston, Philadelphia, and other major cities during the first decades of the nineteenth century. Fleeing the War of 1812 and, later, the Irish famine, these new citizens brought the tradition of bare-knuckle fighting across the Atlantic. According to the historian Jack Anderson, these Anglo-Irish prize-fighters found more supportive conditions for their profession in the United States, where authorities "were less confrontational while the political stakes or purses available on that side of the Atlantic were much more attractive than anything that was on offer in Britain at that time."[16] In the case of John L. Sullivan (1858–1918)—an early celebrity and heavyweight champion with Irish roots—prizefighting granted the opportunity to become white as well.

In the southern, slave-holding states, fighting existed as part of a larger eco-system of recreational activities permitted by planters, granted in the interest of gaining greater control and compliance.[17] Even Frederick Douglass wrote of slaves "ball-playing, wrestling, boxing, running foot races, and dancing."[18] His-torian David Wiggins describes informal boxing matches as a "common occur-rence" on antebellum plantations, but these were of two types. Boxing matches were likely organized by slaves as a form of gambling; such contests were less violent in nature, according to the limited reports available. More formal affairs—where a planter would organize a contest to fight their slaves against those of another planter—were also common, as well as profitable.[19] The events would often coincide with seasonal corn shucking and log rolling, when large numbers of slaves would gather on a single plantation. And these were often brutal fights to the death.[20] As the historian T. J. Desch Obi explains, the ad-vantages to those entering into such violent matches may have outweighed the risks. Framed as gladiators within their respective plantations, fighters may have received special treatment from the owner or preferential work assignments (e.g., driver or overseer). The extremely rare benefit for these fighters would be the possibility of boxing their way to freedom.

Bill Richmond (1763–1829), who was born into slavery in Cuckold's Town (now known as the Richmond neighborhood of New York City's Staten Is-land), provides one example of the potential that boxing offered to Black peo-ple in the antebellum United States. (fig. 1.2). When his owner fled the British invasion of Staten Island, the teenage Richmond enlisted as a stable hand. His first recorded brawl took place at the Red Lion Tavern in November 1776.[21] He entered the world of English boxing after crossing the Atlantic to live with

1.2

———

Stringer Rischgitz, "William Bill Richmond," 1805.
Pen and ink illustration, 8.75 × 9.2 inches (22.23 × 23.37 cm).
Hulton Archive.

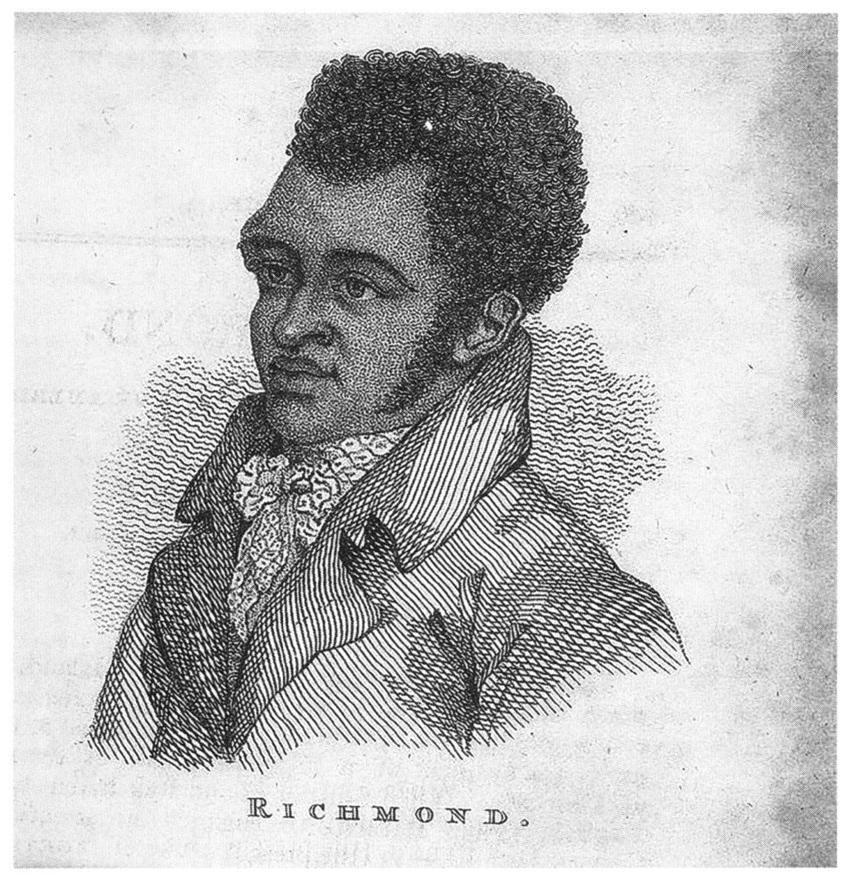

General Percy, who sponsored the former stable hand's education as well as his apprenticeship as a cabinetmaker in York. At forty-one years of age, Richmond entered the world of British bare-knuckle boxing—a sport attended by both the aristocracy as well as the urban working class. Known as "the Black Terror," he quickly distinguished himself with his quick footwork and sharp counterstrikes. In 1805 he unsuccessfully fought the up-and-coming English boxing star Tom Cribb (1781–1848). However, his most significant battle came in 1809, when he defeated the veteran bare-knuckle fighter George Maddox (1756–1811) after fifty-two rounds. Richmond's ascendancy within the boxing profession (not to mention his tendency toward flamboyant dress) attracted criticism as his dominance over white fighters threatened the stability of the established social order.[22]

Despite Richmond's precedence, however, the most infamous example of an enslaved boxer is his pupil, Thomas Molineaux (1784–1818). Born on a Virginia plantation, Molineaux fought his way to freedom (via a battle with a slave from another plantation) and eventually moved to England to face Tom Cribb—then champion of England—at Copthorne Gap in December 1810 for thirty-three rounds.[23] Although Molineaux lost the fight, as well as the rematch against Cribb nine months later, the public appetite for images of Molineaux did not decline. As mass-produced lithographs would not come to dominate the visual record for another decade, the depiction of Molineaux and Cribb in a series of miniature statuary attests to the match's popular appeal (plate 1). Distributed in England for at least a decade after the fight, these glazed earthenware figures were marketed to the middle-class masses, who would have collected them in commemoration of this significant, interracial match. Molineaux's figurine is unique, as the very first Black Staffordshire figure to represent an actual person rather than a fictional character. We could assume that Molineaux remains the most famous of the Black boxers in this period because of the wide availability of his image. His predecessor and mentor exists only in a few known etchings. And although he fights just a decade after Richmond's championship fight, Molineaux literally assumed the form of a household object via his transformation into a Staffordshire figurine; the collection of his image by white, middle-class patrons transgressed the boundaries of race that would not have typically allowed the presence of a Black person in such domestic spaces.[24]

Molineaux, a Black fighter, could only have faced a champion by moving (as he did in 1809, and as Bill Richmond did three decades before him) to England. Aside from sporadic matches across southern US plantations, most organized prizefighting in the United States during the early nineteenth century excluded Black participants. An exception would be the Battle Royal—a popular attraction that started in England in the early eighteenth century and proliferated in the United States after the Civil War. Such matches involved multiple combatants inside the ring without regard for rounds or divisions by weight class. Fighters were sometimes blindfolded or had one or both arms tied behind their backs. In almost all US cases, the participants in these fights—whether taking place on a plantation or organized independently within individual communities—were Black. In Molineaux's time and after, a collection of Black American boxers (most formerly enslaved men) similarly crossed the Atlantic to fight, such as Sam Robinson, Henry Sutton, and George Head.[25] But despite their fame in England, these fighters were predominantly ignored by the American press. Given the political tensions between England and the United States at this moment, we could imagine that if Richmond (who defeated the English champion George Maddox in 1808) was white he may have been cast as an American hero. Instead, white athletes dominate representations of boxing in colonial America. But, as we will see, this does not necessarily mean that such images escaped racist classification.

The first major American boxing celebrity, "Yankee" Sullivan (also known as James Ambrose, Frank Murray, and Francis Martin) rose to prominence in the midst of heated debates about race happening across Anglo-America (fig. 1.3). Born in Bandon, County Cork, Ireland, in 1813, James Ambrose (as Sullivan was named at birth) moved to Liverpool in his teens. While in England, he began his fighting career as a member of the criminal underworld, before being deported to Australia in 1837 for theft. According to one biographer, he was once arrested on the charge of murder because his wife suffered severe burns and died while quarreling with Sullivan. The case, however, never came to court.[26] While in Australia, Ambrose fought with other convicts, and soon stowed himself away on a ship bound for New York. After a brief, initial stay in the United States of less than a year, Ambrose departed for the London prize ring, where he took up the assumed name of Sullivan. After securing a surprise victory over an English fighter named Hammer Lane in 1841, Sullivan soon gained a reputation in the United States. Supporters called him across the Atlantic, hoping that the fighter could similarly defeat English fighters on American soil. The success of Irish over English fighters was, after all, increasingly important amid growing nativism.

Upon his arrival in America, "Yankee" Sullivan satisfied expectations by defeating the English fighter Vincent Hammond in Philadelphia, winning $100 in prize money. The next year, in November of 1842, Sullivan defeated the native New Yorker Tom Secor in a brutal sixty-five round fight, followed by another win eight months later against another Englishman, William Bell, for a stake of $300 in front of a crowd of more than six thousand spectators.[27]

1.3

James "Yankee" Sullivan, ca. 1846. Print, 17 × 24.4 inches
(43.18 × 62 cm). Prints and Photographs Division,
Library of Congress, Washington, DC.

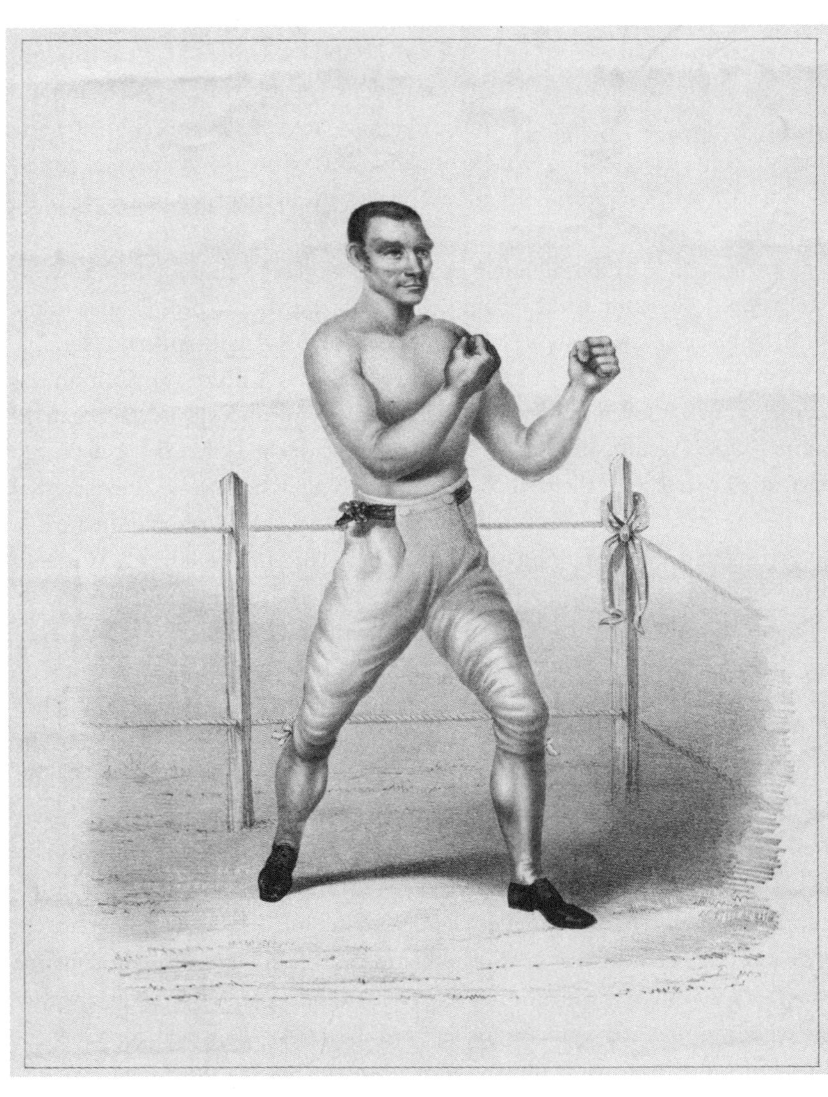

Just two weeks after his fight against Bell, "Yankee" Sullivan found himself in the midst of a legal argument about prizefighting due to his participation (as a bottle holder, rather than as a fighter) in a bout outside New York City that left one fighter dead. According to the sports historian Jack Anderson, the fight between Christopher Lilly and Thomas McCoy took place near Hastings, New York, and went on for 119 rounds, only ending with the death of McCoy, who (according to the coroner's report) choked to death on his own blood. The minister who presided over the trial summarized the social ills so commonly associated with prizefighting during the issuance of his judgment before the court:

> A prize fight brings together a vast concourse of people … the gamblers, and the bullies, and the swearers, and the blacklegs, and the pickpockets, and the thieves, and the burglars are there. It brings together a large assemblage of the idle, disorderly, vicious, dissolute people—people who live by violence—people who live by crime—their tastes run that way.… You can readily perceive the influences which such assemblages are likely to exercise on the public peace, and morals and taste; and you can therefore estimate correctly the propriety and necessity of that law which forbids their existence.[28]

For many so-called respectable audiences, prizefighting offended Victorian propriety. The reliance on brutal violence and the mixed audiences of "gamblers, bullies, thieves" were perceived as a threat to both public safety and morality.

This would not be the first open debate about prizefighting in a court of law. In fact, attempts to distinguish the more controversial prizefighting (associated with gambling) from boxing or sparring continued throughout the nineteenth century. Despite the adoption of Queensbury rules in the late 1860s—which stipulated that fighters wear gloves and fight in a twenty-four-foot ring (or one of comparable size) for rounds of three minutes duration with one minute between rounds—scholars of the sport contend that nineteenth-century America still struggled to accept the sport.[29] The Commonwealth of Massachusetts issued "An Act to Prevent Prize Fighting" in 1849, with another two cases brought before the court in 1865 and in 1871—each found fighters guilty of assault and battery.[30]

From the earliest days of the sport, many feared that the violence of the match could not be contained within the four corners of the ring. The fighter Ned O'Baldwin (a.k.a. "the Irish Giant," 1840–1875) was shot in a saloon by his business partner in November 1868, and in 1879 (before his recognition as bare-knuckle heavyweight champion), gangsters reportedly attacked and stabbed

Paddy Ryan (1851–1900) for his failure to perform at a sparring exhibition. Other fighters were prosecuted for violent crimes. In 1870, for example, a court convicted the Irish-American bare-knuckle fighter Jimmy Elliot (1838–83) for the attempted murder of the Black minstrel singer Hughey Doberty. The fighter Joe Coburn (1835–90), who immigrated to the United States from Ireland in 1850, passed more than five years in Sing Sing Prison, from March 1877 to December 1882, for assault with intent to kill. As the historian Michael Isenberg argues, "outlawed, excoriated, harangued from pulpit and press, the bare-knuckle breed as a commercial spectacle found no home in American life."[31]

In fact, prizefighting initially provided amusement for the lower classes. Contempt for the crowds that supported this form of blood sport abounded in early fight coverage. For the Bell-Sullivan fight, for example, the *Spirit of the Times* described the steamboats "with their heaped masses, rocking to and fro in the stream." They "looked like some infernal cortege seeking the waters of the Styx, or a savage eruption bursting forth for ravage and plunder."[32] Such coverage illustrates the disdain for not only the sport itself but the types of spectators it produced. These were exploits that best suited the saloon, and promoters catered to an urban underclass willing to skirt the law to attend matches on Hart's Island—a favored spot for prizefights and located just twenty miles north of Manhattan by steamboat. The *New York Express* openly rebuked the steamship operators who transported the "ruthless vagabonds" to view these fights under the headline "Demoralization in New York."[33] The fighters, the spectators, the promoters, and even those who transported audiences to the matches were all to blame for the supposed erosion of polite New York society.

Driven by an immediate need to distance wealthy elites from the reputed barbarism of the prize fight, Americans as far back as Thomas Jefferson worked diligently to stem the supposed infection of prizefighting among well-born men. The essay "On Pugilism," reprinted in the *Literary Magazine and American Register* in 1806, described a basic hierarchy of leisure activities—with art and music reserved for the most refined tastes, and pugilism relegated to a brutal and vulgar expression of debased men. Prizefighting, by design, provoked "nothing but brutality, ferociousness, and cowardess [sic]," and threatened to "debase the mind, deaden the feelings and extinguish every spark of benevolence." The writer further implored: "The force of laws, as well as the persuasion, example, and influence of all the good should be vigorously exerted to outroot every kind of violence, all contests of brute force and lawless passions, among the members of human society."[34] Given the deterioration of rank and title brought about by democracy in the New World, the growing popularity of prizefighting made social upheaval appear imminent. Many thought the turn to such a brutal sport among the lower classes would create a wild, out of control populace. Others argued that prizefighting inevitably led to a man's indulgence of other vices, such as drinking and gambling. In other words, in the early nineteenth century, prizefighting symbolized the very corruptions that a new republic should endeavor to avoid.

Early Prizefighting and the Power of Whiteness

Despite the illicit and illegal associations of the sport, champion fighters were living examples of the American dream—the unlimited potential available to a man willing to test himself, the making of one's way exclusively through hard work and bodily strength. But for most, their immigrant status complicated their rise to fame. Between 1820 and 1860, 3.7 million immigrants flowed into New York Harbor, overwhelming the city's existing population, which at that time was just under one million. Overwhelming anxiety surrounded these "new immigrants." Scholars like Matthew Jacobson have outlined how courts, academics, reformers, and others eventually developed a new racial language (i.e., Caucasian) in order to navigate the influx of Greek, German, Italian, Irish and other European races and to unify them as "white" in the twentieth century.[35] But the scene was much messier in the nineteenth century, and (as we will see) not all immigrants were created equal. In the absence of any legislation regulating the influx of newcomers, including more than a half million Irish fleeing famine from 1845 to 1861, the New Yorker Samuel F. B. Morse (inventor of the telegraph) formed the first political party against immigration—the Native American Democratic Association—in 1835. Due to their religious practices, Irish and German Catholics were particularly targeted. Over the next two decades other nativist clubs and political parties formed in an effort to restrict citizenship and voting rights, and to prevent immigrants from holding political offices or competing against "Americans" for employment.

The Order of United Americans, a nativist organization originally named the American Brotherhood, was founded in Philadelphia in 1844 with the explicit aim of opposing foreign labor.[36] A large, illustrated membership certificate for the Order, created around 1848 by the artist Charles Parsons and printed by New York's G. & W. Endicott, shows a central vignette of the female goddess Liberty elevated on a pedestal. A portrait of George Washington (dead for nearly fifty years at the time) and a banner with the nativist motto "Beware of Foreign Influence"—a phrase often mistakenly attributed to President Washington's farewell address in 1796—appear on the pedestal's base (fig. 1.4).[37] The allegorical figure of Liberty bears a crown of stars. She holds a wreath of flowers

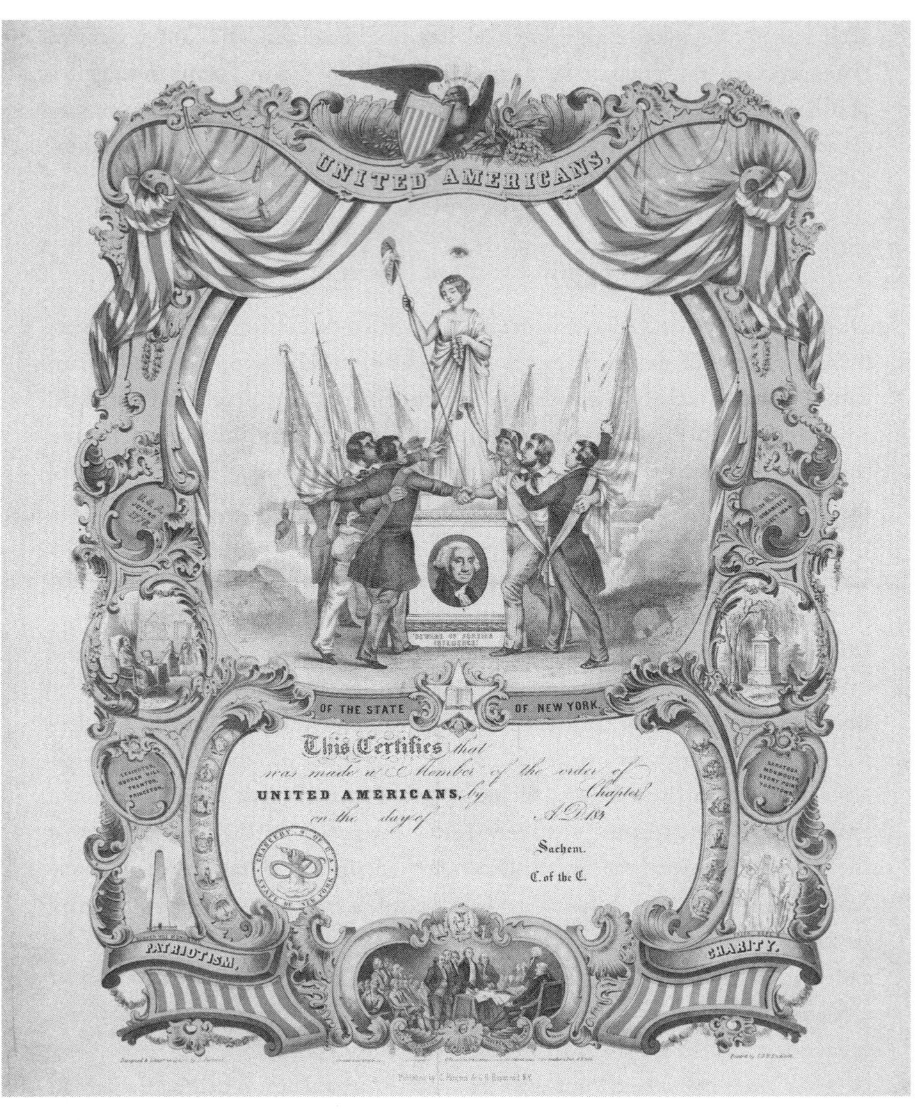

1.4

Charles Parsons, "United Americans of the State of New York,"
ca. 1848. Lithograph on wove paper, 20.8 × 15.5 inches (52.83 × 39.37
cm). Published by C. Parsons and G. H. Raymond, New York.
Library of Congress, Washington, DC.

in one hand, and grips a staff with Phrygian cap in the other. Above her head we see an eye (a symbol of vigilance) as well as a crescent of stars. Along the bottom of her pedestal are several men — soldiers, seamen, and civilians — wearing colored membership sashes and holding up flags; their hands join in solidarity to their cause. In the background of this image, two Native American bodies turn away from us, facing instead a large waterfall. The two white men in the foreground, presented to us as committed advocates, are the central focus, while the non-white bodies figuratively and literally occupy the margins. Surrounding this large vignette, we find several scenes meant to demonstrate the superiority of whiteness — its charity toward the ill, its sacrifice for the greater republic, and, above all else, its commitment to organized government. Parsons has made a great effort here to align the cause of nativism with progress and patriotism, and to depict the new immigrant as a threat to democracy itself.

The nativist movement in the nineteenth century, and its drive toward whiteness and class privilege (i.e., the American bourgeoisie), happened directly alongside the rise of prizefighting. This runs directly counter to the myth of the United States as a generous melting pot — perhaps the most powerful romantic fiction of all. The influx of Irish immigrants were of primary concern, and nativist rhetoric positioned them as the necessary "savage" component to English colonialism, frequently lumping the Irish together with the urban poor, Africans, and indigenous Americans that composed the labor pool. The rise of industrialization in the United States between 1820 and 1860 had also radically transformed the economic life of the urban citizen. This included the erosion of the apprenticeship system, in which a young boy would learn a trade, then work to acquire those skills as a journeyman, and eventually become a master. The decline of small-scale shops eroded the almost patriarchal, familial relationship between the shop owner and his workers, while capitalism reinforced a marked division between them. Industries that adapted machine technologies were suddenly reliant on cheap "sweated" labor, which proved threatening to American workers, many of whom accused new immigrants of undercutting their wages. The prizefight allowed the tension of immigrants versus so-called native-born citizens to play out in a spectacular way.

Despite its early association with illicit crime, white American boxers were marketed as neighborhood heroes as early as 1823, when the *New York Evening Post* described one young fighter — a butcher by trade — as "the champion of Hickory Street."[38] But it is more complicated than that when one considers the nationalistic overtones of the fight and its preceding events. As sports historian Elliot J. Gorn describes, just one day prior to the 1823 match described in the *Post*, the butcher had beaten a foreigner (probably Irish) after a public quarrel. The foreigner's fellow countrymen immediately accused the butcher of foul play, and in response he challenged any one of them to a prizefight. The match took place the following day.[39] Above all, this early fight demonstrates that boxers were public representatives of their neighborhoods (and their racial groups) from the earliest accounts. In the midst of pronounced antagonism between the English and the Irish in particular, the immigrants from these groups introduced the sport to the American context. In the words of Gorn, "*boxing* did not immigrate, *boxers* did," and as a result, "pugilism thrived where ethnic communities were largest, in New York and Philadelphia and, to a lesser degree, Boston, Baltimore, and New Orleans."[40] In the ring disenfranchised men had a way to earn prize money, to play out nationalist conflicts among various European ethnic communities, and to reassert their masculinity.

A particularly impactful match in this regard was the 1849 fight between the Irish immigrant "Yankee" Sullivan (by now a political strong-arm boy and saloon keeper) and the native-born American Tom Hyer (1819–64)—a butcher by trade, who had a reputation as a fierce street fighter and a political "shoulder-hitter," a name given to ruffians brought in to intimidate sympathizers of opponents in electoral politics.[41] The match, one of the few to be staged following the death of a fighter in Hastings, New York, in 1842, signaled the long-awaited return of prizefighting in the United States and the first championship fight.[42] In fact, between 1842 and 1849, only a handful of matches took place in the country. Most were held in and around New Orleans, Louisiana. Naturally, periodicals fomented excitement among their readership during the six-month lead up to the Sullivan-Hyer match.[43] Coverage of the fighters' training regimens and other speculations about the potential outcome of the match appeared in several media outlets, despite the illegal status of the sport. The *New York Herald*, for example, proclaimed: "We do not remember ever to have seen so great an excitement among certain classes of society, as has been developed during the last few days in relation to the approaching prize fight between 'Yankee Sullivan' and Tom Hyer. It is similar in some respects to the agitation produced in the public mind by the first accounts of the Mexican War."[44] The hyperbolic connections drawn between warfare and the impending prizefight underscore the stakes of the match. According to the *National Police Gazette*, the public wagered more than $300,000 on the fight (i.e., more than $10 million dollars today, adjusting for inflation).[45] For six months, "a man could scarcely enter a saloon without being asked his opinion of the two gladiators."[46]

On the afternoon of the fight in Still Pond Heights, a town located in Kent County, Maryland, Hyer and Sullivan appeared before a crowd of hundreds and stripped down to their boxing tights. Newspaper accounts reveal a public fascination with the bodies of the fighters, exposed to the cold February air as well as the gaze of the gathered spectators. According to one report:

> They were finely developed in every muscle as their physical capacity could reach.... Sullivan, with his round, compact chest, formidable head, shelving flinty brows, fierce glaring eyes, and clean turned shoulders, looked the very incarnation of the spirit of mischievous genius; while Hyer, with his broad, formidable chest, and long muscular limbs, seemed as if he could almost trample him out of life, at will.[47]

The emphasis here on describing the physical form of the fighter and their embodiment is of particular interest, as it indicates the alignment of the body—or more specifically the image of the body—with an emerging definition of masculinity.

Although the championship match included less than ten minutes of actual fighting time (with Hyer defeating Sullivan), according to sports historians this landmark event had major ramifications for urban and racial politics. However, my interest lies in the proliferation of visual imagery that followed. Hyer ended up a celebrity, followed around the city by reporters, while in saloons men sang "The Pleasant Ballad of Tomme Hyer and Ye Sullivan."[48] After the fight, hundreds of papers were distributed and lithographers sold pictures of the combatants as fast as they could be printed. The public embrace of this fight—in print, in image, and in song—is a surprising outcome for an illegal activity, but one that lasted for decades. Even as late as 1948 the writer William Riordan reported that the battle lived on, as Hyer and Sullivan appeared frozen in perpetual opposition, in lithographs that continued to hang on the walls of working-class taverns.[49]

As we look at one of these images from our contemporary perspective, we may only see a landscape of whiteness (plate 2). Two shirtless men appear at the center of the ring and the composition with fists raised. Tom Hyer, the fighter on the right, appears taller, reflecting his four-inch height advantage over Sullivan. We note that several of the figures in the scene are numbered, their names and identities corresponding to the legend below the image.[50] Inside the corners of the ropes the fighters' seconds—Tom Burns and John McCleester—appear on bended knee, while the managers and promoters stand at their sides. Spectators surround the ring, and it seems that great attention has been paid here to depicting their individual faces, their clothing; some gesture and point at the central action, with their mouths open mid-shout. From our present circumstance we may in fact linger on the seascape that comprises the top half of the composition, underscoring perhaps the wildness of the scene before us. That is, looking out onto this watery horizon we may interpret the brutality of the fight as simply another manifestation of "nature."

It is doubtful that the original viewers of this scene, however, would overlook what is almost imperceptible to contemporary eyes—the swaths of blue and green cloths that appear on opposite sides of the composition. The figures to the right of this scene are wearing blue scarves with stars (a visual shorthand for the stars and stripes of the US flag) and those on the left bear emerald green with white spots for Ireland. Although both fighters would certainly have tied their colored sashes to the ropes of the ring before the fight began, we see that for the purposes of this illustration they wear them during the match. This division of blue and green symbolizes the sharper line between native-born Americans and Irish during this period, who were engaged, as we know, in a deeper political, economic, and social antagonism. From the perspective of a nineteenth-century viewer, then, what we see here is not simply a historic match between two prominent white fighters. Every viewer of this match—both in real time and in retrospect via this lithograph—would have understood this as not only a fight between an American and an Irishman but as an example of the superiority of the American race, exemplified by Hyer's defeat of Sullivan. Early prizefighters, like Tom Hyer, came to be nationalist symbols, which, of course, required a careful negotiation (or whitewashing) of European ethnic identity. Though it may not appear so at first glance, we are viewing a "battle of the races" that predates the more well-known match between Jim Jeffries (1875–1953) and the Black boxer Jack Johnson (1878–1946) sixty years later.[51]

The first years of prizefighting in the United States were tumultuous. As a sport associated with gambling and other vices, many openly debated its virtue (not to mention its legality). But by the 1850s, in part encouraged by the landmark fight between Sullivan and Hyer, it had grown into a popular sport, practiced dutifully among the working classes and promoted by doctors, ministers, and even politicians. Sports were promoted as a path to improving the spiritual and mental health of an urban public overwhelmingly focused on the intellectual at the perceived expense of the physical. Bolstered by the Victorian obsession with hard work, many pointed to athletics in general as a way to teach "Christian" values, to build moral character, and to instill lessons in leadership and cooperation. The type of fighting practiced by most American men in the later nineteenth century, however, was not the bare-knuckle prizefighting popularized among immigrant communities. Referred to as "professors of pugilism," these boxers wore gloves and did not fight for prize money; they referred to their style of fighting as "sparring."

Sparring masters publicly exhibited their skills in pugilistic "science" on stage and provided lessons on boxing in private gymnasiums. These boxers were not the prizefighters of the underclass but had a modicum of respectability in the greater public sphere. Public advertisements from the early nineteenth century took great pains to align boxing with the more elegant (and noble) practice of swordsmanship and promoted pugilism as a mode of self-defense or more gentlemanly way to settle disputes than dueling, further distancing it from the vulgar entertainment of prizefighting. Many considered sparring a way to invigorate both the mind and body of the modern man, and these "professors of pugilism" made great efforts to maintain the honor of their profession. Sparring lessons were marketed to individuals engaged in a sedentary (read: respectable) lifestyle as a way of "opening the chest, strengthening the arms, and adding strength to the valetudinarians."[52] Instructors who worked to distance themselves from the barbarity of prizefighting were certainly not helped by ring fighters who did double duty—fighting in bare-knuckle fights for a purse while also exhibiting and giving lessons.

Evidence of the increasing public appetite for athletes includes a wide range of examples from both visual and material culture. For example, after John C. Heenan defeated Tom Sayers of England in 1860, more than five individual lithographs produced by Currier & Ives featured him as subject, while the other four fighters commemorated received only a single image. To celebrate Heenan's defeat over Sayers, F. B. Smith & Hartmann in New York City issued a series of commemorative medals, where Heenan (identified as "the Champion of America") and Sayers (labeled "the Champion of England") appear in profile on one side of the coin with the details of the fight printed on the obverse. The early representations of prizefights circulating in the late nineteenth century via a diversity of media demonstrate how these events exceeded the specifics of any one fight.[53]

Boxing and the Media

As illustrated by the example of John Heenan, a well-established visual culture of boxing already existed in the mid-nineteenth century. Over the following decades, public support for and representations of prominent boxers continued to increase. The rise of print media and, more specifically, newspapers allowed for the proliferation of boxing within the visual culture of this period. The mid- to late nineteenth century was indeed a transformative moment in mass media.[54] In the colonial era, for example, newspapers were produced by and for the government, and supported by wealthy patrons, usually those with an interest in politics, or actually employed in politics themselves. The prose would not have been accessible to the common people. Writers used pseudonyms, referred to public people with elided letters, and generally assumed that their readers were already well informed about events and familiar with every edition of the newspaper. But following the American Revolution, newspapers developed into a more explicit instrument of propaganda. They presented a picture of a public united first against Britain, and then in favor of a new democracy. By the turn of the nineteenth century the development of the marketplace was a central concern. Newspapers were critical tools in advancing the market revolution. Providing a way to bear the expenses associated with publication, many bought into the sale of products wholeheartedly. News periodicals distributed information about the market through stock quotations and price currents. Sophisticated tables, originally developed to cover election returns, also began to include economic news (especially after 1840), including share prices, local currency, and so forth. To become a vehicle of the public sphere, the size of the newspaper increased, giving writers more room to essentially treat the paper as a public forum in which to present and debate ideas. By 1860 newspapers expanded to accommodate an increasing number of advertisements. These newspapers doubled in size—from four pages to eight—with eight columns per page and a slight variety in font and text size.

Newspapers also began to organize news matter to appeal to specific demographics, such as women, youths, sports fans, and businessmen, in an effort to increase readership. Advertisements, as well as cartoon illustrations to accompany fictional stories, were a key strategy for newspapers to do this, and were often interspersed between news matter—with the separation between the two demarcated with lines and labels. Some newspapers were primarily image based, while others would have issued a weekly edition with more images. Stock etchings for staple images such as horses, houses, and stores allowed for the standardization of image production. In the mid-nineteenth century, news printers used woodcuts to print images; later, they would switch to wood engravings. Portraits would be engraved from a photograph, whereas large scale depictions of events were amalgamations of individual drawings. Artists—in this case sketch artists or photographers—would be sent out into the field to gather pictures for a specific article. An in-house chief artist would consolidate the images and select the most effective ones to be printed.

Sporting images and sports coverage gained popularity in the last quarter of the nineteenth century, a period similarly characterized by sweeping changes in attitudes about masculinities. The *New York World*, for example, began sports coverage in 1890. Baseball received the most coverage, consuming three to five columns of the six-page paper each day. Boxing news appeared in alternating issues of the Friday edition, with between one and four articles on fights and athletes. Prior to the 1880s, sports reporting had more typically been assigned to fans, local correspondents, or the most novice newspapermen.[55] The most popular sport covered early in the century was baseball, followed closely by horse racing.[56] But the news media provided inconsistent coverage of these sports, due not only to the lack of organized events in the winter months but also the political news of the Civil War, which began to consume a majority of news columns in 1860. After the war, dedicated sporting journals emerged.

For example, *Turf, Field, and Farm*, founded in 1865, was an authority in the world of horse racing—a sport that had begun in the antebellum South but was soon popularized in the urban North and Midwest. With three dedicated sports reporters, *Turf, Field, and Farm* (one of a dozen publications devoted to turf sports) emphasized the propriety of horse racing and the respectability of its fans. The editors advertised their position on prizefighting, stating, "The paper denounces pugilism, and all low, disgusting sports."[57] Such publications argued for the moral superiority of certain sports. In the opening issue of *Forest and Stream* (founded 1873), for example, a letter from the publishers proclaimed: "*Forest and Stream*... will pander to no depraved tastes, nor pervert the legitimate sports of land and water to those base uses which always tend to make them unpopular with the virtuous and good."[58] The emphasis here on intelligence and virtue creates a difference between these more "legitimate" sports and the wantonness of prizefighting, alongside its attendant attractions of drinking and gambling.

Grandstanding aside, publications dedicated to field sports were not particularly lucrative. At least twenty-eight of these journals and magazines were defunct by the last decade of the nineteenth century.[59] Even moves to cover other sports news—cycling, yachting, tennis—were not enough to sell more than (at best) 94,000 issues.[60] This would all change with the rise of prizefighting and the concurrent shift in mainstream news publications to appeal to the common man, rather than to the gentleman. Founded in New York in 1845, the weekly newspaper *National Police Gazette*, for example, prided itself on its ability to answer many of the questions that men faced at the end of the nineteenth century, as both workplaces and gender roles underwent dramatic changes. According to the historian Guy Reel in his study of the newspaper, "Its blend of crime stories, sporting promotions, woodcut illustrations (and later, photographs) of scantily clad, often athletic, or talented young women helped create a national culture of male fans."[61] Many of the illustrations were just as salacious as the stories.

Alongside its competitors, such as Joseph Pulitzer's *New York World* and William Randolph Hearst's *Morning Journal*, the *Gazette* built a reputation for its reporting on the debaucheries of urban life, particularly the crimes and the follies of the underclass—positioning it somewhere between a newspaper and tabloid.[62] The *Gazette* billed itself as the "most lurid journal ever published in the United States."[63] As proclaimed on the cover of the November 8, 1845, issue: "We offer this week a most interesting record of horrid murders, outrageous robberies, bold forgeries, astounding burglaries, hideous rapes, vulgar seductions, and recent exploits of pickpockets and hotel thieves in various parts of the country."[64] The *Gazette* covered corrupt subjects, which included not only reportage on scandals but also an illustration program that threatened the laws of Victorian propriety. Boxing would become a perfect subject for cultivating this new class of reader.

The editor, Richard Kyle Fox, who took over in 1876, famously stewarded the *Gazette* into its position as the most sensational newspaper of its era. Under Fox's guidance, the weekly transformed into the leading sports journal of its time, providing readers with information on prominent fights, profiles of popular athletes, as well as advertising, promoting, and sponsoring individual sporting events. According to its own self-promotion, the *Gazette*, also known as "the Barber's Bible," was "required reading for any sports fan."[65] Its subtitle was the *Leading Illustrated Sports Journal in America*. Along the bottom of the tabloid-sized pages the editor proclaimed: "There is only one sporting paper worth considering—The Police *Gazette*" and "Sporting people who know a thing or two say the Police *Gazette* is the very best." Boxing provided a natural subject for the *Gazette*, as the newspaper remained extremely popular among the male patronage of taverns, where these matches were often held. The *Gazette*'s coverage of the championship fight between Irish-American boxer Paddy Ryan and the English-born Joe Goss in 1880, for example, kept the presses hot and generated an unprecedented 400,000 copies.

The success of the Ryan-Goss coverage prompted Fox to commit explicitly to sports reporting. He introduced a sporting news column titled "Our National Game," where discussions of the newly professionalized sport of baseball appeared alongside gossip about its athletes. To get the paper into as many hands as possible, Fox offered discounted subscription rates. The average circulation of 150,000 copies reached almost every city in the United States. We can well imagine that the readership numbers were at least five times more, as many would have accessed a copy of the *Gazette* in a public space—saloons, barber shops, and hotels—rather than via individual subscription. To further support interest in sports (and thereby his publication), Fox began to sponsor belts, trophies, and prizes for competitions; this investment paid off in increased sales of his paper. Fox's *Gazette* delivered an early model of journalism that persists today—one that not only reports on the news, but creates it as well.

Unlike the sporting newspapers devoted to the more gentlemanly pursuits, the *Gazette* catered specifically to an immigrant readership with limited literacy skills. This required a mode of communication based on images, and the illustrations were a vital component of the *National Police Gazette*, which included a full-page illustration on the front and the back of every issue. In fact, the front page of the *Gazette* from 1876 until 1906 (i.e., the years corresponding to Fox's editorship) included only a giant woodcut and the *Gazette* flag. Occasionally a headline would appear on the cover, but never a story.[66] The illustration enticed readers—a convincing testament to the importance of the image in this new age of mass media. In the words of Elliott J. Gorn, "the *Gazette* existed to display spectacles, to appeal to individual's lusts, fears, hatreds, fantasies and desires with viscerally moving images that transformed the world's utter incomprehensibility into readily consumable visual information."[67] Publications like the *Gazette* were at the center of a new, large-scale visual culture in the nineteenth-century United States.

Sporting illustrations slowly increased in popularity throughout the early 1880s, averaging a half page per issue in 1880 and nearly a full page in 1883. By the mid-1880s the space devoted to pictures made up more than half of the total paper, and illustrations of boxing and bodybuilding began to appear with increasing frequency, averaging two pages per issue. By the early 1900s sports were even more prominently featured, with nearly five or six pages devoted to sporting images—the number split predominantly between boxing and bodybuilding. This increase in the illustration of sports coincided directly with the rise of heavyweight champion John L. Sullivan. According to Reel, 30 percent of *Gazette* headlines from 1879 to 1906 covered boxing, with a peak in 1889 at 60 percent of all headlines that year. Even when a boxing illustration did not appear on the *Gazette*'s cover, Fox often included a headline to promote inside coverage of the popular sport.[68] Fox also advertised engravings of prizefighters deemed "suitable for framing." An issue in November 1880, for example, offered to hopeful collectors a scene from a match involving John Heenan and Tom Sayers. In March of the following year, Fox again advertised an engraving—free to annual subscribers—of Heenan vs. Sayers. Fox proclaimed, "No Saloon, Restaurant, or Sporting House should be without it."[69] An advertisement for Fox photographs, published in the *National Police Gazette* on March 31, 1894, listed thirty-three boxers (the most popular out of Fox's collection of 30,000 cabinet photos); each cabinet photo could be purchased for ten cents.

The Celebrity of John L. Sullivan

Born in Boston to Irish parents, the Irish-American boxer John L. Sullivan appeared right at the center of this drive toward the promotion of prizefighting—in both print and visual media. A favored subject of the *Gazette* (fig. 1.5), Sullivan "drifted" into boxing at the age of nineteen, when he was invited onto the stage at a variety show at the Dudley Street Opera House to fight a young pugilist named Tom Scannel. After knocking Scannel across a piano on the stage, Sullivan moved to fighting in theaters and music halls around Boston. He faced middleweight champion Mike Donovan (1847–1918) and the former English champion Joe Goss (1837–85) in four-round matches; he also fought (and defeated) Johnny "Cockey" Woods and the "Champion of Massachusetts" Dan Dwyer. Despite his lack of formal training, Sullivan's success led almost immediately to profitability. By the age of twenty-one, he decided to devote himself to the sport full-time. In late 1880 Sullivan traveled to Cincinnati to face John Donaldson (1853–97), and defeated the "Champion of the West" in twenty-one minutes. In what would become his typical theatrical style, Sullivan issued his challenge to any fighter who dared to face him in the pages of the *Cincinnati Enquirer* on December 9, 1880. Sullivan's letter to the editor of the *Enquirer* proclaimed: "I am prepared to make a match to fight any man breathing for any sum from one thousand dollars to ten thousand dollars at catch weights. This challenge is especially directed to Paddy Ryan and will remain open for a month if he should not see fit to accept it."[70]

The Irish American, bare-knuckle heavyweight champion Paddy Ryan rejected the widely reprinted call, reportedly advising Sullivan to "go and get a reputation."[71] And so Sullivan ended up in New York, making his debut in March 1881 in Manhattan's Lower East Side at Harry Hill's Dance Hall and Boxing Emporium, one of the most popular sporting venues in the city, frequented by men like Thomas Edison, P. T. Barnum, and Oscar Wilde. He offered fifty dollars to any man who could last four rounds with him in the ring.[72] Without question the most popular sports hero of the nineteenth century (and perhaps the nation's most famous citizen), Sullivan's reign as heavyweight champion lasted ten years, as did his media celebrity. Sullivan often published challenges to the public in newspapers, and his fights filled Madison Square Garden. According to historians of the period, Sullivan "endorsed everything from boxing gloves to beef broth."[73] He even had his own catch phrase, which he cried aloud from nearly a thousand stages: "My name's John L. Sullivan and I can lick any son-of-a-bitch alive."[74]

When Ryan finally agreed to a match with Sullivan in February 1882, Fox backed Ryan with a $1,000 stake, and also guaranteed half of the $5,000

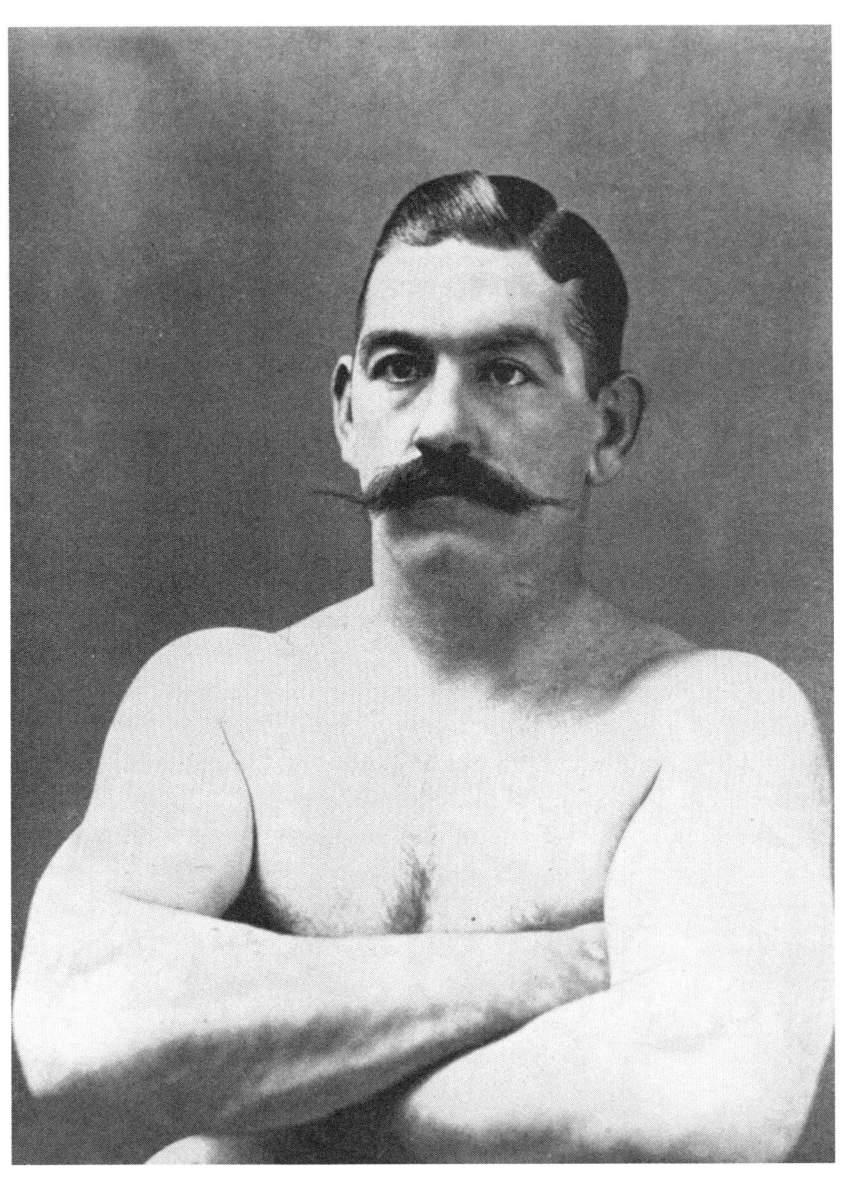

1.5

——

John L. Sullivan, ca. 1894. Photograph by Bob Thomas,
6.6 × 9.25 inches (17 × 23.5 cm). Popperfoto Collection.

purse—perhaps a consequence of Fox's reported dislike of Sullivan following a run-in between the two men in 1881.[75] The press coverage devoted to this one fight included everything from the training regimens of the athletes to a detailed analysis of their fighting colors in weekly reports leading up to the match on February 7. The *Gazette* even doubled its normal page count—from eight to sixteen pages—to manage the amount of exposure given to the bout.

Sullivan prevailed in the ninth round of the fight, wrenching the bare-knuckle heavyweight title from Ryan, who had held it since May 30, 1880. However, we might consider Richard K. Fox the real winner of the match. Fox boasted in the *Gazette* that the paper's special supplement, published the week prior to the match, had sold more than twice its normal print run of 150,000. The Sullivan-Ryan fight, however, was just the beginning of the *Gazette*'s popular (and lucrative) coverage and outright sponsorship of Sullivan's fights, as well as those of other prominent fighters, including the women's champion Daisy Daly and the Cincinnati-based fighter Harry "the Black Diamond" Woodson (1852–87), shot dead after only five years of professional fighting.[76] By the late 1880s, sports coverage made up more than half of the written copy in most issues of the *Gazette*.[77]

John L. Sullivan emerged as an unprecedented commercial success. He completed two US tours in 1883–84 and 1886–87, offering $1,000 to any challenger who could last four rounds in the ring with him. Sullivan's biographer estimates that he earned between $80,000 and $100,000 on just one of these tours.[78] Moving outside the boundaries of the ring, the reporting on Sullivan began to include the fighter's personal life as his fame grew throughout the 1880s. This included stories about Sullivan and his wife, who were rumored to fall into violent drunken quarrels quite frequently. Again, as Elliot Gorn has explained: "Sullivan rejected the routine world of work and family to live by his fists and his wits. . . . To turn of the century American men, Sullivan symbolized the growing desire to smash through the fluff of bourgeois gentility and the tangle of corporate ensnarements to the throbbing heart of life."[79] The overwhelming interest in Sullivan attests to his status as a symbol of manhood for Gilded Age America.

Given his status as the child of Irish immigrants, Sullivan's infamy was particularly poignant. Only three decades earlier, native-born Americans described members of the Irish "race" as savage, bestial, and lazy; many writers argued that the Irish were a separate caste, a "dark" race with potential connections to the African continent.[80] A cartoon published in *Harper's Weekly* in 1871, just ten years before Sullivan's first fight, depicts the hostile threat of Irish-American control from the nativist perspective (fig. 1.6). We see a man perched atop a powder keg; one arm is raised above his head, clutching a bottle of rum. His

1.6

Thomas Nast, "The Usual Irish Way of Doing Things."
Harper's Weekly, September 2, 1871. History Project,
University of California, Davis.

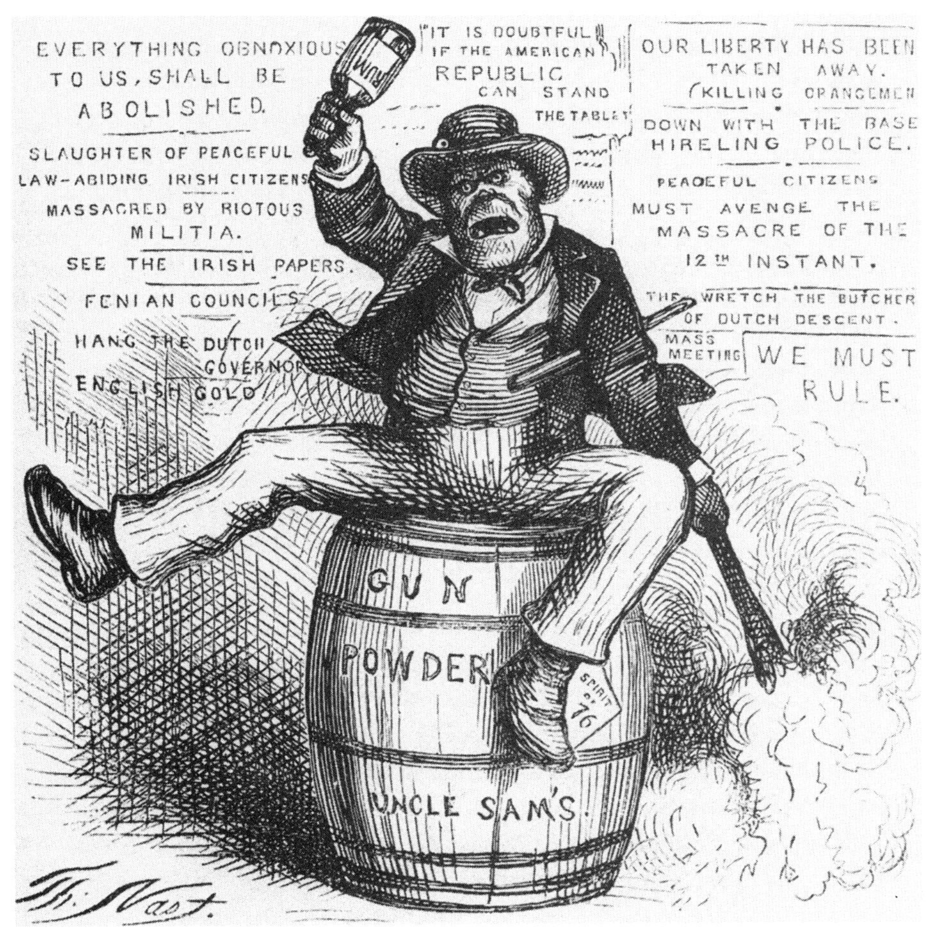

race is ambiguous, as he appears more like an ape than a man—with small eyes, a flattened nose with wide nostrils, and a wide-open mouth revealing sharpened incisors in the bottom jaw. Sarcastic slogans cover the background of the image; to his right appears the phrase "WE MUST RULE." Even at the end of the nineteenth century, popular myths continued to circulate about the inferior intelligence of the Irish, aided by widespread acceptance of physiognomy that linked them to an African rather than the presumed superior Anglo-Teutonic heritage. According to the historian David R. Roediger, the comparisons (and equivalences) drawn between African Americans and the Irish were a result of their shared experiences of displacement and longing as well as their similar positions within domestic service and the transportation industries.[81] But despite these similarities, Irish-Americans held little sympathy for African Americans and did little to advance the abolition of slavery. "Instead of seeing their struggle as bound up with those of colonized and colored people around the world," Roediger writes, "they [Irish-Americans] came to see their struggles as *against* such people."[82] Irish-Americans, then, focused on their own transformation into whiteness, capitalizing on their ability to organize and the power of the immigrant vote. The reconstruction of Sullivan's race was a social campaign with a markedly visual component. Dr. Dudley Sargent, a professor of physical training at Harvard, evaluated the fighter as an ideal example of "the brawn and sinew that conquers both opponents and environments and sustains the race."[83] Sullivan's body was measured, evaluated, and photographed as a specimen of excellence.

An image from near the end of Sullivan's career underscores the extent to which his celebrity depended on his heritage as the children of Irish immigrants being usurped by his affiliation with American identity and values. In the image, taken in 1898, we can see Sullivan poised to confront an unseen opponent out of the frame. His growing mid-section (a reality for most in their fourth decade of life) is partially obscured by his raised fists (fig. 1.7). The position in which they appear—curved, one arm slightly lower with its fist pointing in toward the torso and the other arm, extended outward with the knuckles perpendicular to the ground—reflects the rushed, straight punches he famously used in bare-knuckle fights. But we also notice that Sullivan here wears an American flag at his waist in place of the traditional silk sash.

In the midst of a contentious political battle between Irish descendants and the so-called nativists, boxing presented Sullivan with an opportunity to assert himself as white. Sullivan, through his repeated defeat of white fighters, disproved the myth of Irish inferiority in a public arena. His success in the ring translated to wider acceptability of Irish Americans within the estab-

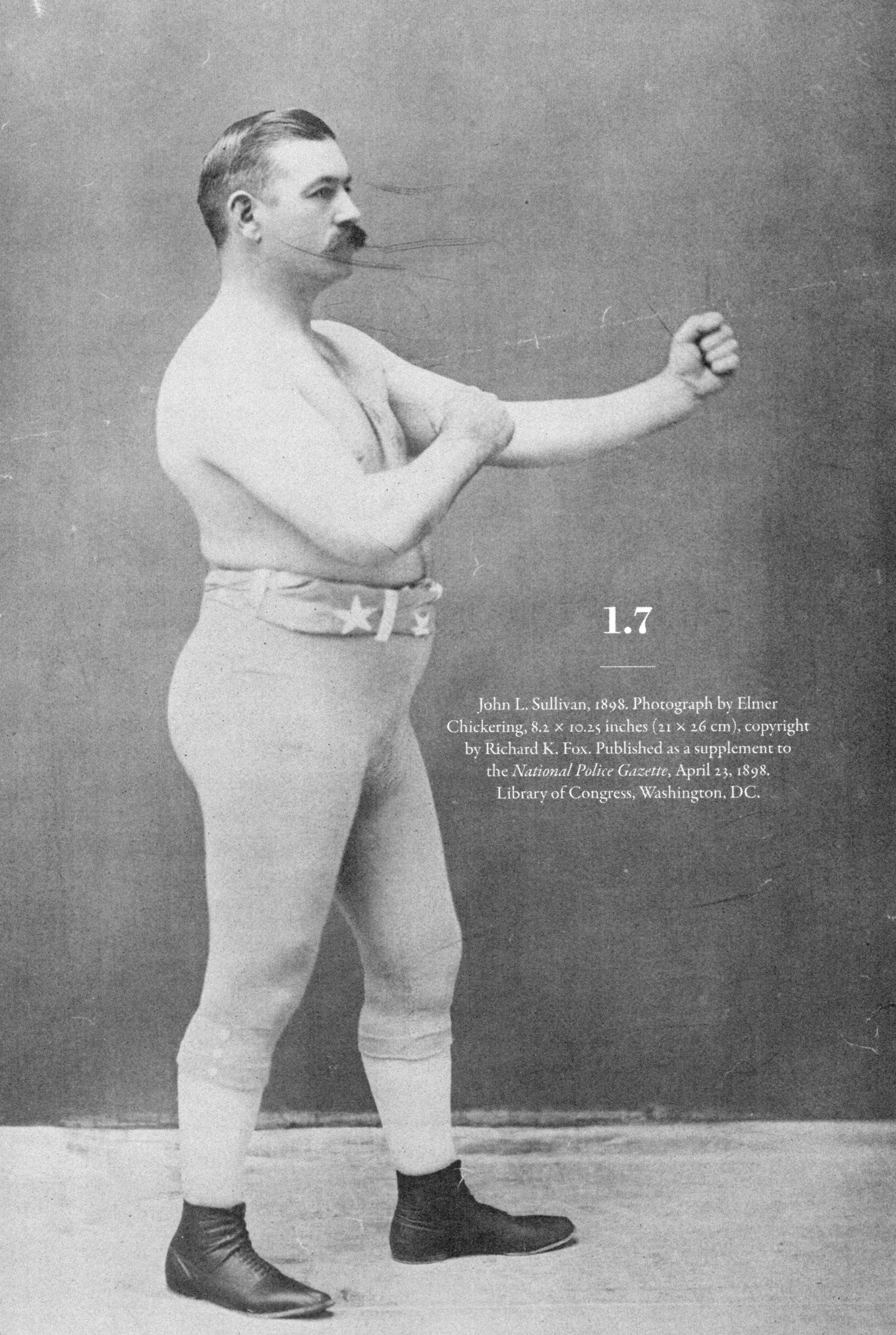

1.7

———

John L. Sullivan, 1898. Photograph by Elmer Chickering, 8.2 × 10.25 inches (21 × 26 cm), copyright by Richard K. Fox. Published as a supplement to the *National Police Gazette*, April 23, 1898. Library of Congress, Washington, DC.

lished structure of white supremacy. During the period of Sullivan's reign as heavyweight champion (1882 to 1892) his visage appeared in the *Gazette* almost weekly. The popularity of Sullivan's image inspired Fox to sell subscribers individual cabinet cards of the boxer for ten cents, alongside images of scantily clad actresses. While many white, middle-class men quickly claimed Sullivan as an American hero, we will later see that this was not the case for Black fighters who succeeded him.

The bodies of fighters were integral to the promotion of the sport, as, in the words of the historian Louis Moore, late nineteenth-century white audiences "yearned to see big, strong, muscular white bodies perform" to assuage their own anxieties around racial superiority.[84] The fighter's body was, in short, a physical display of the power of whiteness.[85] At the 1893 World Columbian Exposition in Chicago, visitors to the fair would also have encountered the sparring performance of the white heavyweight champion, Jim Corbett (1866–1933), who fought African and "Oriental" savages in the Midway portion of the fair—a section of villages intended to represent "primitive" cultures in contrast to the exhibits in the White City. The sculpted musculature of fighters like John L. Sullivan were frequently discussed in the press as specimens of white manhood. As instruments of the social and political power of whiteness, sports writers often produced effusive descriptions of the fighter's bodies, using terms like "hard as a rock" and comparing them to gods.[86] The ritual of a fighter disrobing inside the ring at the start of the fight often whipped fans into a frenzy, as evidenced by one description of Sullivan's appearance in Chicago: "When the magnificent proportions of the Boston pet loomed up in the crowd the audience cheered hastily—He was stripped to the waste [*sic*], and his giant proportions excited wonder and admiration."[87] The most widely circulated images of Sullivan during his reign as champion show him nude from the waist up, poised for battle with his fists raised or with arms crossed in front of his chest with his eyes locked on something just beyond the camera's frame (figs. 1.5, 1.7). Both compositional standards encourage the viewer to focus on the physical form of Sullivan's body, a celebrated "ideal" that provided an (aspirational) model for the viewer—undoubtedly white, middle-class, and male.

The historian Amy Lippert has argued that the technical innovations in the mid-nineteenth century resulted in a dramatic increase in the inherently visual cult of celebrity.[88] Prior to this period, stars were mostly unrecognizable to the general population, and their image remained inaccessible to the majority of America. Celebrity status had been confined to cosmopolitan centers, and most stars were connected to the theater. Photographers specifically began capitalizing on celebrity images as soon as the daguerreotype was invented, and celebrities quickly took advantage of the way that these images could increase their popularity. The price of these photographs was based on the fame of the sitter. According to Lippert, "by the late 1850s and early 1860s, theatrical stars were posing for *cartes de visite* that could be circulated through the mail, posted in public storefronts, and sold for a quarter—about the same price as the cheapest (gallery or pit) ticket to a live show."[89]

In her study of nineteenth-century San Francisco, Lippert argues that the proliferation of bodily imagery played a key role in the process of commodifying and providing intimate access to these performers. San Franciscans, already comfortable with the circulation of photography in familial and romantic contexts, simply added photos of celebrities to the mix. While Lippert focuses in her study on female theatrical stars, we could argue that the images of male athletes operate on a similar register. The proliferation of the boxer's image was partly responsible for the production of male identity (and sexuality) as well. This is particularly the case for boxers, who unlike the athletes of team sports, are the sole focus of the spectator. Their facial expressions, vocalizations, and movements are all easily tracked by the audience, which looks up onto the elevated ring not unlike the viewers seated in the audience of a theatrical stage play. Like the actors in Lippert's study, these men similarly circulated as cabinet cards, which allowed the consumer not only to collect these images but also to attribute value to certain bodies—templates for the creation of a new self.

Conclusion

Throughout the early days of prizefighting in the United States, print coverage of the sport almost always included visual information. Portraits of fighters—posed either clothed or in their boxing trunks—circulated with increasing frequency as the century progressed and as the technology of the camera advanced. The images of the fighter "Yankee" Sullivan for example, most frequently circulated as engravings or lithographs. But with the next generation of fighters, including John C. Heenan and Tom Sayers, we see the introduction of photographic representations as well. By the time we arrive at John L. Sullivan, the advancement of reproductive technologies allowed for the dissemination of the boxer's image across newspapers and broadsides from coast to coast.

Despite the proliferation of these images, a closer examination finds that most adhere to a strict visual regime. In many cases, we find a simple frontal portrait showing the fighter from the waist up with their arms crossed in front to highlight the bulging of both pectoral and bicep muscles (fig. 1.5). Other examples show us a full-length image of a fighter posed in boxing tights with his torso exposed—and this is the example upon which I would like us to linger. In some cases, the figure may face the front of the picture straight on, while more often the body turns slightly so that we have a three-quarter view (fig. 1.8). In both examples, one foot appears in front of the other, suggesting the dynamic movement of the figure. He raises both arms and extends them, bent at forty-five-degree angles, fists clenched and pointed toward an unseen opponent; one arm closes the body of the figure at mid-torso, while the other extends in space. The head turns in the same direction as the poised arms; the fighter's gaze never meets our own. We see this pose rehearsed across decades and across media. As Black boxers come into the sport, we see them adopt the same arrangements—body slightly turned, fists cocked, gaze averted (fig. 1.9). The pose even persists into our current moment, rehearsed by everyone from a child trying to look "tough" to professional fighters. It is a trope that often goes unnoticed, accepted instead as part of the visual economy of the sport.

While prolific, the boxer's pose is far from neutral. As later chapters will demonstrate, the boxer is but one component of a wider visual regime surrounding the white male body in this period, which included the rise of the physical culture movement as well as an intersecting interest in the classical ideal. In his analysis of physical fitness trends at the end of the nineteenth century, John F. Kasson has argued that looking closely at these masculine symbols of strongmen and athletes tells us "about how modernity was understood in terms of the body and how the white male body became a powerful symbol by which to dramatize modernity's impact and how to resist it.... They also tell us that hopes and fears, aspirations and anxieties are often difficult to distinguish."[90] In a new urban and political environment under the influence of immigrants, these men were looking for a way to gain social autonomy and reclaim white patriarchal authority, and they did it through the cultivation of the physical body. As its image circulated and traded among the male, middle-class public, the boxer's body performed as a stand-in for ideal form. Moreover, the specific arrangement of the boxer in the frame of these images allows for the direct observation (or consumption) of his body.

In psychoanalytic terms, the function of these representations would have been the *objet petit a* (or object of desire), an image set up for (and consumed by) white middle-class men in an attempt to compensate for their own loss of political, economic, or cultural capital. While waves of immigrants, and later free Blacks, enter the urban metropolis, men like "Yankee" Sullivan, John L. Sullivan, and later in the century Jim Jeffries, allow for the continued narcissistic projection of the fantasy of white superiority. This was so effective, in part, because of the overall interest in the body itself as a site for moral and psychic

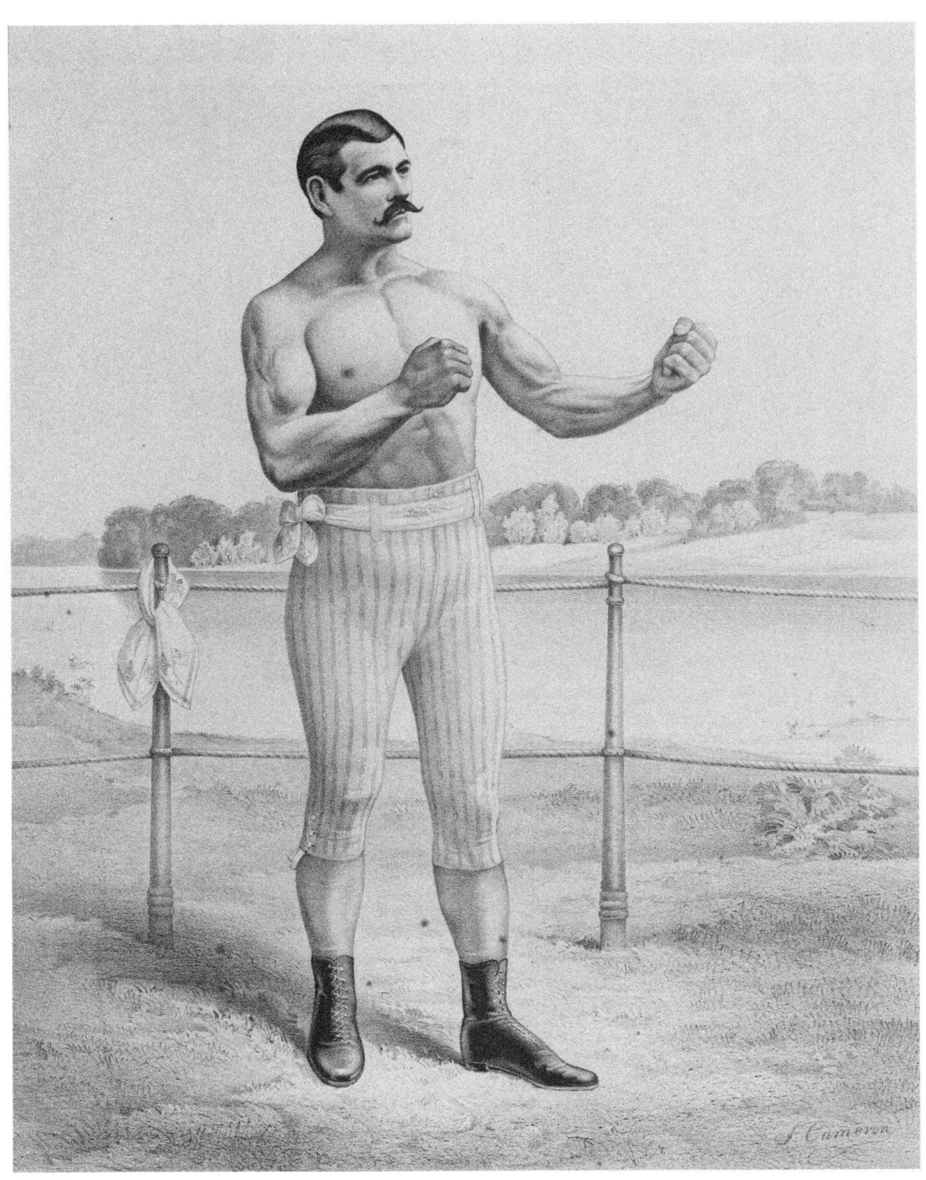

1.8

"John L. Sullivan: Champion Pugilist of the World," 1883.
Hand-colored lithograph, 14.5 × 19.25 inches (36.83 × 48.9 cm).
Published by Currier & Ives, New York. Gift of Lenore B.
and Sidney A. Alpert. Springfield Museums, Massachusetts.

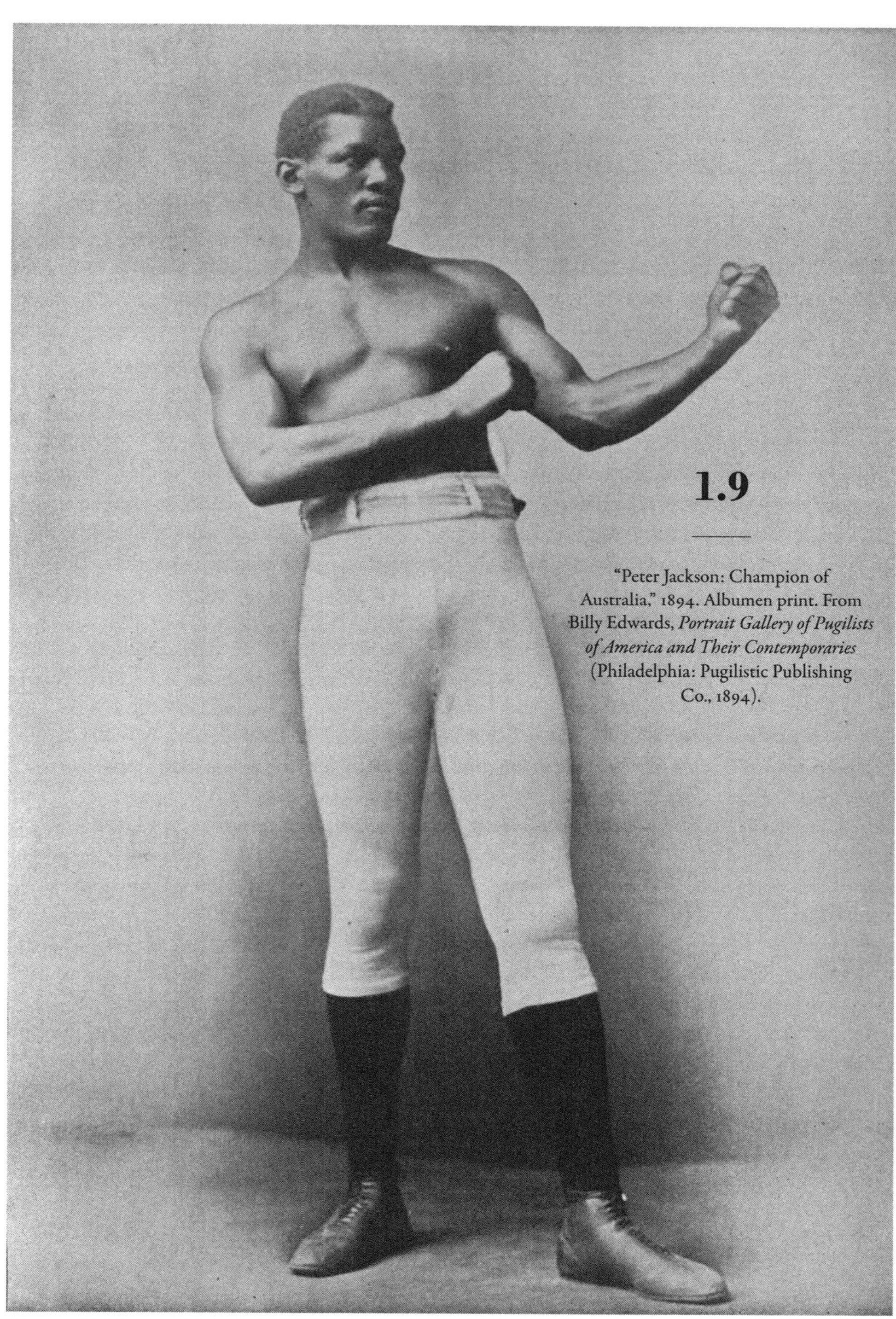

1.9

———

"Peter Jackson: Champion of Australia," 1894. Albumen print. From Billy Edwards, *Portrait Gallery of Pugilists of America and Their Contemporaries* (Philadelphia: Pugilistic Publishing Co., 1894).

authority. We can imagine that the frenzied consumption of the images of these men—illustrated in newspapers, sold as cabinet cards and lithographs, even engraved onto medals—connected to the desire or the need for reassurance in an increasingly complex world. While these boxers may have functioned in part as cultural heroes, their images were formally constructed in order to cohere an ideology of whiteness.

But what happens when the boxer in the frame is Black? I want to consider the boxer's pose as a careful formal construction whose ideological effectiveness is made possible by repetition. And when replicated later in the century by Black fighters, we begin to see its complications. On one side we might read the poses of Black fighters as a form of mimicry. As Homi Bhabha argues in his 1984 essay "Of Mimicry and Men," mimicry is a tool of colonial power and control. In Bhabha's terms, the colonizer can control and repress the native by encouraging them to imitate the habits or behaviors of the colonizing authority. However, as Bhabha examines mimicry in practice, he discovers that its effect is not unilateral. To exemplify the inherent ambivalence of mimicry, he focuses on the problematic situation of the Indian living under British rule. No matter how hard the Indian may try to imitate English behavior and habits, he will never be an Englishman. Neither does the English colonist, in fact, wish him to be. Effectively, it is as if the colonist says: "Be like me, but don't be exactly like me, because then you'll be me. Be like me with a difference." This "demand for identity" thus produces "a subject of difference that is almost the same, but not quite."[91] In other words, mimicry results not only in identity, but also in difference, and a difference which is, in effect, a parody of the colonist. The colonist looks at the native and sees a distorted vision, a partial representation of himself which he perceives to be "at once resemblance and menace."[92]

We might interpret that the rise of the image of the Black boxer after Reconstruction—the primary subject of this book—as a "demand for identity" that will always (in part) be a failure. Despite the prevalence of Black boxers in the ring and in popular culture, they may never quite reach autonomy in wider political culture. But nevertheless, they always impose a threat to the established social order. As Bhabha explains, "the menace of mimicry is its double vision which in disclosing the ambivalence of colonial discourse also disrupts its authority."[93] The ambivalence of mimicry produces what Bhabha calls a "space for agency," a means for subversion of the dominant order. The ambivalence of the gesture (i.e., the Black boxer posed for the camera) produces a space for agency which is subversive. These men are not simply repeating a pose; rather, they are simultaneously reinforcing and destabilizing a visual ideology of white masculinity. And here the threat of Blackness appears.

In the last two decades of the nineteenth century, all but one of the boxing champions were white. These bodies, according to the historian Gail Bederman, were evidence of the limitless abilities and racial superiority of white men.[94] The public victories of these men and their attendant publicity consistently connected their success to their whiteness. But we cannot forget that Black fighters were part of this history as well. The concept of mimicry may be a necessary undercurrent for this book, because the athletes themselves occupy an ambivalent position with regard to the normativity of white masculinity. Mimicry primarily deals with representation, which reveals the performative aspect of paradigms of power. The site of negotiation, antagonistic or otherwise, always provides a space for agency. The remaining chapters attempt to reevaluate the question of culture from the perspective of power and authority, and to examine how these are expressed and exercised.

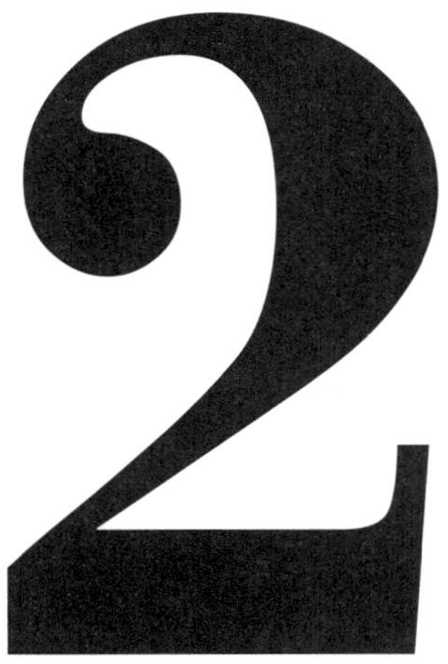

BOXING IN THE FRAME

The young amateur heavyweight boxer Ben Bailey stepped into the makeshift photography studio of Eadweard Muybridge (1830–1904) on the University of Pennsylvania campus on June 2, 1885. He would have seen up to three batteries of twelve cameras, each arranged alongside, and in front of, a track where Bailey was to perform his movements (fig. 2.1).[1] The cameras were managed by electrical triggers, which moved a magnet to control the opening of the shutter so quickly that Muybridge was able to make exposures of a thousandth of a second—that is, almost instantaneously.[2] As the subject passed in front, each camera was triggered, a quick succession of sharp sounds that must have startled anyone unfamiliar with the relatively new technology. Bailey appeared in Muy-

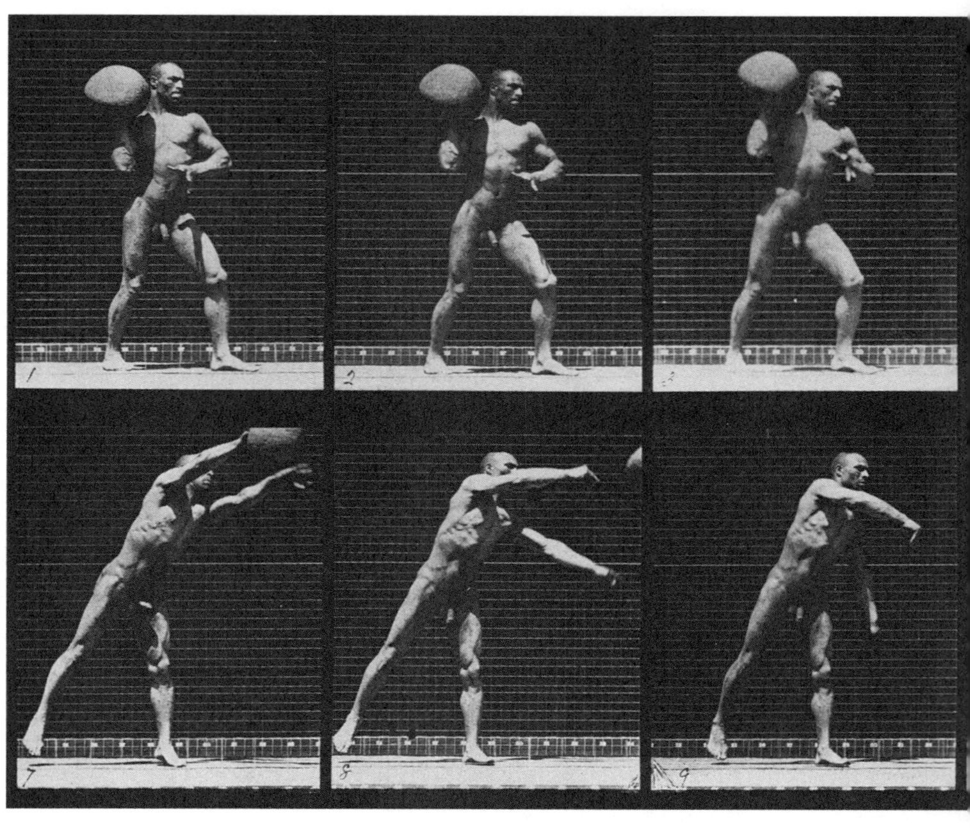

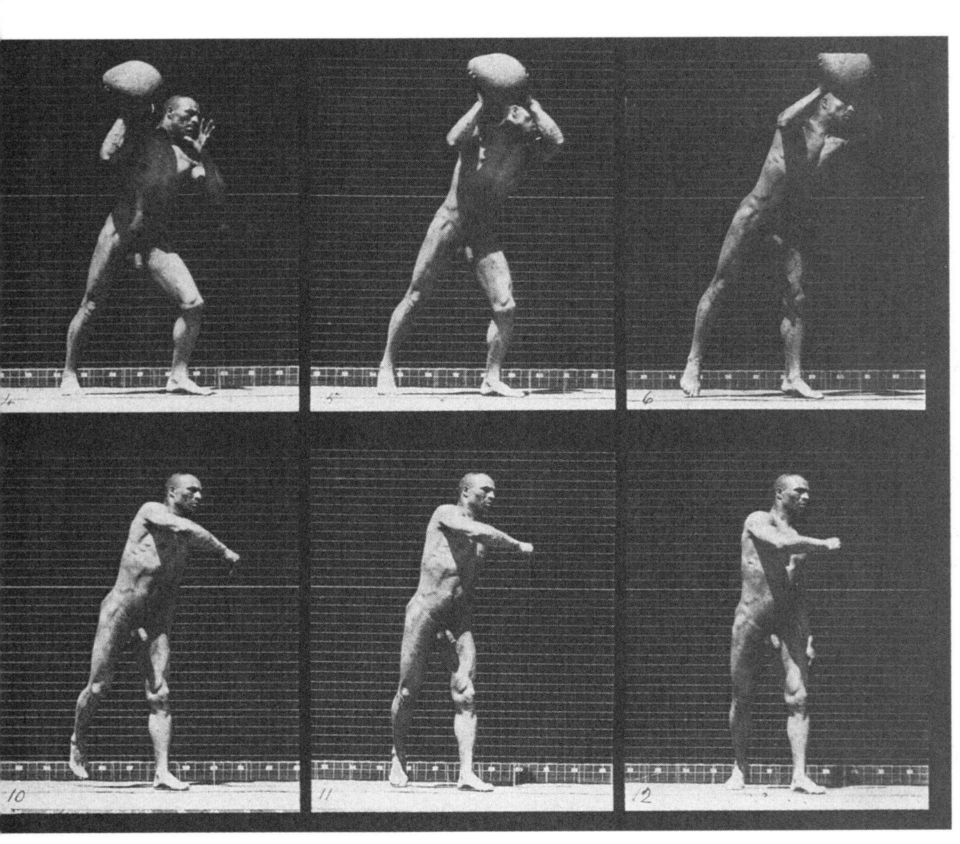

2.1

Eadweard Muybridge, *Heaving a 75-Pound Rock*, 1885,
printed 1887. Collotype print, 15.9 × 6.8 inches (40.4 × 17.3 cm). From
Animal Locomotion (Philadelphia: J. B. Lippincott & Co., 1887),
plate 311. Boston Public Library.

bridge's studio/shed on the first day of the photographer's second summer of work. Muybridge had returned to Philadelphia to continue the motion studies that he had begun the previous year under a commission overseen by nine men, including doctors and engineers, a professor at the university, and the Philadelphia painter Thomas Eakins (1844–1916). Bailey, like the other models for Muybridge's studies, had been recruited from the local community and asked to perform specific movements in front of Muybridge's battery of cameras; they pictured him from the front, back, and side simultaneously. But unlike the other ninety-four models featured in Muybridge's project, Ben Bailey was Black.[3]

Although he spent less than a day in the studio, Bailey's presence in Muybridge's series reveals much more than the mechanics of motion. These photographs are not documents but a performance (of not only the sitter but the photographer as well). This chapter argues for an interpretation of Bailey that foregrounds his athleticism and its intersections with themes of race, gender, and desire in his contemporary moment. I will consider Bailey within the ideology of manhood being actively constructed (and defended) within the visual grammar of Black violence in the late nineteenth century.[4] While we tend to write a visual history of the Blackness in the nineteenth century with the lynching photograph as the gravitational center, I would like to shift our attention elsewhere. These images of Bailey are a violent effort to control and manage the excess of Blackness.

In this chapter I will explore the racial politics of Muybridge's so-called empiricism, and their entanglement in a network of social and cultural assumptions that make these images legible.[5] In the case of Bailey, that network includes the tension between the scientific, the popular, and the artistic rhetorics of photography in the late nineteenth century, and the role of the medium in fixing (pun intended) notions of the Black male body. In fact, as I will explore further below, many of the funders for Muybridge's study went on to found the American Anthropometric Society in 1889, which played a key role in the circulation of ideas about race science in the nineteenth century. The specific treatment of Bailey's penis in these images, the use of the grid, and the isolated presence of Bailey within the frame (the only athlete shown in Muybridge's voluminous collection *Animal Locomotion* to box alone) will all be considered. It is my contention that Muybridge's photographs of a Black boxer, alongside the implicit associations of the sport with violence and eroticism, work differently than the other motion images in this project. More specifically, in looking at Muybridge's images alongside subsequent fine art representations of Black men by the photographer F. Holland Day (1864–1933) and Robert Mapplethorpe (1946–89), we see that photographs of Black boxers produced outside commercial contexts expose a continuum of both gendered and racial politics of representation. Rather than attempt to write a history of photography that covers the century between Day and Mapplethorpe, I instead locate within both examples a continued genealogy of the eroticization of the Black male body that Muybridge's own images of Bailey provoked. In reference to the mode of historical inquiry adopted by Michel Foucault and derived from the "critical history" in the second of Nietzsche's *Untimely Meditations* (1874), the genealogical approach provides an alternative to the traditional historical or linear approach to history. The frame of genealogy will allow for us to consider these nineteenth-century images alongside the reception of works by Day (produced in the decade after Muybridge's study) and Mapplethorpe (working a century later).[6] Further, the more recent interpretations of works by Day and Mapplethorpe provide a vocabulary for articulating the stakes around representations of Black masculinity. This will require that we look also to the affective dimension of the images and consider how the visual articulation of (potential) violence gives visual form to widespread fantasies (and fears) about Black male bodies in the public sphere.

Ben Bailey was the twenty-second model out of the ninety-five that Muybridge photographed in Philadelphia, and the first athlete.[7] The published prospectus for Muybridge's *Animal Locomotion* project describes him as a "mulatto pugilist." Unlike Muybridge's other models, he has remained until now largely unknown—his identity, his involvement with this photographer, his life outside the frame all unspoken and outside the archive.[8] Bailey was most likely born into slavery or to a family of low-wage laborers in the early 1860s in Virginia, making him approximately twenty-five years of age at the time of his first public heavyweight match in March 1885.[9] On July 18, 1886, the *Philadelphia Times* recorded Bailey as being "of the eighth ward"—an area of central Philadelphia.[10] The easternmost edge of the Eighth Ward would have been only a seven-minute walk from the University of Pennsylvania campus. Most of the athletic clubs, where Bailey was known to fight under the moniker "the Black Diamond," were also located in central Philadelphia; in these clubs, exclusively white audiences indulged in the brutal spectacle of the boxing match.[11]

Just two months before appearing in Muybridge's studio, Bailey had gained the attention of the local press with his defeat of Toby Brown, "the colored champion of Baltimore."[12] However, his fight performances were rather erratic. Bailey was knocked down eighteen times in four rounds in a match against the mulatto heavyweight fighter Amos Scott (1859–1925).[13] A month later Bailey faced Frank "Clipper" Donahue (1852?–1910) in six rounds uptown, fighting "with soft gloves until the cry of 'police' went up stopping the match," and the referee called a draw.[14] Bailey won only four of twelve recorded bouts. In an 1890 article titled "A Plucky 'Coon,'" the *Morning Oregonian* proclaimed that he was "no fighter," relying instead on stamina in his April bout against Amos Scott.[15] In 1891, the *Philadelphia Inquirer* went so far as to describe one of Bailey's matches as "comical."[16] Nevertheless, for Black men like Bailey, boxing was a brutal but effective way to earn a living (and perhaps even financial autonomy) outside traditional means. But by late spring of that year, Bailey's opportunities to fight were limited, and like many others he was forced to make do in a labor market that offered few viable options for working-class Black men.[17] Muybridge's unconventional study provided Bailey with the rare opportunity to earn money, and in exchange he provided the photographer with his first non-white model.[18]

While at the University of Pennsylvania, Muybridge photographed several white students, teachers, and tradesmen performing athletic feats (fig. 2.2). The *Animal Locomotion* project included models "running, jumping, throwing the javelin and discus, pole-vaulting, wrestling, lifting weights, rowing and fencing."[19] In fact, local audiences may have been the most interested in the athletic dimension of Muybridge's project. The student newspaper *Pennsylvanian* revealed in 1886, during Muybridge's third year on campus, that

> the part most interesting to University men is the delineation of athletic sports, foot-ball and base-ball, running, jumping, vaulting, and wrestling. Nearly every well-known University athlete of the past two or three years has served as a model in the nude, many of them showing magnificent physiques, and exhibiting exquisitely the play of every muscle.[20]

Such descriptions of Muybridge's project, with an explicit focus on the "magnificent physiques" recorded by his camera, underscore the emphasis within these images on the subjective experience of the viewer.

Although commonly understood within the context of fine art and often discussed in histories of film and photography, sports historian Mike O'Mahony has recently argued for a reconsideration of Muybridge's experiments as fundamentally sports-oriented. Even as early as 1879, O'Mahony points out, the photographer, then resident in California, chose athletes from Charles Nahl's Olympic Club in San Francisco (among one of the first athletic clubs in the United States) as his subjects.[21] The club's boxing instructor, strongman, and several other athletes came down to Palo Alto in August 1879 to be photographed by Muybridge. As reported by the *San Francisco Chronicle*:

> In order to display as completely as possible the movements of the muscles, the athletes wore only brief trunks while performing. Mr. Muy-

bridge, the photographer, had every arrangement made at the racetrack for carrying out the work, and from ten o'clock in the morning until four o'clock in the afternoon boxing, wrestling, fencing, jumping, and tumbling followed in a quick succession and all of their intricate movements were instantaneously and exactly pictured.[22]

Muybridge's technology promised to reveal the mechanics of human motion at a level of detail never before seen. Contemporary accounts of his larger project (including the newspaper report above) focused on the speed of the camera, which made possible incremental views of the body in motion at a level of detail that was previously inaccessible to the naked eye.

In the context of boxing, the technical possibilities of popular photography in Muybridge's moment meant that the action, and true brutality, of the fight escaped representation. We most often see the fighter posing for the newspaper's camera, the victory celebrated after the match, or the contemplation of a tired fighter faced with defeat. We do not see the drama and action of the fight itself; boxers appear as static figures rather than dynamic actors. They are frozen within the frame. One of the defining features of Muybridge's experiments with photography, and indeed his main contribution to the history of the medium, was the ability to capture motion and the dynamic movement of his subjects. Given the limitations of early photography, which could only portray the still (or slow) world due to the length of exposure time required to make an image, Muybridge's accomplishments were singular for his time. As Rebecca Solnit argues, "The bustling nineteenth century had come to a halt for the camera, until Muybridge and his motion studies."[23] Muybridge's images laid the foundation for early cinema, allowing him to capture a world in motion—gymnasts flying through the air, models ascending and descending stairs, fencers captured in dramatic lunges toward opponents. His innovations allowed for a new kind of vision, which would prove essential for the photography of sports. In the context of boxing specifically, Muybridge's experiments with motion photography would eventually allow for the capture of images showing the most violent encounters within the ring.[24]

The fourteen "boxing" plates from the *Animal Locomotion* project in Philadelphia (numbered 329 to 342 in Muybridge's portfolio) all conform the same essential formula, showing two white men in some form of combat.[25] But, upon closer examination, we might also notice that the fight here is more theatrical than scientific. Plate 330, *Boxing, Cross-Counter*, for example, contains a sequence of twenty-four frames (fig. 2.3). Reading the suggested narrative from left to right, and top to bottom, we see that in the first two rows, the models

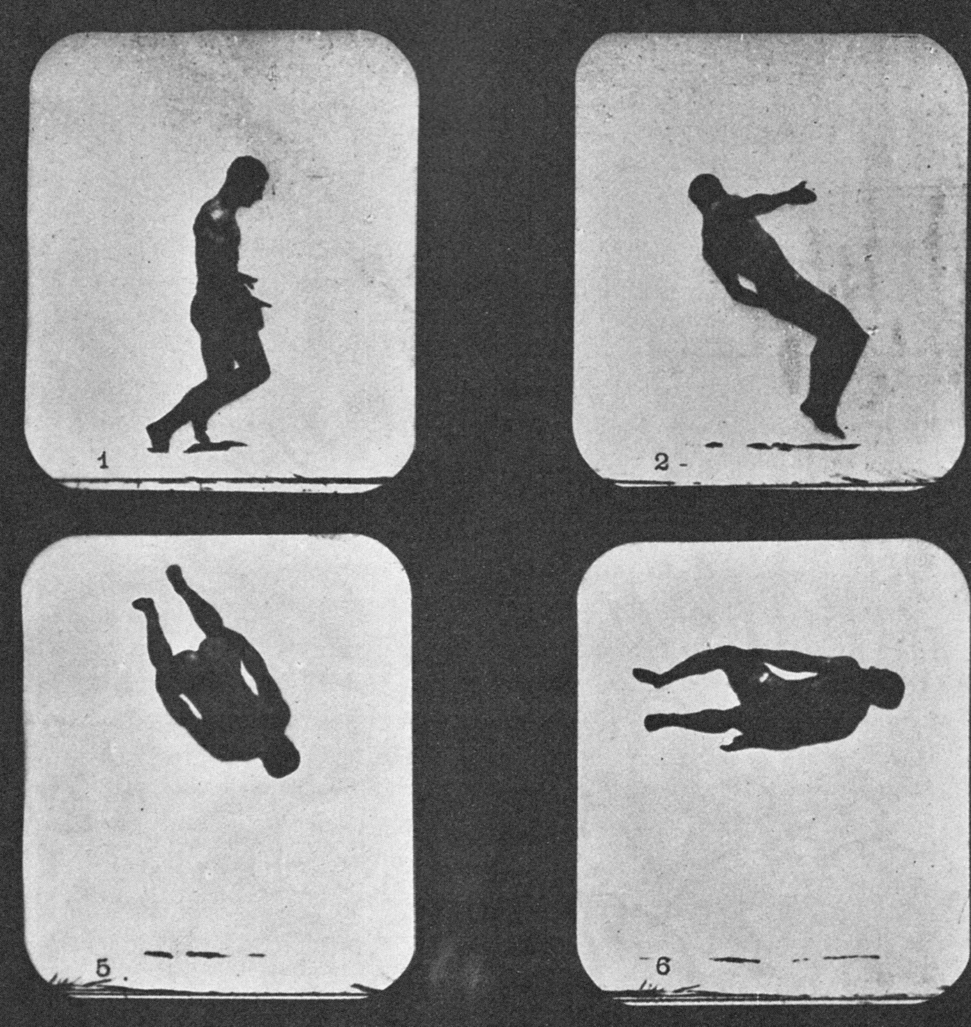

2.2

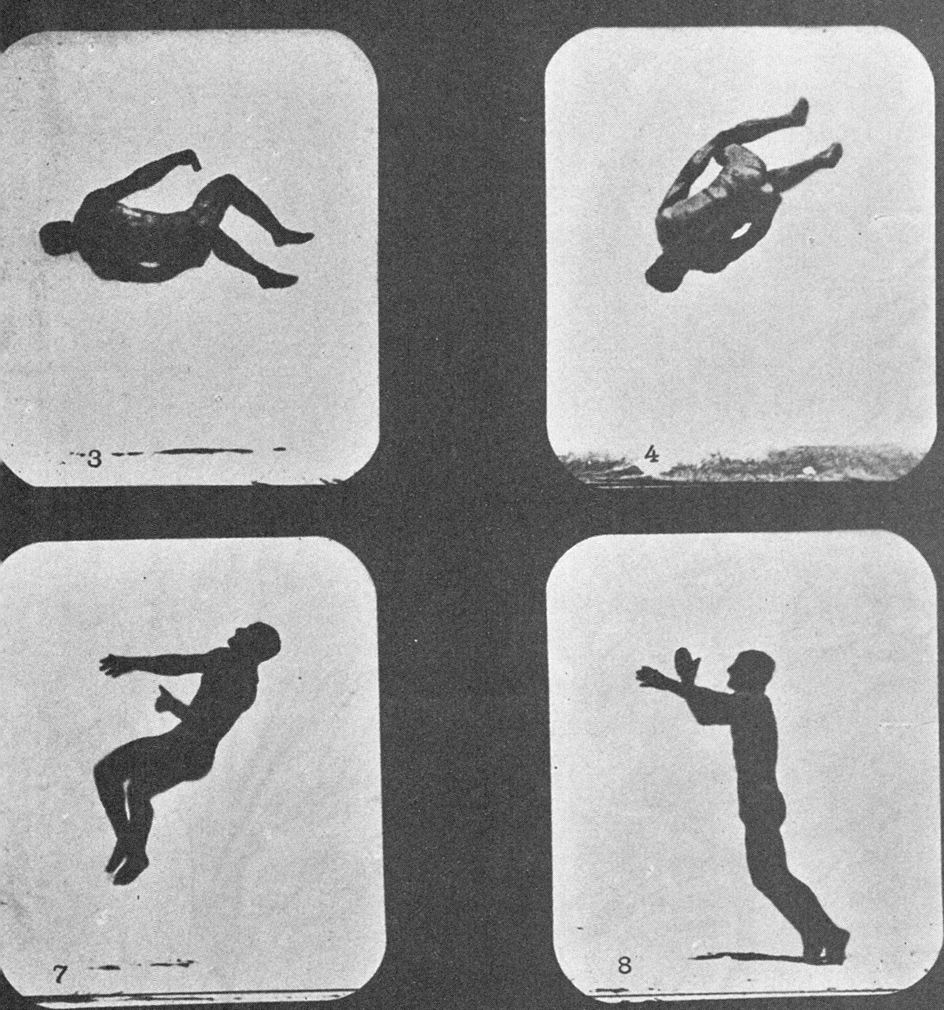

Eadweard Muybridge, *Twisting Somersault*, 1878–79,
printed 1887. Iron-salt process print, 8.8 × 7.4 inches (22.4 × 18.7 cm).
J. Paul Getty Museum, Los Angeles.

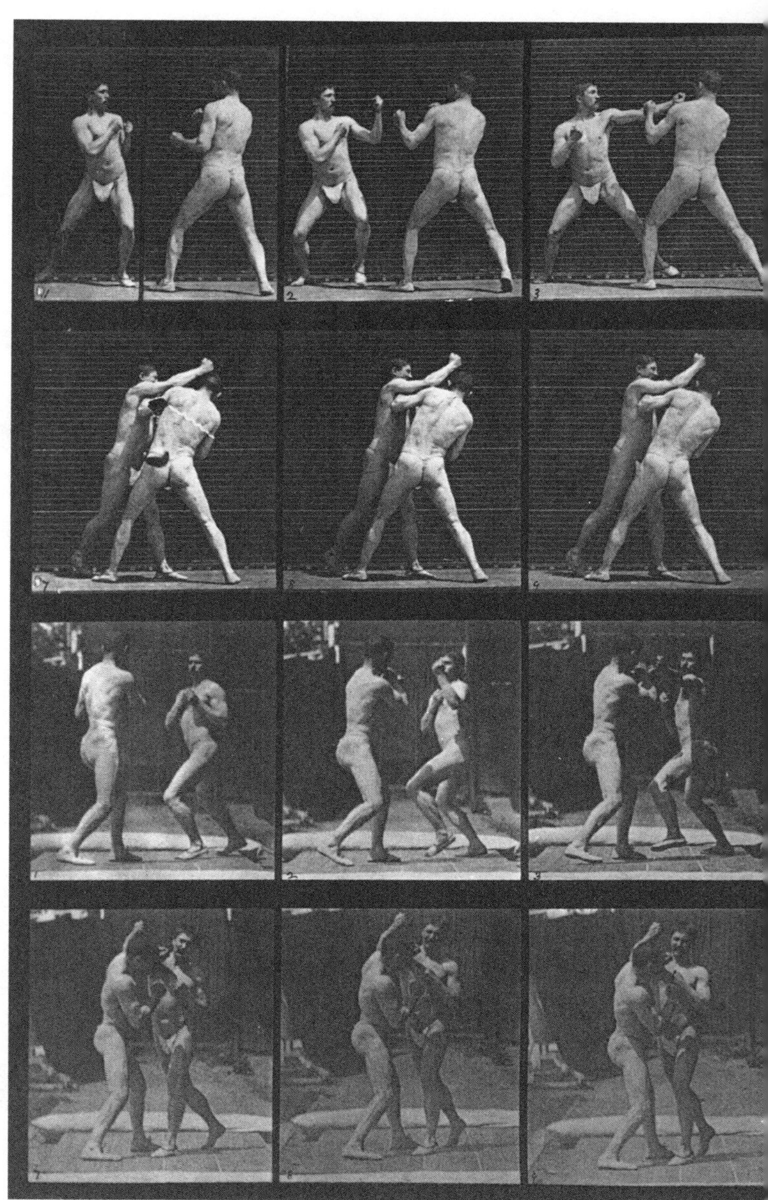

2.3

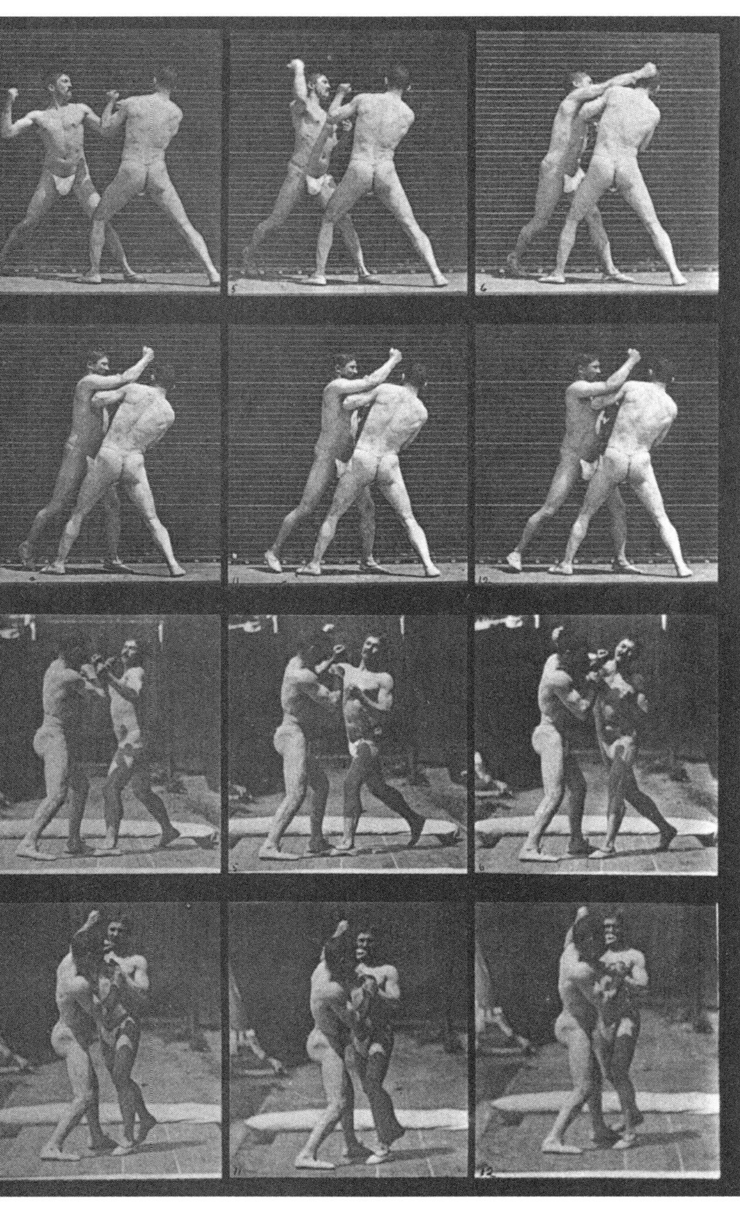

Eadweard Muybridge, *Boxing, Cross-Counter*, ca. 1885, printed 1887. Collotype print. From *Animal Locomotion* (Philadelphia: J. B. Lippincott & Co., 1887), plate 330. National Gallery of Art, Washington, DC.

begin by squaring up to one another. The model on the left appears from the front (his genitals covered in a light cloth) and the model on the right from the back; both have raised their fists slightly to shoulder level rather than up around their head, as would be expected. However, when we look at the second frame we see that the "on guard" position of both figures show their legs widely splayed; their knees bend toward a squatting position and their feet are parallel, rather than the suggested stance: "feet from twelve to fifteen inches apart . . . the right heel on a line with the left, toes slightly turned out."[26] The model on the left throws the first punch (in the third frame), but it appears rather unnatural. As the left arm stretches toward the face of the model on the right, the model leans back onto his right leg. This is the exact opposite of what would be needed to deliver a true cross-counter, which requires that the right leg bend in the front position while the left leg pushes forward (even rising up to the toe) to drive power to the left extended arm. The footwork has been corrected in the fourth frame, as the front-facing model pulls back his right arm and drives it forward, leading with the elbow, which strikes the left shoulder of his "opponent" as the arm extends and the fist lines up with the back of the other model's head. So, while the placement of the feet for this second cross-counter punch appears to be more feasible, the position of the striking arm remains unconventional.[27] Although this sequence bears a slight resemblance to what might happen if one opponent ducked the punch, the arm overextends so that the elbow reaches over the shoulder. Frames five through twelve follow this awkward punch. The model on the left presses downward onto the shoulder and head of the model on the right, who leans farther and farther away. The bodies of both men come closer together, forming a series of intersecting diagonal lines at the center of the frame. A cross-counter punch such as this (i.e., aimed at the head) would have been less common in bare knuckle matches, where fighters would aim at softer spots of the opponent's body to protect their hands.

Looking at just one more frame from Plate 330, where now the men seem to have shifted locations (no longer appearing against the flat, gridded background), we see another encounter between the two men that similarly violates the conventions of the sport.[28] Here, the men have reversed positions and the striking model now appears on the right of the composition. His left arm extends out toward the other man, perhaps in a jab, but again he leans backward with his left foot lifting off the ground. Throughout the "boxing" images we see similar errors and inconsistencies. These actions are performed by novices, unfamiliar with the basic conventions of the sport.

Ben Bailey is the only experienced boxer pictured within Muybridge's Philadelphia project. Across the six plates in which he appears, he walks, ascends and descends stairs, and even throws a heavy rock, but Muybridge does not highlight his sparring ability. Instead, Bailey appears alone in the plates titled *Striking a Blow with the Left Hand* and *Striking a Blow with the Right Hand* (figs. 2.4 and 2.5). In the first example, we view him from the side, as he lunges (or does he stumble?) awkwardly forward. As we read the top row of images tracking his movements from left to right, we see a punch in reverse.[29] The left arm extends outward and points down; its position runs parallel to a bent thigh, creating almost an abstract shape with the body in this frame. The weight of the left arm pulls the entire body downward, coming slightly off balance as the right heel raises. Following the narrative action of the sequence, this left punch moves upward until it appears raised, the angle between the thigh and the bicep growing progressively obtuse. In the next frame, the elbow bends and the arm moves backward, and finally, the arm passes the torso, cocked at an angle that exposes the shoulder and brings the fist into alignment with the head. It is almost like watching a tape being rewound, as the left-hand jab reverses, with its power and force reabsorbed. As we look at the second row of images we see the punch played forward. The arm moves from its bent acute angle at the shoulder to full extension again.

At first glance, this is a study of motion—a useful analysis for both scientists and artists with a deep investment in the mechanics of the body and its presentation. It seems that Bailey illustrates here the performance of a standard body blow—a punch meant to land squarely on the torso of the opposing fighter. However, Bailey's performance (and indeed all of the boxing shown in the *Animal Locomotion* project) has been altered in order to meet the expectations of Muybridge's audience. In *Striking a Blow with the Left Hand* for example, we detect the photographer's manipulation of the motion sequence, which interrupts the narrative or cinematic quality of the images and places them instead in a series of discrete moments—better perhaps for the close observation of the individual movements of the figure on display. This is a feature unique to the collotype prints made of Bailey; the original negatives of the sparring boxers in *Animal Locomotion*, by comparison, reveal a direct correspondence to the sequence of the final collotype prints. We also see that Bailey's blow itself appears awkward in that he leans farther forward than would necessarily be required, creating deeper strain (and thereby more pronounced flexion) on the muscles of the legs, buttocks, and back.[30] And, as other scholars have noted, the fact that Bailey, the only identifiably Black subject within Muybridge's oeuvre, is the first model in the *Animal Locomotion* project to appear in front of the anthropometric grid complicates his presence in the frame.

We do not know the exact reason for Muybridge's deployment of the grid in images of Bailey. Perhaps, as I argue below, Muybridge was directly influenced

2.4

Plate 343.

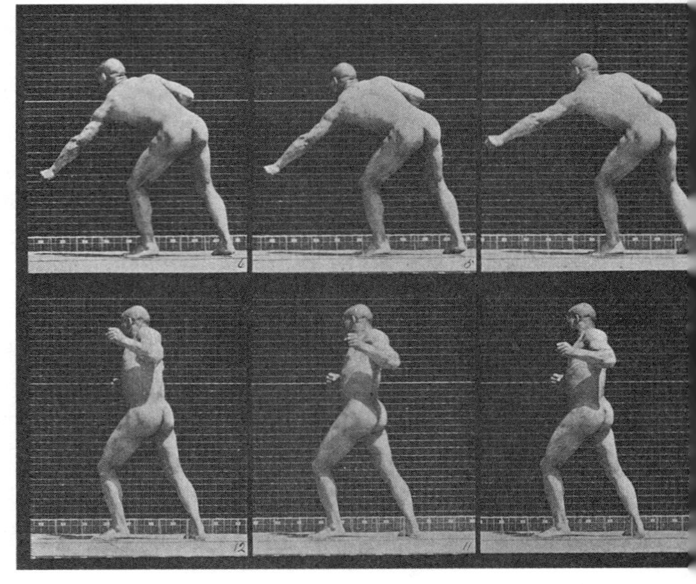

2.5

Plate 344.

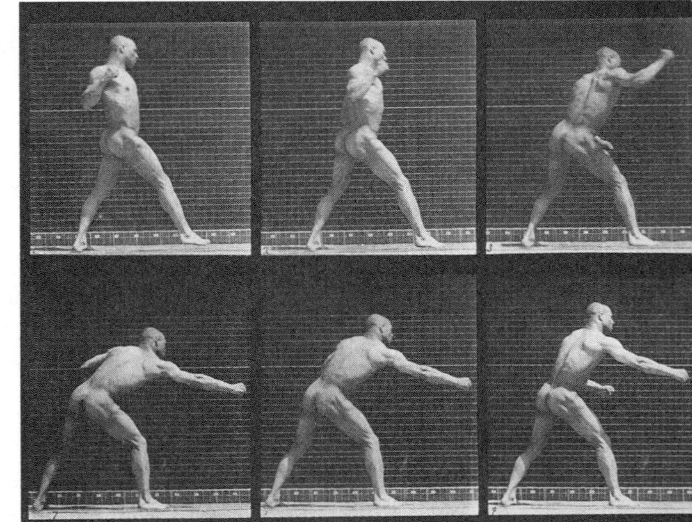

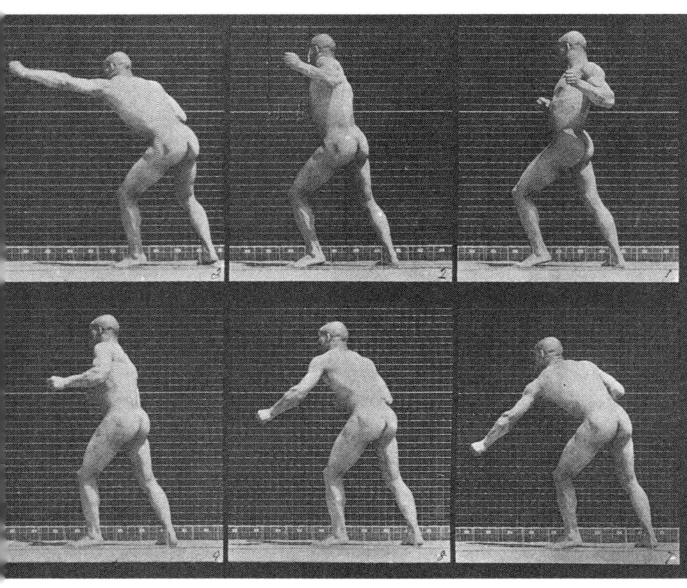

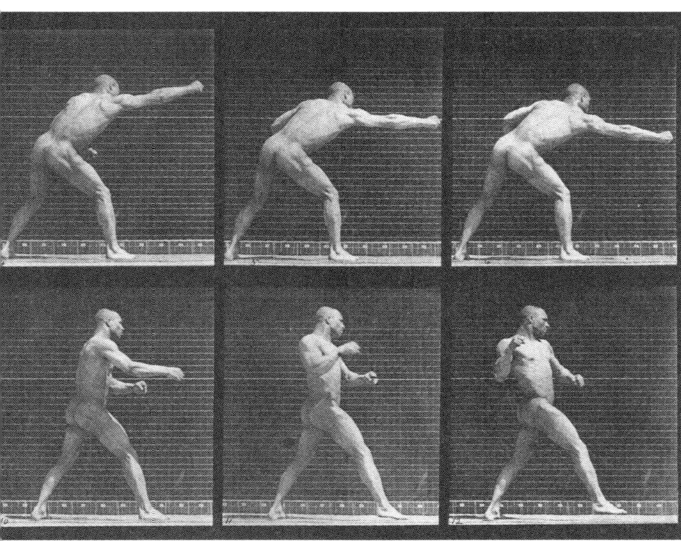

Eadweard Muybridge, *Striking a Blow with the Left Hand*, 1885, printed 1887. Collotype print. From *Animal Locomotion* (Philadelphia: J. B. Lippincott & Co., 1887). Boston Public Library.

by the work of Lamprey and others, who used the grid in previous decades in order to identify (and by extension exclude) a "type." Nevertheless, those grids haunt this image, creating an association with racist science and in turn tying Bailey to an ideological structure. Artist and art historian Hannah Higgins has written on the ideological power of the grid, which connotes a sense of order that predates modernity. Higgins describes the grid as a "mythological form"—"a visualization of... faith in rational thought and industrial progress comprising everything from the urban landscape to the power grid, from modernist painting to modernist physics."[31] The grid's use in photographs of the human body was a method of standardizing human form, of denaturalizing and of stripping the subject of individuality. As Ben Bailey moves in front of Muybridge's cameras—straining forward in a pretend jab—he becomes a type rather than an individual. I argue here that Muybridge's study of Bailey specifically does not explore motion, but instead fixes Bailey's body to an ideological structure. The individual frames of the collotype prints, and the individual units of five-centimeter squares that divide his body, constrain Bailey, unlike the other subjects of *Animal Locomotion*, within a white supremacist gaze.[32] And in the context of Reconstruction-era politics, the denial of Bailey's individuality here is in turn a denial of his right to be human.

Muybridge and the Veil of Science

In many ways, Muybridge's Philadelphia project conformed to the template of his famed motion studies, which he began in 1872 under the direction of the former governor of California and racehorse breeder, Leland Stanford. Stanford employed Muybridge in the hope of gaining more information about the gait of his racehorses, which he could then use to improve their performance. The key question for Stanford was whether all four legs of a galloping horse left the ground at the same time. The photographer worked for five years, producing images of Stanford's horse Occident flying through the air that were widely appealing to audiences across Europe and the United States and were published in May 1881 under the title *The Attitudes of Animals in Motion: A Series of Photographs Illustrating the Consecutive Positions Assumed by Animals in Performing Various Movements* (fig. 2.6). It seemed almost magical; Muybridge had manipulated the mechanical exposure of his cameras to reveal a characteristic of nature inaccessible to our vision. As Phillip Prodger, a historian of photography, has argued: "With his first photographs of the galloping horse in California, Muybridge had pushed photography beyond the threshold of what is visible and made time stand still. As a result, natural and photographic vision had

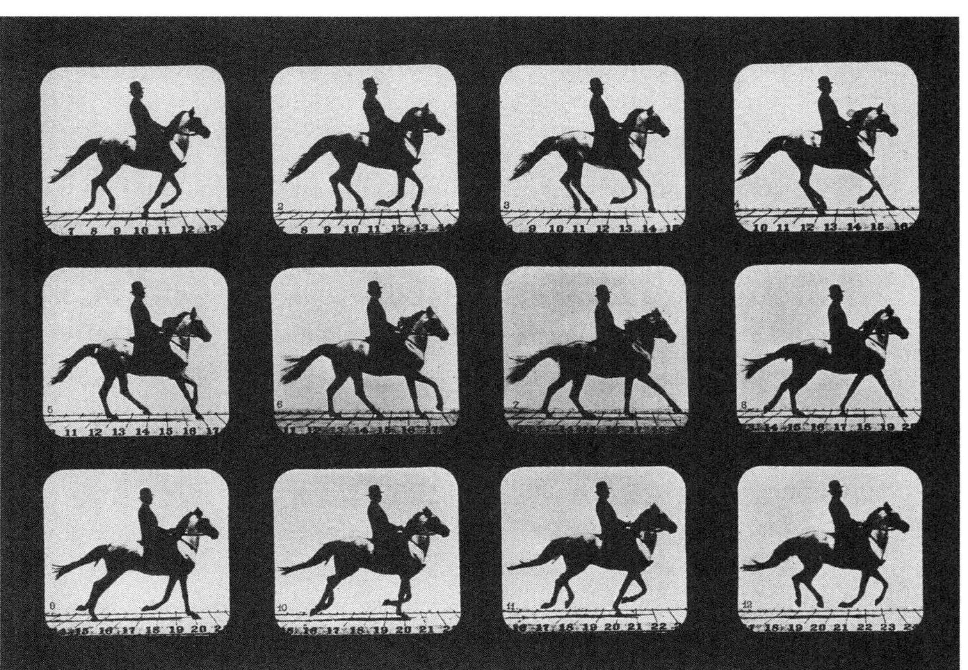

2.6

———

Eadweard Muybridge, *Attitudes of Animals in Motion*, 1879.
Albumen print, 6.3 × 9.3 inches (25.3 × 16 cm). Metropolitan
Museum of Art, New York.

diverged forever."[33] Audiences in Europe and the United States were immediately fascinated by Muybridge's results. In June 1878 a group of reporters came down to Palo Alto to see these new motion photographs. One described the experience of viewing Muybridge's images:

> There is a feeling of awe in the mind of the beholder, as he looks at the glass plate which is half before the yellow curtain, and he sees the miniature of the flying horse so perfect that it startles him. Reduced in size until it would do for the scarf-pin of a lady, and yet in the weird opal-tinted light it is as distant as if cut on a gem. The eye runs rapidly over the series, and there are positions which could never be explained by hypothesis, but that which cannot be questioned by those who have witnessed the operation.[34]

Such accounts confirm that Muybridge's images inspired both wonder and delight among their audience, encouraging their proliferation across a range of popular media. In 1878 *Scientific American* reproduced Muybridge's *Horse in Motion* photographs on the cover of its October 19 issue. Two months later, the French journal *La Nature* followed suit. Muybridge's images revealed the limits of human eyesight, and further positioned the camera as a closer approximation of the real. Muybridge was himself on the precipice of becoming an international celebrity.

The tension between the documentary and artistic functions of photography defined the early history of the medium, starting with the first permanent photograph (a direct positive image) produced by Joseph Nicéphore Niépce around 1826. It was Niépce's collaborator Louis-Jacques-Mandé Daguerre who brought his experiments with capturing images to the attention of the French Académie des Sciences in January 1839—a little over three decades before Muybridge's studies with Leland Stanford. Daguerre demonstrated the process for making an image (a daguerreotype) in front of a joint session of the Académie des Sciences and the Académie des Beaux-Arts a few months later on August 19, 1839. From this moment, photography had a dual identity—as a scientific tool and as an artistic medium—and Daguerre played both sides. He made microscopic and telescopic daguerreotypes (none of which survive) that allowed for the close study of anatomical or astronomical features that could not be observed with human sight alone. But alongside the photographed arrays of shells and fossils, Daguerre also photographed still-life compositions that referenced antique sculpture. While post-Enlightenment scientists praised the exactitude and detail provided in the daguerreotype, artists celebrated the artistic effects of light made visible by the medium. The French painter Paul Delaroche wrote to the French government: "Daguerre's process completely satisfies all the demands of art, carrying certain essential principles of art to such perfection that it must become a subject of observation and study even to the most accomplished painters."[35] As photography became more popular through the end of the nineteenth century, this dual identity persisted.

Muybridge's early experiments with taking photographs of horses in motion were received by both scientific and artistic audiences with great enthusiasm. Even the French physiologist E. J. Marey, who had encountered Muybridge's photographs in a December 1878 issue of *La Nature*, concluded that the technology held great promise for scientists and artists, writing at once of the possibility that "one could see all imaginable animals during their true movements" and of the "revolution" these images would create for artists, "since one could furnish them with true attitudes of movement; positions of the body during unstable balance in which a model would find it impossible to pose."[36] As Muybridge toured Paris and London, giving lantern slide-shows and demonstrations of the zoopraxiscope—an invention debuted by Muybridge in California in 1879. The zoopraxiscope (also called the zoogyroscope) was a combination of photography, the magic lantern, and the zoetrope (a spinning toy that placed a band of images inside a drum so that when set in motion it gave the illusion of the image moving). It created large projections of moving images praised by both scientists and academic artists of the period. At a lecture in Paris, hosted at Professor Marey's home in September 1881, those in attendance represented a collection of the foremost scientists of the era, including the German physicist Hermann von Helmholtz (known for his explanation of the first law of thermodynamics), the Norwegian physicist and meteorologist Vilgelm Bjerknes, the editor of *La Nature* (and builder of an electrically powered airship) Gaston Tissandier, and the photographer Nadar. Two months later, the audience was almost entirely artists. Hosted by Jean-Louis-Ernest Meissonier on November 26, Muybridge's audience included the French painters Léon Joseph Florentin Bonnat, Jean-Baptiste Édouard Detaille, and Jean-Léon Gérôme, along with the dramatist Émile Augier and writer Alexandre Dumas.[37] Muybridge's photographs appealed to both scientific and artistic audiences, as he outlined how the images might be used both by scientists in the further study of animal mechanics and by artists to elucidate the movement of the animal body.

Despite his dual appeal, Muybridge was by no means a scientist; he never studied medicine, anatomy, or physiology. When he traveled and lectured, he stayed within artistic circles and, more often than not, artists composed the majority of his public audiences. In fact, the scientific opinion of Muybridge's photographs was that they were inexact, lacking in a constant approach to either the subject (viewed from multiple angles) or its capture (using more than one camera and at random temporal intervals).[38] He openly manipulated photographs in previous projects, combining negatives for expressive effects. It was the prominent Philadelphia painter Thomas Eakins, himself a devotee of photography and an acquaintance of Muybridge, who pressured the University of Pennsylvania to bring the photographer to the campus for a continuation of his motion studies.[39] Nevertheless, his project at the university was specifically positioned as "science." The university oversaw the entire project, prescribing the conditions of Muybridge's work and the specific nature of the experiments. A university commission was appointed to uphold the "thoroughly scientific character" of the work, particularly since Muybridge would be employing naked models—a discomfort for his late Victorian backers.[40] The photographer's placement on the new grounds of the veterinary department underscored the scientific tone of the overall project. The bodies included in the project were solely examples of the human capacities for movement. The final publication of *Animal Locomotion* presented Muybridge's models without names, describing them simply as "male" or "female," or by the action they performed (*Running at Full Speed* or *Baseball, Catching and Throwing*). Most appeared naked, foregrounding the sexual difference of their anatomy as well as their presence as specimens rather than as subjective individuals. In the second half of the project, the sequences of the models' actions are shown to us against the backdrop of a grid, applying the structural logic of geometry onto the unruly body. Muybridge then arranged the final images in sequences of horizontal rows. The close arrangement of the individual exposures, separated by a thin black bar, compels us to interpret the sequence as uninterrupted motion, despite the reality of their static construction. The scientific logic of these photographs was constructed outside Muybridge's images, but brought inside through his use of the anthropometric grid.

Photography and Difference in the Nineteenth Century

In the nineteenth century, both scientists and citizens in Britain and the United States were committed to removing the threat of immigration and miscegenation. The demarcation of difference was imperative to the management and the marginalization of immigrant and Black populations in both contexts. In Britain, the main concern centered on improving the birth rate of the wealthier classes in a period of rapid immigration, while in the United States the consequences of race mixing compounded these concerns. In the British context the issue was class based, while in the United States any worries about class were always overdetermined by race as well. The rise of eugenics and its accompanying imagery was part of a larger attempt to manage white anxiety around these social, political, and economic upheavals. In the United States, for example, early eugenic photography was popularized in the 1880s by Professor Henry P. Bowditch, dean of Harvard Medical School. Bowditch's studies of physiology centered on the relationship between height and heredity; he wanted to prove that the increased height of white American children was due to genetics rather than superior nutrition. Although Bowditch's methods were criticized at the time, the historian Anne Maxwell has argued that the results of his growth studies remained popular into the 1930s. Bowditch's theories, in her words, "underscore the correlation between good genes, physical beauty and wealth on the one hand, and the importance of curbing foreign immigration and racial mixing on the other."[41]

This was the era of positivism—a time when many devised methods to define the perceived universal laws that governed both body and spirit. More specifically, the body appeared as the primary symptom, the universal sign of everything that still remained veiled—both at the level of the individual and within the wider social body. The nineteenth century was thus the first period in which the individual was submitted to scrutiny by a whole range of agencies (medical, judicial, moral, etc.) that measured the degree of deviation from an undeclared statistical norm. The body was interpreted as the visible proof of human differences. Criminal tendencies, pathology, and delinquency could all be discerned through close observation of the physical form.

The concerted efforts to align Muybridge's project with science, to position his photographs as objective facts, must be read within this larger context of nineteenth-century photography, in which the bourgeois classes looked to the medium, with its strong associations with "truth," for evidence to support their preoccupations with the classification of difference and a general drive to regulate, even criminalize, the presence of an unwanted underclass in the new urban environment.[42] The popularization of photography in the late nineteenth century coincided with a wider cultural obsession with classifying racial or ethnic types intended to reveal a hierarchy of race and class with the white middle class on the top rung and "urban savages" on the bottom. So, at the same time that photography offered a tool by which to affirm the social position of many of its middle-class subjects via the portrait, it simultaneously functioned as a way to define the Other generally, and to establish the inferiority of the non-white Other more specifically.[43] Fin de siècle studies in anthropology, psychology, and medicine all relied upon the assumption that the body was the primary symptom for underlying deviance, but while positioned as "objective records," the photographs produced in the pursuit of establishing this difference were anything but.

While Muybridge's studies of Bailey at first appear to follow the codes and conventions of Muybridge's other human studies, these were also the first to introduce the anthropometric grid, rather than the plain backdrop he had used previously and for the other ninety-four models who were white. Muybridge used a backdrop divided by silk threads into five-centimeter squares—a format derived from the techniques of the French photographer John H. Lamprey, also a member of the Ethnological Society of London. Lamprey developed this procedure in the 1869 as a way to transform the photograph into a scientific document. As he described it:

> A stout frame of wood, seven feet by three, is neatly ruled along its inner side into divisions of two inches; small nails are driven into these ruled lines, and fine silk thread is strained over them, dividing the included surface by longitudinal and latitudinal lines into squares of two inches every way. Against this screen the figure is placed, the heel fairly on the line with one of the strings; the iron prop to support the object is pressed firmly in its place at some distance from the background; for, by this means better defined outlines are secured than if the man stood directly against a solid screen on which lines might have been scored.[44]

Lamprey's scrupulously described system allowed for the accurate measurement of the body and its proportions. But perhaps more significant for Muybridge, the implementation of the grid behind the figure meant that the body could be posed in less rigid ways.

Chinese Male provides us with one example of Lamprey's use of the grid in photography (fig. 2.7). Here, a male subject stands atop a wooden platform, his body turned to the right of the composition. The figure's left hand stretches across the body and rests on the right side of the chest; the right arm remains extended down the side the torso, with fingers gently holding the end of a long braid. The head is in profile so that the viewer's gaze may proceed unobstructed over the terrain of the figure's body. The standardized grid—in Lamprey's example, spaced at two-inch intervals—that covers the background of the image allows the viewer to measure and assess the body in the frame, as well as to make comparisons across images to other bodies. In sum, the grid is part of a visual iconography of empiricism, positioning the photograph as scientific evidence and truth. The nudity of the figure, the static pose, the gridded background, and even the refusal of the subject to meet the camera's lens with his own look

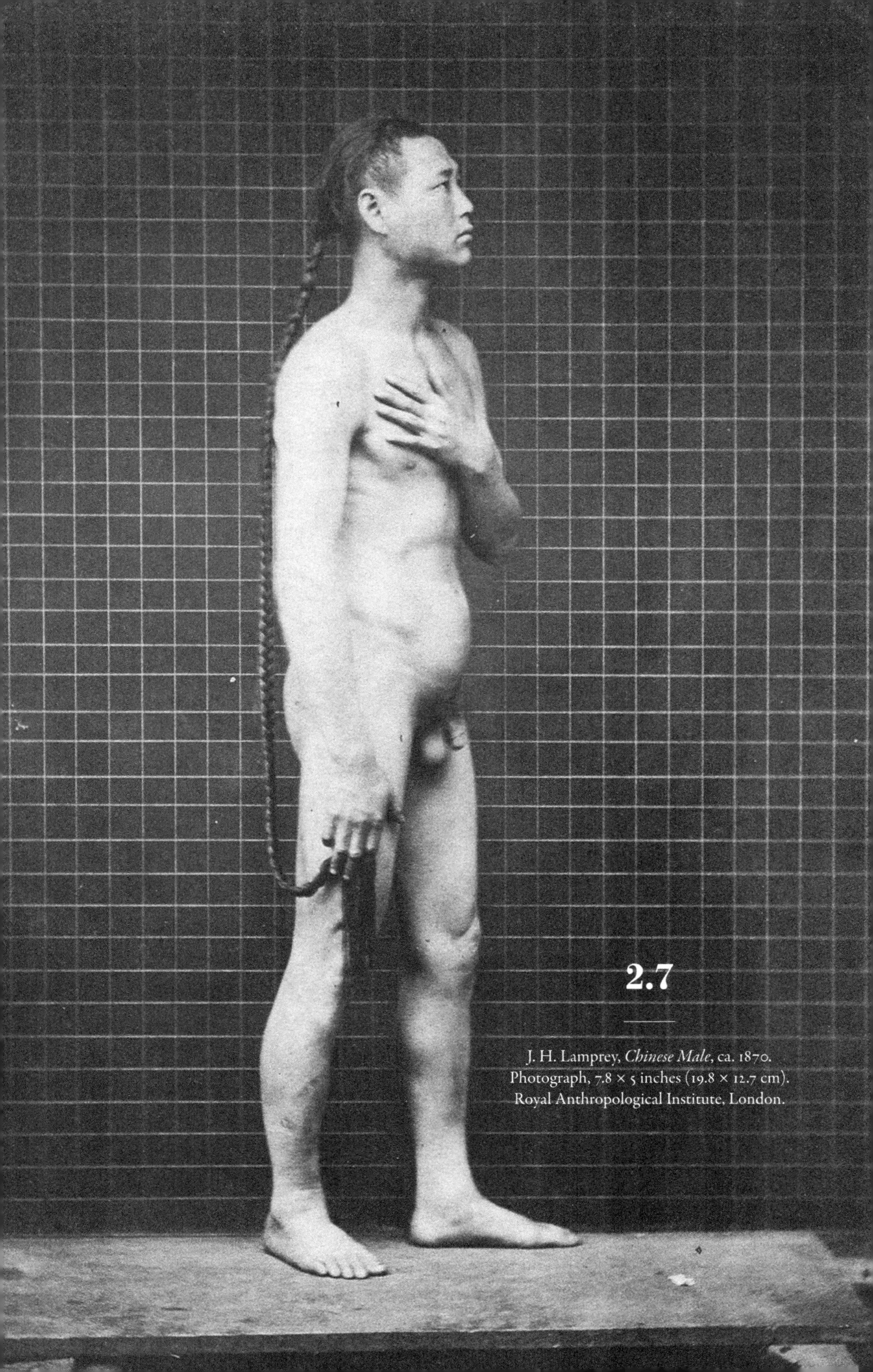

2.7

J. H. Lamprey, *Chinese Male*, ca. 1870.
Photograph, 7.8 × 5 inches (19.8 × 12.7 cm).
Royal Anthropological Institute, London.

all position this image as "scientific," and the pictured body as a specimen to be observed. Lamprey's system was published in English in the *Journal of the Ethnological Society* in 1869, and Muybridge deployed it for the first time in his negatives (numbered 524 through 531) of Ben Bailey for the University of Pennsylvania project.[45]

In this period, photography became a tool used by both scientists and lay people to explore their interest in and to reaffirm the theories of eugenics that were popular at this moment. Relying on previously established associations with truth, the photograph provided a method to visualize these differences, and the medium was deployed in a wide variety of contexts. The techniques of anthropometry (the measurement of the body) and ethnology (the classification of people into groups) were applied to the medium with the goal of identifying simple human types. The work of Francis Galton, for example, centered on creating photographic evidence of deviant types. In his 1878 submission to the journal *Nature*, Galton described his method of combining several drawings or photographs of people and superimposing them on one another in order to extract their common features. In Galton's estimation, these composite photographs made it possible to discern the common features of criminals or even syphilitic patients with great accuracy. "The merit of the photographic composite," he argued, "is its mechanical precision, being subject to no errors beyond those incidental to all photographic reproductions."[46] Under the guise of scientific accuracy, such images modeled physical traits, which either the photographs' subjects or their commissioners could compare and categorize across numerous faces and bodies. Both professional and amateur scientists collected these images, seeking to map character traits onto specific features. These collections contributed to the popular science of phrenology, as well as political efforts to improve society through the policing and recording of physical characteristics, particularly with regards to race.

The very first racial-type photographs appeared in the decade following the invention/discovery of the daguerreotype. By the time of Muybridge's investigations at the University of Pennsylvania, the production of such images relied upon the standards set by anthropological photographs made by Thomas Henry Huxley and John Lamprey in Britain.[47] Both men sought a specific method for racial photography that would allow for a systematic comparison across bodies. As Huxley, then the president of the Ethnological Society of London, wrote in 1869:

> Great numbers of ethnographical photographs already exist . . . [but] they lose much of their value from not being taken upon a uniform and

well-considered plan. The result is that they are rarely measurable or comparable with one another and that they fail to give that precise information respecting the proportions and the conformation of the body, which ... [is of paramount] worth to the ethnologist.[48]

As part of an effort to create "measurable or comparable" ethnological records, he designed a standardized/systematic method for capturing the subject, posing them in similar ways and photographing them at the same scale. Huxley's method involved photographing naked subjects from a fixed distance; he also inserted a measuring stick (Huxley called it an "anthropometer") on the same plane of the figure. His method required two full-length photographs of the subject, one showing the body from the front and the other of the body in profile. For the first, frontal pose, the subject stood with their heels together and with their right arm stretched horizontally away from the body with the palm facing the camera. For the profile photograph, the subject would be turned with their left side facing the camera, the left arm bent slightly to reveal the shape of the figure's torso (and in the case of female subjects, their breasts). Huxley's methods were used to photograph subjects of the British Empire—prisoners, Indians, Bushmen of South Africa, Aborigines from Australia, and Sri Lankans— in part to justify their colonial subjugation.[49] Huxley's bodies are presented to us as specimens, relying on the visual index of "science" through the repetition of poses, the inclusion of measuring tools, and the presentation of the naked body.

When comparing Muybridge's motion study images with those of Huxley and Lamprey, we can see that they share an implicit focus on pathology, on the marking of difference. It was in this distinctly racist context that Muybridge took up the example of the grid in his own photographs. By introducing the Black body alongside the anthropological method of the grid, these photographs of Bailey automatically become a racial project. Muybridge's experiments at the University of Pennsylvania brought these debates about photography and difference to an American public. While Huxley and Lamprey had previously photographed non-white bodies in the course of their research into colonial populations, Muybridge's incorporation of a Black figure functioned differently.

In using the grid, Muybridge aligned himself with race science, including the work of J. T. Zealy three decades earlier. Zealy's project, commissioned by the Harvard University professor Louis Agassiz, was part of a concerted effort to prove the latter's theory of polygenesis or separate evolution. Agassiz (the most famous race scientist in the United States at the time) was searching for evidence to prove that each race did not in fact evolve from a single source (i.e., monogenism) but rather was the result of separate, multiple creations—a theory espoused by Dr. Samuel Morton, whose publications *Crania Americana* (1839) and *Crania Aegyptiaca* (1844) were foundational texts in nineteenth-century conceptions of race in the United States. Agassiz hired the photographer J. T. Zealy to travel to Columbia, South Carolina, in 1850 and photograph several slaves who were of identifiably African origins, a challenge given that imports of slaves to the United States had effectively stopped more than four decades earlier, in 1808. Zealy's subjects included a Fulani male named Alfred, along with several other slaves that Agassiz had identified on his tours of plantations in and around Columbia. The resulting images reveal that Zealy took great care to stage the photographs themselves as objective views of physical specimens, rather than as subjective individuals (figs. 2.8, 2.9). They bear a striking resemblance, in fact, to the anthropological photographs of the French daguerreotypist E. Thiesson, who had previously photographed Brazilians and Africans in Portugal in 1845 for anthropological study. While lacking the grid used in Lamprey's images, this is not a typical portrait photograph, which would show the subject confidently meeting the gaze of the camera, surrounded by objects or scenery that reaffirmed their social position. Instead, Alfred appears naked before the camera, positioned perpendicular to the lens in a profile view, and in another image positioned with his back facing the camera. In both photographs the figure fills the full length of the composition and appears in front of a nondescript backdrop with only a simple stool sharing the frame. In these images we see the efforts made to construct a visual typology that would transform a human subject into an object of scientific study.

Looking at Muybridge's motion studies from 1884 and 1885, we see a sustained effort to align the photographic image with these earlier "scientific" models. In plate 526, for example, Muybridge has placed his unclothed model in a similarly nondescript space, framed only by a black curtain. In this series of images, titled *Stumbling* by the photographer, we see a white naked female walking forward with her arms extended out in front and her head down (fig. 2.10). We can barely make out the surface of the walking track along the bottom of each composition. The darkness of the surrounding space not only prevents the viewer from locating the body in a specific space, but also highlights the contours of the body before the camera. Looking at six different exposures of the same moment, we are meant here to observe solely the body and its movement (as the woman lurches forward in space); even the face appears obscured, further emphasizing the status of *this* body as an object rather than a subject.

Muybridge's photographs of boxers (plates 329 to 342) are not portraits or studies of fighters, but rather studies of the sport itself.

Looking at the boxing images in Muybridge's *Animal Locomotion* project, which include not only Ben Bailey but also sparring white college students, we see that the photographer emphasizes the actions or motions of the body, rather than the individual fighter (fig. 2.3). Like the early anthropologists, Muybridge commits to showing only the general outline of the figure; we do not have access to the fighter's face or other defining features, which occludes their individuality to present them instead as physiological specimens. One could argue that the introduction of the grid in 1885, which Muybridge would continue to use for the remaining two years of the *Animal Locomotion* project, provided a tool by which the photographer could further highlight the objective function of his images. While this is certainly one story we could tell about these images, we must also consider the indexical relationship of the grid to pathology and that of photography to race.

Because race is itself a sociological rather than a biological construct, its definition (and, as I argue, its power) depends upon wider social and cultural forces to make it visible. And while the concept of race organizes our national, political, and social lives, its legibility depends almost exclusively on the visual perception of difference (e.g., skin color). In his 2003 essay "The Shadow and the Substance: Race, Photography, and the Index," Nicholas Mirzoeff discusses the relationship between photography and discourses of race. In his estimation, both function as an index. In the case of photography, the medium itself is indexical—a sign that designates the presence of something which was once there. Race operates in a similar fashion in that the skin color (or another external, physical difference) is thought to represent some inner quality of difference. "The photograph," he writes, "became a prime locus of the performance of the radicalized index," and the viewer "consciously or unconsciously decides whether and how it indexes the race of its object."[50] We should ask, then, in what ways do Muybridge's photographs of the Black boxer Ben Bailey and his explicit introduction of the grid connect to the wider social impulse to locate race for nineteenth-century audiences?

Previous scholars have addressed the unique presence of Bailey in the *Animal Locomotion* project. For example, in her study of Muybridge, Sarah Anne Gordon contends that the introduction of the grid in the photographs of Bailey was mere coincidence, or rather evidence of the increasingly empirical approach taken by Muybridge when he returned to Philadelphia in the summer of 1885. The day that Bailey was in the studio "was also the first day he [Muybridge]

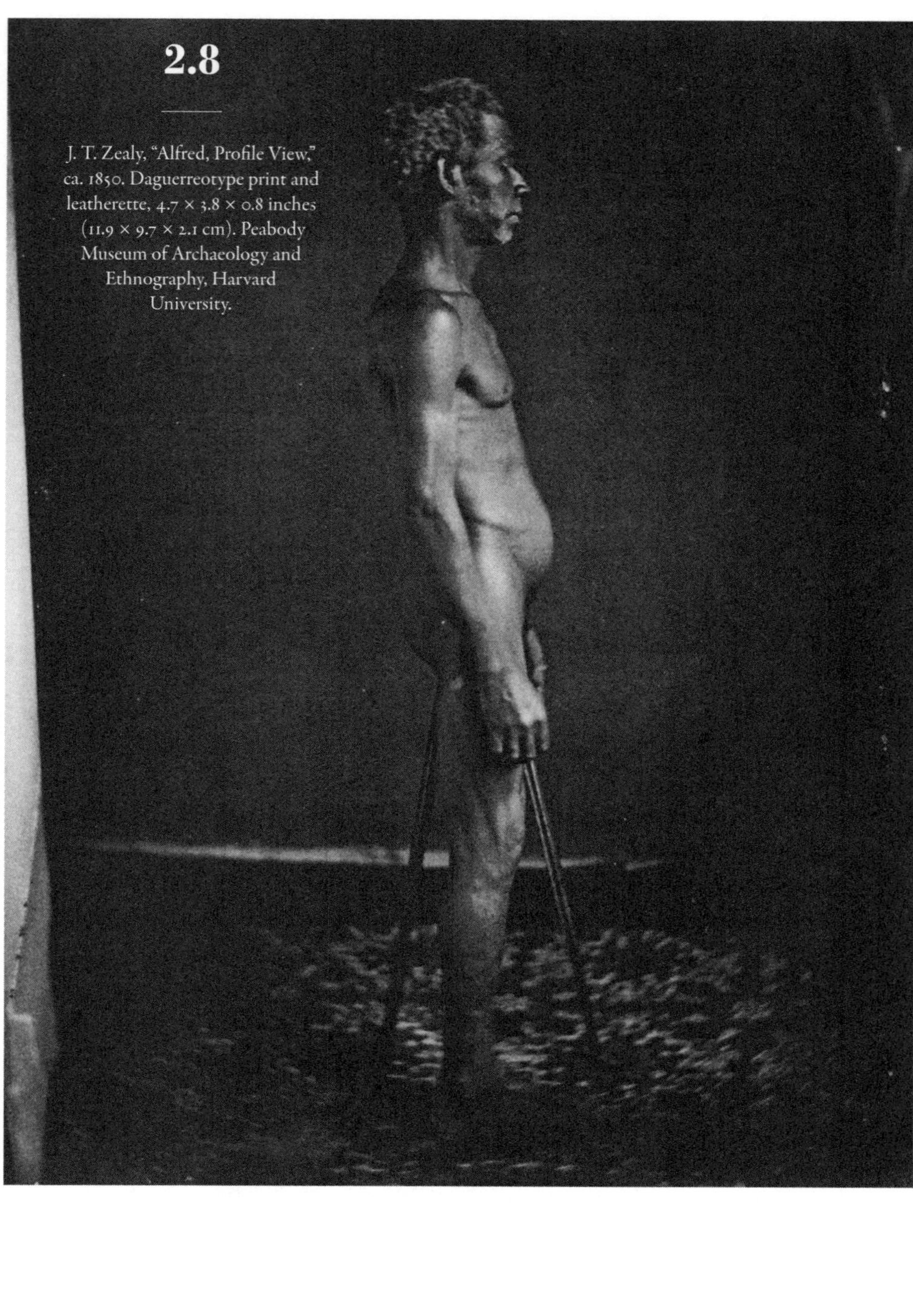

J. T. Zealy, "Alfred, Profile View," ca. 1850. Daguerreotype print and leatherette, 4.7 × 3.8 × 0.8 inches (11.9 × 9.7 × 2.1 cm). Peabody Museum of Archaeology and Ethnography, Harvard University.

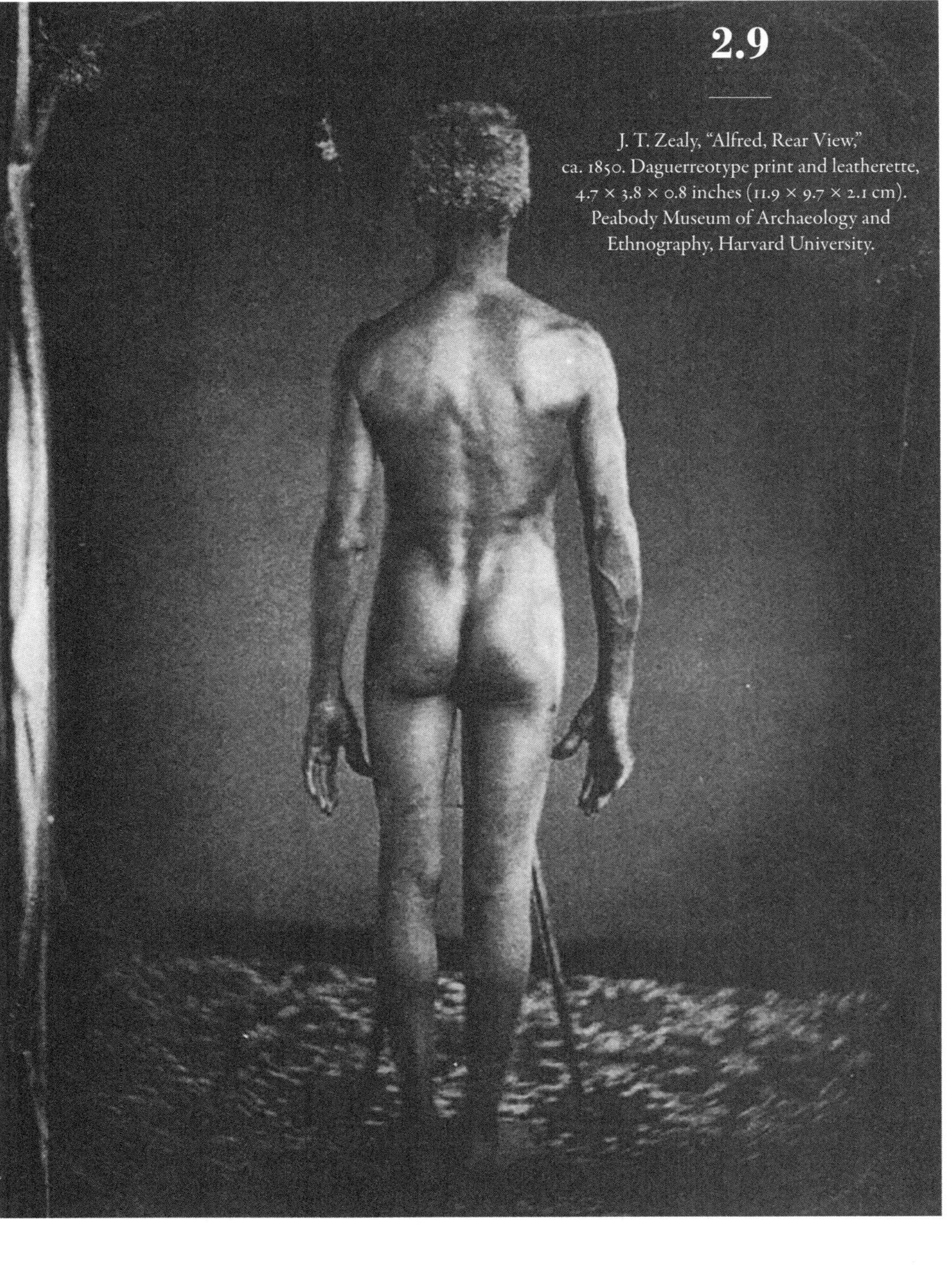

J. T. Zealy, "Alfred, Rear View,"
ca. 1850. Daguerreotype print and leatherette,
4.7 × 3.8 × 0.8 inches (11.9 × 9.7 × 2.1 cm).
Peabody Museum of Archaeology and
Ethnography, Harvard University.

——

Eadweard Muybridge, *Nude Woman Stumbling*, ca. 1884/1886, printed 1887. Collotype print. From *Animal Locomotion* (Philadelphia: J. B. Lippincott & Co., 1887), plate 526, detail. Boston Public Library.

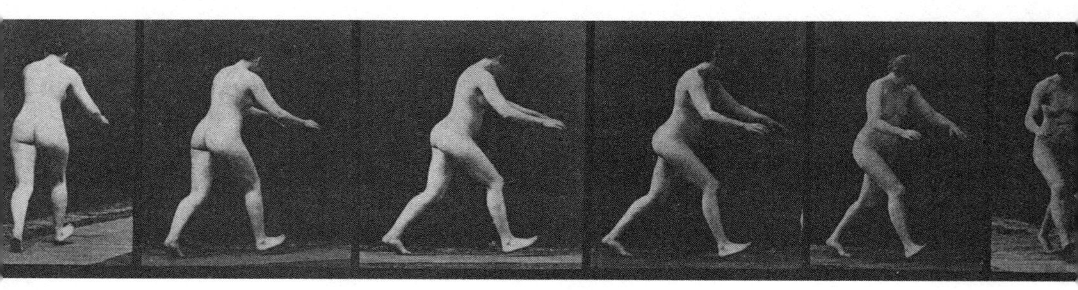

recorded data in his notebook, thus marking the true beginning of the investigation." "The initiation of the grid," she argues, "likely had to do with this starting point rather than with Bailey's race."[51] Gordon declares that the images of Bailey do not deviate from the representations of white boxers in Muybridge's study, and may in fact simply indicate the growing popularity of the sport.[52] In Gordon's estimation, then, the selection of Bailey as a subject connected to the contemporary, middle-class interest in and promotion of the sport. His placement in the published volume ("interspersed" with white athletes) aligns rather than separates Bailey from his white counterparts.

The historian Elspeth Brown, on the other hand, has described these images specifically as part of "a historically situated racial project in which 'human bodies and social structures are represented and organized' in order to create, inhabit, transform, or destroy racial categories."[53] In these images we see how the social categorization of Blacks played out via the manipulation of the photographic medium, and more specifically via the introduction of the grid that accompanies Bailey's image. Speaking of Muybridge's introduction of the grid in the photographs of Bailey, she claims, "It is as if the non-white 'other' cannot be understood, scientifically, without the anthropometric grid, a technology for mapping racial difference."[54] In Brown's reading, the presence of the grid cannot be read separately from nineteenth-century race science, which relied heavily on anthropometry—the physical measurement of difference—and the technology of photography to visualize racial and ethnic difference.

More recently, Shawn Michelle Smith has read Muybridge's photographs of Bailey in even more urgent terms. Smith contends that the grid presented the possibility of managing white anxieties around the Black body through the constraint of its perceived physical and sexual excess. "Perhaps," she writes, "Muybridge's grid was first used to restrain the Black male body, to break it down into manageable, little five-centimeter square parts."[55] Muybridge's presentation of this particular body, and its translation of Bailey's dynamic movement into a series of discrete and identifiable poses, rehearses an attempt to fix and constrain the Black body within the photographic frame. For Smith, the (presumed) precision of each of these photographs underscores their investment in pathology. She convincingly connects the shadow boxing we see performed by Bailey in these images to the "shadow archive," first theorized by Allan Sekula in his 1986 essay "The Body and the Archive." The shadow archive includes the entire field of representation, within which every photographic image (fine art or vernacular) takes its place as part of a wider social hierarchy.[56] Sekula argues that the meaning of an individual photograph is not held exclusively within the image; instead, meaning and coherence are found in the contemplation of that individual photograph in relation to all others. For Smith, the shadow archive for Muybridge's photographs of the Black boxer Ben Bailey includes all the men, women, and children that follow him in this project and who are also subjected to the anthropometric grid. Focusing on the sequences of female subjects, for example, Smith reads the emphasis on gender differentiation within the series—where women perform domestic tasks (often with props)—as a commentary on both race and class. This project, and its overwhelming presentation of ideal white bodies (graceful women and powerful, athletic men) was an argument for the superiority of whiteness.[57]

Bailey's presence marks his difference as well as reflects wider cultural anxieties around the Black body. The anthropometric grid visually distinguishes Bailey's body from those preceding it in the series, and his isolation within the frame as he shadow boxes an invisible opponent points to the fragility of racial hierarchy. Given the politics of the moment, it would have been impossible for Bailey to have appeared with a white opponent in these images. Muybridge avoided bringing in two Black models for these scenes, although it would have presumably been quite easy to locate a second fighter. Like Smith, I believe that Bailey's appearance alone has consequences for the ways we read his presence within the series—for one, the framing of his figure quite differently from the white boxers photographed by Muybridge. As the film scholar Jesús Costantino has pointed out, the fixation of the camera on Bailey alone could be read along the lines of "Laura Mulvey's account of the fetishistic close-up."[58] Bailey occupies the center of the frame, and unlike the sparring images of two white fighters, the square format of the composition does not allude to the four corners of the boxing ring.

However, I argue that we must consider connections between these images of Ben Bailey and an ideal, white manhood consciously constructed through and reinforced by a rising culture of athleticism.[59] What existing scholarship has failed to produce is a genealogy of these images of Bailey that takes into account his own position as a precursive figure—in both boxing and visual culture. Ben Bailey is a product of intersecting ideas around race, sexuality, violence, and sport. I am interested in this image because it brings together all these discourses simultaneously. As Allan Sekula has argued, every photograph exists in relationship to a network of social and cultural assumptions that make the image ultimately legible. In the case of Bailey, that network includes the hermeneutic paradigm of anthropological study, the culture of ideal Victorian manhood, as well as associated beliefs about the threat of the Black body to ideas of white supremacy. I will also extend these readings through a deeper consideration of the subject. In other words, what does it mean that the first Black body is a boxer's body? I will consider the intersectionality of Bailey's identity as a Black boxer, as a Black man, and as a Black photographic subject.

The Art of Boxing in Philadelphia

Because there was no formal boxing club at the university, Bailey most likely came into Muybridge's orbit via the artist Thomas Eakins (1844–1916), an ardent fan of boxing and the man who introduced Muybridge to Philadelphia. Several members of the athletic program at the university were professional or amateur boxers.[60] Eakins himself had boxed casually as a student in France at the Académie des Beaux-Arts in 1866; he also went to the gymnasium several days a week to wrestle.[61] Following his return to America, Eakins began attending boxing matches in Philadelphia in the 1870s. By the 1890s, he attended matches multiple times a week at the encouragement of Samuel Murray—Eakins's favorite student and an avid boxing fan. Eakins invited several boxers to his studio and became friends with them. He was also introduced to local fighters by his friend, Clarence Cranmer, an aspiring sportswriter who advised him on the selection of boxing models for his 1898–99 paintings.[62] Cranmer was a member of the Quaker City Athletic Club, where Ben Bailey boxed in 1890 and 1891.[63] In the mid 1890s, Eakins went to matches at the Philadelphia Arena Athletic Club, located at Cherry and Broad Streets in the Tenth Ward of central Philadelphia and only a seven minute walk south from the Eighth Ward (where Bailey lived in 1886).[64] The Arena Athletic Club most likely opened in 1892.[65] This was just after Bailey presumably stopped boxing, since he goes unmentioned by local newspapers after 1891; however, their proximity demonstrates that Bailey and Eakins were in the same neighborhood at the same time. Furthermore, Eakins also rented a studio at 1330 Chestnut Street from 1884 to 1900, which was located in the northern center of the Eighth Ward.[66] If he wanted to walk into a nearby gym to find a model for his friend Muybridge, Eakins likely would have encountered Bailey.

Eakins's interest in boxing is well documented. He painted boxers three times during 1898 and 1899 after attending boxing matches at a public arena. The canvases *Taking the Count* (1898), *Salutat* (1898), and *Between Rounds* (1899) all show intimate views of boxing matches set inside large amphitheaters. As early as 1883 Eakins also photographed subjects boxing in the service of his paintings. There are four known photographs showing naked men, perhaps Eakins's students, in a forest clearing. Two of the men box with padded gloves, while four men sit around them and observe (fig. 2.11). In 1884 Eakins began a series of photography experiments independent of Muybridge but under the

Thomas Eakins, *Six Males, Nude, Two Boxing*, ca. 1883. Albumen print, 4.13 × 3.1 inches (10.5 × 7.9 cm). Charles Bregler's Thomas Eakins Collection, Pennsylvania Academy of Fine Arts, Philadelphia.

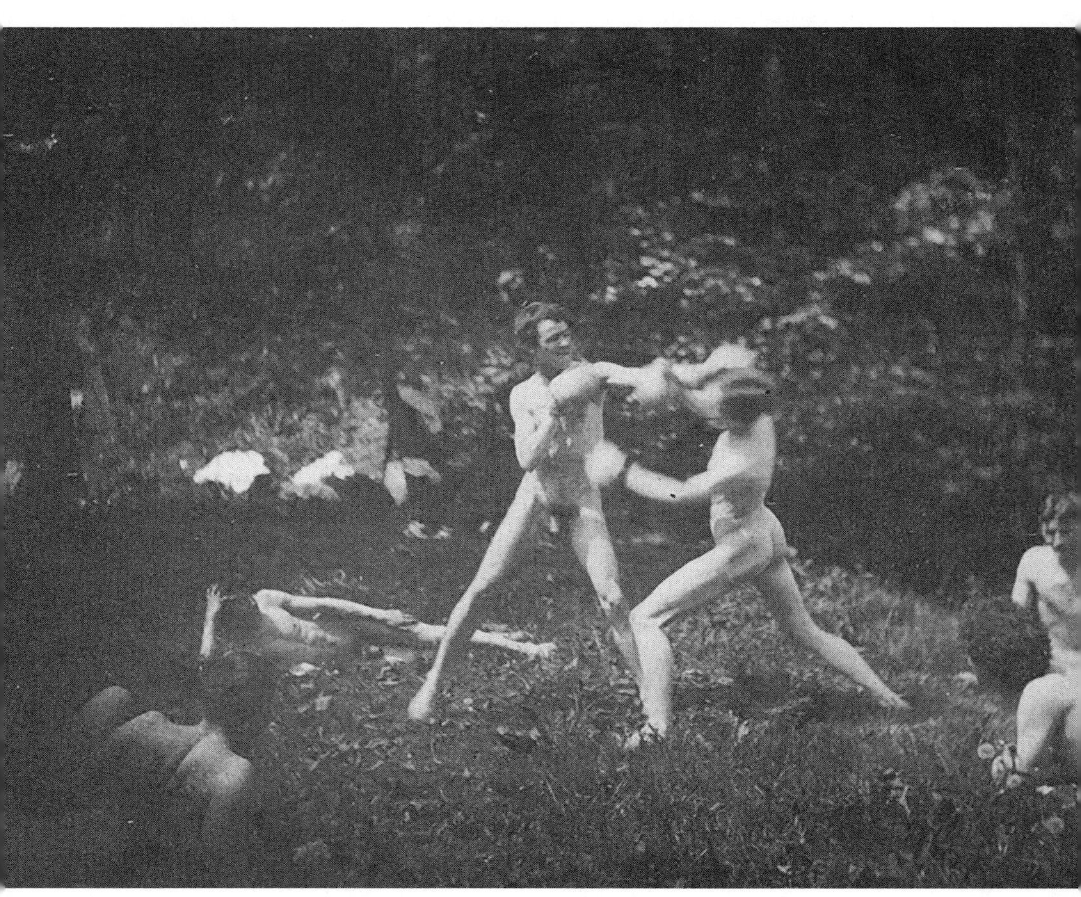

oversight of the University of Pennsylvania. Working with Dr. Harrison Allen, the chair of physiology, Eakins photographed running horses as well as athletes running, jumping, and walking.[67] This project ended in 1885. However, Eakins subsequently received little credit for contributing to Muybridge's work.[68]

Thomas Eakins's paintings give us a unique view into late nineteenth-century boxing—a new, urban phenomenon, whose representation until this point had been overwhelmingly confined to newspapers and other print media. The fighters in Eakins's canvases are not engaged in direct combat, but are instead shown at moments of inaction. The paintings fail to show us blood, a referee, or even an opponent. In her close study of Eakins's boxing paintings, Marjorie Walter has argued his choice of subject was tied to his own interest in the sport, particularly the connection of the physical body (strength) with the mind (strategy) that it required. The theme of boxing—with its explicit focus on male aggression and violence—was an ideal subject for the exploration of masculinity at the end of the nineteenth century.

I argue that Muybridge's and Eakins's choice to focus on boxing shored up contemporary constructions of the (white) masculine ideal as intrinsically connected to the body. Unlike other popular sports of the late nineteenth century—baseball, tennis, even football—where there is a focus on a ball, in boxing the body itself is at play. The physical body of the fighter, left exposed to the view of the audience, acts as the primary focus. Even the language used to describe the boxer's body in popular media of the nineteenth century revealed an enjoyment of its beauty. The sexual prudishness of the Victorian era was cast aside in detailed descriptions that bordered on the homoerotic. Take as an example the following coverage of a fight in *Spirit of the Times*:

> Burke presented an iron frame, in which all superfluous flesh seemed excluded. His broad and extended chest, his outward turned knees, that take off from beauty to add so much to muscular power, his muscular and well-knit lower limbs left no doubt in the minds of the spectators that no common skill or bodily strength would be sufficient to overpower or vanquish the possessor. O'Connell stripped to greater advantage than expected. His upper frame is large and muscular, but it wants compactness and tension. His sinews hang loose, and his frame is far from being well banded together.[69]

It may be surprising to the contemporary reader that sporting coverage in this period frequently failed to record the action of the match, describing instead the form of the boxer in exquisite detail. Elliott Gorn has argued that the new and explicit focus on the boxer's body "grew less from narrowly defined homosexuality than from a common male aesthetic."[70] In this aesthetic, the view of the male body as a thing of beauty was connected to a homosocial bond between working-class men, who were themselves struggling to define masculinity—not by their relationships with women, but instead through their comparisons with other men. The widespread emphasis on the physical development and muscularity of the male body, as well as the standards of measurement promoted by celebrities like Eugen Sandow (1867–1925) and Bernarr Macfadden (1868–1955) all fed into this larger project to discover a male aesthetic. And the body of the heavyweight boxer in particular was promoted as the ideal body. According to the historian Gail Bederman, the culture of late Victorian America had already identified the body of the heavyweight boxer as the perfect example of manhood; at this moment, bodily strength and social authority were inextricably linked by a series of metonymic social processes (rather than any logical reason). The boxer's body was a physical expression of prized, middle-class masculine values—strength, power, and stamina.[71] Bailey was himself listed as a heavyweight boxer in his matches, weighing 198 pounds in 1889.[72]

The display of the physical body has always been integral to the sport of boxing. The partial nudity of the athletes and the dramatic lighting of a boxing ring intentionally highlights their form. The male boxing costume, first short pants and later briefs or trunks, leaves the torso exposed, often increasingly slick with perspiration. When fighters are pictured outside the boxing ring in photographs, illustrations, and other publicity, the central focus often becomes the symmetry of their musculature—a feature highly valued in the burgeoning physical culture movements of the nineteenth century. Convention in the late nineteenth century dictated that these bodies frequently appeared either in a frontal position with the arms crossed in front, highlighting the enlarged pectorals and flexed biceps. For example, if we look at the 1882 photograph of the heavyweight champion John L. Sullivan (1858–1918), also known as the "Boston Strong Boy," taken in the same year as his famous defeat of Paddy Ryan (1851–1900), the composition has been constructed to train our focus on the bare torso of the fighter (fig. 1.5). Sullivan appears, with short hair and his trademark handlebar mustache, with his arms crossed in front. His head and upper body are centered in the frame with the majority of the composition devoted to the somewhat abstract shape formed by the shoulders, arms, and torso. Looking closely at this shape we notice above all the symmetry of the body. The creases and folds of the figure's skin are mirrored on both sides, the size of forearms and biceps appear equal and balanced. The position of Sullivan's hands, tucked beneath each opposite arm, pushes his biceps slightly outward to give the appearance of a more developed musculature. Our focus is meant to be trained on the beauty and power of Sullivan's body and its classical form. Sullivan's head is even turned slightly toward the right so that his gaze falls just out of the frame. The boxer's gaze does not confront the viewer, in the position of an opponent, further underscoring the voyeuristic offering of the boxer's body for our pleasure.

Artists like Eakins and Muybridge sought out the boxer as an ideal model for explorations of white, middle-class masculine identity. What remains less obvious is the impact of Bailey's presence, as the only visibly Black subject within Muybridge's larger project. While there were several Black boxers fighting in Philadelphia (or in nearby Camden, New Jersey) in the last decades of the nineteenth century—along with Ben Bailey we know of Amos Scott, Jake Carter, and "Dusty Frank" Gorman—whom Eakins may have chosen as models for his artistic studies, the boxers in his paintings and drawings remain exclusively white. This is even though the Black population of Philadelphia skyrocketed during Eakins's time, growing from 34,000 in 1850 to 480,000 by 1950.[73] Speaking to the absence of Black boxers in Eakins's oeuvre, Walter has argued that the body type of African American fighters of Eakins's moment would not have fit his preference for "young men with slim builds." Eakins, she imagines, "probably found [the Black heavyweight fighter Joe] Walcott and other, larger fighters too muscular for his taste."[74]

Martin A. Berger has convincingly argued that the Black figures that do appear in other works by Eakins, such as *Rail Shooting* (1876) and *The Dancing Lesson* (1878), do not fit the progressive or race-neutral readings preferred by present-day scholars. Instead, Berger contends that these Black figures, once placed into a predominantly white visual landscape, reinforce "the model of white patriarchal control" through their reliance on a "genealogy of figures" reaching back to the era of Jim Crow and minstrelsy.[75] Gilded Age audiences would have read *any* Black figure from a racist vantage point, interpreting the dancing figure in Eakins's 1878 watercolor, for example, as a comedic rather than a sympathetic view of Black life. Berger calls attention here to a contemporary review of *The Dancing Lesson*, which referred to the work's "goblin humor" and declared it a "comedy of plantation life."[76] While Black figures do not often appear in Eakins's works, their presence is always already "overdetermined as Black."[77] And, more importantly for this study, we can say the same for Muybridge.

The conscious effacement of Blackness from most late nineteenth-century representation makes Muybridge's choice to insert a Black model into the *Animal Locomotion* project even more radical. This is, above all, complicated by the wider context of nineteenth-century physical culture, which equated the muscular body with white, middle-class conceptions of manhood and programmatically excluded Black bodies (both from representation and from professional sports). The body of the heavyweight boxer was specifically bound up in the definition of white, middle-class masculinity, so much so that Black fighters were barred from competing for championship titles. Bailey's presence underscores the issue of race within these wider debates surrounding white Victorian manhood. In the late nineteenth century, men like Ben Bailey boxed as amateurs (sometimes professionally overseas), but were unable to compete professionally or be recognized as champions in the United States. Their lurking presence—in the sport and in visual culture—was always conditioned by their exclusion. In addition, these images of Ben Bailey are produced in a post-Emancipation US landscape and must be read within the context of wider questions of race and the overall perceived threat of Blackness.

Race, Violence, and Representation in the Nineteenth Century

The violent encounter that takes place inside the four corners of the ring endures as the main attraction of boxing. In Muybridge's era—that is, in the decades after slavery—boxing moved (like Ben Bailey himself) from the plantation and from beneath the shadows of urban immigrant communities to a wider stage. Middle-class men began to practice boxing in local gymnasiums; boxing became a club sport at prestigious universities like Harvard, and was even promoted by doctors, ministers, and politicians. By the end of the nineteenth century, prize fighting specifically, and boxing in general, had been sanitized just enough to make it legal, while still retaining the grittiness and brutality that promised to give spectators a view of "real life."

Yet outside the widespread efforts to disassociate boxing from the rough underclass and establish it as a gentlemanly sport, boxing remained a violent and brutal affair. A thin line exists between a boxing match and attempted murder; the fight itself makes a spectacle of cruelty. As audiences looked on, two fighters on a brightly lit, elevated stage beat each other to a pulp (or sometimes to death). Men in evening dress attended fights for the cathartic release that witnessing such violence promised. It was a compelling combination of control and base impulse. And despite the attempts at organization or respectability that came about in this period, we must remember that alongside the civilized sparring taking place at Harvard, fighters still met each other in punishing bareknuckle fights. Between 1890 (the earliest year for which we have recorded data) and 1899, approximately 103 men died in the ring.[78] Even as the sport became more professionalized, these moves toward organization did not mitigate the true violence of boxing, which was itself overdetermined by class. We can imagine that the club matches at Harvard were decidedly tamer than those taking place in the backrooms of bars in urban centers.

It was perhaps impossible to represent by photographic means the violence and chaos inside the ring, as opponents lunged at and punched one another in quick rounds. But Muybridge's photographs at the University of Pennsylvania had the potential to change that. Suddenly, we could see not only the impact of the fighter's punch, but trace its movement. The violence of Muybridge's method transforms the individual subject into a photographed and measured object, connecting the resulting image to a wider context of violence. More specifically, the photographer's choice of representing a boxer produces associations with the brutality so characteristic of the sport. We read the threat of violence in Muybridge's photographs of Bailey, as these images markedly differ from those of the white fighters. In contrast to the other images of boxing from Muybridge's series, where we see two fighters somewhat playful sparring (fig. 2.3), Bailey appears alone. He also consumes a much larger proportion of the photographic frame; his body stretches and lunges in one continuous movement from the left foot in the back to the right arm that punches forward. We see the pronounced musculature of his body, whereas the white amateurs appear thin and even underdeveloped. And while the white fighters wear a white cloth to cover their genitals, Bailey's anatomy remains exposed.

The violence of boxing, both inside and outside the ring, was made palatable for white middle-class audiences despite its murderous energies. For these predominantly Anglo-Saxon viewers, boxing in the late nineteenth century was a spectacle of brutality, its ultimate goal to render one of the men unconscious before the roaring crowd. As in the words of Joyce Carol Oates, "boxing is the only sport in which the objective is to cause injury: the brain is the target, the knockout the goal."[79] In her writing on the sport Oates calls into question the ethics of viewing a fight:

> The spectacle of human beings fighting each other for whatever reason, at certain well-publicized times, staggering sums of money, is enormously disturbing because it violates a taboo of our civilization.... In this way boxing as a public spectacle is akin to pornography: in each case the spectator is made a voyeur, distanced, yet presumably intimately involved, in an event that is not supposed to be happening as it is happening.[80]

In other words, viewers become voyeurs in the most literal sense, taking pleasure from the pain of others. Homoeroticism is also at play here, as the two men at the center of the ring negotiate the areas of the body they can touch; both men appear bare chested, glistening with sweat.

In the same way that Oates points to pornography as a means for consuming taboo sex, boxing acts a socially acceptable mode by which to consume violence. In the nineteenth century, as Black fighters entered the ring and white spectators confronted their own fears and fantasies about these bodies, the fragility of racial superiority was at stake. The widespread racial tensions following Emancipation and Reconstruction often played out in the boxing ring. White audiences interpreted the participation of Black people in this violent sport as being connected to their intrinsic savagery. As Frederick Douglass wrote in his autobiography "only those wild and low sports peculiar to semicivilized people were encouraged."[81] We can imagine that to white audiences the presence of Black fighters may have in some ways seemed a natural consequence of their inhumanity. After all, a conception of the Black body as one incapable of suffering and immune to pain was an underlying principle of slavery. An examination of boxing and its audiences reveals, to borrow the words of Saidiya Hartman, "the precariousness of empathy and the thin line between witness and spectator."[82] Although Hartman discusses here the violence of slavery, we can imagine that some white audiences in the era of Jim Crow saw parallels between the beatings on the plantation and the punches in the boxing ring, perhaps recognizing the shared virtue of interchangeability (wherein the Black body becomes "an abstract and empty vessel") peculiar to both institutions.[83]

While the violence of boxing may have reaffirmed some ideas about Black suffering, victories by Black boxers, and their overall dominance in the sport, contradicted much of the racist pseudoscience popular at the turn of the twentieth century that suggested Blacks were both mentally and physically inferior to whites, too lazy and undisciplined to be successful athletes. As Black fighters began defeating white opponents in public view in the last decades of the nineteenth century, audiences began to worry about Black domination in other spheres. "If the negro is capable of developing such prowess in divisions of boxing," wrote one reporter in the late nineteenth century, "what is going to stop him from making the same progress in the heavier ranks?"[84]

The fears of Black dominance whipped up by these matches certainly extended beyond the four corners of the boxing ring. More specifically, we must also consider the fear of Black boxers alongside the myth of the Black man's insatiable sexual desire for white women—a threat to the supremacy of whiteness. The 1863 pamphlet "Miscegenation: The Theory of the Blending of the Races, Applied to the American White Man and the Negro," published by the

New York World, was a popular piece of anti-Lincoln rhetoric (disguised as an argument *for* racial equality) that fomented a fear of Black sexuality. This fear not only legitimized the alienation of African Americans from national culture, but also connected racial exclusions of race to issues of sexuality and gender.[85] The Black boxer's performance in the ring, therefore, was more than a performance of athleticism; his body called forth the objectification of Blackness and denials of Black sentience. It carried an implicit threat to white authority, and the threat of race mixing. In Muybridge's images of Bailey boxing alone, naked, measured against a grid, we see the photographer's attempt both to manage this threat and to make the violence palatable for his audiences.

Reading into the implied violence of Bailey's punch and into the careful manipulation of his naked body I want to consider the "lurking, objectifying inverse" of these images.[86] This will require that we look carefully at contemporaneous visualizations of violence, including images of lynching, which, alongside eugenics photography, worked toward the formation of racist ideology and the production of race as a "visualizable fact."[87] We must also consider the eroticization of the Black male body that occurs alongside this violence, looking at the work of F. Holland Day, whose fetishistic images of Black men are another integral part of the visual record of the late nineteenth century. In what remains of this chapter, I explore the intersections between these two types of photography (popular and fine art) and their place within a visual discourse that positioned Black men as objects of desire and of violence simultaneously.

Both boxing and lynching (and their representations) cultivate and even condone violence against Black bodies. In the 2010 book *Embodying Black Experience: Stillness, Critical Memory, and the Black Body*, Harvey Young considers the origins of boxing on plantations in the American South, where slaves sparred with one another for entertainment and for the profit of their slaveowners. These matches were above all else a demonstration of white superiority, at times requiring that white slaveowners themselves enter the ring. In William Faulkner's *Absalom, Absalom!*, principally set during the period surrounding the Civil War, the white protagonist Thomas Sutpen uses boxing to establish his own supremacy:

> It seems that on certain occasions, perhaps at the end of the evening, the spectacle, as a grand finale, or perhaps as a matter of sheer deadly forethought toward the retention of supremacy, domination, he [Thomas] would enter the ring with one of the negroes himself. Yes. That is what Ellen saw: her husband and the father of her children standing there naked and panting and bloody to the waist and the negro just fallen evidently,

lying at his feet and bloody too save that on the negro it merely looked like grease or sweat.[88]

Faulkner's fictive event calls out the very real stakes of boxing—for both Black and white fighters. These fights, according to Young, "'instructed' not only the captive body in the ring but also those outside of it, the witness to the ring event, to accept the Black body's position as inferior and subordinate."[89] The Black boxer experiences physical subjugation but is also reduced to the object of the white spectator's look.

We can locate similar performances of white supremacy and of the objectified Black body in the visual culture of the late nineteenth century and, more specifically, in the photographs of lynching that circulated throughout the United States in this period. The ritualized execution of Black men and women in the United States goes back as far as the first slave ships to arrive at its shores, and in the 1890s an average of 139 people were victims of lynching annually, 75 percent of them Black.[90] Between 1877 and 1950, estimates hold that 4,084 Black people were murdered by acts of racial terror. Although the highest numbers of lynchings come from the states of Mississippi (654), Georgia (589), Louisiana (549), and Arkansas (492), non-Southern states were not immune to these events. Fifty-six Black people were lynched over the same period in Illinois, for example, and "even in states with sparse Black populations, violent attacks terrorized small and vulnerable Black communities."[91] In 1885, the year that Muybridge photographed Ben Bailey in Philadelphia, seventy-four Black people were victims of lynching across the United States, a nearly 30 percent increase over the year before.[92] In January 1884 the *Philadelphia Inquirer* reported on the trial of John H. Brown, a Black man, who allegedly chased and attacked a boy of unlisted age who spoke to him using a racial slur. A police officer chased Brown, attacked him with a club, pulled a revolver on him, and would have shot and killed him were the officer not wearing "mittens." Brown was sentenced to a year in prison.[93] And just a few hours before Bailey walked into Muybridge's studio, a white mob lynched Townsend Cook in Westminster, Maryland, a city less than a dozen miles from the Pennsylvania state border.[94] According to the report published that day in the *Baltimore Sun*:

> The mob took Cook out the Mt. Airey [*sic*] road about a mile and hung him to the limb of a tree beside the road. They fired two bullets into the back of his neck. No one was allowed to accompany them, and when, about 3 o'clock some citizens found the body, life was gone. Blood was streaming down the body from the bullet-holes in the neck. The mob had stripped

off all his clothes except his trowsers [*sic*], and had tacked the following
note to the tree: "This man confessed his crime."

News of Cook's spectacular and violent death, witnessed by approximately
thirty men in Mount Airy, reached thousands of readers across the country in
the morning papers, including the *Lancaster Intelligencer*.

The newspapers provided an outlet for advertising (some announced the
time and place of a planned lynching) and for memorializing the executions.
As photography's popularity grew in the late nineteenth century, the camera
became another tool by which these sensational events were preserved, a testament to both "their openness and the self-righteousness that animated the
participants," in the words of American historian Leon F. Litwack.[95] The photographs captured the execution of Black bodies, as well as the proud spectators that surrounded them. Many of these photographs (of lynchings and
of burnings) were circulated as postcards, traded among the overwhelmingly
white public along with fragments of rope or locks of hair, as souvenirs to com-
memorate these events, and as affirmations of white power over Black bodies.[96]
One such postcard from 1899 is of Frank Embree, who was captured by a white
mob on July 22 on the way to his trial for the alleged rape of a fourteen-year-
old white girl in Fayette, Missouri (fig. 2.12). Nineteen-year-old Embree was
stripped naked and whipped before a large crowd in an attempt to extract his
confession. After being lashed more than one hundred times, Embree, to the
satisfaction of the gathered spectators, finally offered his confession. He was
hung from a black oak tree "about 150 yards east of where the crime was committed," dying after "several more violent jerks and convulsions" before a crowd
of 1,000 onlookers.[97]

Embree's death received widespread news coverage, and stories appeared in
the United States as early as the day following his death (in the *St. Louis Dispatch*) and circulated in international news media several months afterward.[98]
The images of Embree's arrest and execution circulated widely in the form
of photographic postcards. According to Leigh Raiford, "to consider lynching through the cultural logic of photography compels us to recognize such
violence as wholly part of modernity, as not simply endemic to the southern
United States but able to travel, like the expanding modes of transportation,
to spread as far and wide as the photograph (or the stereograph or the film or
the audio recording) might take it."[99] As we look at the photographs of Embree's body, we must also consider their circulation or, in Raiford's words, "the
constant mediated repetition of 'the Black body in pain for public consumption.'"[100] Images of Black bodies like Embree's are inherent to white American

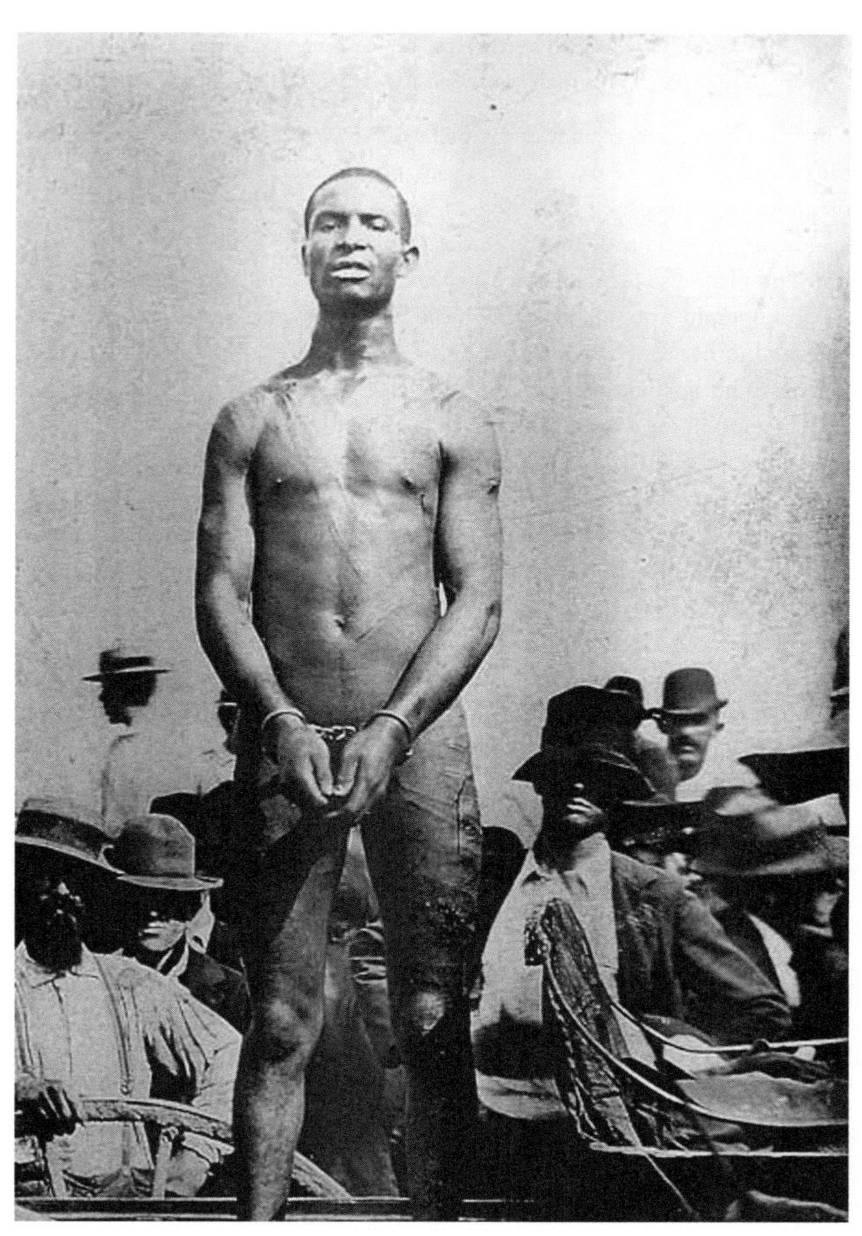

2.12

———

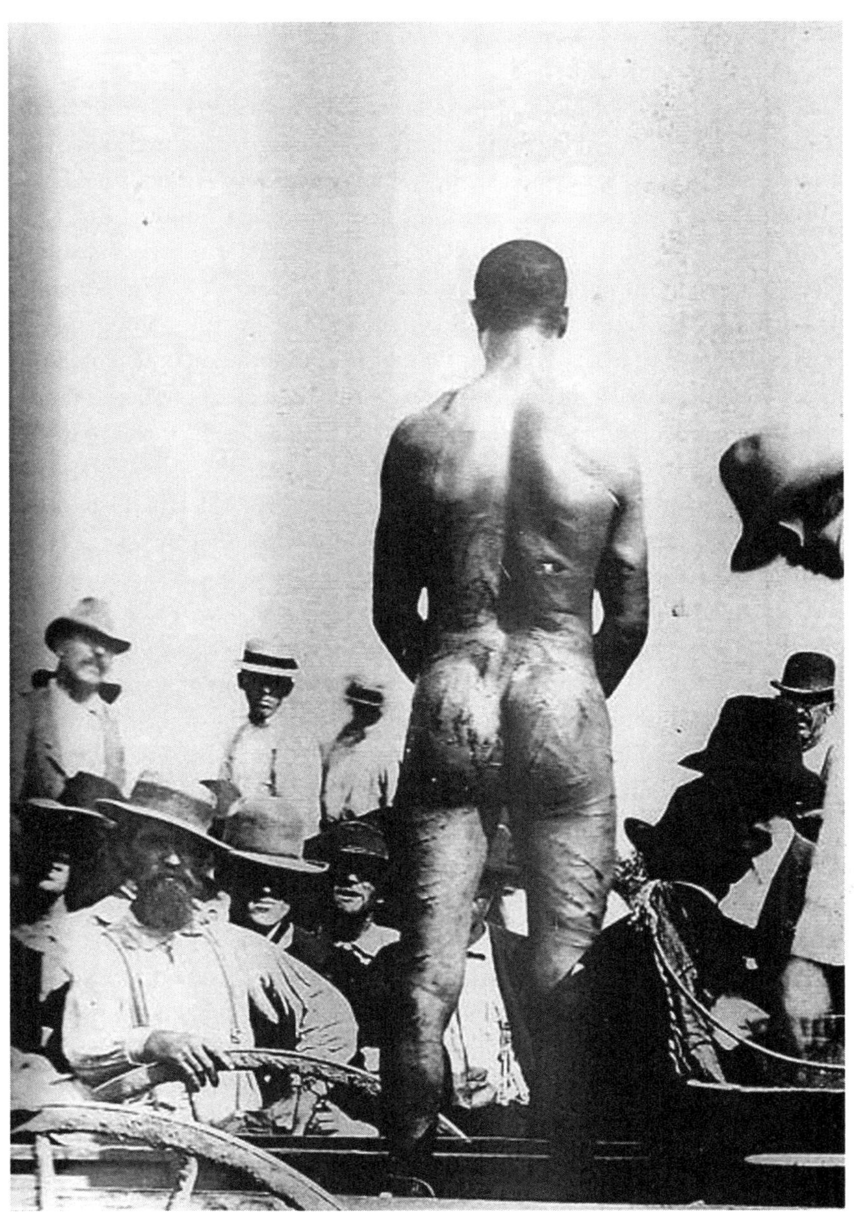

"The Lynching of Frank Embree, July 22, 1899."
Photographer unknown, postcard, 9.4 × 6.8 inches (23.8 × 17.3 cm).
Equal Justice Initiative, Montgomery, Alabama.

identity, which has always depended upon the affirmation of Blackness as inferior, passive, and abjected.[101]

The photographs of Embree that remain show his naked body covered in lashes that weep blood. He stands in the back of a wagon, elevated above the crowd of white spectators who gaze up at him from below. His body has been turned for the camera so that he may be photographed from the front, and again from the back. In the frontal view, Embree's handcuffed wrists meet directly in front of his pubic area, blocking his penis from view. While images of lynching victims are unfortunately common in this era, this photograph of Embree stripped of his clothing for the camera and the audience before him underscores the sexual dimension of this execution. Embree's body here is transformed into an object of violence, and into the location of the threat of Black sexuality.

Litwack has argued that the lynching of Black men, regardless of the accused crime, always bears the trace of sexuality. "To endorse lynching," he writes, "was to dwell on the sexual depravity of the Black man, to raise the specter of the Black beast seized by uncontrollable, savage, sexual passions that were inherent in the race. The inhumanity, depravity, bestiality, and savagery practiced by white participants in lynchings would be justified in the name of humanity, morality, justice, civilization, and Christianity."[102] The lynching of the Black man, then, was an attempt to control the invented threat of Black sexuality. Alongside the theatrics of minstrelsy, which was similarly rooted in white racialized anxiety, these public murders acted out both the panic and the pleasure associated with Black bodies in the post-Emancipation era. We must therefore read lynching, minstrelsy, and even Muybridge's photographs of Ben Bailey within a wider "landscape of stereotypes" about Blackness—many of which have origins in the nineteenth century and persist into our present moment.[103] These stereotypes—arguably derived from the desires of white men—served above all to regulate and to oppress a newly emancipated populace, while legitimizing the racist actions of the systems of power. In particular, echoes of the over sexualized Black buck—the stereotype of a violent, rude, even lecherous Black man who refuses to submit to white authority—are inescapable.[104]

We cannot legitimately consider racial exclusions as separate from gender and sexual exclusions. The motivations underlying racial exclusion are marked not only by politics and economics (i.e., the disenfranchisement of African Americans from a capitalist structure and its potential rewards) but also by a desire to regulate gender and sexuality driven by the fear of miscegenation.[105] In Roderick Ferguson's view, the mythology of the Black man's desire for white women played a formative role in the exclusion of African Americans from national culture. In the case of Ben Bailey, then, any analysis must consider both race and sexuality; these photographs are not about Blackness *or* about sexuality, but about both simultaneously.

Imaging Black Sexuality

One of the common threads in the violence of the images discussed thus far is the emphasis on and/or exposure of the penis. For Embree standing captive before the leering crowd, the implicit threat of his anatomy is at the center—of both the composition, and of the controversy. In Muybridge's image of Bailey walking, the locomotion of the figure, recorded from the side, illustrates Bailey's dynamic musculature as well as the movement of his penis (fig. 2.13).While the presence of male genitalia is not a feature unique to Muybridge's oeuvre, the fact that we can measure it using the five-centimeter squares of the photographic background, which as discussed instantly transforms Bailey into an anthropological object, marks his penis as different. As we look even closer at the photographs of Bailey boxing, we see that he lunges so that the leg on the same side as the outstretched arm moves forward as well, as would be required for a jab to the torso (figs. 2.4 and 2.5). The resulting pose, however, appears awkward. Bailey begins the punch with his arm extending backward and the elbow flared, rather than tucked in close to his body. As he delivers the punch, he continues to lean farther and farther forward until he is nearly horizontal; his fist and opposite foot touch alternate sides of Muybridge's frame. His knees exceed the "slight bend" we would expect and are spread in excess of the recommended "twelve to sixteen inches." It is unlikely that Bailey would have punched in this way naturally. It seems then that this awkward pose was contrived specifically for this photograph, potentially at the invitation of Muybridge himself who frequently orchestrated the movements of his motion-study subjects.

Whatever the motivation for this unconventional punch, the result is that Bailey's penis is partially shielded from our view in his sporting poses. This is not the case, however, for the other white boxers that appear in Muybridge's series. In fact, most the men performing athletic feats—shown jumping (plate 157), lifting weights (plate 321), lifting and heaving a heavy rock (plates 319 and 320), fencing (plate 350), and sparring (plates 329 to 342)—wear a cloth covering of either white or black fabric (fig. 2.3).[106] While Bailey does appear naked in the other plates (as do most of the other models walking and ascending/descending stairs), it is curious that in the "boxing" poses, Bailey's genitalia have been shifted just outside our view. Something similar happens in the photographs of Embree, whose hands obscure his exposed genitals as he stands

Eadweard Muybridge, *Walking*, 1885, printed 1887. Collotype print.
From *Animal Locomotion* (Philadelphia: J. B. Lippincott & Co., 1887),
plate 6. National Gallery of Art, Washington, DC.

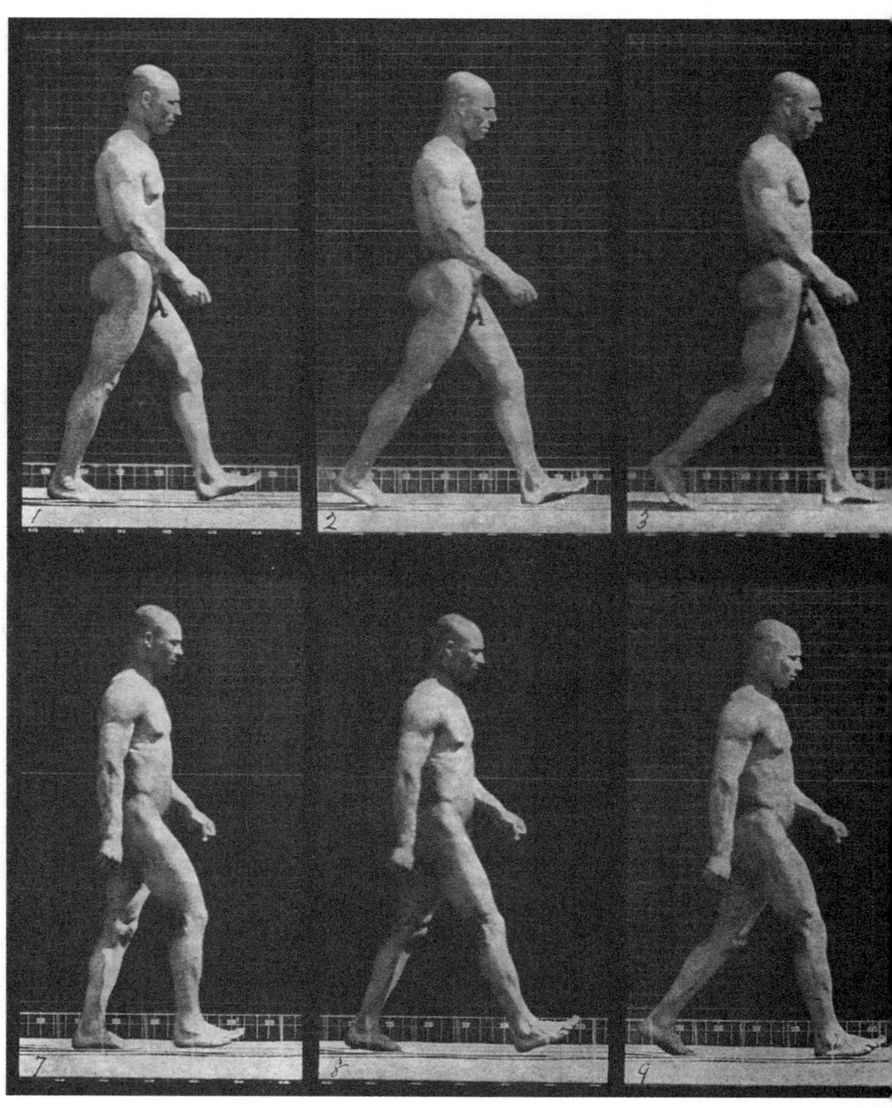

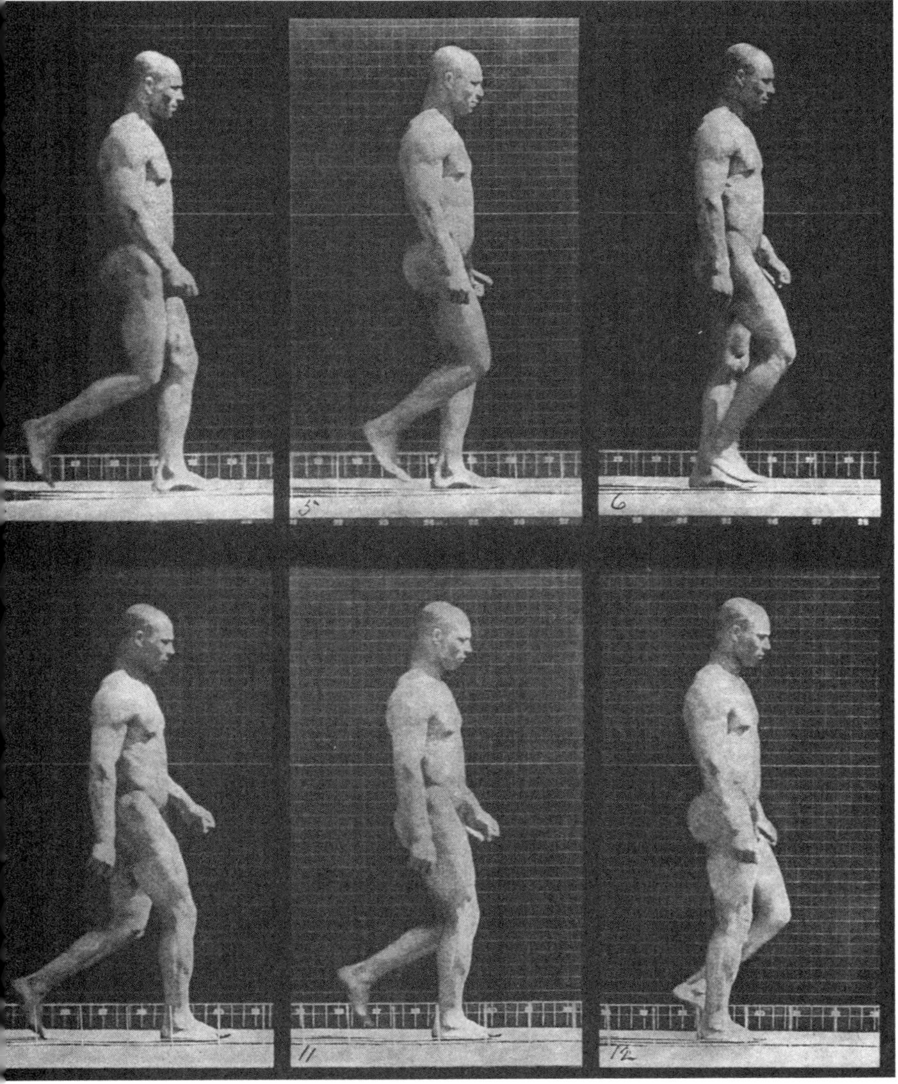

on the back of the wagon before his execution. In another photograph, taken postmortem, Embree hangs from a tree (fig. 2.14). He is still stripped naked, but the lower half of his body has been covered with a blanket fastened at the waist. What are we to make then of these traces of Black sexuality?

The photographs of Bailey and of Embree are constructed as "documents." The repetition of Bailey within the frame and the introduction of the grid position the images of his body as objective representations. In Embree's case the rotation of his body, which shows him from the front and then the back, similarly draws on the traditions of anthropological photography to position him as a specimen. Yet the penis here is not simply a fact of anatomy; it is a complex site of fantasy and anxiety for many white audiences. This is an equation described by Kobena Mercer in the late twentieth century as "Black + Male = Erotic/ Aesthetic Object," wherein "Black men are confined and defined in their very being as sexual and nothing but sexual, hence hypersexual."[107] Such stereotypes rely both on the artistic tradition of the nude, which emphasizes the body as a site of visual pleasure, and on a Cartesian mind-body separation that reduces the Black male to a mere physical specimen. The Black male body is reduced to an object of difference and an object of desire simultaneously.

Alongside Muybridge, we can look at the work of his contemporary F. Holland Day, whose photographs of Black men similarly sexualize their subject and emphasize the aesthetic over the scientific dimensions of the image. The defeat of the Italians in Ethiopia in 1896 inspired Day's creation of a series of figure studies (*Menelek, Nubia, An Ethiopian Chief*) using the aspiring artist J. Alexandre Skeete as his model. *An Ethiopian Chief* from ca. 1897 shows Skeete dressed in a long North African robe, which hangs open above his waist, exposing his torso and shoulders to the viewer; he wears a headdress made of pigeon feathers (fig. 2.15). One hand extends outward parallel to the picture plane, holding a sword that stretches up to the edge of the photograph's frame. The "chief" gazes downward at the viewer (having been photographed slightly from below), which grants a magisterial air to the image. The viewer is meant to linger here on the soft focus, the effects of light, the emphasis on the velvety surface of the skin—all key components of Day's interest in the artistic effects of photography.

Like other American pictorialists, Day emphasized aesthetic effects in order to stand apart from the more scientific associations of the medium. The blurred effects of atmosphere challenged the supposed transparency of photographic evidence. Of particular interest is Day's almost exclusive focus on the unclothed male body, which was uncommon at this time outside anthropological or scientific contexts. According to Shawn Michelle Smith, Day's allegorical

2.14

———

"The Lynching of Frank Embree, July 22, 1899." Photographer unknown, postcard, 4.7 × 6.8 inches (12 × 17.3 cm). Equal Justice Initiative, Montgomery, Alabama.

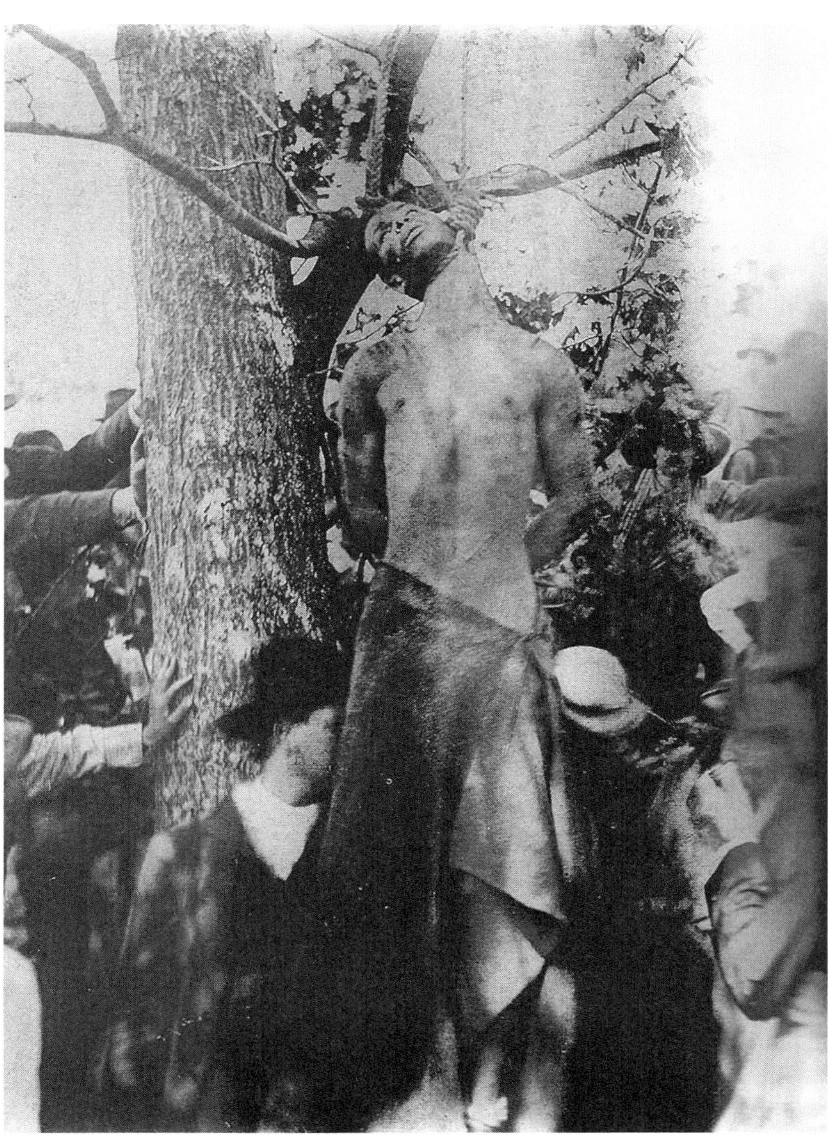

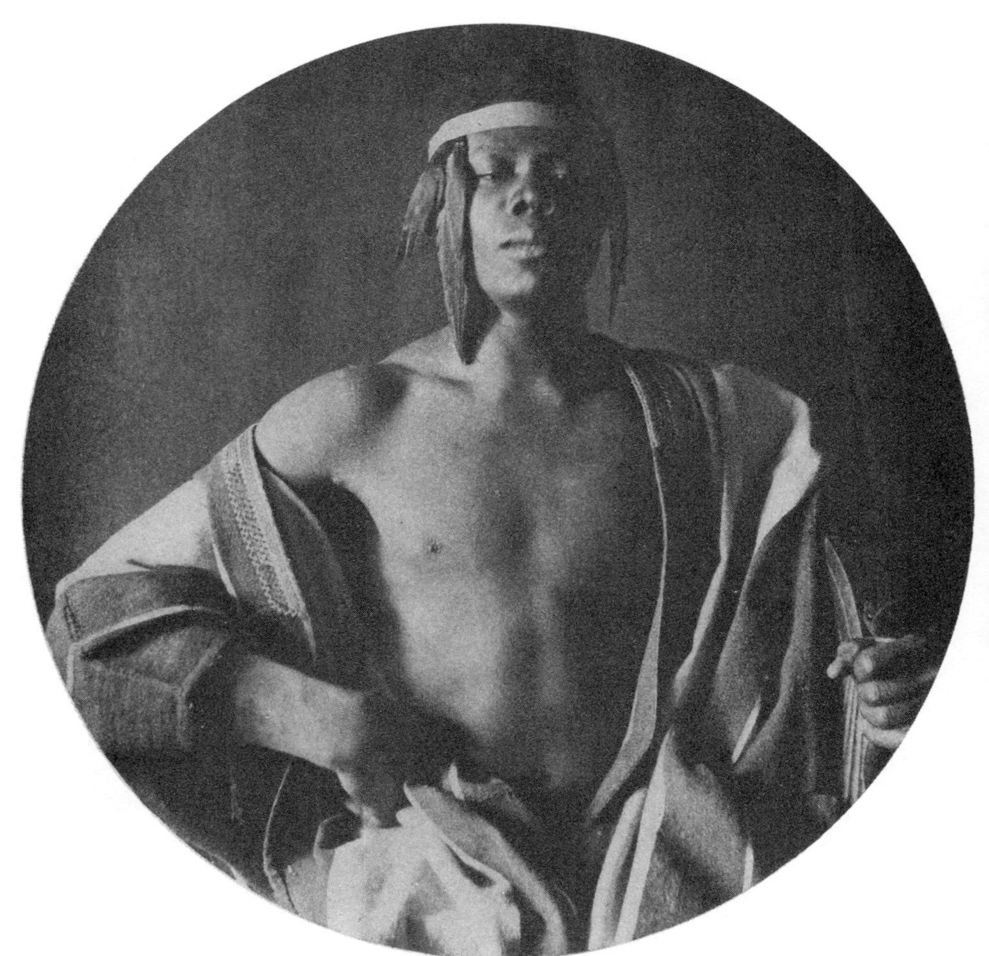

2.15

———

F. Holland Day, *An Ethiopian Chief*, ca. 1897. Gum
bichromate print, 7.1 × 7.25 inches (18 × 18.5 cm).
J. Paul Getty Museum, Los Angeles.

nudes in fact "liberate the body from the disciplinary archive: in many of his images soft focus obscures detail, and figures provide platforms for imagination rather than observation."[108] Smith further encourages a reading of these images in homoerotic terms, wherein the photographs themselves "solicit a homoerotic gaze."[109] Day's 1906 photograph *St. Sebastian* is a particularly apt example in its display of the partially clothed model Nicola Giancola bound to a tree with his arms behind him (fig. 2.16). As he strains against the ropes, we see the flexion of the muscles in his arms and torso. His head is thrown back with eyes closed as the lips part slightly. The viewer is invited here to linger on the surface of the body, to revel in the soft light that touches Giancola's chest and face. By the turn of the century Saint Sebastian had already transformed into a homosexual icon—as both an object of homoerotic desire and a homosexual subject—and Day's photograph builds on this to further encourage erotic desire.

But we must also consider the ways that Day's images of homoerotic desire are complicated by the inclusion of Black male bodies.[110] As discussed above, these photographs were made at the height of lynching, in a moment where Black male sexuality engendered violence. Looking at Day's *Ebony and Ivory*, we see a counter narrative to the racial sexual discourse of the Black male body as a threat to white supremacy (fig. 2.17). In the image, an undressed model sits atop a table, covered with a leopard skin; he holds in his right hand a small white sculpture, and his face is turned away from the camera. The whiteness of the statue (a Greek model) contrasts sharply with the darkened background of the image and with the exposed skin of the model; its presence renders the model as another "object" in the frame.[111] We can also note here again the reliance on the classical model to emphasize the beauty of the body. Day has rendered his model as a passive object; there is a "dialectic of power [that] is embodied and encoded in the image."[112] The Black male becomes an aesthetic (and powerless) object. His face is turned away from the camera in a denial of his agency and his identity. The figure instead appears as a series of interlocking, geometric shapes. We are meant to linger here on the surface of the sitter's naked body, to take pleasure in the silky, dark skin. The model in Day's photograph poses specifically so that he might be consumed.

Mercer drafted his grim equation in response to the work of Robert Mapplethorpe, whose erotic portraits of Black men generated deep controversy in the 1980s. Many, including Mercer, regarded Mapplethorpe's images as public rehearsals of the stereotypes of the oversexualized Black stud (or buck) established more than a century earlier. The studio lighting, stylized compositions, and slick, polished surfaces combined to create a fetishized view of the Black male body. Mapplethorpe's 1981 photograph *Ajitto*, for example, is similar in

2.16

F. Holland Day, *St. Sebastian*, 1906. Platinum print, 9.75 × 7.75 inches
(24.8 × 19.7 cm). Library of Congress, Washington, DC.

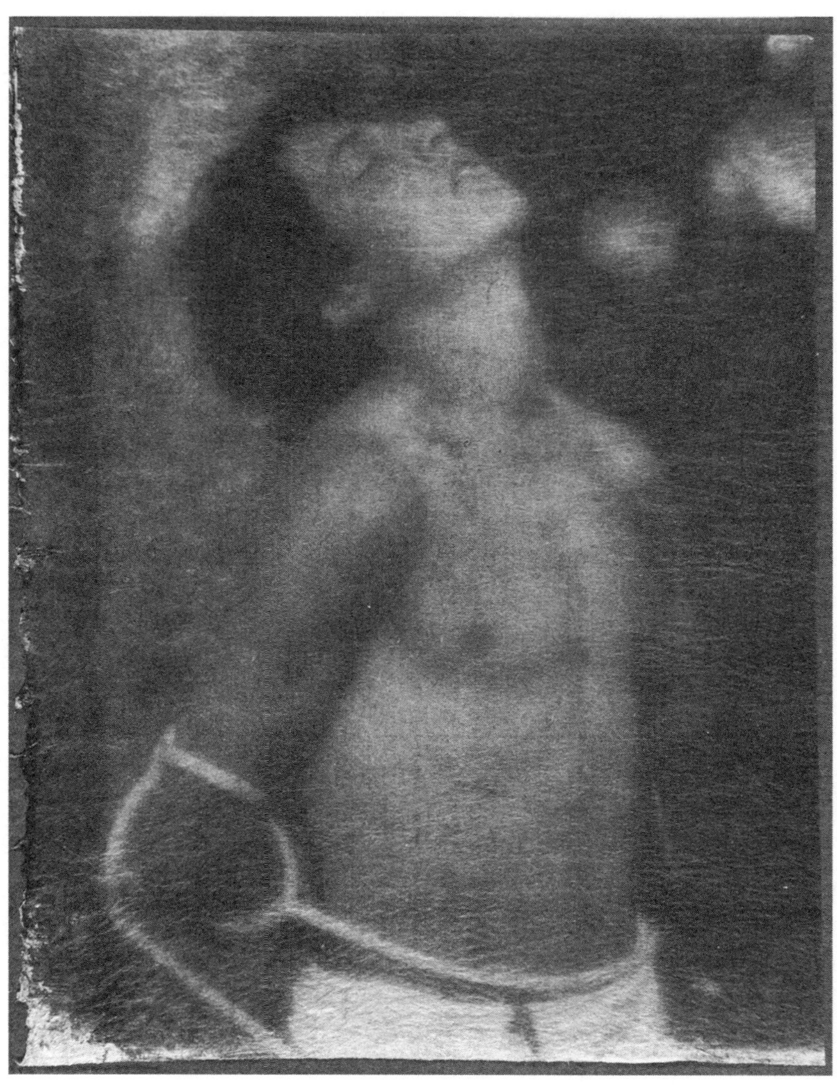

F. Holland Day, *Ebony and Ivory*, ca. 1897. Platinum print, 7.2 × 7.9 inches (18.3 × 20 cm). J. Paul Getty Museum, Los Angeles.

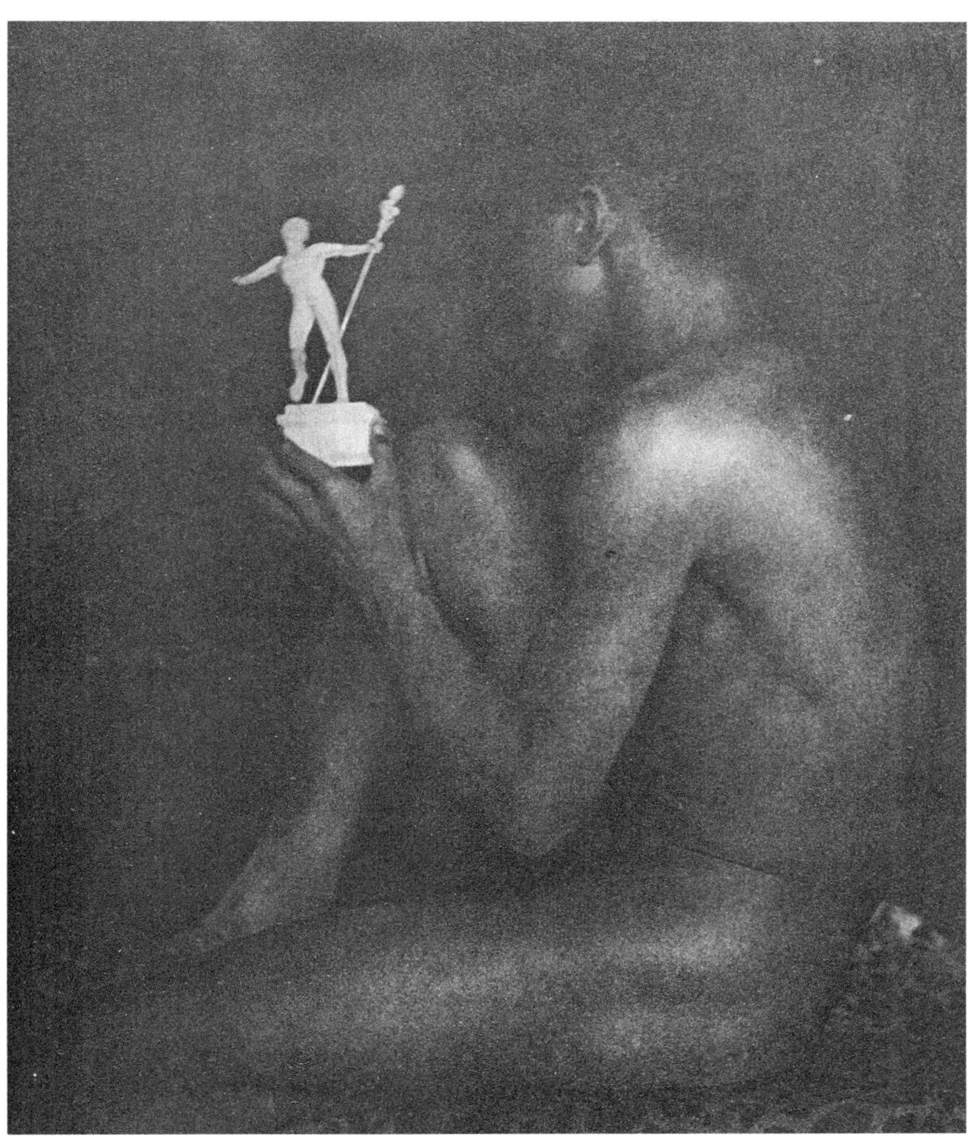

its composition to Day's *Ebony and Ivory* from a century earlier, where again a Black model appears seated on a fabric-covered pedestal with their face hidden from the camera (fig. 2.18). In Mapplethorpe's version, the comparative presentation of ideal sculpture and the Black body has been collapsed into a single figure perched high upon a pedestal. He hugs both legs toward his chest with knees bent while his back curves outward. His head is slightly tucked between his parted knees. The emphasis here falls on the abstract form of the body, the dappled light that falls across the model's smooth skin, and the rich, velvety surface of the gelatin silver print. But we also see, at the lower center of the composition, the exposed testicles and (a partial view of the) penis of this figure. This implicit focus on the penis reiterates one of the most persistent stereotypes in the white imagination, regarding Black male sexual prowess. The arrangement directly echoes the words of Frantz Fanon: "One is not aware of the Negro, but only of a penis; the Negro is eclipsed. He is turned into a penis. He is a penis."[113]

Mapplethorpe's images have been controversial largely because they render the Black male body, commonly perceived as a threat to white masculine power and control, "safely" an object, locked into a position of passivity. His 1983 exhibition *Black Males* at the Institute of Contemporary Arts in London presented Black men as erotic (and, arguably, almost wholly aesthetic) objects, projections of the artist's own fantasies. The controversial 1986 publication *The Black Book* included ninety-six eroticized and formalist images of Black men, the most extreme of which effectively reduced each man to objecthood. It was essentially a catalog of stereotypes, wherein Black men were reduced to overtly physical and stereotypically virile specimens and viewers automatically positioned as xenophilic white, male, homosexual subjects. But while Mapplethorpe's photographs certainly objectify and sexualize Black men, it would be unwise to simply reject them as fetish objects, or evidence of the white supremacist gaze. Although produced a century after Muybridge's images of the Black boxer Ben Bailey, the criticism that emerged around Mapplethorpe's images helps us to understand the consequences around the representation of the Black male body in photography. Kobena Mercer has argued that these photographs function not only as art objects, but as cultural artifacts as well. It remains nearly impossible, according to Mercer, to look at Mapplethorpe's image without considering the "racialized dynamics of power and pleasure in the gaze," wherein the Black body within the image elicits the scopophilic instinct of the white viewer.[114] "The glossy, shining, fetishized surface of Black skin," he writes, "serves and services a white male desire to look and to enjoy the fantasy of mastery precisely through the scopic intensity that the pictures solicit."[115] Mapplethorpe's images illustrate the ways that Black bodies are viewed by white audiences (regardless of gender

Robert Mapplethorpe, *Ajito*, 1981. Gelatin silver print, 17.7 × 14 inches (45 × 35.6 cm). Museum of Modern Art, New York.

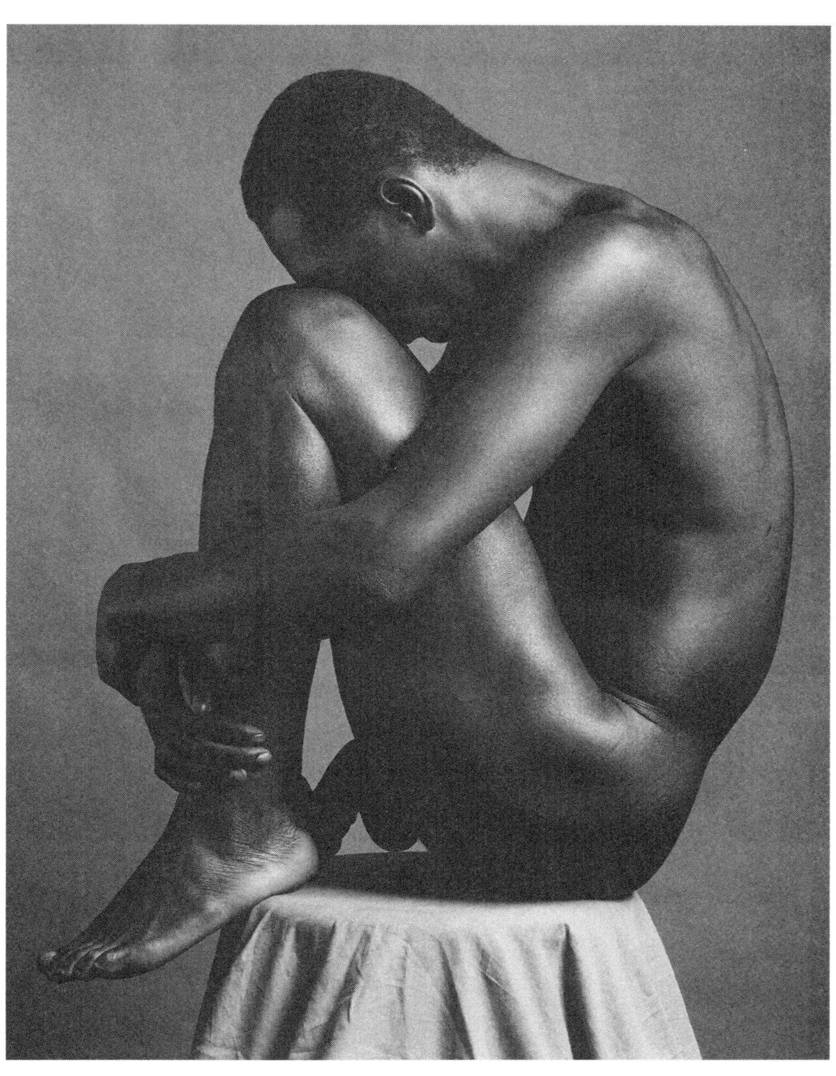

or sexual orientation), connecting back to the history of minstrelsy and its relationship to white, mainstream anxieties about the Black body.

Writing about Mapplethorpe (or rather the discourse around his photographs) in 1989, Stuart Hall positions the Black critics who have written about these images—Kobena Mercer among them—and their lamentations around the tropes of fetishization, the fragmentation of the Black body, and its subjection to the white, homosexual gaze as only one side of what he calls "the play of identity and difference." He writes:

> The continuous circling around Mapplethorpe's work is not exhausted by being able to place him as the white fetishistic, gay photographer; and this is because it is also marked by the surreptitious return of desire—that deep ambivalence of identification which makes the categories in which we have previously thought and argued about Black cultural politics and the Black cultural text extremely problematic.[116]

In looking at these photographs we recognize an oscillation between race and sex, between repulsion and attraction, between Mapplethorpe's gaze and our own.

Both Day's and Mapplethorpe's images of Black men provide a vocabulary and a critical framework for thinking about Muybridge's work from a century before. These white photographers attempt to enact power over the Black body, to lock it into passivity. We see an illustration of the fear of the Black body, wherein the photographers' models are reduced to aesthetic objects and stripped of their individual identities. But we also see how these images are marked by erotic desire. We are invited to take pleasure in the gaze, to linger on the flexion of musculature and on the smooth, dark skin. The pleasure, however, is inextricably tied to the violence of objectification. This is a paradox famously voiced by Kobena Mercer, who later revised his rejection of Mapplethorpe's photographs as purely exploiting ideas about racialized sex fetishes. Mercer argued for a productive ambivalence in reading these images, claiming that an alternative reading in which Mapplethorpe's photographs of Black men hold the potential to subvert the dominant tradition of the nude in a wider history of representation.[117] While I do not wish to argue that Muybridge similarly subverts the traditions of representation in the same ways as Mapplethorpe, I want to highlight the value of looking at these images of Ben Bailey as violent, as racist, and as sexualized simultaneously. There is an ambiguity embedded within these images, as they operate between the anthropological, the scientific, the aesthetic, the pornographic, and the artistic.

Conclusion

When Ben Bailey walked into the studio on that early summer day in 1885, the first and only Black model to be photographed by Muybridge, he must have been aware of the role he would be asked to play that day. As the subject of the photographer's study, the focus of a sustained inquiry into animal and human locomotion, Bailey may have expected to perform as a scientific subject. His punches before the camera indeed record the traces of his gestures, the flexions of his musculature, and the coordinated movements of his limbs as he traversed the space in front of Muybridge's cameras.

But as he posed inside Muybridge's studio, moving his body at the command of the photographer, Bailey was not simply a passive object before the camera, an image for us to consume. As a Black subject within *Animal Locomotion*, Bailey maintains a hyper-visibility, and we cannot look away. In his 1952 text *Black Skin, White Masks*, Fanon presents race as historically constructed and defined within social experience. The central metaphor of the text—that Black subjects must wear "masks" in order to function in the overwhelmingly white world—reaffirms the investment that every subject has in whiteness. Fanon then takes on an analysis of the psychological conditions of colonization that this racist phenomenology incites, or in other words how the subject encounters the trauma of being seen as inferior—a process he calls the "historical-racial bodily schema" of individual subjects. Fanon argues for two distinct experiences of race: race as an erasure, or invisibility, and race as matter, always opposed to the default of whiteness as the universal subject position. These modalities are a way to understand the contradictory experience of Blackness, that state of "being over-determined from without." "The Black body," Fanon claims, "is hyper-visible and invisible at the same time."[118] We might say the same for Bailey's presence within Muybridge's project. Despite the attempt to make him invisible, despite the deployment of the grid in an attempt to render him the subject of science, his Blackness exceeds the frame and makes him hyper-visible. We cannot fail to consider Bailey's own subjective power and agency within Muybridge's project, as he commands our gaze.

In this chapter I have not attempted to write a history of Bailey's image, but rather to trace a genealogy that positions these photographs within a complex web of images. Comparing Bailey's image to other types of photographic representation—anthropological images, lynching photographs, and even fine-art nude photography—provokes reconsiderations of the relationship between masculinity and whiteness, as well as between photography and pathology, and between the scientific and the aesthetic. Moving through these examples allows us to understand the complexity of Bailey's place within Muybridge's study of motion. He is not simply a Black body, but a Black boxer. And while Bailey has been interpreted within Muybridge studies and within the history of photography, he has never been considered within the history of the sport.

I have positioned Bailey here as an emergent figure, emblematic perhaps of the spectacle that the Black body would later become. In the decades following Muybridge's project, the image of the Black boxer would be circulated in popular media—the beginning of a visual culture of Blackness intrinsically tied to sports. In the next chapter I will look at the example of Peter Jackson, a Black boxer from Saint Croix who won the Australian heavyweight title in 1886, a little more than a year after Bailey's trip to Muybridge's makeshift studio. Although unable to fight for the American (and by default the world) heavyweight title due to the reluctance to host interracial matches in the United States, we will see how discourses of sexuality and race shaped the public appetite for Jackson's image in the popular press and provided a way to manage the threat of the Black body in the post-Civil War era.

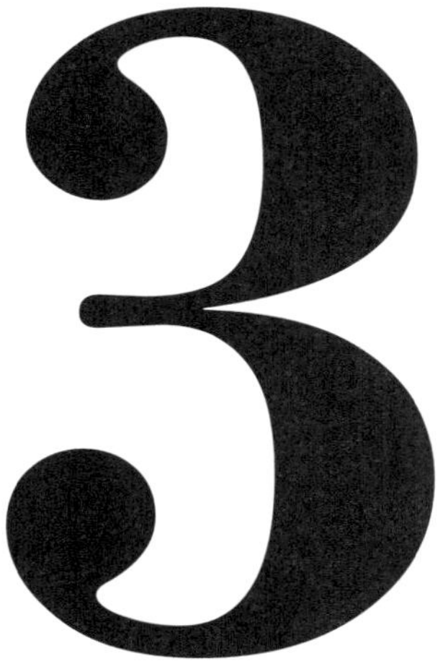

THE BLACK PRINCE

The heavyweight boxer Peter Jackson lived many lives and between worlds. He circulated—both physically and via representation—across the Caribbean, the United Kingdom, Europe, the United States, and Australia. He was born on a sugar plantation in 1860 to former slaves in Saint Croix (then the Danish West Indies) and died forty years later (and more than 11,000 miles away) as a champion heavyweight fighter in a small Australian town.[1] In the years between, he was a competitive swimmer and coach, an apprentice and cook on Dutch merchant ships, a hotel owner, and an actor. Perhaps most shocking for American audiences, who became aware of Jackson shortly after his arrival in the United States in 1888, he was also a gentleman educated in the British tradition with a penchant for quoting Shakespeare, Tennyson, and Edgar Allen Poe. When twenty-seven years old, he arrived in the United States as the first gloved heavyweight champion of Australia. While known to most as "Gentleman Jackson," "Peter the Great," and "the Black Prince"—an aristocratic boxing moniker likely connected to Jackson's insistence on fighting under the new Queensbury rules of boxing—when he left the country twelve years later, he was called "Uncle Tom." Unable to consistently secure opponents in the ring, he turned to the stage as a featured performer in the hit play *Uncle Tom's Cabin*, based on the best-selling novel by Harriet Beecher Stowe; in the process, he became one of the most famous Black men in America. The story of Jackson's time in the United States has been, up to this point, one of transformation—from boxer to actor, from heroism to humiliation.

Let us start, then, with a few images in mind. The first is a poster advertising Jackson's 1893 performance as "Uncle Tom" (plate 3). Under the title "Chas. E. Davies' Spectacular Production *Uncle Tom's Cabin*," we find a visual representation of the central character, "Tom," as he progresses from well-dressed servant (and friend) of the Shelby family on the left of the composition to the abused slave of the vicious plantation owner Simon Legree on the right. At the center there is a pedestal, adorned with what appear to be palm leaves, bearing a plaque inscribed with a poem by the English writer Alexander Pope (1688–1744). At the top of the pedestal, we find a bust of Peter Jackson, awkwardly attached at the waist so that the podium stands in for the fighter's lower extremities. In this image, we are meant to connect Jackson to his performance as Tom in this production, and perhaps even to transfer the honorable nature of Stowe's literary character to the boxer. But the poster also transforms Jackson into an object, taking a fight portrait (bare torso, arms crossed in front) and cutting his legs off. He is disembodied and (like Tom) disempowered. And while our impulse more than 130 years afterward may be to read these images as singularly evident of Jackson's objectification, or even exploitation, I would like to position these images instead as entangled within wider discourses of aesthetics and desire.

Just a few years prior to his theatrical debut, Jackson made it a point to travel to the studio of the London Stereoscopic Company on Oxford Street to have his portrait made—one that showed Jackson as he wanted to be seen. In the resulting photographic portraits from 1889, the twenty-seven-year-old man appears as a typical nineteenth-century gentleman. All three portraits show Jackson fully dressed and from the knees up. In the first image, he appears in a clean, three-piece suit with collar and tie, a smart vest, pocket watch, starched trousers, and even a pocket square. Standing confidently (if not casually) before the camera (fig. 3.1), he shifts his weight to the right leg, slightly elevating his left hip. Jackson, freshly shaven, looks just outside the camera's frame, turning his head in a classical three-quarter view; his right hand is tucked gently into his right trouser pocket, while his left hand grazes the trouser fabric with his fingers loosely held and curved inward. In the next image, a top hat covers Jackson's smart haircut; his suit jacket is again buttoned at the top and spreads outward toward the bottom of his torso so that we can see both the underlying vest as well as the pocket watch that dangles from a delicate chain at his waist. Jackson peers out directly at us with a confident gaze (fig. 3.2). Rather than folding his arms in front, or even posing with fists raised—as would be expected in any portrait of a prizefighter—Jackson instead places his hands inside the deep pockets of his pinstriped trousers. In a third shot from this session, Jackson appears ready for the streets of London, wearing an overcoat with fur lapels and cuffs; he holds in his right hand the top of a walking stick and clutches in his left hand (where we also see a shining pinky ring) a pair of leather gloves (fig. 3.3).

In all these examples Jackson appears as a classic London gentleman, a dandy even—smartly dressed, confidently posed. But, aside from the fact that he appears clothed and outside any contextual suggestions of his brutal profession, what also strikes me across this series of portraits are Jackson's hands. They are hidden in pockets, loosely held open, limply clutching a pair of gloves, and any exposed fingers curl back toward the figure. We see a contrasting version of Jackson's public persona—not the boxer, but the gentleman, a businessman perhaps that we might ordinarily pass on a crowded city street. He appears in the photographer's studio without any identifying scenes or props. There are no ropes or punching bags, only a nondescript light background. What we see instead is Jackson's attempt to fashion an image of himself *outside* his identity as a boxer, no more than a year into his fighting career outside Australia. In the months that passed between his arrival in San Francisco in 1888 and this image, Jackson had already successfully defeated three Americans—Mike J. Sullivan (1878–1937), Joe McAuliffe (1864–1926), and the "colored" heavyweight title holder George Godfrey (1897–1947)—at the California Athletic Club. In August 1889, Jackson traveled to London at the invitation of Hugh Cecil Lowther—the fifth Earl of Lonsdale—who introduced him to the National Sporting Club.[2] In November, while in London, Jackson fought the British champion Jem Smith (1863–1931) in a nontitle fight at the Pelican Club for a purse of £1,000 (more than £163,000 today) before a crowd of nearly a thousand spectators.[3] But he had another purpose during his time in London. That is, in the middle of what would be one of the most successful runs of his career (Jackson fought twenty-eight of the best boxers from England and America

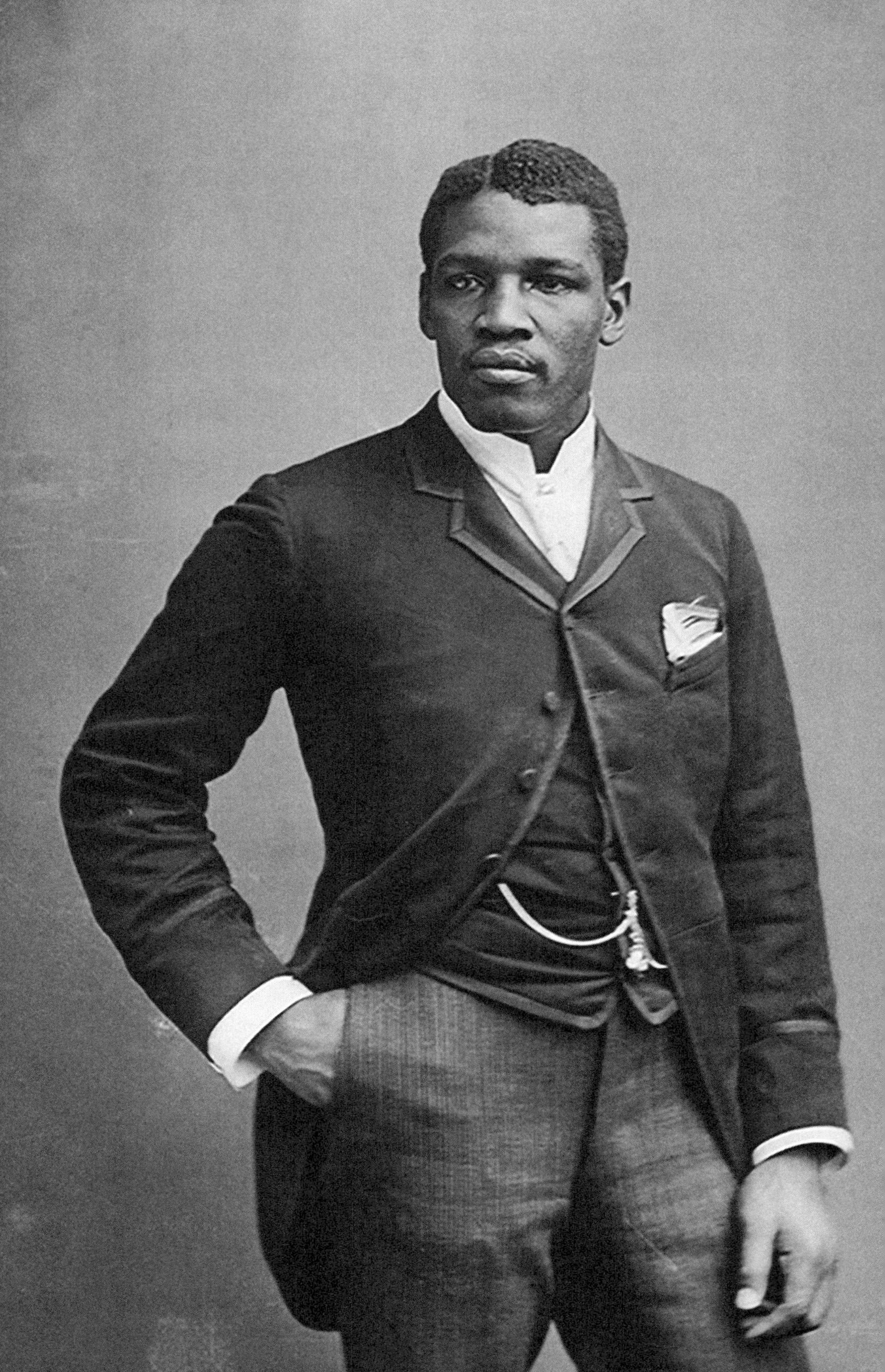

3.1–3.3

"Peter Jackson," 1889. Photographer unknown, silver gelatin dry half-plates, 4.75 × 6.5 inches (12 × 16.5 cm) (approximately) each. Published by the London Stereoscopic Company. Image courtesy of the Hulton Archive.

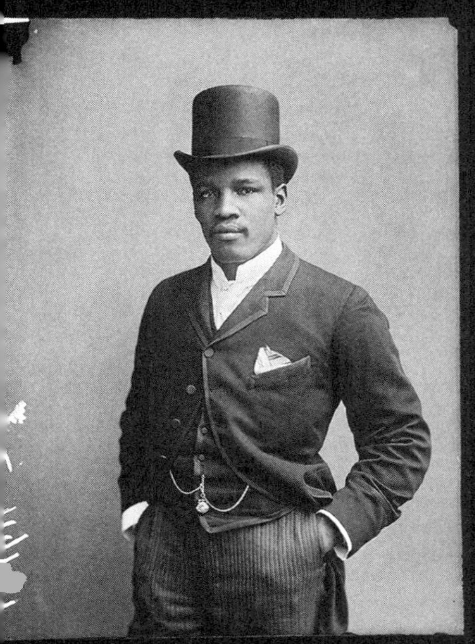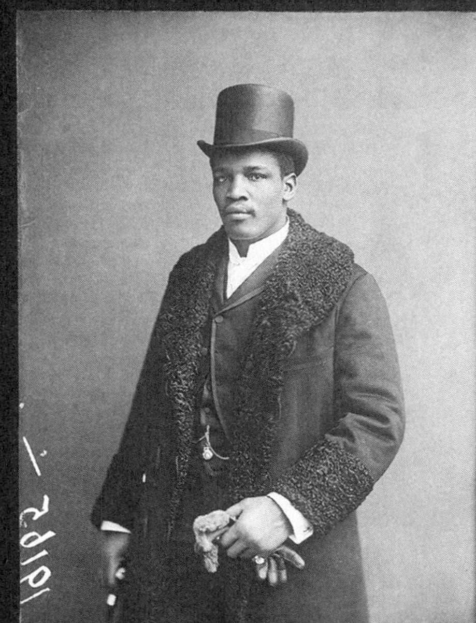

between 1888 and 1892, losing to none), Jackson walked into a photography studio at 313 Oxford Street and posed in his most fashionable clothes.

These two sides of Jackson's personality—the boxer and the gentleman—were in constant tension, and throughout his life Jackson attempted to reposition himself outside the stereotype of the Black brute. In her analysis of Black dandyism, Monica Miller, a scholar of religion and Africana studies, asks us to consider how the overt stylization of Black men is a performance of self-actualization and self-determination, a survival strategy even, in the context of hostile social, political, economic, and cultural conditions. I would like to read Jackson himself as a dandy, as (in Miller's terms) a "creature of invention who continually and characteristically break[s] down limiting identity markers and propose[s] new, more fluid categories within which to constitute themselves."[4] His overt manipulation of his appearance in the London photographs indicates not only an awareness of the social order of the nineteenth century, but also a desire to transgress the boundaries of Black identity.

Dressed in a cutaway, fur-lined coat (parted to provide a view of his gold chain and pocket watch), morning vest, and matching trousers, and clutching white gloves, Jackson's performance and self-presentation invites us to consider the consequences of what art historian Richard Powell (relying on the philosopher Henri Bergson) has called the "Negro in disguise." I am building here on Powell's study of antebellum sartorial trends, which he argues exceed the stereotypes ("Dandy Jim" or "Zip Coon") to perform as a challenge to the outside world.[5] Powell considers the example of Frederick Douglass, writing:

> Standing before an audience at public antislavery events, filled with the emotional fire and fervor of advocates representing a people maligned and unfairly treated, these black men dressed in what would have been considered "white men's clothing"—a formal suit, vest, dress shirt, and cravat—and thus challenged their audiences even before uttering a word.[6]

Powell asks us to consider how Douglass's sartorial choices reinforced his oratory. His conscious self-styling as a dandy—that is, in "white men's clothing"—challenged social expectations about Black men. We can imagine that Peter Jackson shared a similar motivation.

For historians of the nineteenth century, Douglass serves as a compelling example of the ideological dimensions of style, wherein one's physical attire communicates a social desire to be seen. Douglass is also held up as a unique case of a Black man who capitalized on new technologies (lithography and photography, in particular) to disseminate his image. He is frequently cited, in fact, as the most photographed man of the nineteenth century; he sat for more than 160 portraits before his death in 1895. And while all this is true, it fails to acknowledge the efforts of other Black subjects to challenge social expectations and to take up the model of the dandy in their pursuit for recognition. There is little difference, in fact, between Douglass's presentation and that of Jackson; both align squarely with more traditional representations of white men of the late nineteenth century. Take, for example, the 1890 cabinet card of a gentleman taken by E. S. Nellis (fig. 3.4). Comparing it with Jackson's portrait we see a similar coat, vest, trousers, and overcoat; we see the same gold chain and pocket watch, the topcoat cradled in gloved hands. As discussed later in this chapter, we can imagine that the differences in the reception and representation of Jackson may have been due in part to his status as a Black immigrant to the United States (rather than as a descendant of slaves) and/or to the white public's tendencies toward Anglophilia in the late nineteenth century. As a product of the African diaspora, and more specifically a citizen of the British Commonwealth, Jackson was not locked into a singular logic of representation, as we would typically expect of Black men in the United States—silenced, objectified, and violently evacuated of their subjectivity. This is a logic exemplified by the photographs of Ben Bailey, addressed in the previous chapter, and by the existing narratives of Black representation in the nineteenth century.[7] But what if we considered a different history of Black visual culture—one in which the Black male body was an object of desire and fantasy rather than one of abjection? Unlike representations of the more well-known Black heavyweight fighter, Jack Johnson, that would come in the twentieth century, images of Jackson showed him as a fighter, as a dandy, as a businessman, as a specimen, and even as an aesthetic object.

As he began to defeat white fighters in the United States, Jackson (unlike the more sensational Johnson) was positioned within the rhetoric of the ideal. Images did not present him as monstrous, but rather as emblematic of the American obsession with classical models. As reported by one writer in 1894, nearly six years after Jackson's arrival in the United States, "If I were a sculptor and wanted a model of a perfect figure to illustrate the happiest possible combination of strength and agility—a between of Hercules and Mercury—I would choose Peter Jackson."[8] While the media positioned Johnson (the first Black champion) as a pariah, an explicit threat to white America and its values, Jackson instead was "the perfect man." This was a perfection based on Jackson's physical body, which was measured, imaged, and reproduced across a wide range of media. Looking at photographs of Jackson introduces another condition of possibility for Blackness. I would like to specifically ask how the gaze is transformed via these encounters with Jackson's image from one of opposition (characterized by violence) to one of desire. To do this, we must consider the intersections between

3.4

E. S. Nellis, "Gentleman," 1890. Cabinet card, 3.88 ×
5.75 inches (10 × 14.6 cm). Collection of Erik Genalo and
Laura Laubenthal, Little Falls, New York.

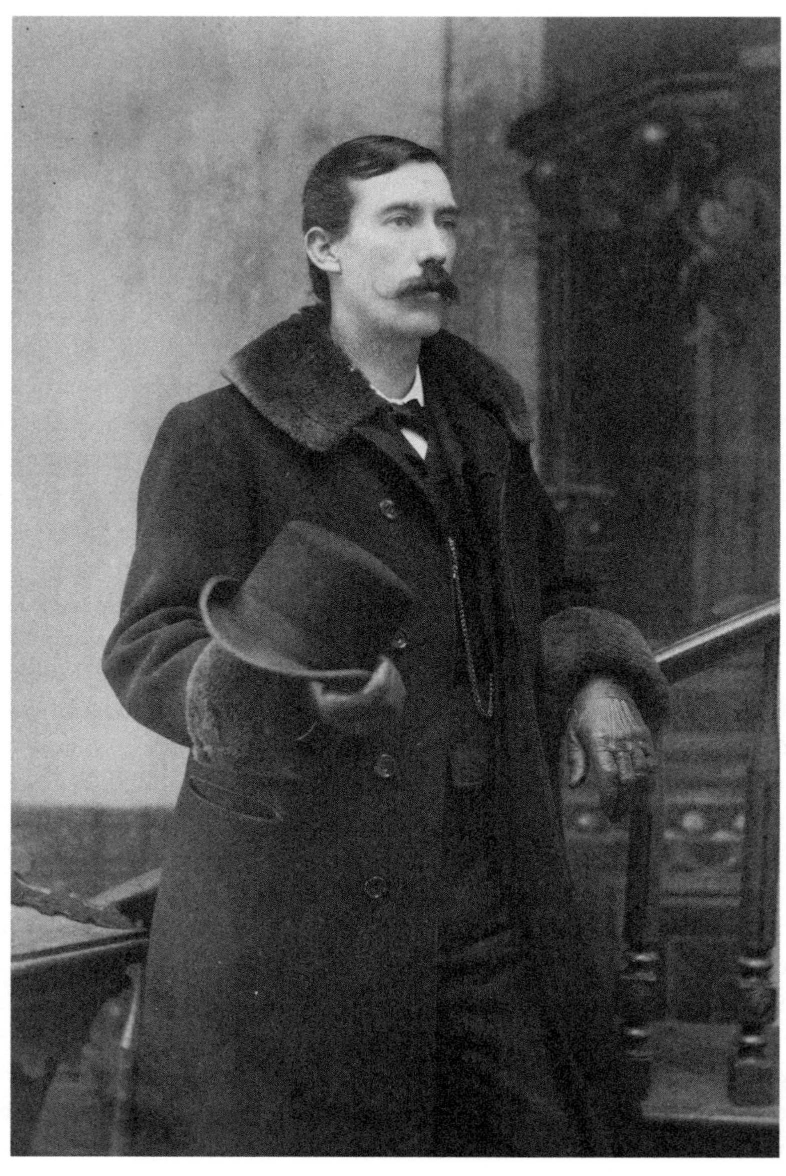

race, culture, politics, and ideology at play in the late nineteenth century—all of which were produced and reinforced through visual culture.

As this chapter will show, the complexity of Jackson's representation was compounded both by the concurrent development of print culture, which was itself producing a new mode of spectatorship and identity formation, as well as the transformation of boxing from a violent blood sport to a middle-class activity. One writer for the African American newspaper *The Freeman* boldly declared in 1890 that "Peter Jackson is the best advertised Afro-American in the country, with T. Thomas Fortune as a close second."[9] As the first Black heavyweight champion in the United States, although not a citizen himself, Jackson's circulation (both physically and visually) was also entangled within the politics of race during the era of Reconstruction. I would like to consider all these elements—boxing, the development of a modern media culture, and race—not only in relationship to Jackson's rise to celebrity but also in terms of their investment in vision. Looking closely at several images made in the first few years after Jackson's arrival in the United States will allow us to reconsider the intersections of power, desire, and vision at play. My aim is to interrogate the assumptions we make about Black subjectivity and to highlight Jackson's awareness of the creation and performance of his image across media that would be consumed by a diverse public—in lithographs and newspapers, of course, but also in cabinet cards that would be purchased and collected by his fans. I want to consider how the erotic dimensions of boxing map onto representations of boxers. In her landmark book *On Photography*, Susan Sontag discusses the photograph as an apparatus that collects and appropriates its subjects, transforming them into objects. In Sontag's view, the photographic body is always already observed and controlled.[10] This is a perspective that certainly informs this chapter. However, I wish to also present the photographic subject *as* subject and to reconsider Jackson's own role in being seen. We see here the complexity of desire, which oscillates between the viewer who wishes to consume Jackson's image and the boxer's own compulsion to be seen.

Rather than consider images of Jackson as either objectifying or perhaps even indexical to an archive of Black men, I am interested in looking at how Jackson's image shows us the subject resisting iconicity. In this way we might consider the degree to which the Black boxer brings to life that "closed field of forces" named by cultural and literary critic Roland Barthes. In a particularly relevant passage of *Camera Lucida*, he writes:

> In front of the lens, I am at the same time: the one I think I am, the one
> I want others to think I am, the one the photographer thinks I am, and

the one he makes use of to exhibit his art ... In terms of image-repertoire, the Photograph ... represents that very subtle moment when, to tell the truth, I am neither subject nor object but a subject who feels he is becoming an object.[11]

We must acknowledge that in becoming an image, Jackson was also making an image.[12] He takes up the visual codes of white dandyism, cracks them open, and then uses that raw material to reframe—pun intended—his position from minority (excluded) subject to that of active agent. I am relying here on the concept of "disidentifications," first presented by José Esteban Muñoz in his 1999 book of the same title. He writes: "Disidentification is about recycling and rethinking encoded meaning. The process of disidentification scrambles and reconstructs the encoded message of a cultural text in a fashion that both exposes the encoded message's universalizing and exclusionary machinations and recruits its workings to account for, include, and empower minority identities and identification."[13] In these photographs Jackson oscillates between a desired object and a desiring subject.

The relationship between fine art (in this case sculpture) and the physical body of the athlete is here expressed as intertwined. Perhaps one reason for this is the simultaneous emergence of photography with the rise of physical culture—that is, the focus on the development of the human (read: white, male, heterosexual) body as dynamic, strong, agile, and muscular.[14] In this chapter I will take up the body of the athlete, and specifically that of the boxer Peter Jackson, as "social sculpture," a term put forward by the German artist Joseph Beuys in the 1970s.[15] Beuys understood the potential of art to transform society, and believed even mundane acts (e.g., peeling a potato) could create new, revolutionary structures within society. The frame of "social sculpture" allows us to highlight both the physical and the ideological shaping of the body.[16] I deploy this concept to demonstrate ways in which Jackson's body (and its representation across a variety of media) is written by discourses of gender, race, and sexuality in the late nineteenth century, and how the circulation, interpretation, and the judgment of that body tells us something about the performance of Blackness that subverts more typical narratives of abjection.

Becoming "the Black Prince"

Unlike the other subjects of this book, the biography and personal life of Peter Jackson is fairly well documented.[17] He was born in Frederiksted, Saint Croix, on September 23, 1860 (a date that he himself did not know), the sixth of eight children to former slaves Joseph and Julia Jackson—a carpenter and washerwoman.[18] Peter first worked as an apprentice to Danish merchant Captain Herluf Heering, who took an interest in the boy when he was only ten years old.[19] During his time aboard Herring's vessel the *Svanen*, Jackson "made several journeys to and from Denmark, and remained for two or three years on an island near Copenhagen," before joining another Danish ship, *Dagmar*, serving as an apprentice for almost two years.[20] The depth of Peter's maritime experience and training would have in most cases led to a career as a merchant marine or a post in the Danish Navy; however, both options remained closed to Black colonials. His only plausible career path would have been as a merchant seaman or perhaps a fisherman, following in the steps of his older brother Samuel. After a brief return to Saint Croix at the age of fifteen or sixteen, he left the Danish West Indies as a sailor sometime after 1876 and arrived in the United States for this first time in 1878, landing in New York to look for his older brother James.

Unable to locate James in New York, Peter soon found passage on the *H.J. Libby*, a relatively new ship that hailed from Portland, Maine, and headed to the island of Java in the Dutch East Indies. Stopping first in Calcutta, where Peter was reassigned to the position of cook and steward, the ship sailed down the Bay of Bengal toward Java, then went on past New Guinea and arrived in Port Jackson—the port of Sydney, Australia—on February 19, 1879. A week or so later, at just seventeen years of age, Peter Jackson made the risky decision to desert the ship with another crew member, Harry Slaughter.[21]

Jackson and Slaughter were walking alongside a railroad track when a man driving a four-horse bus stopped to pick them up. After hearing their story, the driver offered to drop them at the Greengate Hotel, where the hotel licensee, Tom Waterhouse, appeared sympathetic to the boys' plight.[22] Waterhouse offered them food and a place to sleep without charge and connected them with jobs in nearby orchards. Jackson's transition from sailor to orchard laborer to boxer was punctuated by brief stints as a lumberjack, a fireman, a machinist, a longshoreman, and even a deckhand for a paddle steamer. He was first introduced to the sport of boxing by the Waterhouse family, known for their investments in drinking, gambling, and horse racing. Tom himself had fought in several bareknuckle fights in the 1860s, including one twenty-eight-round match against the Australian champion of Victoria, "One Eyed" Burke, which was called as a draw. Another Waterhouse son, Billy, opened Waterhouse Hall— a venue for both boxing and dancing—in the 1880s. Peter was known to spar with the local pugilist George Swarzas on Saturday afternoons, and by the end of 1879 he was hanging out at the Athletic Hall near his boarding house on Market Street, located close to the harbor.

Peter fought his first opponent, Jack Gregory, also known as "Cigarette Kelly," with gloves at the Athletic Hall in 1880. Wanting to move intentionally into the world of prizefighting, Peter purchased a boxing instruction manual: "Professor" Ned Donnelly's *Self-Defense; or, The Art of Boxing*, published in 1879.[23] In the book, Donnelly, a former fighter turned professor of boxing at the London Athletic Club, opens with a brief historical overview before moving on to technical descriptions of boxing technique and hints for successful sparring: "The mouth ought to be firmly closed. The slightest tap on the lower jaw when it is hanging loose with be remembered for long afterwards, while a more severe blow may dislocate it."[24] Seeking to supplement his readings, Peter also sought out a mentor. He met the Baltimore-born Black fighter Harry Sallars, and the two men became close friends, despite the more than four decades between them. Peter recounted that the sixty-year-old Sallars "appeared the picture of health and the personification of strength," and told of his admiration for the elder champion's "movements and utterances."[25] With Sallars's introduction, Peter then moved on to train with the Australian champion Larry Foley, who invited Peter for a sparring match against Jack Hayes at the Queen's Hotel.[26] Under Foley's tutelage, Peter (still employed at the wharf) fought an average of three men per week. Of course, considering the precarious legal status of the sport, the records and details of these early bouts are scarce. There was also very little mainstream press coverage of boxing in Sydney at the time; the *Sydney Morning Herald*, for example, did not report on boxing as a policy, although they did accept money to advertise matches.

Jackson's early career in Sydney, in fact, developed in parallel to the Australian sporting press. In 1880 the weekly newspaper the *Bulletin* was founded, publishing a sports column under the title "The Referee." A little more than five years later, in 1886, the weekly paper the *Referee* started up. It was quickly one of the most well-respected sporting publications in the world, and often printed excerpts of other international sporting papers. A cheaper sporting paper, the *Dead Bird*, began in 1889. Eventually, even the *Sydney Morning Herald* acquiesced. This early sports coverage in Sydney was a blazing success. By September 1891, the *Referee* was selling 22,777 copies (to a population of about 100,000 adult males), and it could be found in every barbershop in Sydney. Unlike US-based publications, boxing coverage in the *Referee* and the *Dead Bird* tended to focus primarily on the excitement of the prize fight as well as its pure entertainment value, rather than its dubious legality.

Peter received a considerable amount of attention in the *Referee*, as well as from the *National Police Gazette*—a weekly paper based in New York—via its Australian correspondent, Frederick Egerton Diamond, an ardent fan who also spent some time as an honorary referee for boxing contests.[27] These papers retrospectively recorded his earlier fights and covered his first major bout in Melbourne in July 1884 against the (somewhat disputed) Australian champion, Billy Farnan (1851–91), known as the "Emerald Hill boxer."[28] The fight itself was something of a disaster for Peter, who later reported that he suspected he had been drugged. According to the story he would later tell, he suddenly found himself weak and tottering, reportedly calling out to Ned Powell, who was in his corner, that his legs were "useless." Later that evening he fell ill and "retched violently for some time."[29] Peter returned afterward to Sydney and continued his work at the Port Jackson Swimming Club (where he offered swimming and diving lessons).[30] Less than a year later, in April 1884, he appeared in news coverage devoted to a boxing match turned fatal.[31] Accused of harboring the accused (the fighter Peter Lawson), Peter was charged as an accessory to murder. Although the charges against him were later dismissed, the event apparently led him to seek a more reputable income.

By July 1885 Peter took over the license of the Sydney-based United States Hotel, where he served as a bartender and host. In July 1887 he also took over as licensee of the Lighthouse Hotel. But Peter's legitimate business was only one of his professional ambitions; in March 1887, the *Referee* announced: "Professor Jackson has disposed of his public house, and is willing to fight any man in Australia for £200 and the belt."[32] Peter proceeded to refurbish the dining room of the Lighthouse Hotel, turning it into a boxing training facility with large mirrors, a punching bag, and a roped ring.[33] His opponents ranged from everyday men, who came to train and spar, to professionals like Dick Matthews (1858–1893)—the future champion of New Zealand. Peter stayed busy. As he recalled in March 1894, speaking to a reporter from the *Herald-Despatch*: "I don't remember all the men I have fought with and probably would not know them on the street if I ever met them. Fighting is my business. I never see the man with whom I am to fight until we get into the ring. They are dressed different on the street and I wouldn't know them."[34]

Peter Jackson continued to fight in boxing tournaments—both at the Lighthouse Hotel and in other temporary public venues. He spent several nights in the summer of 1885 fighting as an opening act to a traveling circus; his final night (boxing William Miller) was billed as the "Great Boxing Tournament" and reportedly attended by three thousand spectators. On September 25, 1886, Peter, now known as the champion of New South Wales, fought his former pupil Tom Lees, the Victorian champion, for the championship of Australia. Prominent politicians mixed with the crowd of spectators, many of whom were Black.[35] Sydney's weekly newspaper the *Bulletin* described the crowd in its report on the fight the following week: "White predominated, but darkies attended so largely as to give the hall of sort of piebald appearance."[36] Peter's victory over Lees earned him his first championship belt. The belt was a prized possession for Peter, who apparently carried it with him throughout his life, even depositing it in a local bank for safekeeping wherever he traveled (fig. 3.5). It was fastened to his waist with a dark-blue silk sash when he was photographed by W. C. Norman of the Electric Photo Engraving Company (fig. 3.6).

The following year, Peter appeared, dressed for work at the United States Hotel, in an ink sketch by Samuel Calvert in a book titled *Australian Sporting Celebrities with Biographical Sketches of Their Careers* (fig. 3.7). This early representation by Calvert is a rare example of a Black athlete represented outside competition. And it gives us some indication how Peter's image existed outside the logic of representations for athletes in this period. Rather than shown wearing boxing tights and in competition—real or imagined—he instead appears to us as a businessman. We, in turn, identify him differently, forced to consider him and his abilities on intellectual rather than physical terms. This emphasis on his intellect is further underscored by his appearance in bust-portrait format, showing only his jacketed shoulders, a knotted tie, a pointed collar at the neck, and his head with a crown of hair parted in the center.

After being named the Champion Boxer of Australia, Peter decided to capitalize on his new-found fame and put together a boxing troupe to go on tour throughout the coastal towns south of Sydney in mid-1886. The fights took place in a tent that Peter and his buddies erected in the center of each small town; local guys fought one from the troupe for four rounds. According to Jackson's biographer, the venture was extremely lucrative and often the only form of entertainment in these remote areas. A few months before his final departure from Sydney, Peter entered a swimming competition, stunning the audience with his ability to stay submerged for fifty-eight seconds while swimming 240 feet. Such demonstrations of his athletic abilities were further evidence of his explicit choice to pursue boxing instead of other sports. Nevertheless, the pull of America was unmistakable, and Peter, at this point having no one left to fight, decided to travel to California in the winter of 1887 to try his luck.[37]

Boxing, Celebrity, and Photography in San Francisco

Almost a decade after this first arrival in New York, Peter Jackson returned to the United States. He traveled from Sydney to San Francisco aboard the Spreckels Pacific Mail ship the *Alameda*, which docked at Brannan and First streets in the southern part of the city on Saturday, May 12, 1888.[38] His seven-thousand-

P.1

Tom Cribb and Tom Molineaux figures, 1812–1815.
Staffordshire earthenware (pearlware), 8.37 × 4.8 × 3.75 inches
(21.27 × 12.19 × 9.52 cm). Mr. and Mrs. Thomas Norton Bernard
Collection, Winterthur Museum, Garden and Library, Delaware.

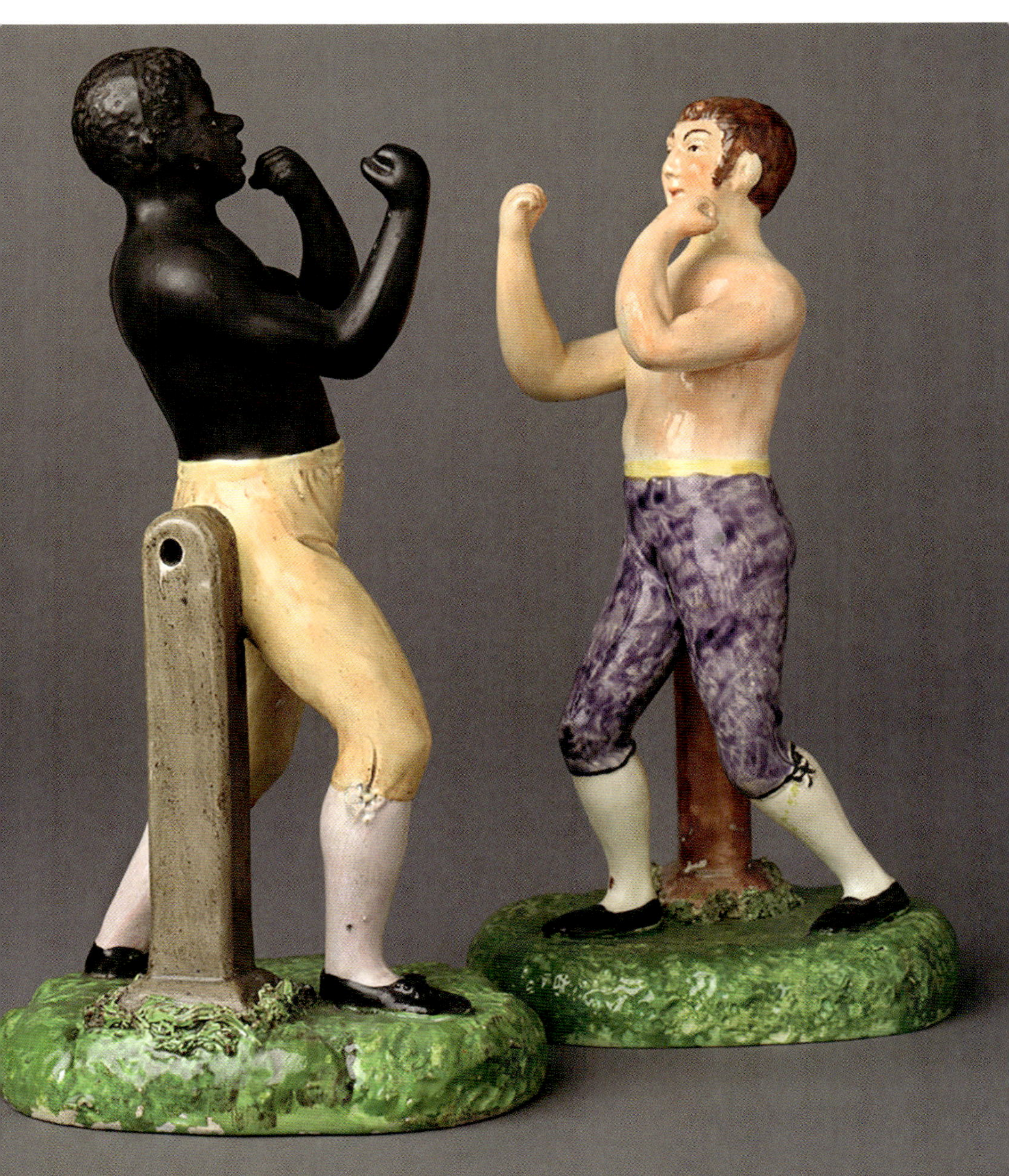

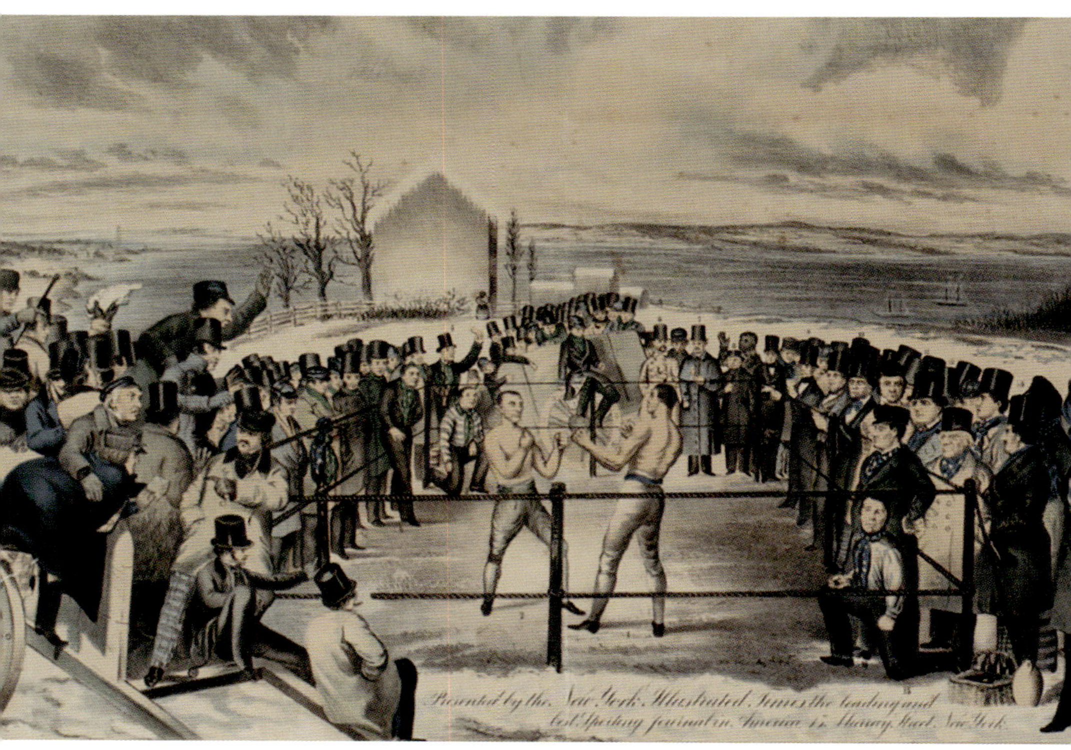

P.2

James S. Baillie, Ingalls Studio, "The Great Fight between Tom Hyer and Yankee Sullivan for $10,000," 1849. Lithograph, 17 × 20.25 inches (43.18 × 51.44 cm). Harry T. Peters "America on Stone" Lithography Collection, National Museum of American History, Washington, DC.

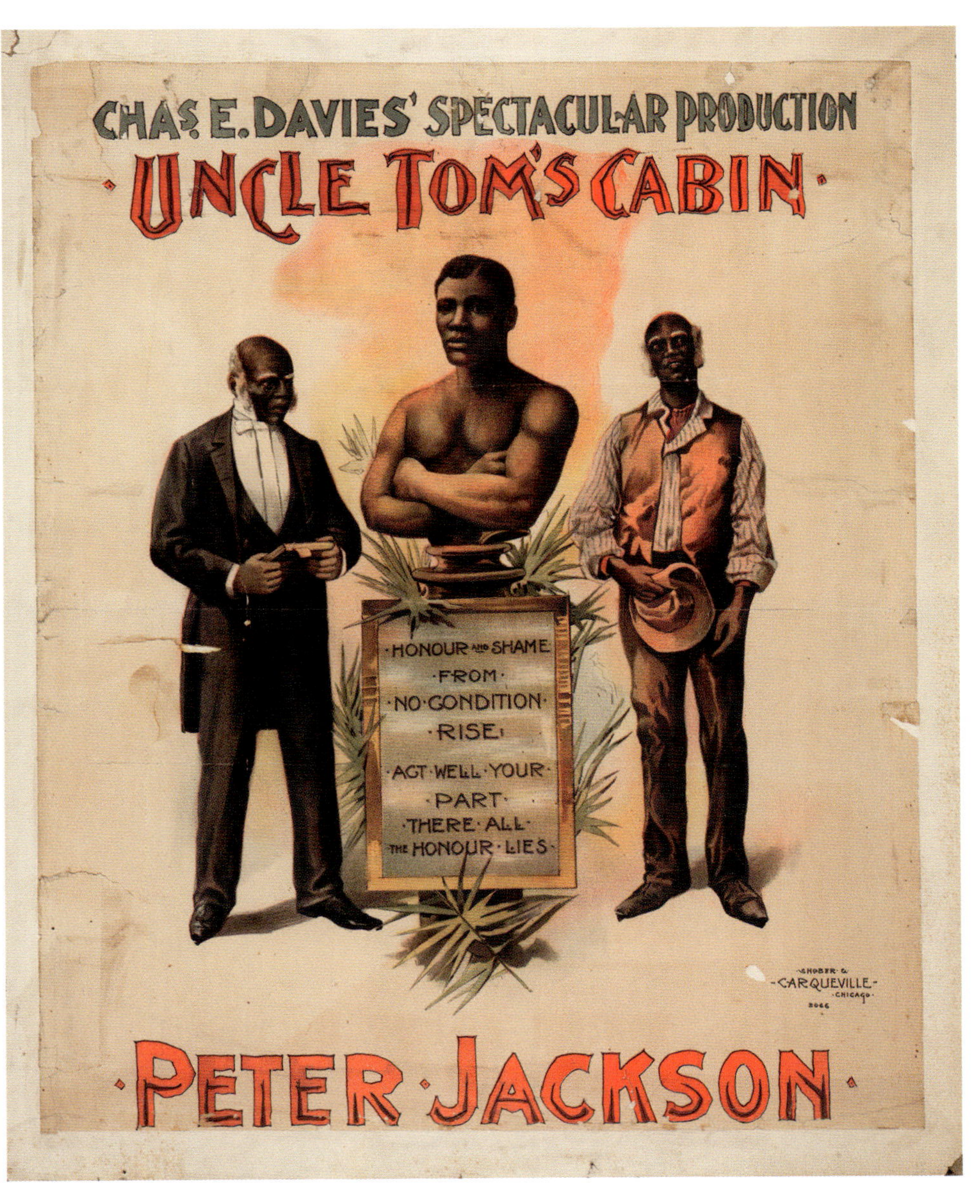

P.3

Poster for Chas. E. Davies's production of *Uncle Tom's Cabin*, ca. 1893.
Published by Shober and Carqueville, Chicago. Courtesy of the Harry
Ransom Humanities Research Center, University of Texas at Austin.

George Bellows, *Both Members of This Club*, 1909.
Oil on canvas, 45.25 × 63.2 inches (115 × 160.5 cm).
National Gallery of Art, Washington DC.

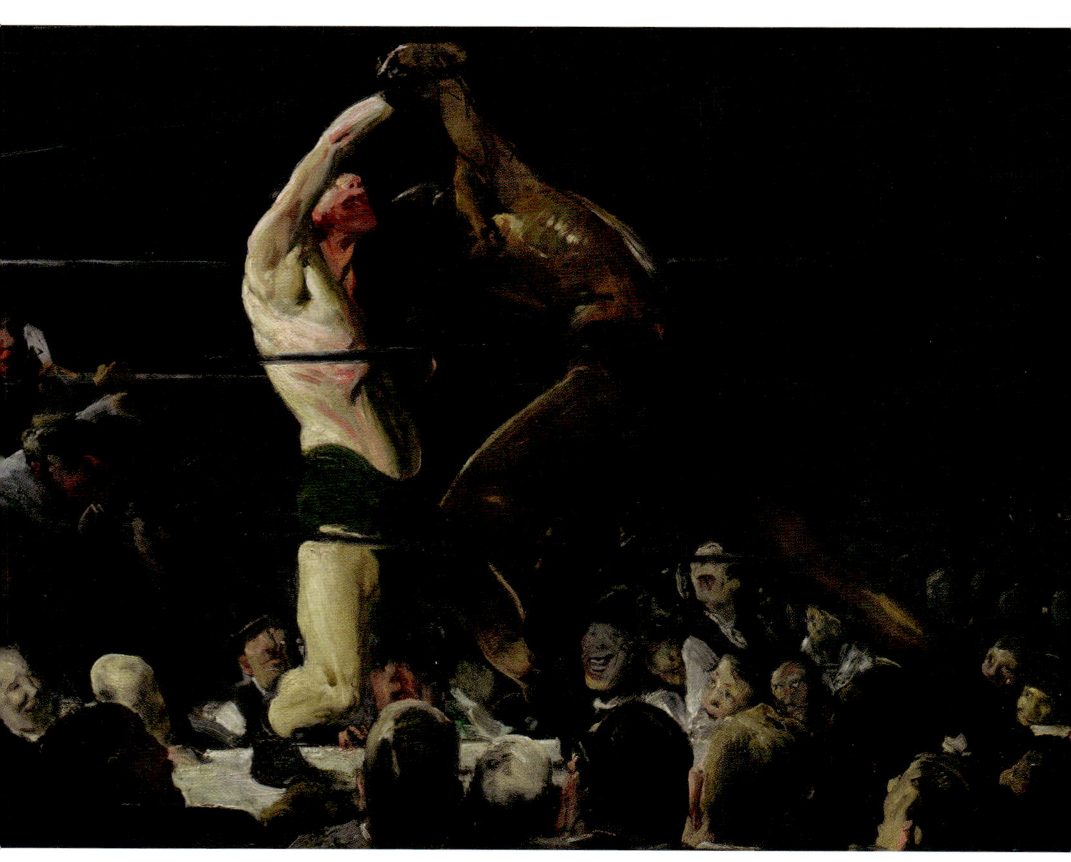

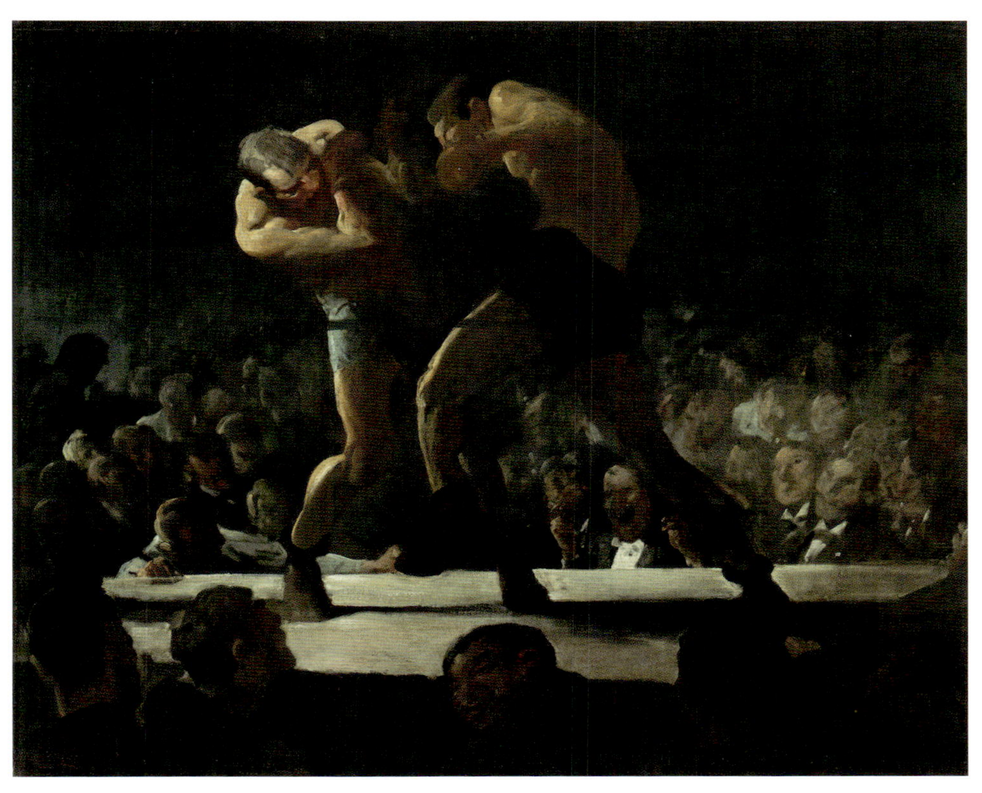

P.5

———

George Bellows, *Club Night*, 1907. Oil on canvas,
43 × 53.13 inches (109.2 × 135 cm). National Gallery
of Art, Washington DC.

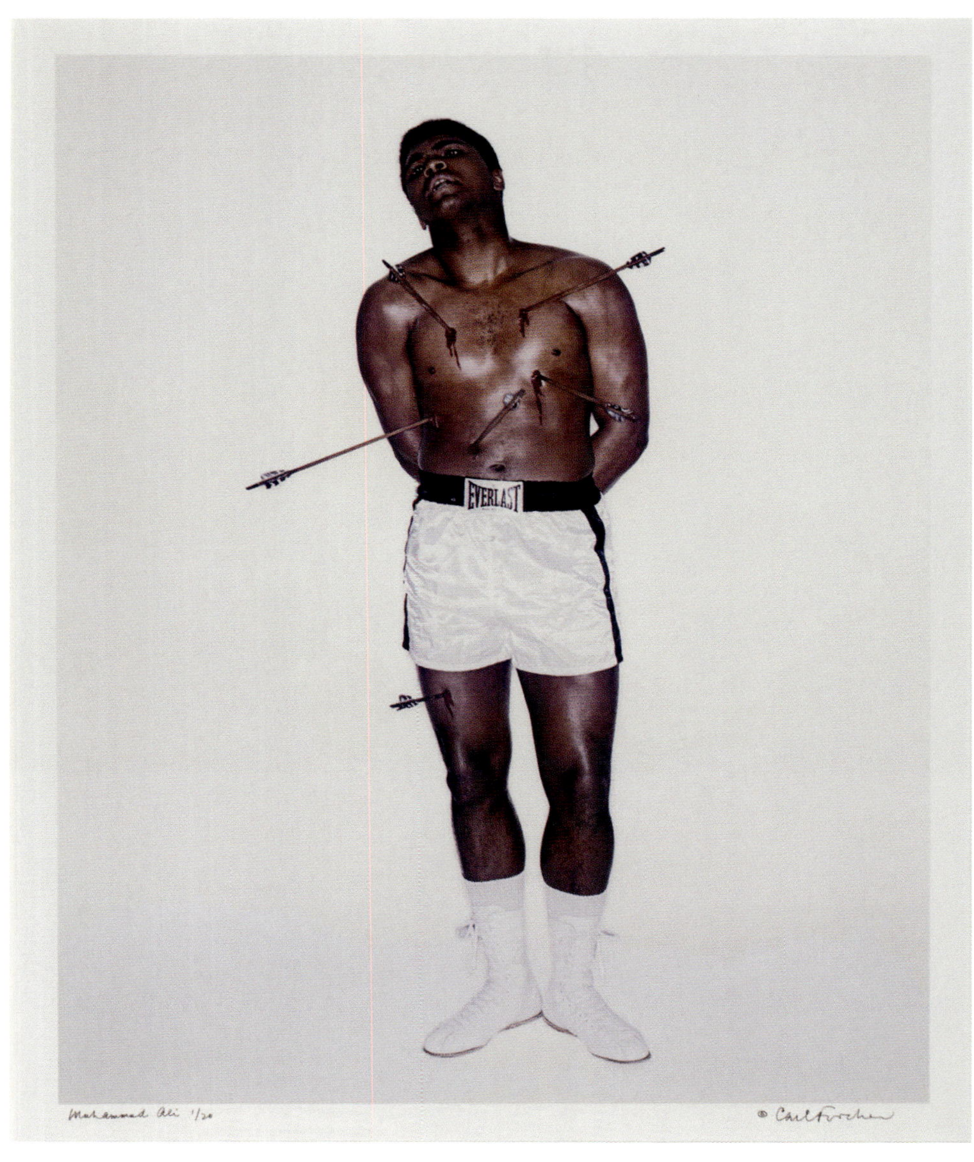

P.6

Carl Fischer, *Muhammad Ali as Saint Sebastian*, 1967.
Printed ca. 2004. Chromogenic print, 32.7 × 26 cm. Victoria &
Albert Museum, London. Copyright 1967 Carl Fischer.

P.7

Glenn Ligon and Byron Kim, *Rumble Young Man Rumble (Version #2)*, 1993. Paint stick on canvas punching bag, metal, 36 × 13 × 13 inches overall installed. Butler Family Fund, 1995. Walker Art Center, Minneapolis.

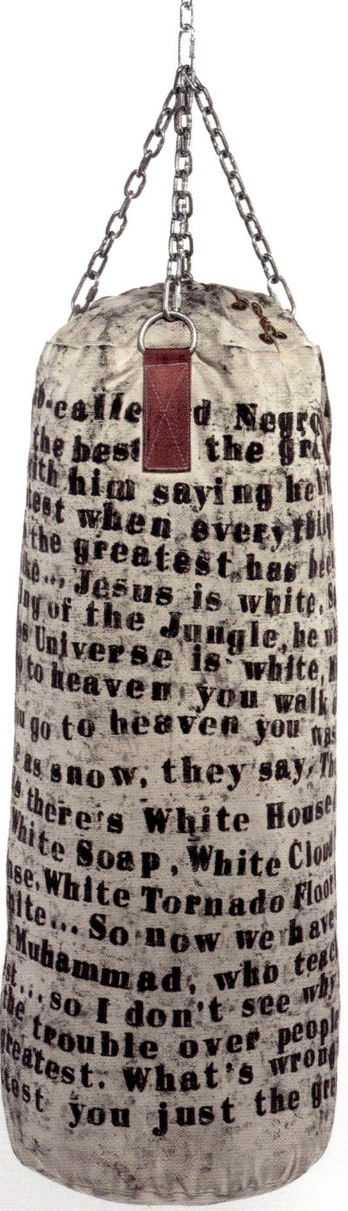

P.8

Lyle Ashton Harris, *Memoirs of Hadrian # 17*, 2002.
Monochromatic dye diffusion transfer print (Polaroid),
24 × 20 inches. © Lyle Ashton Harris.

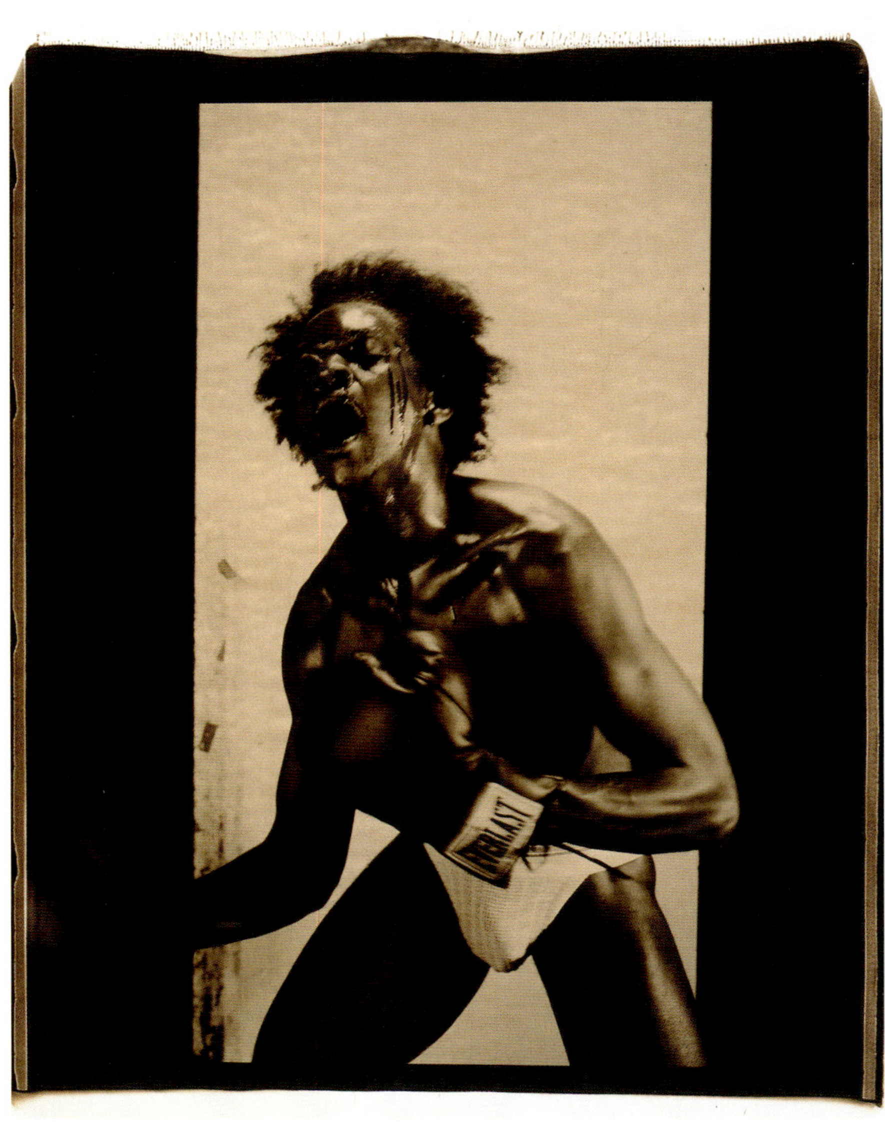

mile journey was prompted by a search for a more tolerant atmosphere as well as a way to earn some cash.[39] As Peter disembarked, he may have walked into the continued commotion that had effectively shut down that part of the city the night before. As was expected in a city built primarily of wooden structures, a fire had erupted two blocks south of the port around 8:30 p.m. the previous evening. One of two reported fires that evening, this one started in a shared building occupied by a cigar factory and a lumber mill, quickly expanding to consume a nearby furniture factory, a cooperage, and several single-story tenement buildings. We can imagine that Peter, arriving less than sixteen hours after firefighters contained the flames, would have trudged through the waterlogged streets and alleys, the distinct scent of burnt ash filling his nose.

In 1888, San Francisco was a city undergoing rapid transformation. In the years following the 1849 Gold Rush, the forty-two-square-mile area became a city of immigrants. By 1880 its population had reached nearly 234,000, making it the ninth largest city in the nation and the largest metropolitan area west of the Mississippi. A little less than half of its residents were classified as "foreign-born" in that year's census—a proportion higher than any other city in the United States. In addition to those who arrived overland from Mexico, tens of thousands landed in San Francisco from China (21,790 in 1880), France, Germany, and the British Isles. As a port city, San Francisco was a nexus of commerce and trade, and the rise of the metropolis coincided with an increased technological capacity. In the first half of the nineteenth century, residents witnessed the arrival of the railroad, the telegraph, and even the first steamships to bring mail to the California coastline. But it was the arrival of the wet plate photograph that perhaps left the most durable imprint on the city.

The historian Amy Lippert has described late nineteenth-century San Francisco as a city uniquely obsessed with the concept of the self. "New conceptions of the self," she has argued, "emerged from this capitalist crucible of ambition, anxiety, masculinity, and curiosity."[40] And photographs, in particular were central to this enterprise. In Lippert's words:

> Forty-niners commodified and fetishized images of the individual— images produced by a bourgeois industrial base and circulated within the public spaces of San Francisco that offered new possibilities for identification before a wide audience. They were visualizations of self and of others, new and exotic, at once familiar and mysterious.[41]

In Lippert's view, visual media—lithographic prints and photographs, most specifically—were key components of this emergent, bourgeois society. The affordability and reproducibility of these images led to their widespread prolif-

3.5

Peter Jackson's first championship belt, made by
John J. Cohen, 1886. Engraved and stamped sterling silver,
11.8 × 6.3 inches (16 × 30 cm). National Gallery of Australia.

3.6

W. C. Norman, "Peter Jackson," 1889. Newspaper print, 13 1/2 ×
19 9/64 inches (34.3 × 48.6 cm). Published by the Electric Photo
Engraving Company. National Library of Australia.

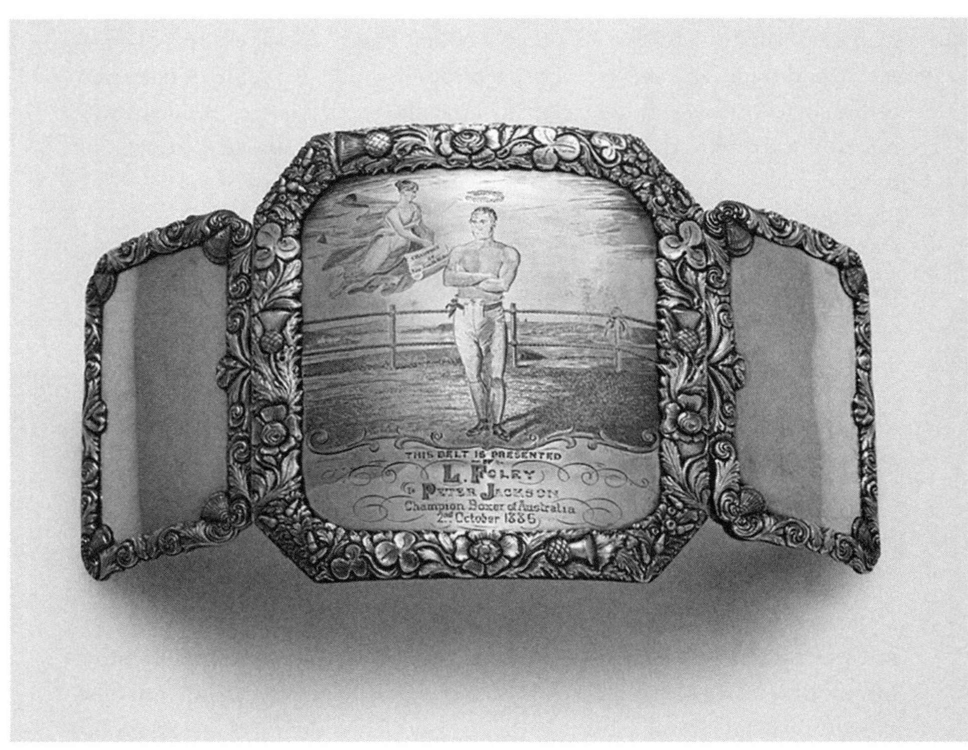

Our Australian Sports.—Boxing.

(Continued from last issue.)

AS 'the sport of kings,' as horseracing has been termed, has its seamy side, it would be too much to expect that prize fighting could be carried on free from unsavory surroundings. These gradually became so pronounced that it was deemed necessary in the interests of the public for the legislature to interfere, with the result that the sport, as formerly practised with the naked fists, was prohibited by Act of Parliament. After that, although it had been previously regarded as a most fashionable pastime, it fell into disrepute like bull-baiting, bear-baiting, dog-fighting, cock-fighting, or any other branch of sport that can only be indulged in in defiance of the law. Yet so strong is the natural admiration of Britons for brute courage that a combat between two men who have been specially trained for the encounter still forms one of the most powerful attractions it is possible to place before them. This inherent fondness for witnessing the ordeal of battle between brave men it was that induced members of Parliament, of the Church, and even Her Majesty's Ministry itself, it was believed, to risk the terrors of the law by being present at Farnborough on the ever-memorable morning when Sayers and Heenan contended for the championship, now nearly thirty years ago. The enthusiasm created by the contest it would be almost impossible to describe. For weeks afterwards a gaping crowd followed each of the combatants whenever they took their walks abroad. When Tom Sayers sat at the window of his hotel at Chester during the race week, nearly a month later, the street in front was almost impassable, and Heenan attracted almost equal notice. Many people then went so far as to suppose that that sensational fight would serve to revive the fallen fortunes of the prize-ring, but it proved only a flash in the pan. They were certainly a very fashionable crowd that went into Kent by special train to see the fight between Heenan and King; but when an army of roughs arrived by the ordinary, before a blow was struck, the swells found they had been betrayed, and a death-blow was dealt to the high tariff of charges that alone made prize-fighting profitable to the promoters. After that matters went from bad to worse, and the business gradually died out until a new generation arose, to be treated to the farcical fight for the championship between Jem Smith and Jake Kilrain, and the made warfare between the bragging John L. Sullivan and the bouncing Charlie Mitchell. Whether the advent of Australia's champion (Francis P. Slavin) in England will serve to alter the present unsatisfactory state of affairs in the old country for the better, remains to be seen; but of this much we feel certain—that whoever meets him will have to fight, and very, very hard, before they beat the native-born Australian, who now aspires to the Championship of England.

Whatever may befall Slavin, either in England or America, to which last-named continent he is sure to find his way eventually, it is safe to assume that prize-fighting, as formerly carried on, is practically a thing of the past. The old order of things has given place to the new. Boxing with gloves is not prohibited by law either in England, America, or Australia, a fact of which a few ardent admirers of the fistic art have taken advantage to supply the national craving of the public for personal encounters in which they are not primarily concerned. Glove fights are essentially the fights of the future. In America, the Californian Athletic Club of San Francisco, as we have previously stated, offers most valuable prizes for competition by professionals, and through that club Peter Jackson has been able to earn both wealth and fame, and to do credit to the teaching he received in this colony, mainly at the hands of Laurence Foley. The

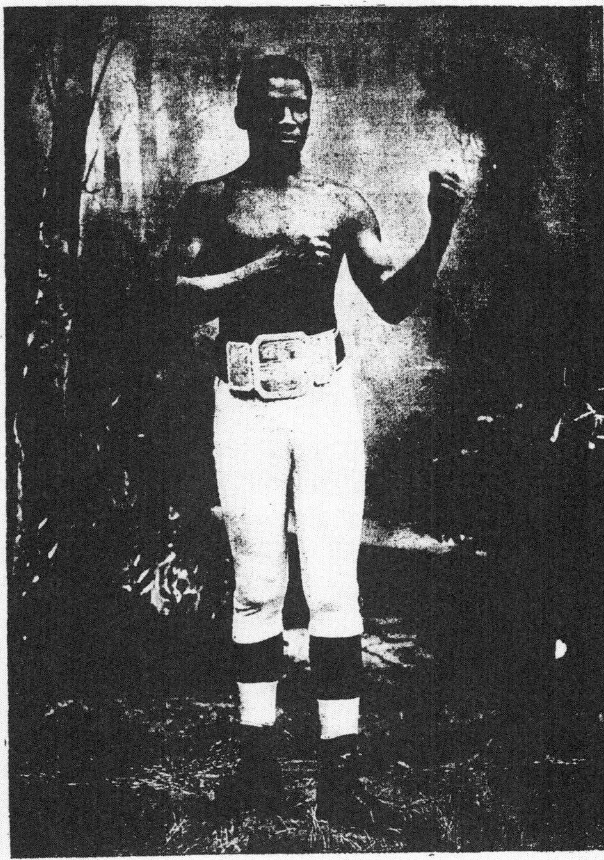

PETER JACKSON.

business of the Association is most admirably conducted, as only members are admitted to its entertainments, and the greatest good order and decorum are maintained throughout the proceedings. There are many other kindred associations throughout that country, but none of the same order of importance. The entertainments of the rather high-toned Pelican Club in London are of a somewhat different kind, as the contests promoted by its members are decided by superior skill rather than powers of endurance; being limited to a few rounds under the Queensberry rules, the victor being the competitor, who, in the opinion of the judges, scores the most points. In Australia such associations are yet in the womb of the future, but in each of her principal cities private enterprise supplies the residents with a regular series of glove encounters, in which both amateurs and professionals take part, and many of which are in the highest degree

entertaining. In fact, we have no hesitation in saying that boxing—even professional boxing—as now carried on in Australia, is deserving of much better patronage than it at present receives; and that it would be for the benefit of the community to have amateur boxing displays more generally encouraged. We feel sure that in Sydney there would be very little difficulty in forming an athletic association that would make the noble art of self-defence the most prominent feature on its programme; and of its ultimate pecuniary success there is no reason whatever to be afraid—under capable management. Whether it should be conducted upon the lines of the Californian Club in 'Frisco, or the Pelican Club in London, so far as the sparring entertainments are concerned, would be a matter for the consideration of the members; but whichever was adopted would command an amount of patronage that would speedily render it self-supporting. We have pleasure in commending the project to the favourable consideration of our readers, and for their information we also publish the revised Queensberry rules of boxing, and those governing contests for endurance.

REVISED QUEENSBERRY RULES.

1. The ring shall be roped, and 24 feet square.
2. Competitors to box in light boots or shoes (without spikes), or in socks, with knickerbockers, breeches or trousers, and to wear jerseys.
3. The result shall be decided by two judges, with a referee, or by a referee only.
4. The number of rounds contested shall be three. The duration of the first two rounds shall be three minutes, and of the final round four minutes, and the interval between each round shall be one minute.
5. Any competitor failing to come up when 'time' is called shall lose the bout.
6. Where a competitor draws a bye, he shall be bound to spar such bye for the specified time, and with such opponent as the judges or referee may approve.
7. Each competitor shall be entitled to the assistance of one attendant only, and no advice or coaching shall be given to any competitor by his second, or by any other person, during the progress of any round.
8. The referee shall have power to give his casting vote when the judges disagree, or to stop the contest in either the second or third round in the event of it being very one-sided; and he can further order a fourth round, limited to two minutes, in the event of the judges disagreeing.
9. The decision of the judges, or referee, as the case may be, shall be final, and without appeal.
10. The referee may, after cautioning the offender, disqualify a competitor who is boxing unfairly by flicking or hitting with the open glove, by hitting with the inside or

(Continued on page 25.)

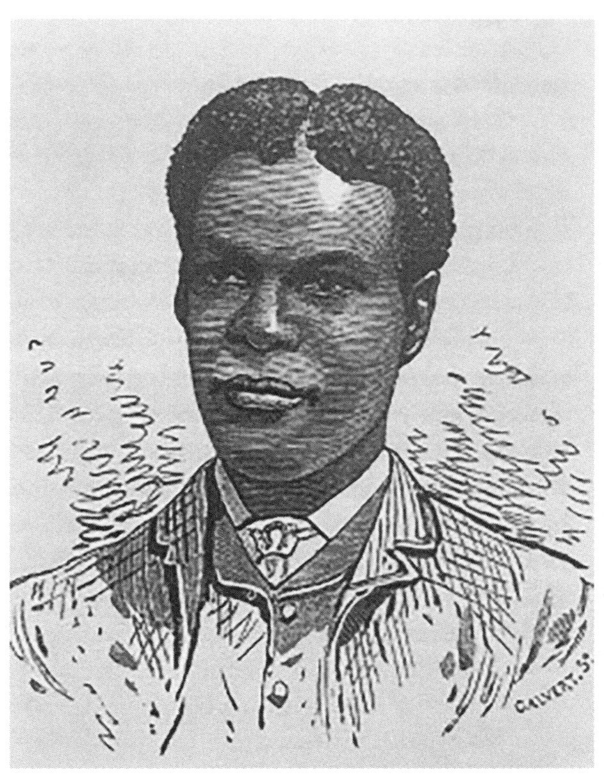

3.7

———

Samuel Calvert, "Peter Jackson," 1887. Ink sketch, 6 × 8 inches (15.2 × 20.3 cm). From *Australian Sporting Celebrities with Biographical Sketches of Their Careers* (Melbourne: A. H. Massina, 1887).

eration and, most significant for the purposes of this study, their subsequent influence in shaping public personas. As Lippert has shown, these circumstances created a distinct (and not to mention lucrative) market for performers and entertainers, who took advantage of photography to promote their public personas at times when they were not on stage.

While Lippert's study focuses (in part) on the role of photography in the celebrity culture of San Francisco's theater, this chapter explores the photographs of Peter Jackson that were produced in San Francisco during the years of his residency there. We find in this story that Jackson's image raises questions both about the politics of performance in nineteenth-century professional boxing and the conditions of possibility for Black men in a nation deeply divided by race. As an immigrant living in San Francisco, Jackson was in some ways part of the majority, but his Blackness would have immediately and consistently separated him. When he arrived in a late spring afternoon in 1888, he was one of only 1,600 Black people living in the city. Within two years he would be the most famous Black man in the United States.

Nevertheless, most histories of visual culture of this period neglect images of prizefighters. Even Lippert, who has produced one of the most detailed analyses of visual culture of the West Coast in the nineteenth century, fails to acknowledge the centrality of San Francisco within the sport of boxing and its resident celebrities. This is a surprising oversight considering that many of the sport's stars, including Peter Jackson and James "Gentleman Jim" Corbett (1866–1933) also worked as actors in traveling theater productions. Other boxers that called San Francisco home included John L. Sullivan (1858–1918), Joe Choynski (1868–1943), the middleweight champion "Nonpareil" Jack Dempsey (1862–95), and the first Olympic boxing champion, Samuel Berger (1884–1925). San Francisco (and the neighboring city of Oakland) contained nearly a dozen boxing clubs. The amount of talent within and attention given to boxing in San Francisco in the nineteenth century led to its being known as "the Cradle of Fistic Stars."

To date, few studies of visual culture consider the athletic dimension of nineteenth-century social life. However, we must write a history of this period that acknowledges the profound effects of sports and athletic culture on the visual register, and by extension on the making of white, middle-class identity. While I do not seek to deny the real impact of family photography or portraiture on the making of American subjectivity, I argue instead for a reconsideration of the primacy of images in the mass media and their role in shaping a rhetoric of white masculinity that is explicitly focused on the individual white, male body as a required component for social authority. Sports images—both those published within newspapers and magazines and those sold separately as lithographs or cabinet cards—were a significant part of the emergence of this new cult of masculinity. This was a masculinity that circulated on a massive and national scale via publications like the *National Police Gazette*, the output of printmakers like Currier & Ives, cabinet cards sold by Fox and others, and even via theatrical performances. Boxers were an ideal subject for visual media; the individual character of the sport and its close emphasis on the actions of two singular bodies translated well to visual representation.

The sport of boxing in San Francisco was incredibly popular in the late nineteenth century. Like the rest of California, most residents of San Francisco were newcomers in some way or another. Spectator sports provided a way for these residents to build a sense of community and to develop a mass civic culture. Along with theaters, festivals, and dance halls, prizefighting areas were spaces of cultural contact and even a celebration of masculine ideals. At the start, prizefighting in San Francisco (as in other major urban centers) was considered a disreputable and illegal activity. However, unlike the East Coast, where fights were organized in off-site locations outside city limits, most San Francisco prizefights before the 1880s took place in "slogging dens"—dark basements, back rooms, and other hidden spaces.[42] By the time of Jackson's arrival in 1888, prizefighting was undergoing a transformation into a respectable sport. As the historian Matthew Andrews writes, while boxing was becoming less popular in the East due to the pressures of moral reforms,

> San Francisco leaders gladly enlisted the sport into the larger enterprise of civic promotion and began hosting high-profile and profitable prizefights in places like Mechanic's Pavilion, Dreamland, and the Orpheum Theater—modern edifices that accommodated a larger crowd and, importantly, added an aura of opulence to the proceedings. Boxing entrepreneurs converted these grand civic arenas into fantastic palaces of pugilism, draping colorful bunting from steel-beam supports, hanging woodcuts depicting the glories of prizefighting's past on newly whitewashed walls, and scheduling brass bands and minstrel shows as pre-fight entertainment.[43]

Attempts at cultivating respectability for boxing through these "palaces of pugilism" was reinforced by the transformation of its audience. Suddenly, white bourgeois men—doctors, lawyers, and those from other "white collar" professions—were joining athletic clubs, undergoing pugilistic training, and even watching fights. The professionalization of baseball two decades prior—which included the adoption of behavioral regulations for players and associated fines, the establishment of professional membership organizations for teams, and the cultivation of middle-class (and female) audiences—may have provided the template.[44]

Peter Jackson surely would have appealed to these new audiences. He was remarkable for his (at that time) strange insistence on fighting with gloves and under the Queensbury rules. And we know that he liked to dress up. He would have spoken English with a British-inflected accent—a product of his schooling—and was an avid reader of classical literature. As noted by one newspaper article: "Peter is also a fine Shakespearean reader, and many times has corrected the persons who were rated high in that line while they were giving quotations from the bard's immortal works. He carries a large volume of the plays with him, and during his leisure moments, when not playing checkers he reads them."[45] Jackson's background and self-presentation connected to an overall atmosphere of Anglophilia in the nineteenth century. This included not only the concept of the "British gentleman" promoted by those like the French art historian and critic Hippolyte Taine, whose 1872 book *Notes on England* explicitly praised the British gentleman—as opposed to the French *gentilhomme*—for their sense of decency and honor.[46] When speaking with reporters, Jackson made great efforts to position himself as the gentleman athlete rather than a senseless brute. As Jackson told a reporter in 1889: "I follow fighting and sports in general purely *as a business* and not to satisfy a brutal nature. I can row, swim, and run as well as box, and whatever I do I try to be a gentleman. I make it a point of my fights never to administer a knock-out blow unless I am compelled to do so. It is no satisfaction to me to render an opponent insensible with a blow when he is whipped and at my mercy."[47] Even amid raucous public support, Jackson remained wary of appearing arrogant. The historian Geoffrey C. Ward noted that "when Black admirers staged a parade for [Jackson] in Baltimore, he refused to take part unless a hand-painted banner proclaiming [John L.] Sullivan a coward for avoiding him had been removed."[48]

The news coverage surrounding his first few years in the United States attests to Jackson success in molding a gentlemanly image of himself for both Black and white audiences. After knocking out Joe McAuliffe in San Francisco in December 1888, hundreds of cheering spectators marched on Market Street. Most mainstream coverage described Jackson as polite, even taciturn. The *Newark Advocate* and the *Commercial Gazette* praised his refinement, describing him, respectively, as "a perfect gentleman" with above-average intelligence and "always polite."[49] The limited record we have from the African American press in this period positions Jackson as an emblematic example of Blackness. The recently introduced sports column of *The Freeman*—the first illustrated African American newspaper—announced in April 1890: "Peter Jackson does this generation a service by proving that a man can be both a prize-fighter and a gentleman."[50] Certainly, Jackson's habit of quoting Shakespeare—a not so subtle reminder of his education—did not hurt. Any doubts that the Black bourgeoisie may have had about associating with the lowly sport of boxing were cast aside; they were, in the words of Jackson's biographer Bob Petersen, "forced to accept that the best advertisement around for black talent was a prize fighter."[51] We cannot forget that eventually even Frederick Douglass displayed a photograph of Jackson in his Washington office, where he would tell visitors: "Peter Jackson has done as much as any Negro to solve the race problem."[52]

While my focus in this chapter in on Jackson, he was not the only Black pugilist fighting in the late nineteenth century; George Dixon (1870–1908), George Godfrey (1853–1901), and Joe Gans (1874–1910) were all champions during this period. George Dixon and Joe Gans fought across the bantamweight, featherweight, and light heavyweight categories; Dixon weighed a mere eighty-seven pounds at the start of his professional career. The only notable heavyweight to precede Jackson in the United States was George Godfrey, also known as "Old Chocolate," who fought in twenty-eight bouts (mostly around Boston) before Jackson's arrival in 1888.[53] We can imagine that Godfrey's career, like Jackson's, was made possible due to his perceived distance from American Blackness and the specter of slavery. Born in 1853 and 1860, respectively, Godfrey and Jackson were both island-born, coming to the United States from Prince Edward Island in the North Atlantic and Saint Croix in the Caribbean. As such, their position as colonial subjects of the British Empire allowed them to circulate in different ideological and social spaces. Jackson, for example, traveled extensively before and after his arrival stateside; he even went to the southern United States, visiting both Louisville and St. Louis without incident in 1890. Two years later, in New Orleans, Jackson was the only Black spectator allowed inside the auditorium of the Olympic Club for the Sullivan-Corbett match.[54] I am reminded here again of the work of sports historian Adrian Burgos, whose study of baseball during this same period showed how certain racial categories at play within the sport—in his example, Latinos—"accommodate the inclusion of nonwhite Others."[55] Such exceptions were made possible by the dominance of colonialism as well as the public reception of Jackson as more British than Black, and the stage for the public lionization of Jackson in a time of deep racial tensions. He operated outside the stereotypes of sambos and savages typically assigned to African American boxers. One journalist at the *Leavenworth Standard* went so far as to remark: "Peter is not an ignorant nigger."[56] Jackson's distinctly diasporic background made possible his promotion as "Gentleman Jackson," which marked him as different from American Black fighters.[57] The question for us, then, is how these messages circulated in the visual field.

In other chapters I have discussed images of boxers in weekly periodicals, such as the *National Police Gazette*, and in fine art such as the photographs by Eadweard Muybridge and the paintings and drawings of the American artist George Bellows (the subject of chapter 4). However, I would like to explore images of Jackson that circulated in other ways. More specifically, aided by technological advances in both lithography and photography, as well as the rising reputation of boxing itself, by the end of the nineteenth century images of these athletes were no longer limited to the select newspapers and broadsides distributed in barbershops or saloons for a mostly white, male, middle-class public. Instead, boxers like Jackson entered the visual field of other audiences—women and people of color—both publicly via a more diverse news media (e.g., African American newspapers) as well as privately via the rising popularity of cabinet cards at the close of the century. I argue that both formats introduce a new relationship between the heavyweight boxer and the viewer. In the case of African American media coverage, we can imagine that the perception of Jackson was less a performance of Blackness fixed in stereotype and more one of possibility, where the boxer came to stand in for the potential and the power of the Black body. And when we consider this image, formatted as the $5\frac{1}{4} \times 4$–inch photograph used for a cabinet card, we introduce a viewing relationship based on intimacy, where the image of Jackson is held in the palm of one's hand, tucked into a purse or breast pocket. Such formats introduce a relationship to the image that is personal, tactile even.[58]

As a result of this increase in media coverage and an expanded readership, representations of athletes (already entangled within an emergent cult of manhood) further proliferated. Illustrations of athletes focused on their developed physiques, modeling for a readership a body that would reflect the corporeal ideal assigned to middle-class men in the nineteenth century. And images of boxers, who competed whilst stripped to the waist, were particularly relevant. Images of these men were more than documentary; they were aspirational for viewers. Starting in the 1840s, woodblock engravings were the most popular visual format for periodicals, often assembled from sketches first made by an illustrator. As the medium of photography became increasingly popular, some woodblock engravings would involve the transfer of both hand-drawn sketches and photographs onto the woodblock; in later years, photographs would be directly exposed onto the block. Before the adoption of half-tone printing (which allowed the direct replication of a photograph), the technical requirements of the engraving process created a series of images that were from the start subject to adaptation and adjustment. This meant that the image of the boxer encountered by the mainstream readership of a periodical would have been less a visual fact and more an interpretation.

The cabinet card, first utilized in landscape photography, was a particular mode of portraiture that began after 1870 and quickly began to replace the more traditional *carte de visite* of earlier decades. These images would have been frequently displayed in homes (in cabinets), and their larger size—an average of four by six inches—allowed visitors to view friends and family from across the room. By the time Jackson arrived in San Francisco, cabinet cards were a popular medium for recording both individuals and their families; however, there was also a strong push toward the use and marketing of popular images—for example, actors or political figures to the public.

The gallery and studio of Isaiah Taber West, located on Montgomery Street, was a place where patrons could commission and purchase images of themselves, the awe-inspiring California landscape, or of celebrities.[59] Jackson appeared several times in Taber's studio, which would have been less than a fifteen-minute walk from where he was living shortly after this arrival in the city.[60] Jackson appeared in Taber's photographs as a subject of both standard boxing portraits sold to fans throughout his career, and of a pseudoscientific inquiry into the standards of the "perfect man." We will return to this later.

The photographer Isaiah West Taber, born in New Bedford, Massachusetts, in 1830, had made his way out to the West Coast first in 1850 for work as a miner before settling there permanently in 1864. The bulk of Taber's business was in portraiture, which he began in 1856 with a successful portrait business in Syracuse, New York. By 1871 he had established his photography studio, the Taber Gallery, at 12 Montgomery Street in San Francisco; as the business expanded, Taber moved down the street to 8 Montgomery—opposite the well-known Palace and Grand hotels. From 1871 to 1906, he ran a thriving business working in both portrait and landscape photography, and at one point he managed up to sixty employees. Taber's studio was a victim of the earthquake of 1906; all his glass plates—twenty tons of view negatives and eighty tons of portrait work—were lost as a result. From what is left of the historical record we know that Taber's studio included several photographic parlors as well as an area where he sold photography supplies and prints to the public, including those of other photographers such as Carleton Watkins. He quickly became one of the most well-known American photographers and was undoubtedly the head of the largest photographic business in San Francisco. In 1893–94 he was awarded the photographic concession of the San Francisco Midwinter Fair, and in 1897 he was sent to London to photograph the pageant of Queen Victoria's Jubilee.

By the time he established his studio in San Francisco, Taber was one of nearly forty similar businesses. However, he soon found several ways to distinguish himself from the competition, using the latest technologies, advertising, and his highly visible location at the intersection of Market and Montgomery streets to establish an advantage. Taber's studio was on the third floor of the Hibernia Bank Building. Anyone riding by in their buggy could easily read the large sign: "I. W. Taber Photographic Parlors," pointing them to the place where they might have their portrait made. Once inside the building, customers could take a short elevator ride to the third floor, where they would encounter a series of elegantly decorated parlors and sitting rooms with thick carpets, lush ferns, and several framed portraits resting on easels.[61] They could take advantage of Taber's electrically operated camera that shortened required exposure times—ideal for children or pets—and have their portraits mounted and framed in the latest fashions. According to the *Oakland Tribune*, Taber's company photographed more than 100,000 individuals over a forty-year period.[62]

Taber built his reputation by placing his name in periodicals and other directories; he displayed his work in several fairs and expositions throughout the United States and in Europe, even winning medals that he would repeatedly reference in his advertising. When he traveled, Taber somehow managed to photograph prominent locals—for example, Queen Victoria in 1897—and by the turn of the twentieth century he had established studios in London and Paris. A major source of Taber's success was in creating likenesses of celebrities—political figures, musicians, actors—that could be sold and traded in his galleries. He photographed seven US presidents. When the former president Ulysses S. Grant visited San Francisco in September 1879 on his world tour, Taber produced a souvenir portrait of both the former president and his wife. Such images would be offered as cabinet cards—a photograph mounted on a thin, card backing, the whole typically measuring 4½ × 6½ inches—and sold in packages. One of Taber's cabinet cards stated on the reverse: "Duplicate Copies at Reduced Rates. Viz: 1 dozen for $5.00—2 dozen for $9.00—3 dozen for $12.00—100 for $30.00." The price of these photographs was based on the fame of the sitter, and many local celebrities were aware of the power of these images to increase their popularity. For example, by the late 1860s many of San Francisco's theatrical stars were posing for *cartes de visite* (a smaller photograph, 2 × 3.5 inches mounted on cardstock) that could be circulated through the mail, posted in public storefronts, and sold to patrons for a quarter. Fans could pur-

"Peter Jackson," 1888. Photographer unknown, tobacco card with
albumen print, 1.4 × 2.6 inches (3.6 × 6.6 cm). Published by S. F. Hess
and Co.'s Cigarettes. Library of Congress, Washington, DC.

chase these small photographs for $1.50 to $3 for a dozen (roughly $50 to $100
today) and would paste them in their family albums alongside images of their
family and friends. And by the early 1860s one could purchase images not only
of performers, but also of politicians, writers, and other types of public figures.

Starting soon after his arrival in San Francisco in 1888, Peter Jackson became
one of the subjects of Taber's celebrity portraits. One of the early Taber portraits, taken at the end of 1888, shows Peter looking directly at the camera with
his arms crossed in front of his bare torso. This image was reproduced on a card
sold by S. F. Hess and Co. as part of a series for Creole cigarettes (fig. 3.8). This
type of image would also have been sold in Taber's studio to Jackson's fans for
a quarter. It would have been the personal, collectible counterpart to the larger
lithographic prints that were sold to bars, barbershops, and other public estab-
lishments. Unlike the lithographs, these smaller cabinet-card images did not
show Jackson during a match, but in a moment of repose; he looks not at an
opponent across him in the ring, but gazes directly outward at the viewer. These
photographic portraits were a new, more intimate way of experiencing the athlete. Tucked into a pocket or displayed on a shelf at home, patrons of these images, who were mostly white, middle-class fans, made the choice to bring Peter
Jackson—a Black man—into their personal, visual space.

The "Perfect Man"

In the summer of 1889—just a year after his arrival stateside—Jackson entered
Isaiah Taber's studio for another kind of project. An article in the *San Francisco Examiner* recounted the details of a photographic study of Jackson's body,
which apparently revealed his departure from public expectations of what a
heavyweight boxer should look like. Jackson was measured by Dr. W. H. Mays,
who recorded the fighter's height, weight, and measurements (of the head,

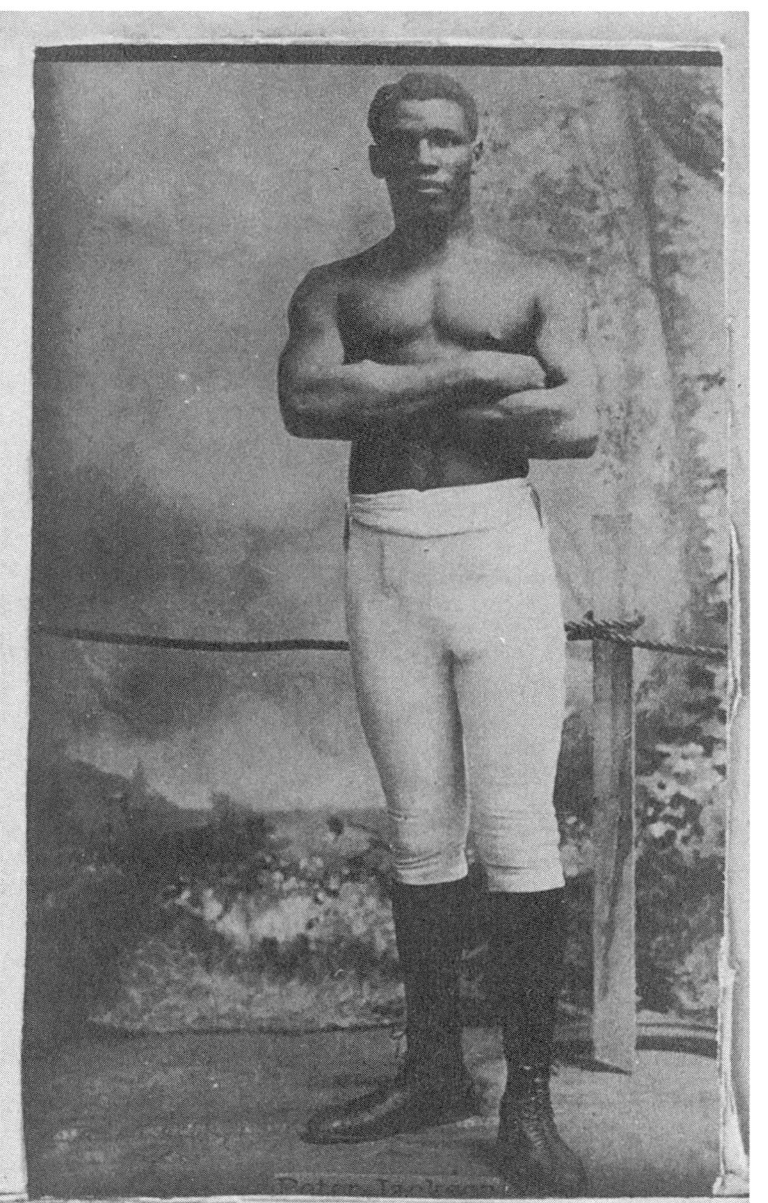

PETER JACKSON.
S. F. HESS & CO.'S
CIGARETTES.

neck, arms, hands, torso, thighs, calves, ankles, feet, and toes).[63] Each detailed measurement—for example, Jackson's head and neck was measured in six different places—was recorded for the newspaper; there were forty-four in all. To take the most accurate measurements, as described by the *Examiner*, Jackson was presented to the doctor dressed only in a short cloth tied around the hips with a long piece hanging in front to conceal his genitals, and he was photographed by Taber's assistant, Frank Davey.

While previous issues of the *San Francisco Examiner* dated December 1888 through May 1889 reveal no other instances of body measurements or references to Dr. Mays, the physical measurement of athletic bodies was a well-established genre in this period.[64] A body measurement craze swept America during the last decades of the nineteenth century, in parallel with a rising interest in physical education.[65] As discussed in the introduction of this book, the rise of physical culture stars like the German Eugen Sandow (1867–1925) and, a bit later, the American Bernarr Macfadden (1868–1955) included a range of publications and images, including how-to instructional manuals and memoirs, as well as the popular magazines *Sandow's Magazine of Physical Culture* (published 1898–1907) and Macfadden's *Physical Culture* (published 1899–1912).

Eugen Sandow, born Friedrich Wilhelm Müller in Germany in 1867, became a celebrity in the United States for his "muscle display performances," and feats of strength promoted by Florenz Ziegfeld. Sandow was even featured flexing in a short film series by Edison Studios in 1894. He published his book *Strength and How to Obtain It* in 1897, and in July 1898 began to publish *Sandow's Magazine of Physical Culture*, which included essays on training techniques across various sports, diet recommendations, illustrated exercises, and even testimonials from Sandow's devotees.[66] His 1897 book contained a chart, which instructed students of his technique concerning the proper methods for taking the measurements of various sections of the body—chest, forearm, thigh—all of which would be ideally developed and muscularized using his techniques (fig. 3.9). Physical culture stars all relied on "success stories" as an integral component of their marketing plans; this often included "before" and "after" photographs but also required another systematic way to demonstrate results. Measuring individual bodies required little specialized training or equipment; in the process, three or four dozen body parts might be measured and recorded. Then, statistical "averages" of these were computed, and charts were prepared with the intention of representing the "ideal" form. Sandow's 1894 publication *Sandow's System of Physical Training*, for example, includes an "anthropometric chart" for "showing the relation of the individual in size strength, symmetry, and development to the normal standard."[67]

The figure will show pupils how to take their own measurements.

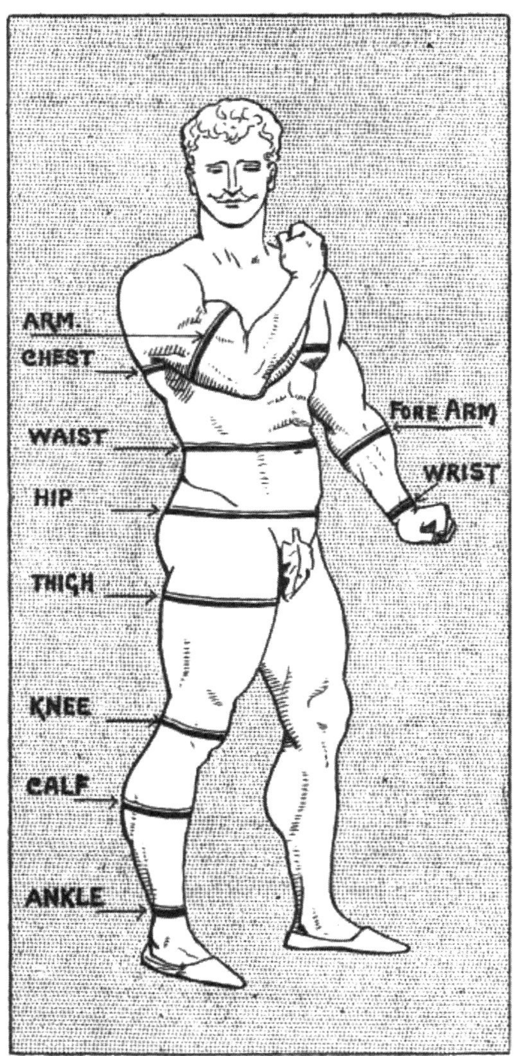

3.9

"Sandow's Chart of Measurements." From Eugen Sandow, *Strength and How to Obtain It* (London: Gale & Polden Ltd., 1897).

In 1887—that is, just a year before Peter Jackson was measured in this way—*Scribner's Magazine* published an article on the physical proportions of the "typical" American male submitted by the physical educator Dr. Dudley Allen Sargent (1849–1924) and illustrated with numerous pen and ink drawings taken from photographs.[68] The *Scribner's* article included a lengthy report of the measurements of athletes (lavishly illustrated), as well as an unillustrated report on the "typical" American woman. Using this data, Sargent identified what he considered to be the "ideal" physical attributes for athletes of specific sports—e.g., distance runners were lean and ectomorphic; wrestlers and footballers were massive and mesomorphic. The message was unambiguous, men whose physiques deviated too greatly from the "ideal" simply did not measure up.[69]

While the measurements of Jackson relate to Sargent's anthropometric system and the headline of the *Examiner* article read "Peter Jackson Measured from the Benefit of Science," the purpose of these measurements was not so much to classify difference as to describe the "ideal." They did not correlate with Sargent's copyrighted measurement system. Jackson's age, weight, height, and measurements of the head, neck, arms, hands, torso, legs, feet, and thighs were all recorded; however, his seated height or arm span (a measurement also typical for boxing statistics) were not. Jackson is not marked here as Other—that is, as an example of what must be avoided or cast out—insomuch as he is marked as a model for readers, as a testament to the cultural obsession with physical culture and fitness, and as a point of comparison with his future opponent, John L. Sullivan. Knowing what we do about the politics of Blackness within the United States during this period, it is nothing short of shocking to find this Black man documented in the pages of a mainstream newspaper as "the most perfect representation of health, strength, and development."[70] Simply put, Jackson is not pathologized; he is idolized.

Four pen-and-ink illustrations accompany this description in the paper, each showing Jackson (wearing only a cloth tied around his hips) in a pose seemingly designed to "secure the best measurements."[71] Here we see Jackson outside the standards of representation established by his celebrity portrait—that is, in standard boxing tights either facing the camera or captured mid-punch. Jackson wears instead a loin cloth tied across his hips. And most of all, Jackson appears in dynamic poses. These illustrations are neither scientific nor commemorative. Each not only demonstrate the movement of Jackson's body but also reify his place in a canon of proportions.

In the first illustration, captioned simply "Peter Jackson," he stands contrapposto with his left leg in front and his arms raised to confront an unseen opponent (fig. 3.10). The second illustration, labeled "Stopping a Rush," shows us the next phase of movement, where the left arm that appeared poised for the punch has been fully extended (fig. 3.11). Another image (the fourth in the series), labeled "Right Hand Lead," details a view of Jackson from the opposite side, punching outward this time with his opposite arm while his left (the arm closest to us) remains bent (fig. 3.12).

As discussed in chapter 2, the middle-class preoccupation with racial difference developed alongside a rise in graphic illustrations (and photographs) of non-white bodies. Drawing in part from anthropological methods, which introduced such devices as the anthropometric grid in photographs to measure bodies within the frame of the camera, illustrations of Black bodies provided visual evidence of difference. But these images of Jackson do not rehearse an anthropometric approach to the athlete's body. We do not see a grid; Jackson does not stand naked in straight profile (see, e.g., fig. 2.7). The explicit positioning of Jackson as a model of masculinity is a curious fact of his time in the United States, and one that runs counter to our understandings of Blackness in the nineteenth century as abject, abused, or invisible. In other words, his performance and self-presentation as "Gentleman Jack" was compounded by his promotion as not just a celebrity but as an ideal body.[72]

The third *Examiner* illustration, captioned "The Quoit Thrower," shows the transfiguration of Jackson into an ideal (fig.. 3.13). Jackson leans slightly forward balancing his left hand gently on his right knee. As he seems to step forward with that right leg, his right arm stretches back in preparation for the throw. But what he holds in that hand does not appear to be an actual "quoit"—a hollow ring that would be thrown onto a spike (placed in the ground).[73] Instead, the circular shape looks solid, covered on the surface by a dark shading in diagonal strokes that run across its diameter. Given these visual facts, it seems likely that Jackson here has been styled in specific reference to the classical Greek sculpture known as the *Discobolus* of Myron. Completed at the start of the classical period, 460–450 BCE, Myron's original does not exist, but there are several Roman copies in marble—currently in the British Museum, the Vatican Museum, and the National Museum of Rome—all of which reproduce the dynamic pose of the athlete (fig. 3.14). The subject of the *Discobolus*, the discus thrower, like Jackson, also leans forward on a right leg with his right arm raised above; he also twists his torso to allow the left hand to cross over the right knee. The pose of Jackson as the classical discus thrower aligns him with one of the most celebrated statues from antiquity, and by extension the boxer's body with the ultimate example of athletic beauty. Moreover, Jackson as "The Quoit Thrower" is just one example of his frequent and extended comparison with Greek statuary—

3.10

———

"Peter Jackson," 1889.

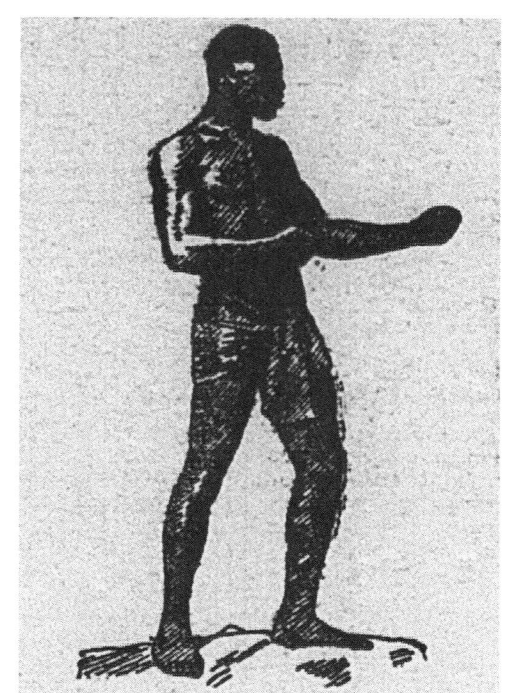

3.11

———

"Stopping a Rush," 1889.

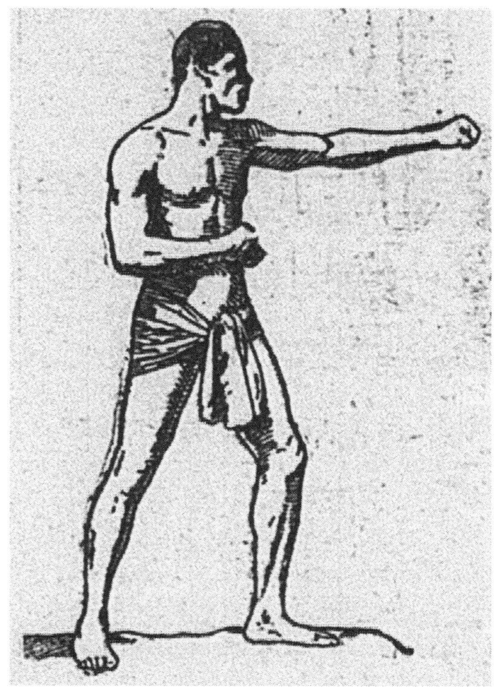

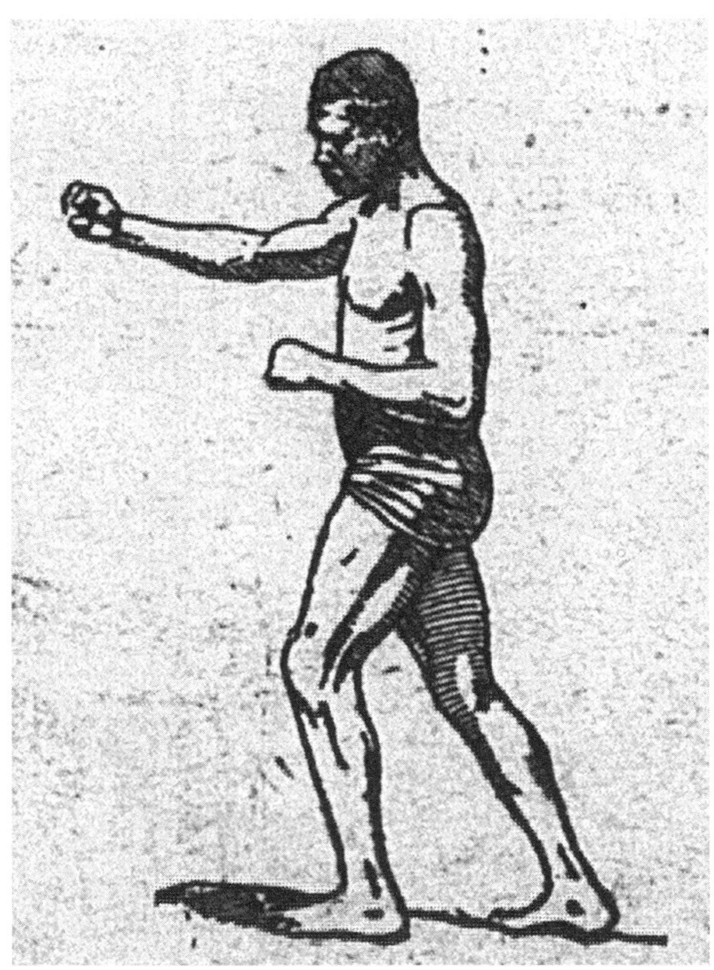

3.12

———

"Right Hand Lead," 1889.

———

Artist unknown, pen and ink drawings.
Published in the *San Francisco Examiner*, May 26, 1889.
Historical Archive, San Francisco Media Company.

3.13

———

"The Quoit Thrower," 1889. Artist unknown, pen and ink drawing. Published in the *San Francisco Examiner*, May 26, 1889. Historical Archive, San Francisco Media Company.

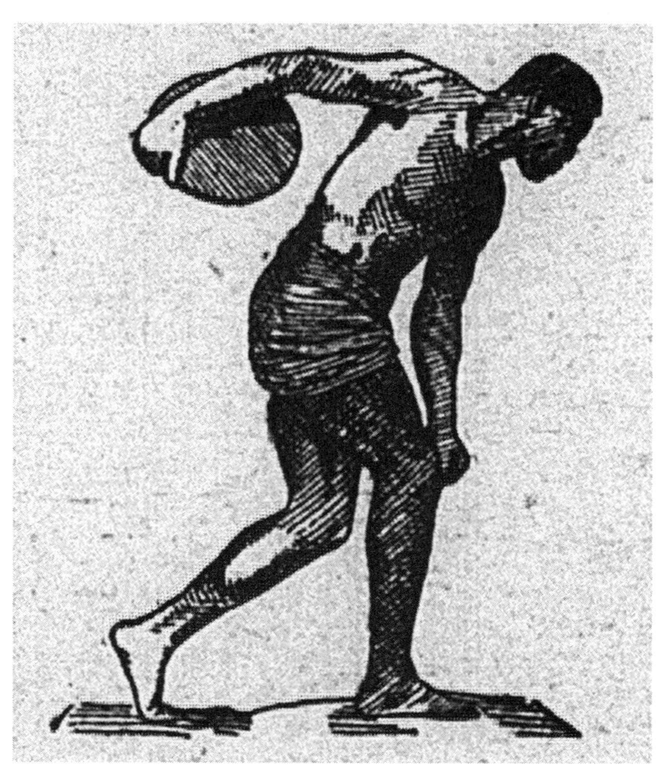

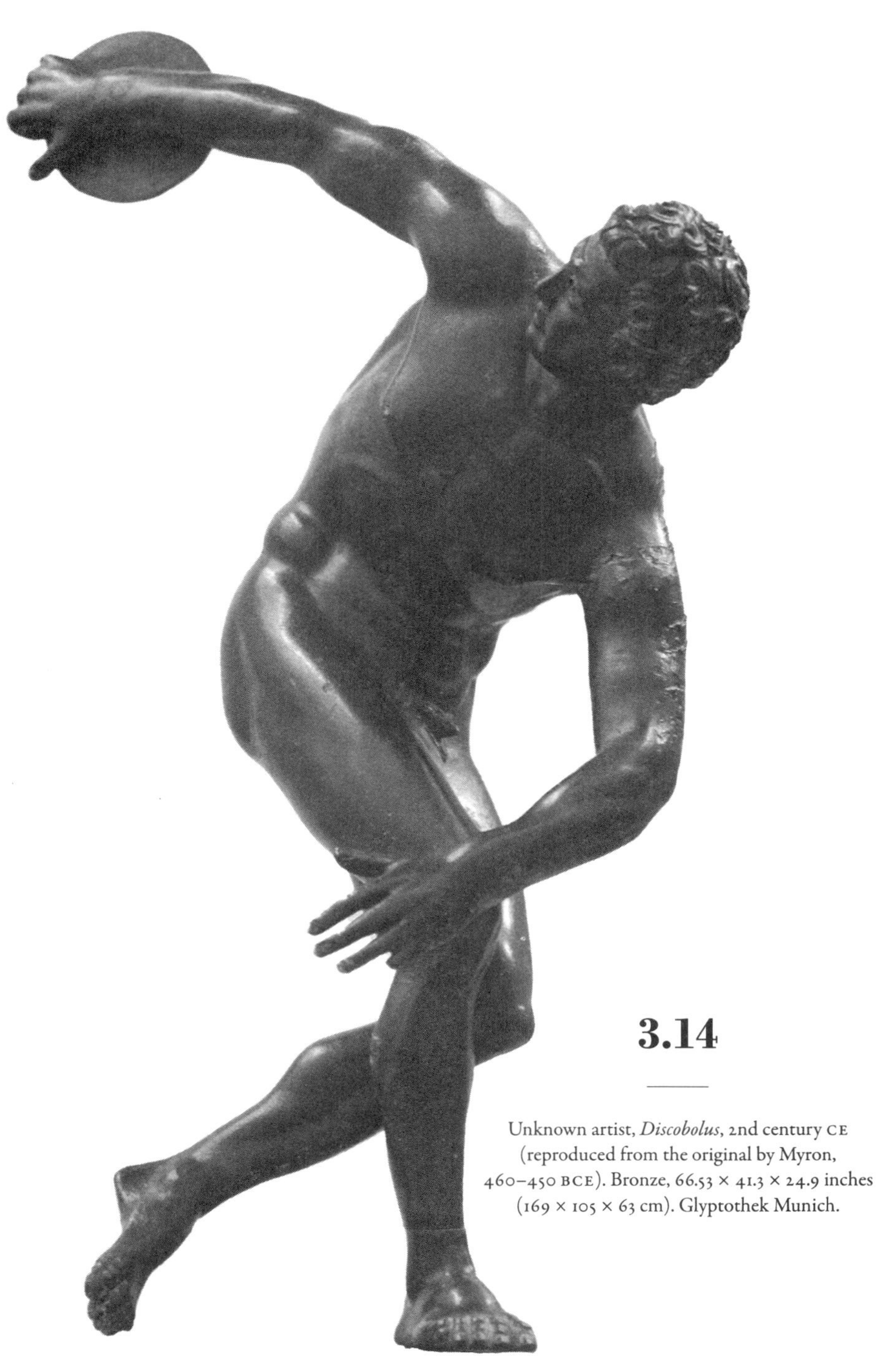

3.14

Unknown artist, *Discobolus*, 2nd century CE
(reproduced from the original by Myron,
460–450 BCE). Bronze, 66.53 × 41.3 × 24.9 inches
(169 × 105 × 63 cm). Glyptothek Munich.

in both word and image. In a contemporary essay, he was called "a living moving bronze statue."[74] Another article in the *Cincinnati Enquirer* called him out as the "Black Hercules."[75]

In the late nineteenth century, classical nude models (specifically those drawn from Greek art) were touted as exemplars, their perfect bodies a metaphor for the greatness of their society.[76] Like other works that highlighted Greek male beauty and male prowess (e.g., the *Belvedere Apollo*), *Discobolus* was well understood in the nineteenth century as an illustration of the relationship between the perfection of one's physical form and one's virtue. Large plaster casts of the statue were sold throughout the late nineteenth and early twentieth centuries to US audiences, who marveled at the discus thrower's athletic beauty. This was a moment in which the white American middle classes were positively obsessed with classical culture and looked to Greece and Rome for its examples of political democracy and ideal aesthetics. The associations with classical culture provided an aesthetic and ideological link to morality and even patriotism, as well as a visual model for the overly muscled physique popularized by men like Sandow. Carried over from Europe, where the discovery of Roman monuments and other antiquities in the eighteenth century inspired a revival of classical aesthetics in painting, literature, and certainly architecture, neoclassicism in the United States reached its peak in the decades before Peter Jackson's arrival in San Francisco. In a testament to the popularity of the style, the 1876 Philadelphia Centennial International Exhibition (the first World's Fair to be held in the United States) positioned the neoclassical aesthetic to fashion a new American identity in the wake of the Civil War. Visitors to the central hall of the art gallery building, for example, would have encountered forty-five pieces of sculpture, many of which were submitted by expatriate artists working in the neoclassical style. These included a large marble sculpture by Edmonia Lewis titled *The Death of Cleopatra* (1875), along with William Wetmore Story's own *Cleopatra* (finished 1869) and Pierce Francis Connelly's *Thetis and Achilles* (1874).[77]

The specific appropriations of the neoclassical style—a visual rhetoric that was well-established in this historical period—were integral to the presentations of "ideal masculinity" that we see emerge in physical culture. In both public and private contexts, the rendering of the classical body in stone, in paint, or via photography was a particular mode by which artists and audiences reaffirmed their commitments to classical ideals—of morality, of democracy, and of beauty. The neoclassical tradition is one which presents the body as an aesthetic object, positioned to be admired and potentially emulated.

The aesthetic ideal of neoclassicism also invites questions of race. In her 2007 book *The Color of Stone*, art historian Charmaine Nelson takes up the 1869 version of Hiram Power's sculpture *The Greek Slave* as an example of how the marble materials rendered these representations (of presumably Black bodies) as somehow outside race, citing "the representational impossibility of the black female body."[78] In her reading of Edmonia Lewis's *The Death of Cleopatra*, Nelson suggests that the sculptor's adoption of a Black historical subject—perhaps a radical subject for nineteenth-century audiences—was complicated by the use of marble, which transfigured the African Blackness of the queen into whiteness. This, she argues, demonstrates the medium's "investment in the bourgeois ordering of the body, which was both patriarchal and colonial."[79] Neoclassicism, therefore, relied on both the rhetorical and the material legacies of the classical world in the fashioning of this ideology.

The curator and art historian Michael Hatt has similarly argued that the presence of naked bodies in this very specific cultural moment required the manipulation of its aesthetic presentation to align with the normative models of Victorian decorum. A constellation of aesthetic conventions, specific to sculptural nudes, was required to wrest these images from reality—the lack of body hair or genitals on female nudes, with skin wiped clean and lacking any wrinkles or scars. Often the results were ambiguous, as Hatt cites in the example of Power's *The Greek Slave*, which was a subject of debate when it was first exhibited in 1851. All these aesthetic conventions were deployed, nevertheless, to distance the body from sexuality, and by extension the artist and even the viewer from accusations of immorality. He writes: "A sense of the individual, of subjectivity even, was drained away in the search for the abstract and universal."[80] This included the use of the white marble preferred by artists during the period, which, although historically an inaccurate representation of the classical preference for polychromy, allowed for the body to transcend mere flesh and operate as a "transcendent form." The alignment of Jackson in such an explicit way with neoclassical sculpture—through his adoption of the pose of these ancient statues, as well as by the rendering of his body in a pen-and-ink illustration that presents him as "white"—is a method by which the boxer's Blackness is not necessarily eclipsed, but certainly neutralized for white viewers.

While the association of a boxer (especially a Black boxer) with classical rhetoric may seem unusual, there was an established precedent in bodybuilding culture of this period. The classicist Maria Wyke has studied, for example, the connections (both formally and ideologically) that popular bodybuilders like German strongman Eugen Sandow made between their own physical pursuits and the overly muscular Greek bodies found in sculptures like the *Farnese Hercules*—a marble sculpture of the Greek God made by Glykon in the third century CE that remains one of the most famous examples of ancient sculptures (fig. 3.15).[81] These were analogies made explicitly by Sandow and other physical culture specialists, who attempted to link highly muscled physique with a classical discourse described by Wyke as "operat[ing] as a multivalent (and sometimes contradictory) signifier of what is natural, traditional, patriotic, spectacular, artistic, and above all valuable."[82] Sandow, for example, openly modeled his own physique on classical examples, which he saw as a child when accompanying his father to art galleries in Greece and Rome. When reporting on this experience as an adult, Sandow emphasized how he "was struck with admiration for the finely developed forms of the sculpted figures of athletes of old."[83] Both the performances and the images of Sandow in the last decade of the nineteenth century show this classical influence. One set of photographs of Sandow, taken in the New York studio of Napoleon Sarony in 1893, for example, records the athlete's appropriation of the Hercules figure (fig. 3.16).

What made the classical Hercules example unique—and thereby suitable for such associations—is not only its massive size (over ten feet tall) but also its excessive musculature; the body here is not the ideal, lithe athlete of other classical models (e.g., *Discobolus* of Myron from the same period) but bulky and perhaps even brutish. Displayed in its original location in the Baths of Caracalla (completed 216 CE), this Hercules would have been studied as an example of athletic form, an aspirational ideal for the patrons who exercised there. And men like Eugen Sandow took up Hercules in the nineteenth century as their own model of an ideal body—a body that presumably any man could achieve. Sandow appears in the same pose of the famous sculpture, leaning against a club that is propped under his left arm and covered with animal skin (a reference to the pelt of the Nemean lion that Hercules slayed). His head droops down slightly with his gaze pointed downward, and his right hand has been tucked behind the torso. He flexes his abdominal muscles, which are centered in the frame of the composition and highlighted by sharp and direct lighting. The only major difference—aside from stature—seems to be the introduction of a leaf to cover the athlete's genitals. Sandow emphatically places himself within the realm of classical (or rather neoclassical) culture and, by extension, its associations with "ideal" form. As with classical Greek sculpture, we are meant to focus here on the nobility of the athlete and the perfection of the human body, which for the contemporary viewer would reflect the corresponding excellence and virtue of the soul.[84]

As argued by Broderick D. V. Chow, a performance studies scholar, such visual cues would have served an important ideological function for viewers. In these photographs, he writes, "the early 20th-century muscular male body ... was posed as an achievable ideal that resembled larger-than-life Greek and Roman sculptures, but which any man could transform into."[85] The magazine *Physical Culture*, published by Sandow's competitor Bernarr Macfadden, often featured classical nude sculptures and paintings on the cover, again explained away by stating that they were to help the viewer achieve a "perfect" body.[86] Viewers of these images (white, middle-class men) were to be inspired by these images, and were encouraged to shape their own bodies in turn. Physical culture was characterized by self-definition, by a fetishization of the desire to fix the self.

Peter Jackson, a boxer, found himself at the center of a debate around "the perfect man" that would continue for at least another decade. Just a few years after his appearance as *Discobolus*, Jackson and Sandow were compared in two consecutive issues of the *San Francisco Examiner* in May 1894, which asked local painters and sculptors to evaluate and compare the bodies of each man in terms of the ideal male physique. In the first issue that appeared, under the title "Sandow, the Imperfect Man," local artists take up Sandow's self-proclamations as "the perfect man," debating his anatomical proportions and their fit within wider artistic standards. The French-American artist Amédée Joullin (1862–1917) forthrightly argues that Sandow "is in no sense a perfect man," going on to list the bodybuilder's defects. "He is not tall enough," claims Joullin, and "the muscles are in bunches," almost as if they are "packages ... tied to him and sticking out all over him." By comparison, Joullin describes Peter Jackson as "nearly perfect" with lines that "are fine and delicate from the wrists to the small ankles."[87] In a follow-up article that appeared a week later, both Jackson and Sandow were interviewed as well. "This inclination nowadays," Jackson replied, "is to compare alleged perfect men with the old Grecian athletes and Roman gladiators. I think these ancients must have looked better in statues than in the flesh."[88] When asked by the reporter to describe the perfect man, Peter proclaimed: "I consider Highland Scotchmen to come as near to my idea of perfection as any. I have also seen splendidly put-up Sikhs and Hindoos for an athletic turn, while if photographs and pictures are to count for anything the Zulus have some splendid specimens of manhood among them."[89] Jackson's response calls our attention to both the invocations of classical sculpture as a standard of beauty in this period, as well as to the subtlety of the fighter's racial politics. The open debate about beauty, proportion, and the classical ideal in the *Examiner* exceeded the texts of these articles.

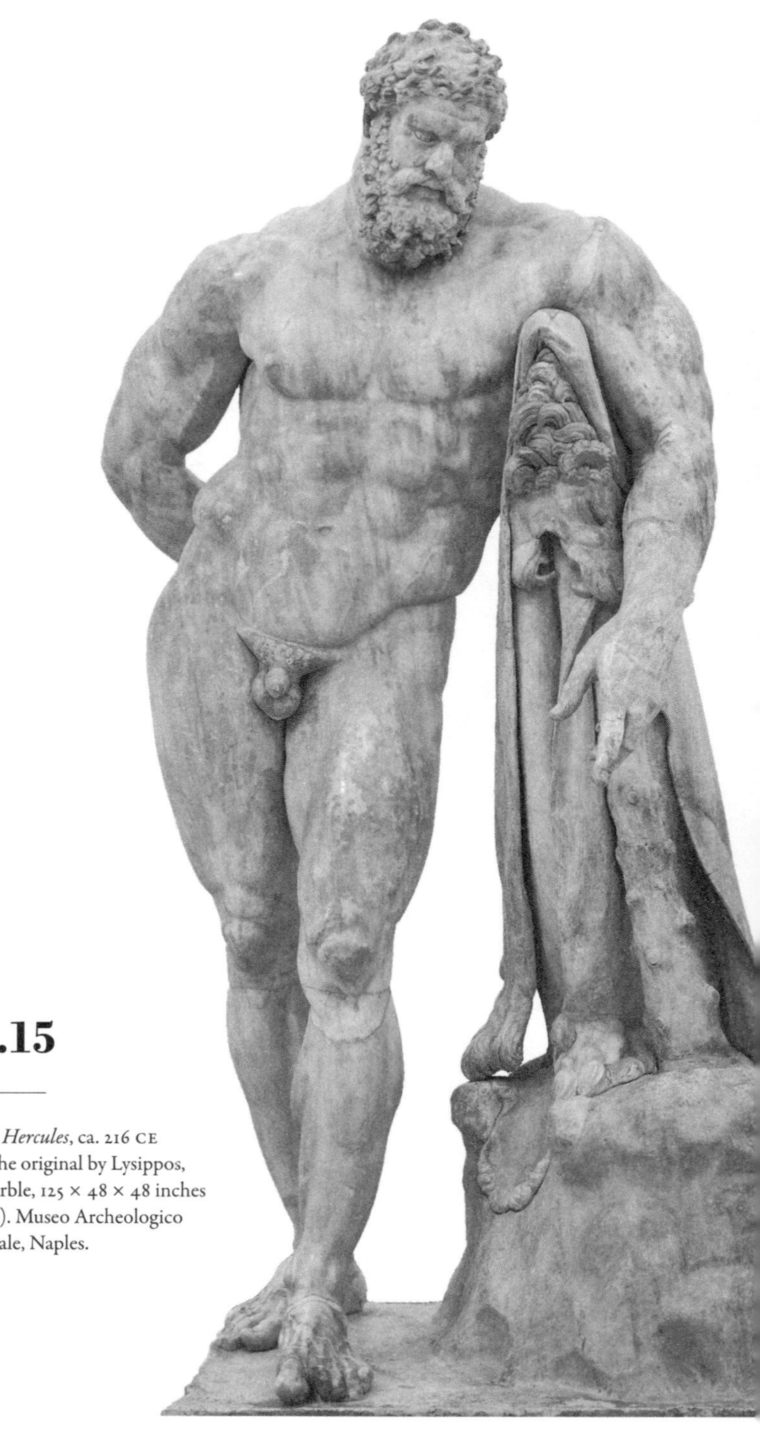

3.15

———

Glykon, *Farnese Hercules*, ca. 216 CE
(reproduced from the original by Lysippos,
4th century BCE). Marble, 125 × 48 × 48 inches
(317 × 123 × 123 cm). Museo Archeologico
Nazionale, Naples.

3.16

———

Napoleon Sarony, "Eugen Sandow," 1893. Photoprint
on cabinet card, 4.25 × 6.5 inches (10.8 × 16.5 cm). Harvard
Theatre Collection, Harvard University.

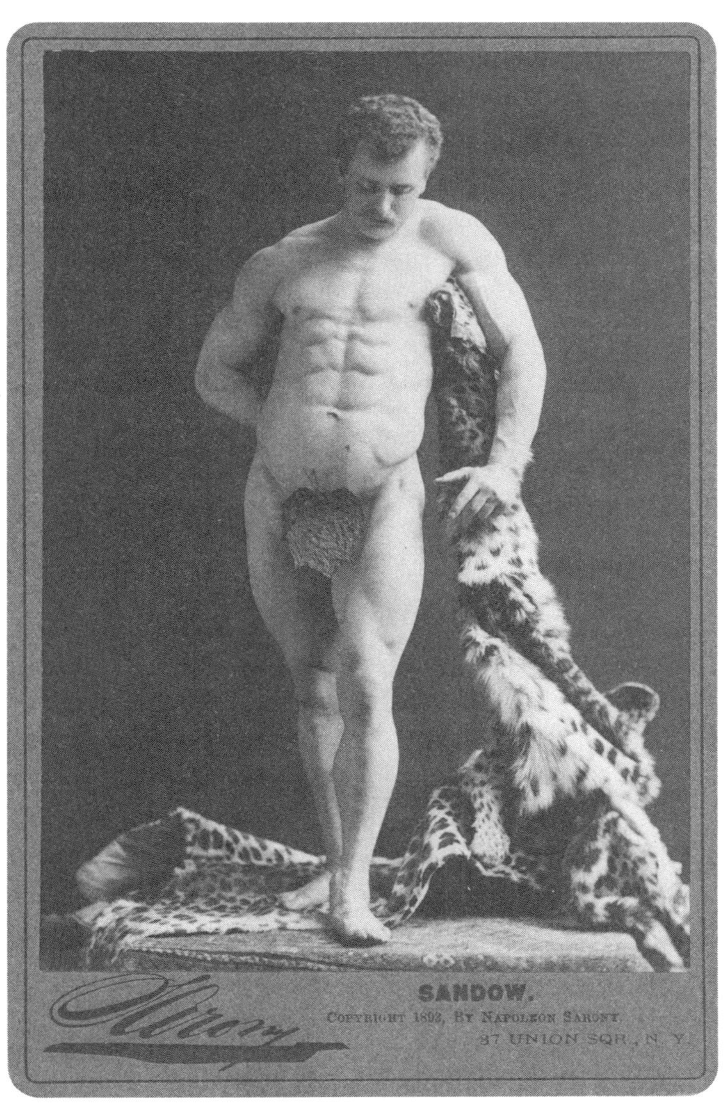

Jackson's image directly engaged with intersecting discourses of classicism and idealism in this period, collapsing the distance between aesthetics and athletics. Just below the article cited above, for example, we see an illustration (the second largest on the page) of Jackson and Sandow flanking the classical statue known as the *Belvedere Apollo* (120–140 BCE); both the statue and the two athletes stand atop small, square pedestals engraved with their names, creating a visual analogy between all three men and perhaps even positioning the two athletes—Sandow and Jackson—as living sculptures (fig. 3.17).[90] Jackson appears on the left. His naked body turns away from us so that we focus on the back of this figure (including his buttocks), while his head appears in profile.[91] Aside from the label on his pedestal, however, Jackson remains difficult to identify based on his positioning in the newspaper. The medium of illustration has even somehow transferred him into whiteness as well. The illustration is based on a photograph, known as *Nubian*, taken in San Francisco in 1889 when Jackson underwent measuring by Dr. Mays.[92] Although the photograph was published (in half-tone) that same year in Australia, it does not surface in the United States until this newspaper article nearly five years later.[93]

To the immediate right of Jackson, we see the *Belvedere Apollo*—a Roman copy of an original bronze statue by Leochares (330–320 BCE); the former has been dated to the middle of the second century CE, and has been held in the collection of the Vatican since at least 1508 (fig. 3.18). The statue was famously celebrated by the German art historian and archaeologist Johann Joachim Winckelmann (1717–1768) as the most sublime example of Greek art. Writing in 1764, Winckelmann claimed: "The statue of Apollo [the *Belvedere Apollo*] is the highest ideal of art among all the works of antiquity that have escaped its destruction. The artist has formed this work completely according to the ideal, and he has taken from the material world only as much as was necessary to carry out his intention and make it visible."[94] Audiences in the nineteenth century eagerly took up Winckelmann's opinion, celebrating this work in marble (as well as many other Roman sculptures) as a perfect example of the human form. Despite the obvious issues with such declarations (this is, after all, an idealized sculpture of a mythological god), men like Sandow directly encouraged the analogy between sculpted ideals and human form via his direct appropriation of classical models. To the right of Apollo we find Sandow in an illustration sourced from an 1894 photograph (fig. 3.19). We see that although the pose of the photograph has been preserved—left arm tucked behind the back and his gaze turned toward the right—the contrapposto stance of the original portrait by Benjamin J. Falk has been lost in its re-presentation here so that Sandow appears, somewhat awkwardly, with both legs extended straight underneath him.

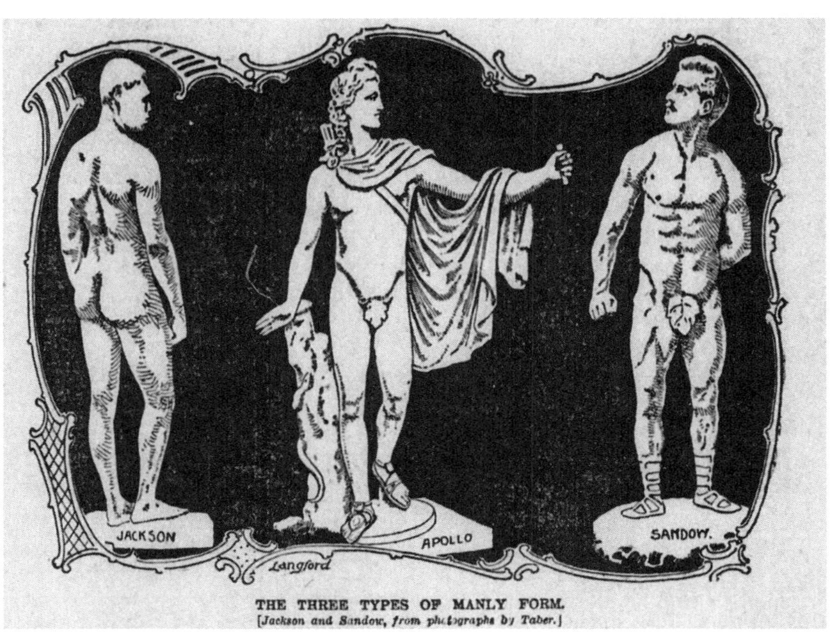

3.17

———

Sam Langford, "The Three Types of Manly Form," 1894. Engraving. Published in the *San Francisco Examiner*, May 20, 1894.

Unknown artist, *Belvedere Apollo*, ca. 120–140 CE (reproduced from the original by Leochares, 4th century BCE). Marble, 88.2 × 46.5 × 30.3 inches (224 × 118 × 77 cm). Vatican Museums, Vatican City.

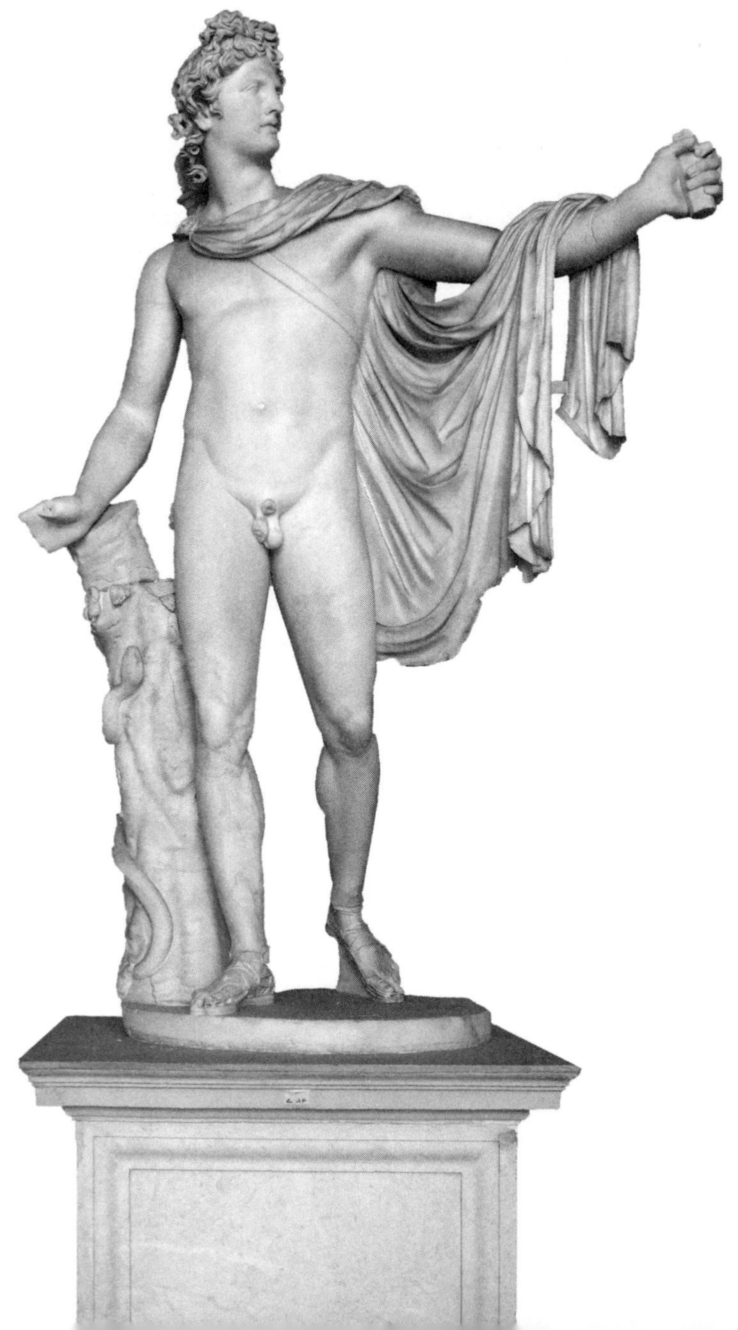

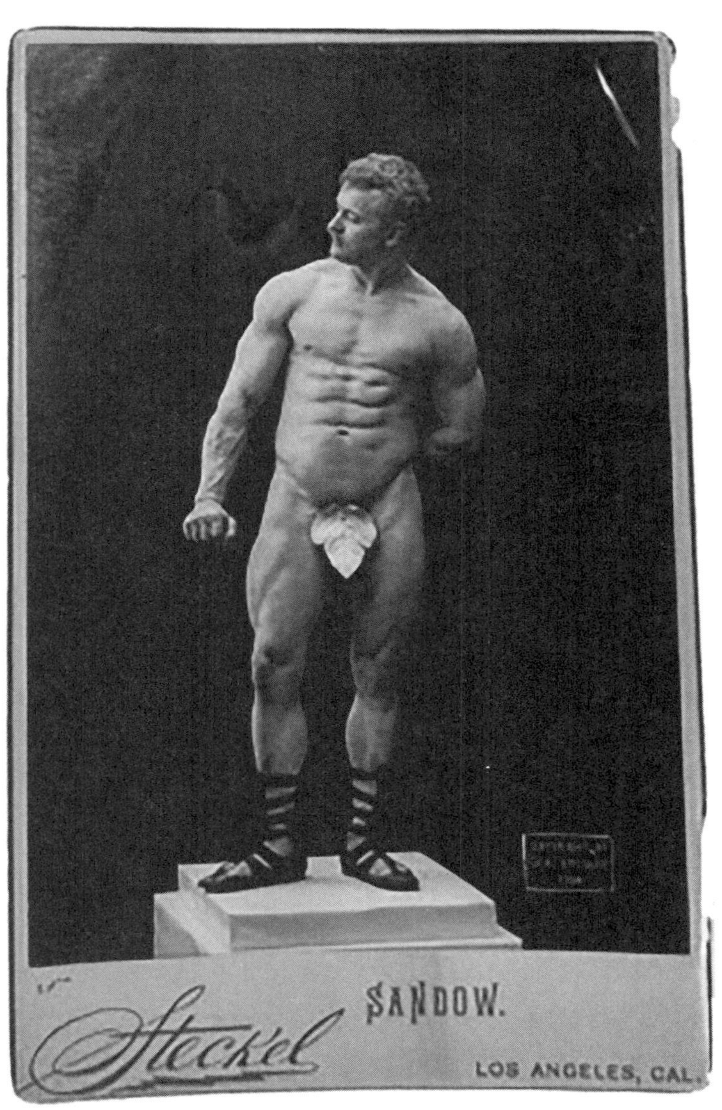

3.19

———

George Steckel, "Eugen Sandow," 1894. Photoprint
on cabinet card, 6.7 × 4.3 inches (17 × 11 cm). Library of
Congress, Washington, DC.

Within the image of Sandow and Jackson flanking the *Belvedere Apollo* we have another example of a mode of Black representation that is less scientific than artistic. Here, the Black body is transformed into a desired body, as a body central to any discussion about beauty, proportion, and the classical ideal. But what does it mean to show a Black man in this lineup of ideal bodies? How might the celebration of Jackson as "nearly perfect" complicate visual histories of Blackness from this period, which overwhelmingly focus on the Black male as either a passive, abject object (e.g., images of slaves or lynching victims) or as an exemplar (e.g., the portraits of Frederick Douglass)? There are other aesthetic and material traditions at play that work to align the figures within these images as objects of desire and potential emulation. In the opening of this chapter, we considered the self-presentation and the self-fashioning of Jackson as a dandy, as a specific product of Victorian culture, and as evidence of the boxer's own desire to be seen.

The Aesthetics of Desire

Nubian was only one of two photographs taken during Jackson's 1889 visit to Taber's studio to be measured by Dr. Mays. Both images were shot by Taber's studio assistant, Frank Davey, who was also known for pictures of athletes and would later move to Stanford. There is no extant copy of the second photograph, which has only been described by Jackson's biographer, Bob Petersen. And while there is also no evidence that this image of the naked Jackson circulated in the United States, we do know that it appeared in 1889 in an Australian newspaper the *Dead Bird*, along with the following caption:

> The portrait which adorns our fifth page will be readily recognized, even without the name on the pedestal, as that of our champion boxer, Peter Jackson, and we venture to assert that never has there been given to the world a more beautiful sample of reproduced living statuary. . . . The marble man should blush to hear himself called a fine shapely man after seeing it, and Australia should be proud to have fed and reared such a model as our champion.[95]

While the editors of the *Dead Bird* attempt to align Jackson with the model of ancient sculpture (i.e., "the pedestal," "the marble"), we cannot deny the overt sexualization taking place here as well. After all, Jackson's naked body is presented to us in passivity; he turns away from the camera, his arms resting by his side rather than raised in defense.

The public appetite for Jackson's body was certainly high. A cartoon published a week after Jackson's photograph appearance in the *Dead Bird* underscores the overt sexualization of the fighter (fig. 3.20). Here we see a woman, coded as a prostitute by her exposed petticoat and loose hair, as she holds the previous week's issue of the paper up to the mirror in a comical attempt to view Jackson's unclothed body from the front. When Jackson returned to Australia from San Francisco in 1890, the photograph was reprinted again in the September 16 issue of *Bird O'Freedom* alongside the caption "The Daddy of Them All." Seven years before the famed "Nubian" photographs of F. Holland Day (see chapter 2), we see the black body both eroticized and exorcized for a white public.[96] The circulation of Jackson's image in these ways forces us to consider the degree to which this image served as an excuse for viewers to gaze upon the male body.

We know already that the bodies of physical culture stars like Eugen Sandow and Bernarr Macfadden were designed with the explicit aim of being seen. The performances of Sandow were explicitly designed to capture the gaze. In his early career he presented himself in a type of *tableau vivant*, moving from the sideshows of European Fairs into the main theater venues of the United States and the United Kingdom.[97] During performances at the Casino Theater (New York), the Tremont Theater (Boston), and the Trocadero Theater (Chicago), Sandow posed on stage as Achilles or the dying Gaul, his chiseled muscles highlighted dramatically by "the white glare of an electric light."[98] In 1893 he performed at the World's Columbian Exposition in Chicago, which led to his becoming a feature act at Koster and Bial's Music Hall in New York City the next year. Sandow was even filmed in 1894 by Edison Studios, using the kinescope. Throughout the short film we see Sandow against a black background, quickly proceeding through a series of poses while wearing only a pair of briefs. Photographs of Sandow appeared as early as 1893—as cabinet cards sold via mainstream portraiture studios in the United States and Britain, as well as within the pages of his periodical, *Sandow's Magazine of Physical Culture*, founded in 1898—and helped to extend his viewership to new audiences. The reliance on a classicizing rhetoric in these cases performed a double function, as both a template for the "ideal body" but also a mechanism for developing the viewer.

The *tableaux vivant*, the photographs, the films—all were excuses for male viewers to gaze upon the male body during a moment of shifting sexual politics. More specifically, at the close of the nineteenth century, as homosexuality was increasingly criminalized, images of men with erotic potential needed to occupy a space of visibility and invisibility. By rendering their erotic status questionable, these images could be easily distributed and purchased by their male clientele. Historian Michael Anton Budd has argued, for example, that the cultural obsession with health culture provided the format for this hidden/

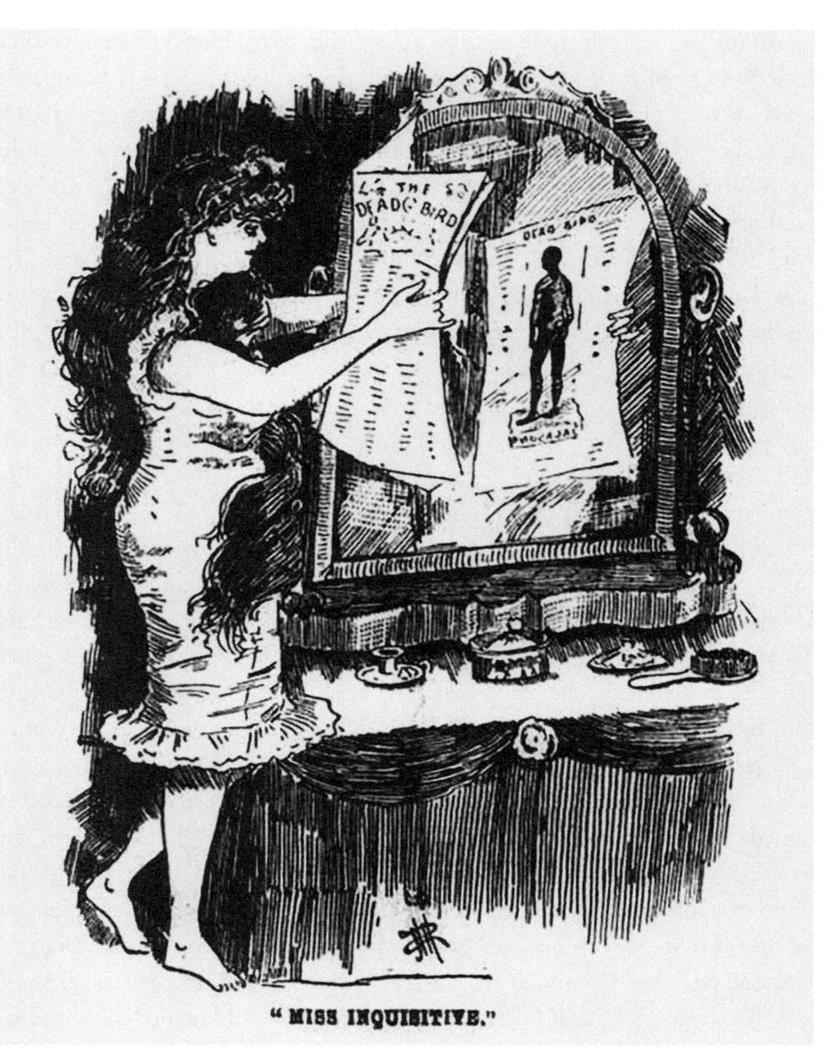

3.20

———

"Miss Inquisitive," 1893. Unknown artist, pen and ink drawing.
Published in the *Dead Bird*, July 27, 1893.

visible distribution, as publishers created a print environment where nudity was admirable, and viewers were encouraged to erotically identify and compare themselves with depicted athletes.[99] Sandow was a key figure in the promotion of such images. In the initial issues of *Sandow's Magazine of Physical Culture*, Sandow organized a "great competition" for which he invited readers to submit photographs of themselves shirtless from the waist up—that is, framing the development of the male body as a participatory process.[100] This was certainly the case for Sandow's public performances, when he would take the hands of male journalists and rub them over his muscles.[101]

We must consider here that these image of naked athletes—whether in live performance or via the multiple photographs that circulated in the Gilded Age—did more than simply record the athletic form. Such representations allowed for these bodies to be seen and for viewers of these images to internalize these bodies as objects of their own desires. In this way I am considering these photographs specifically in psychoanalytic terms—as a specific expression of the indeterminate relationship between the gaze, the subject, and the apparatus of the camera. That is, these images do not reveal as much about the figures represented as they do about the viewers that look at them. We are invited to consider desire as well as the social and aesthetic norms that made such images (and indeed such viewership) possible. In the case of Jackson an overt reliance on Anglophilia and an obsession with neoclassicism (including its promotion of whiteness) allowed for the athlete to circumvent the explicit limitations of Blackness in the American context, and to be billed by his promoter as "the whitest man who ever entered the ring."[102]

We might be tempted to consider Jackson's body as part of a much wider and international visual program that classicized, sexualized, and eroticized the Black body. That is, the body of the heavyweight boxer was just one example of how the Black body's objectification and sexualization functioned to mitigate its threat to the white public after the Civil War via print media. Jackson's nakedness (and comparison with sculpture) is perhaps shocking to the contemporary viewer, who may not have expected a naked Black man to appear in this way within popular culture. We may at first interpret Jackson as just one of many Black men locked into a position of passivity via the photograph, transformed from an active subject to a static object of the anthropological gaze. But instead, throughout this chapter, I have asked us to consider the agency and the subjectivity of Peter Jackson—both desired and desiring. In Jackson's case the body of the Black heavyweight boxer—perhaps the most threatening of them all—was consciously and consistently shaped by discourses of dandyism and neoclassicism, each of which underscores the performative nature of race and of masculinity. And in this way, I premise my understanding of Black masculinity on the theories of Kobena Mercer, who has argued: "Black masculinity is not merely a social identity in crisis. It is also a key site of ideological representation."[103]

The presentation of Jackson as a dandy or a neoclassical sculpture, as an ideal body, does not so much reveal Blackness as it *is* but as it is *seen*. That is, the gaze of the viewer is transformed from one of opposition to one of desire. And in this way these images are what literary and cultural theorist W. J. T. Mitchell calls "metapictures"—"a representation of a representation." The metapicture acknowledges the role of the image not as a translation (e.g., from word to image) but as a "scene of interpretation."[104] That is, these photographs do not picture Jackson; instead, they picture the nation picturing Black men. We see throughout this chapter the tensions between how Jackson *wants* to be pictured and how he *is* pictured. We see a visualization of the ambivalence articulated by Homi Bhabha, who sought to explain how the colonizer psychically portrays the colonizer. In Bhabha's terms, race is structured by ambivalence; Black subjects are feared and desired simultaneously.[105] The oscillation between these positions is a defining quality of colonialist stereotypes, allowing us to recognize the fundamental paradox at play in representations of Black men. On the one hand we have Jackson's image, which reveals circuits of desire for the Black male body that we do not often allow ourselves to discuss; on the other, we have the pathologized, dehumanized, and objectified Black male body that dominates our narratives of Black representation in the late nineteenth century. Peter Jackson casts shadows onto the present, onto the problematics of the Black athlete today—both admired and vilified.

Conclusion

Most stories of Peter Jackson end with a turn toward this theater career. Jackson began acting in February 1893, encouraged by the promoter Parson Davies to take on the role of "Uncle Tom" for an extended run at Stockwell's Theater in San Francisco.[106] Possibly unaware of the racist undertones of the play, Jackson continued to play this role on a thirty-four-week promotional tour through Michigan, Ohio, Pennsylvania, New York, Maine, and Massachusetts, ending in Boston.[107] Susan F. Clark—to date the only scholar to examine Jackson's dramatic career turn—has argued that the move to the stage for Jackson ("billed as the most famous colored man in America") was caught up in Davies's attempts to secure fights for a Black fighter.[108] "If the public could be convinced that Jackson was not a threat to white society," Clark writes, "the racial barriers in his path to the ring might be lifted. What better way to show the white establishment that Jackson was a man who would cause no trouble than to identify him with the very same qualities that distinguished Uncle Tom?"[109] Having Jackson whipped every night on stage before an audience would surely have mitigated his perceived threat to white society. The challenge, however, was finding a way for Jackson to play Uncle Tom without losing his credibility as a heavyweight contender. This conundrum was solved with the insertion of a short, three-round sparring exhibition between the first and second acts of the play. Jackson's performance as Uncle Tom was characterized by a tension between the character and the man. He had reportedly few acting abilities, but the audience was nevertheless always aware they were watching Jackson, the fighter.

Peter Jackson was forced into a theater career because the color line foreclosed other opportunities. He was never able to earn a US heavyweight title or even to secure a championship fight. In 1898, an out-of-shape Jackson was finally granted the opportunity with a match against Jim Jeffries in San Francisco, but he failed to make it past the third round. He returned to Australia in 1900 and died the next year (reportedly from tuberculosis) at the age of forty.[110] But the significance of Peter Jackson exceeds his story as a fighter. Through his repeated representation in popular media, his cultivation of a gentlemanly persona, and his associations with nineteenth-century aesthetic standards, this Black boxer provided an alternative to the stereotypes of Blackness. As James Weldon Johnson observes in his 1991 book *Black Manhattan*, "Peter Jackson was the first example in the United States of a man acting upon the assumption that he could be a prizefighter and at the same time a cultured gentleman."[111] And this is the story I want to preserve—the story of a gentleman, a dandy, a fan of Tennyson and Shakespeare, who spoke in a lilting accent and took every opportunity to assert his individual subjectivity.

Jackson lays in rest today inside the Toowong Cemetery, Queensland, Australia, beneath a stone memorial with a marble lion perched on top.[112] On the front of the eight-foot-high plinth we see a large bust of Jackson carved in relief in white stone. He faces outward with his chin pointed gently downward, as if to engage his viewer below. He is dressed smartly in a collared shirt with ascot tie; we see just enough of his jacket to note its orderly buttons and the pluming fabric of his pocket square. We do not see Jackson here as a fighter or as Uncle Tom. We are reminded by the single-line inscription that runs along the bottom: "THIS WAS A MAN."[113]

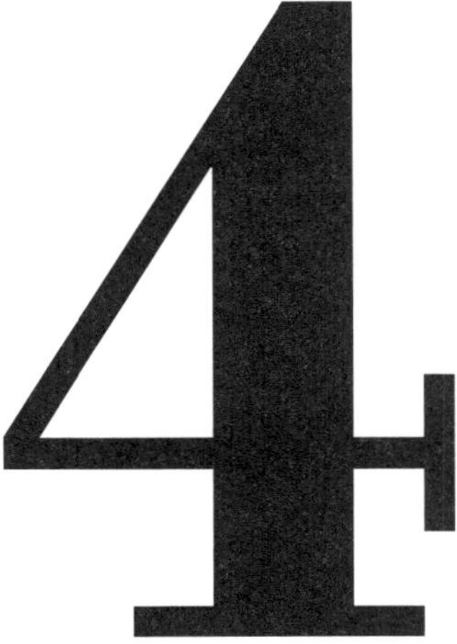

Pretend for just a moment that we are strolling through a gallery when we come upon a painting of a boxing match (plate 4). What do we say to one another? Do you invite me to tell you about prizefighting, encouraging me to talk about the heightened racial and class tensions raging at the turn of the twentieth century? Or do I ask you to tell me the story of Jack Johnson, the "Galveston Giant" who became the first Black champion of the world? At some point we might look closely at the broad strokes of thick paint on the surface, observing the rich, dark brown of the figure on the right and how the arm, stretched upward, is rendered as a sketchy form. We see how the man on the left strains to look up, his face covered in blood and reddened from exertion. On the left of the composition, we notice two similarly red-faced men, who insert themselves between the ropes of the ring, yelling to the fighter before them. Our gaze may drift downward to meet the faces of the bustling crowd. Often no more than a swirl of pigment, these grotesque and distorted visages recede beyond our vision into the darkness beyond; their accompanying bodies squeeze into the very edges of the frame, suggesting the endless expanse of the noisy crowd.

I am interested in "the stories that we compose about paintings."[1] This chapter takes up the story of George Bellows's 1909 painting *Both Members of This Club* and what it might tell us about the relationship between the fine arts, sports, and race in the early twentieth century. Among Bellows's most celebrated works, and indeed one of the most recognizable examples of early twentieth-century American painting, histories of American art often position this work as a transparent example of the artist's challenges to the aesthetic and urban ideals of art in the United States circa 1900. We might, for example, read Bellows's paintings of boxing matches as akin to his realist portrayals of children playing in the East River (*River Rats*, 1906), the dramatic excavations to build Pennsylvania Station (*Pennsylvania Station Excavation*, 1907), the cramped tenements and alleys of lower Manhattan teeming with the bodies of the working class (*Cliff Dwellers*, 1913)—that is, as concerned with providing us an unvarnished view of the city and its inhabitants. The paintings of the Ashcan school garnered critical acclaim for their supposed unfiltered views of city life. We will see, however, that the construction of the "real" was always, already conditioned by race.

This chapter explores how fine art, and specifically painting, of the Gilded Age played a critical role in the pathologization of Blackness. First, we will examine Bellows's embeddedness within artistic discourses of "the real." We will consider how gender specifically figures within discourses of American realism. We look also to the intersecting social expectations around manhood and manliness that provoked Bellows's choice of sports as a subject for both illustrations and paintings in this period. The choice of boxing reveals the artist's engagement with constructions (and articulations) of masculinity. And finally, while *Both Members of This Club* is often celebrated by historians as a socially progressive statement on racial integration, this chapter presents an alternative reading. More specifically, I would like to explore the fear of the Other that materializes in this period and that we see reflected to us in the artist's inclusion of a Black boxer in *Both Members of This Club*. To do so would mean exploring the social dimension of abjection—that is, considering the consequences of the discovery that the "object of the Other" does not come from within the self but from an external force.

Bellows first took up boxing as a subject in 1907 with the large canvas *Club Night* (plate 5); this was followed by two other boxing pictures, *Stag at Sharkey's* (fig. 4.1) and *Both Members of This Club*, both painted in 1909. As with his pervious works, early critics praised the rough brushwork and heavy impasto that characterized these scenes, underscoring the rough nature of the lower classes that were his focus. Responding to *Club Night*, the critic James Huneker's enthusiasm for Bellows's canvas is palpable: "It is a brutal boxing match (surely four-ounce gloves) about to degenerate into a clinch and a mixup [*sic*]. One pugilist is lunging in the act of delivering a 'soaker' to his adversary. You hear, you feel the dull impact of the blow. A sodden set of brute 'mugs' ring the circle—upon the platform the light is concentrated. It is not pleasing this, or edifying but for the artist and amateur the play of muscles and the various attitudes and gestures are absolutely exciting."[2] Bellows's ability to capture the energy of the fight in his loosely painted strokes provided genteel audiences a view into the illicit underworld of the prizefight.[3] Perhaps more important, his choice of subject and style in these new paintings were received as evidence of the artist's own "manliness." *Both Members of This Club* even received a double-page spread in *Harper's Weekly*.[4]

In the century that has passed between then and now, historians and critics have continued the narrative of Bellows as a painter of raw views of urban life and a symbol of emerging discourses around manhood at the turn of the twentieth century. Moreover, Bellows's painting of an interracial boxing match has been specifically praised for its progressive views around racial equality, its mobilization of a classical bodily ideal, and its "realism." But I would like to tell a different story about this painting, one that considers the wider implications of sporting imagery in fine art and popular visual culture, one that highlights the complications of the artist's direct engagement with race, and one that argues for this painting as an illustration of a wider anxiety surrounding Black bodies in the public sphere. I want to show how debates around masculinity—that is, the dominant frame of analysis for Bellows's boxing paintings from the very start—are always racialized as well. Further, I want to show how widespread racial tensions following Emancipation and Reconstruction in the United States played out between white and Black opponents, both in the boxing ring and in the frame.

Black Boxers and White Anxiety

The inclusion of Black *and* white bodies in *Both Members of This Club* reflects the anxiety among early twentieth-century audiences around not only masculinity, but also the fragility of racial superiority. This was an anxiety made real in Bellows's moment through the Black heavyweight boxer Jack Johnson (1878–1946). Born in the port-city of Galveston in Texas, Johnson was just twenty-two years old when his hometown was ravaged by a hurricane, which

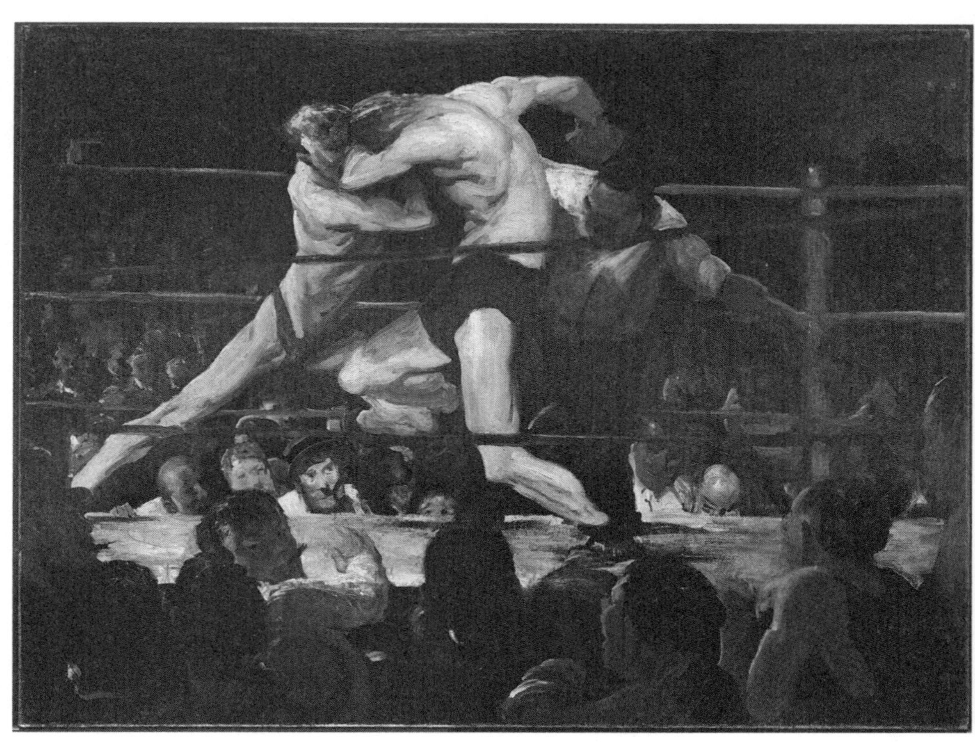

4.1

———

George Bellows, *Stag at Sharkey's*, 1909.
Oil on canvas, 48.25 × 36.25 inches (122.6 × 92 cm).
Cleveland Museum of Art.

killed more than six thousand people and destroyed more than two-thirds of the buildings. Jack's father, Henry, lost everything he owned. At the time the hurricane struck, Jack was living with his parents and fighting professionally at several clubs in the Galveston area, despite the somewhat ambiguous legal status of the sport.[5] Before leaving his hometown for good, Johnson traveled to St. Louis to participate in "scientific exhibitions" of pugilism and fought an additional eight matches back in Galveston (fig. 4.2). By February 1901 Johnson had found his way into a match against the American heavyweight Joe Choynski (1868–1943). Although he was unsuccessful, the men's arrest after the fight, followed by a twenty-four-day jail stay, brought Johnson into the public consciousness. Soon after their release, Johnson left Galveston and traveled to the West Coast, arriving in Bakersfield, California, in the fall of 1901.[6]

Despite his current fame and recognition—as the first African American world heavyweight boxing champion—Johnson's early career was unremarkable. According to one biography, when he arrived in California, "he was known only by word of mouth—generally his own—and attracted little attention."[7] His defeat of Jack Jeffries (brother of Jim) in May 1902 made the California sporting press take some notice, but Johnson's performance was interpreted by the white press as sleepy and lazy. He was "'a good-natured Black animal' . . . no different from the stereotypical slave—lazy, powerful, happy, carefree."[8] Johnson was compared with a "big cat," but posed no immediate threat. He appeared in the press "as a coal-Black, thicker lipped minstrel."[9] Around this time, Johnson also began to publicly goad the heavyweight champion Jim Jeffries, even though Johnson himself had never fought in a championship match.[10] He was helped along by sporting editors, who began running updates on Johnson's pursuit of Jeffries, attempting to lure the champion into a fight. In January 1904 the editor of the *National Police Gazette* opined that Jeffries's avoidance was based on his lack of physical fitness, writing, "Jeffries weighs 247 pounds and is rapidly increasing."[11] A few months later another article titled "Johnson, Negro Champion, Camps on Jeffries's Trail," called out Jeffries for his sudden change in attitude toward interracial fights, given his history of fighting Peter Jackson (the subject of chapter 3), Hank Griffin (1870–1911), and the "King of the Battle Royal," Bob Armstrong (1873–1911).[12] A month later, the *Gazette* got even more aggressive in their teasing of Jeffries, writing, "Taken, on the whole, the color line is looked upon as a pretty shallow excuse for a good fighter to use in side-tracking a good match . . . Jeffries . . . lays himself open to an accusation of cowardice in refusing the meet the husky Negro."[13] Nevertheless, Johnson's baiting of Jeffries was unsuccessful. He traveled east—Philadelphia, Boston, Chicago—for matches over the next few years, and the press in Philadelphia

"Jack Johnson," 1900. Digital file from original
glass negative, 7 × 5 inches (17.8 × 12.7 cm). Bain News
Service. Library of Congress, Washington, DC.

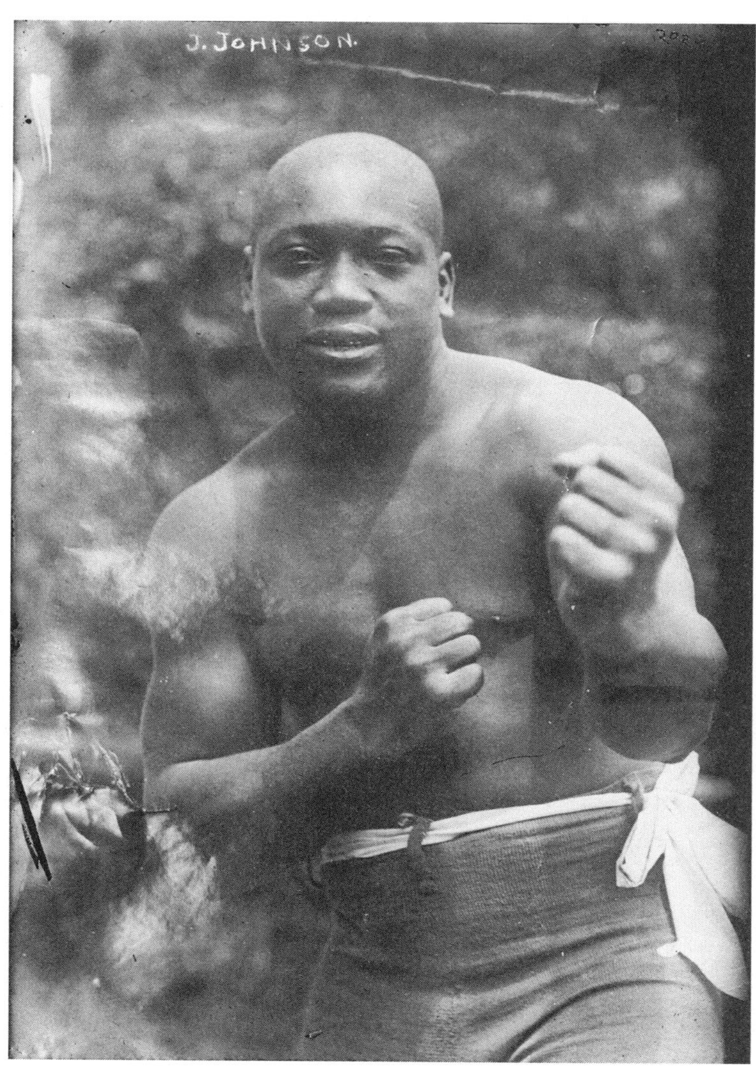

took notice, particularly after Johnson knocked out two heavyweights in a span of ten days in 1905.

As Johnson's victories multiplied in the first few years of the twentieth century, the fears of white audiences began to shift the media coverage toward more racist stories and cartoon caricatures. As he prepared for a rematch against Sam McVey (1884–1921, whom Johnson had bested in February) in Los Angeles, an offensive "biography" of Johnson was published in October 1903. Bearing the title "Texas Watermelon Pickaninny Makes Big Dents," it began:

> About twenty-five years ago one bright, sunny southern morning there was a dull, solid sounding thud heard and felt throughout the state of Texas. A close examination of the face of the commonwealth revealed a large dent on the backbay shore of Galveston which was finally determined to be the place there the stork had severed connection with a wooly little Black pickaninny. The baby set up the characteristic roar and its mammy took care of it.[14]

Such reports—published in the *Los Angeles Times* no less—were indicative not only of the stereotypes circulating about Black people in the early twentieth century, but also of the concerted efforts made by the press to diminish the perceived threat of Jackson specifically. Standing at six feet and weighing in at 200 pounds, Jackson's physical dominance must have been terrifying. But this is not a unique case. The book *Knuckle and Gloves*, published in 1922, describes many of the stereotypical opinions held by the mainstream public concerning Black fighters. Similarly relying on stereotypes of Black men as childlike, ignorant, immune to pain, and primitive, the author Bohun Lynch recounted:

> It was recognized from the first that the African negro and his descendants in the West Indies and America were harder-headed than white men, less sensitive about the face and jaw; most Black boxers can take without pain or trouble a smashing which would cause the collapse of a white man. . . . Niggers are usually children in temperament, with the children's bad points as well as their good ones. The Black man's head is easily turned, and when his personal and physical success over a white man is manifest he generally behaves like the worst kind of spoiled child. In extreme cases, his overwhelming sense of triumph knows no bounds at all, and he turns from a primitive man into a fiend.[15]

Here Lynch deftly regurgitates nearly every myth and stereotype about Blackness to argue that any matchup between Black and white would be a disadvantageous one for the white man, obviously through no fault of his own.

Widespread racial tensions following Emancipation and Reconstruction often played out in the boxing ring between white and Black opponents. One surprising consequence of integrated boxing matches was a public challenge to white supremacy. Victories by African American boxers contradicted much of the racist pseudoscience popular at the turn of the twentieth century, which contended that Blacks were both mentally and physically inferior to whites, too lazy and undisciplined to be successful athletes. As the historian Louis Moore has written in his study of this period, "the toughness, discipline, courage, physicality, and manly aggression white boxers displayed were thought to be inherent racial qualities that proved white authority over the rest of the world."[16] However, the increasing defeat of white opponents by Black fighters at the turn of the twentieth century, proved a challenge to white arrogance. Moore cites the example of the "colored" heavyweight champion Sam Langford (1886–1956), who defeated every white fighter he faced, save one, between 1902 and 1912. By 1910, the perception of Langford was such a threat to whiteness that he was banned from fighting a white opponent in Pittsburgh by the chief of police.[17]

Following the rise of Jack Johnson, Langford's threat was particularly acute, and led many cities and states to ban interracial boxing. White audiences naturally began to worry about Black domination in other spheres. "If the negro is capable of developing such prowess in divisions of boxing," wrote one reporter in the late nineteenth century, "what is going to stop him from making the same progress in the heavier ranks?"[18] The publicity leading up to Johnson's match with Jim Jeffries reflected a wider anxiety around the threat to white supremacy that a Johnson victory on US soil would reveal. Johnson's ultimate defeat of Jeffries in 1910 led to widespread, violent conflicts across the country—in Pittsburgh, Atlanta, Wilmington, Columbus, and New York, among other cities. The film of the fight, which played in cities across the United States, was ultimately banned.[19] As the *San Francisco Examiner* warned, it would be detrimental for white women and children to see "members of their own race beaten into a physical disability by a gigantic negro."[20] But this is just one component of a complicated story. What is most interesting to this study is how popular representation was deployed in the media to temper white anxieties—that is, how the explicit and consistent caricaturizing of Black fighters, like Johnson (and others after him), not only provided an outlet for white voyeurism but also a way to degrade the Black body, to mark it as abject.

Over the first years of his fight career, Johnson's public image became as paramount as his fighting capacity. After his final defeat of Sam McVey (1884–1921), who unsuccessfully challenged Johnson for the World Colored Heavyweight title three times over ten months in 1903–1904, the media coverage of Johnson greatly expanded. Newspapers began to cover Johnson's movements inside and outside the boxing ring; he received (according to one biographer) "the kind of celebrity coverage that had always been reserved for white fighters," reporting on everything from his fashion choices to his domestic life.[21] Indeed, we might claim that he was the most famous Black man of the early twentieth century.[22] Johnson was well-known for his casual attitude and flamboyant attire in the ring (he wore pink pajamas to his fight against Jack Jeffries). He publicly goaded white fighters, daring them to meet him in the ring. He was known for his extravagant spending, staying at luxury hotels and at times even reserving an extra room for his expansive wardrobe. An article in the *Los Angeles Times* in 1903 made special note of the "orderly creases" of Johnson's trousers, which were accompanied by a "modish" shirt with high collar, "a scarf of ermine silk, knotted with a perfect neatness and adorned by a diamond pin," suede gloves, a ring with a "flashing gem of rather more karats than one," and even a walking cane.[23] Johnson openly discussed his love for fine food, motor cars, and, most controversially, white women.

Historians have thoroughly documented the media's positioning of Johnson as an uncivilized savage, particularly as he challenged the social customs of Jim Crow America.[24] When Johnson entered the ring for his 1910 match against Jim Jeffries, the band played "All Coons Look Alike to Me." One particularly colorful press article described Johnson's "courage as white as his skin is Black."[25] And although we may think of Johnson as the best, and perhaps even the first, example of the dehumanization of Black fighters, the media coverage in Johnson's early career was more likely to present him as a docile Sambo with nappy hair, a small head, large eyes, and an impossibly wide mouth with pronounced lips.[26] Johnson was parodied in the popular press, where cartoonists often presented him in typical Sambo style. In one cartoon, published on the front page of the *St. Louis Dispatch* on July 5, 1910—the day following his triumph over Jim Jeffries in a fight billed as "the Battle of the Races"—we see a caricature in boxing gloves and shorts labeled "Johnson" chomping on an excessively large piece of watermelon (whose seeds spell out "Jeff"), his face distorted into a classic Sambo look (fig. 4.3). Johnson's reduction to a caricature countered very real anxieties around his physical dominance. Redrawn as a smiling buffoon, the threat he posed to white masculinity certainly must have felt reduced.

Alternative constructions of the Black fighter—that of the violent savage, or animal—were similarly used to manage the threat to white dominance. The historian Louis Moore has convincingly argued that the comparison of Black boxers, such as Sam McVey and Hank Griffin, with horses was a way to "fetishize over the Black body while denying Black men humanity and equality."[27]

4.3

Robert Minor, "Cutting a Watermelon," 1911.
Pen and ink drawing. Published in the *St. Louis Dispatch*, July 5, 1910.

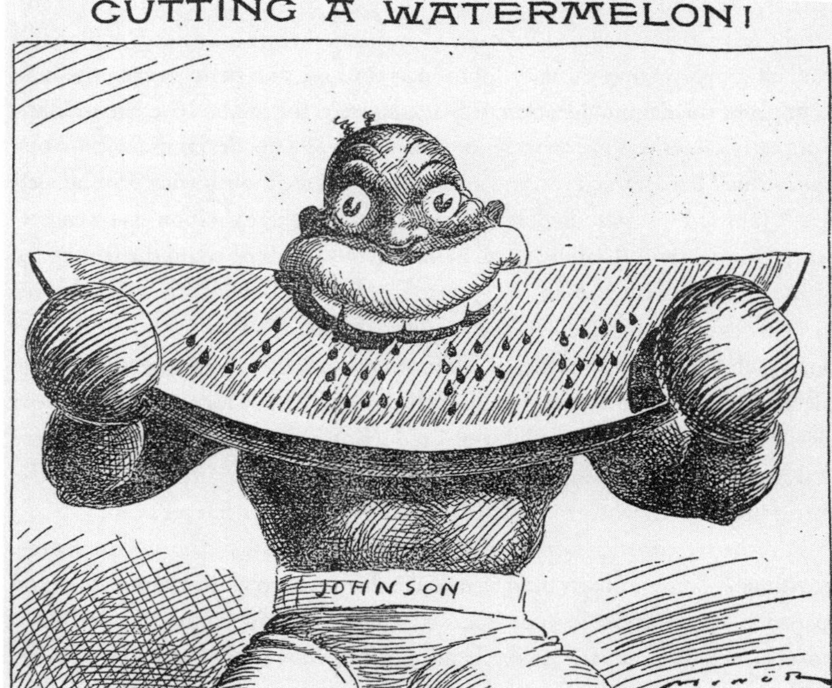

Due to Johnson's cautious fighting style and slighter physical proportions (at just 180 pounds), Moore contends that whites were more likely to target the heavyweight Sam McVey. The media coverage of McVey, in fact, made a concerted effort to create an image of him as the Black savage, focusing on his skin, hair, and aggressive countenance, which, according to one reporter, "would scare back the rising moon."[28] Tip Wright, a writer for the *Tacoma Times*, took his description of McVey to new limits, questioning even the humanity of the heavyweight:

> Imagine a great, big overgrown chunk of black humanity, of the type that sometimes gives credence to Darwin's theory that we are creatures of evolution, with a small, cone line bean, powerful torso and ape-like arms, possessed with little intelligence and as ignorant as a freshly landed Slav immigrant.[29]

In just a few lines, Wright positions McVey on the lowest rung of evolution—an ignorant ape that must be not only rejected, but perhaps even cast out of the wider social order.

Looking at a photograph of McVey from 1910 published by the Bain News Service, one of the earliest news picture agencies in the United States (founded in 1898), we can see how even McVey's image was manipulated to fit these narratives (fig. 4.4). The photographer has positioned the camera so that the lens is pointed upward at McVey, who glares downward at it, and produces a distorted view of the figure. The horizon line of the image is formed by the seam between the wall and the ceiling that runs in an upward diagonal—right to left—behind McVey's head. This positioning leaves the setting of the scene partially obscured; we can see only what appears to be a collection of pennants and photographs tacked to a wall, the partial outline of a window, and a framed support for a punching bag. But we do not see the punching bag itself, or in fact, many overt indicators of McVey's profession. He is not sparring, or even shown in the standard boxing costume (torso exposed). Instead, he is placed as a singular aggressor without context. With his arms folded in front and his stare cast at the camera's lens below him, McVey appears as a larger-than-life bogeyman. Images of both Johnson and McVey demonstrate that visual representations of Black boxers not only gave early audiences a glimpse into prizefighting, but they also (through manipulations of their visual representations) shored up contemporary constructions of the (white) masculine ideal. As we will see throughout this chapter, fine art from this period reinforced such ideals as well.

4.4

———

"Sam McVey," ca. 1910–15. Digital file from original
glass negative, 5 × 7 inches (12.7 × 17.8 cm). Bain News
Service. Library of Congress, Washington, DC.

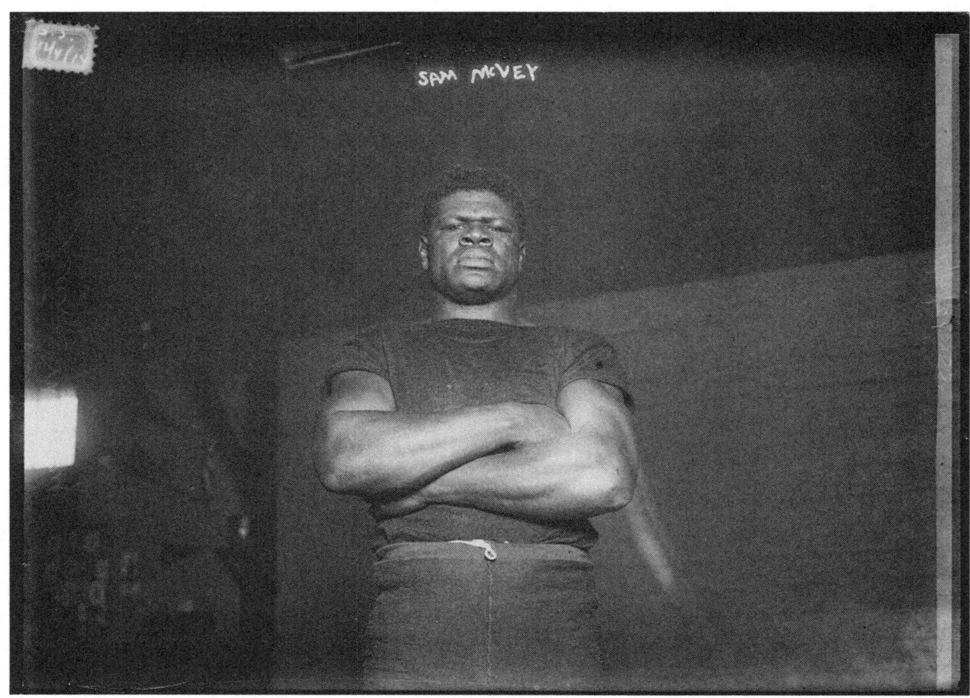

George Bellows and the Pursuit of the "Real"

Like many men at the turn of the twentieth century, George Wesley Bellows, born in Ohio in summer 1882, was obsessed with sports. As a child in Columbus, he was frequently harassed by fellow classmates for his interest in art—classified by them as "sissy stuff." For many of his contemporaries, Bellows was not accepted as a "real man," and he consistently struggled to fit in.[30] The only thing that mattered to his classmates was sports (especially baseball, which was quickly becoming the national game), but the young Bellows was devastatingly uncoordinated. After several years of intense dedication, however, he thrived as a star athlete in both baseball and basketball, winning over his former bullies, who later became lifelong friends.[31] Nevertheless, Bellows was subject to societal pressures around gender norms, and remained ambivalent about his artistic pursuits until his college years.

After two years at Ohio State University, Bellows left Columbus to pursue an artistic education in New York in 1904. He immediately moved into the YMCA (Young Men's Christian Association), which was both inexpensive and close to the school he would attend; it also provided the young Bellows with access to the sporting activities he enjoyed, and satisfied his parents' desire for a morally sound environment.[32] Bellows enrolled at the nearby New York School of Art, whose faculty would have a profound influence on the young artist. William Merritt Chase (1849–1916), a leading American impressionist painter, emphasized technical skill and design sense over sentimental themes; Robert Henri (1865–1929), another faculty member who began teaching at the school in 1902, was similarly interested in formal technique, and encouraged students to celebrate the variety of life and humanity.

A fellow Midwesterner, Henri was himself influenced by the Dutch and Spanish masters, who sought to portray the mundane, even the ugly, aspects of life. He endeavored to portray everyday subjects, like the French impressionists who preceded him. According to American impressionist specialist James M. Keny, Henri felt "that the Impressionists' preoccupation with the serene, composed, and orderly existence of their bourgeois subjects missed much of what is truly important. The important aspects of life were more faithfully revealed through careful observation that ignored the accidental distinctions of class, social privilege, or setting."[33] In place of the boating party or sidewalk cafe, painters like Henri showed the neighborhood bar and the alley.

Henri exhibited works with several other New York painters who similarly focused on urban scenes—the smokestacks, the laundry lines, the crowded alleyways, and even the ashcans of the working class. Known collectively as the

Ashcan school, Henri along with William Glackens (1870–1938), George Luks (1867–1933), John Sloan (1871–1951) and Everett Shin (1876–1953) rebelled against the standards for American art set by the National Academy of Design, which organized annual exhibitions, and bore the consequences. In the winter exhibition of 1906, for example, only paintings by John Sloan (hung conveniently out of view, almost near the ceiling) and Henri were selected. The following year, Henri, disappointed by the jury's evaluation of his three submissions, pulled out of the exhibition and contacted the press. "Robert Henri's withdrawal," reported *American Art News*, "caused a stir in art circles. At a meeting of the jury, of which Mr. Henri was a member, some spirited remarks were made by him . . . that . . . a majority of the judges were not inclined to yield to any innovations in art."[34] Henri publicly and frequently denounced the National Academy's lack of appreciation for original approaches to making art. He apparently convinced a writer at *Harper's Weekly*, who wrote of the Ashcan school in April 1907:

> They seek what is significant, what is real, no matter whither the quest may lead them. . . . There is virility in what they have done, but virility without loss of tenderness; a manly strength that worships beauty, an art that is conceivably a true echo of the significant American life about them.[35]

These comments reflect what many critics at the time identified as the great promise of the Ashcan school's sensibility and approach to making art, as well as its almost immediate associations with manhood. Critic James Huneker, for example, called Henri "the Manet of Manhattan."[36] Following their very public conflicts with the National Academy, Henri and his colleagues organized an exhibition of their own, which opened in February 1908 at the Macbeth Galleries on Fifth Avenue. The group of eight painters were from that point onward known as "the Eight."[37]

Although Bellows was never an official member of Henri's group, he shared their taste for rebellion. Once in New York, Bellows immediately connected with Henri. "It was in the male-oriented atmosphere of the New York School, and with the support of Robert Henri, that Bellows," according to art historian Marianne Doezema, "found a way to reconcile the two seemingly disconnected worlds of his life, the world of artistic sensibility and the world of hard-driving, aggressive action."[38] Robert Henri provided Bellows with a model of a man who could be sensitive and still belong to the cult of manhood; he often told stories of his cowboy past to Bellows as a student. "In Henri's classroom," writes Doezema, "Bellows learned not only to translate his extroverted manner into a free-wheeling, bravura painting technique, but also that 'the world of painting...was definitely a man's world.'"[39]

With Henri's approval, Bellows exhibited a sympathetic study of immigrant street children at the Society of American Artists in spring 1906 titled *Kids*. Its design bore a strong "S" curve down the center of the composition—a device that the artist borrowed from William Hogarth and would deploy again in his more famous painting *Stag at Sharkey's* (1909).[40] Bellows found other subjects among the darkened docks, riverbanks, and shantytowns that surrounded him. For example, the 1906 painting *River Rats*, which Bellows first exhibited at the National Academy of Design in 1907, depicts a group of low-income children swimming and playing at the edge of the water that stretches across the lower border of the canvas (fig. 4.5). Most of the composition is given over to a large mound of earth, which Bellows has depicted using several layers of broad brushstrokes that border on abstract. Despite these natural elements, however, we become aware that this is not a pastoral scene, as we notice the massive buildings and industrial smokestacks at the top of Bellows's canvas as well as the murky color of the unsanitary East River below. Such a scene was typical of the Ashcan school's "urban vision"—a concept developed by the art historian Rebecca Zurier to describe both the subjects of these artists (i.e., urban life) and the set of historical practices that compose sight.[41] Here we see the antidote to the pastoral bathers painted by Thomas Eakins two decades earlier.[42]

Over the next year, Bellows's professional reputation continued to grow, as he focused his view on urban and rural landscapes. He exhibited new paintings *Pennsylvania Station Excavation* (c. 1907–1908) and *Club Night* (executed in September 1907) at the National Academy of Design in December 1907, and his *North River* (1908) at the National Academy, where it won a $200 prize the following spring. Over the next two years, praise for Bellows continued. He entered a prolific period in 1909, producing several major paintings that year, including *Blue Morning* (1909), *Summer Night* (1909), *Riverside Drive* (1909), *Bridge at Blackwell's Island* (1909), *Lone Tenement* (1909), and *Beach at Coney Island* (1908). All these compositions focus on the gritty environments of the new working class, giving audiences a close-up view of the less picturesque sides of urban life.

While it may be simpler to assume narratives of the Ashcan school that highlight their adherence to the so-called democratic outlook of its artists (i.e., a lack of hierarchy in their subjects), I would like to interrogate this brand of realism. We could, for example, interpret the voyeuristic drive of these artists to observe the slums of lower Manhattan in terms of a wider cultural obsession with classifying racial and ethnic types, and ultimately with establishing a hierarchy within the working class. The six-volume sociological study known as the Pitts-

George Bellows, *River Rats*, 1906. Oil
on canvas, 38.5 × 30.5 inches (797.8 × 7.5 cm).
Private Collection.

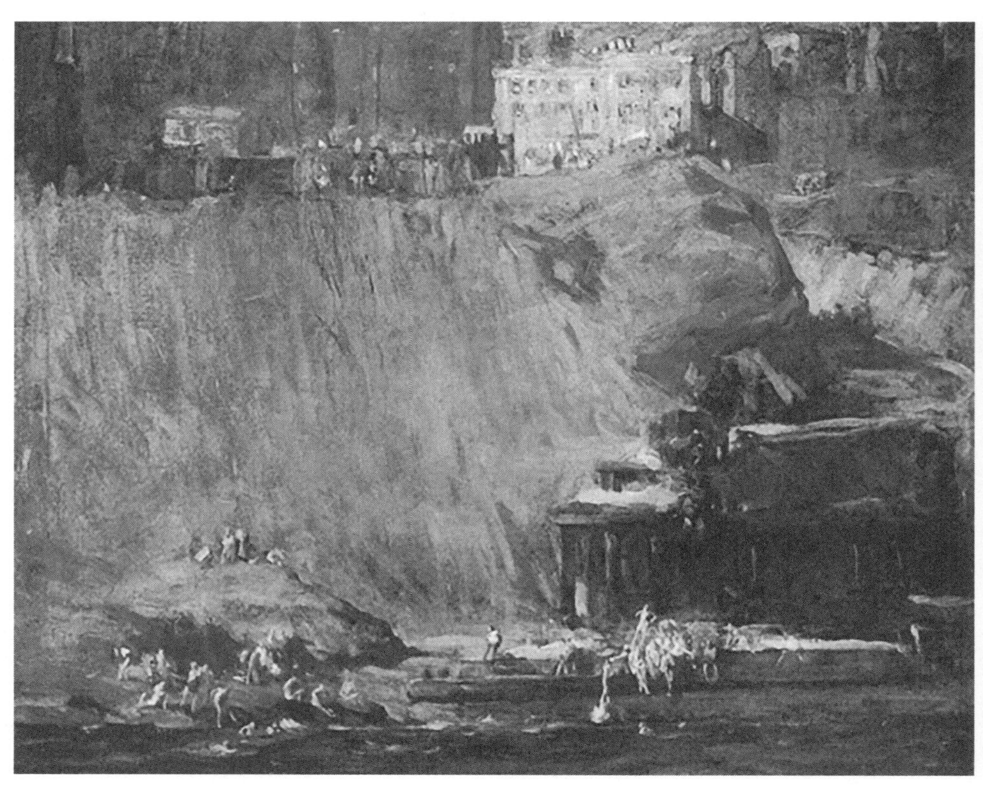

burgh Survey—a collaborative project between academics, social reformers, urban investigators, and activists—provides a comprehensive record of this drive toward classification.[43] Within the Pittsburgh Survey (started in 1907) authors "described and pictured grimy cellars, fearsome furnaces, exotic immigrants, and downtrodden workers" with the aim to demonstrate "the depth of poverty and degeneration in the center of American urban industry."[44] Although framed as a study of immigrants, the Pittsburgh Survey revealed hierarchies of race and class, with "urban savages" at the bottom.[45] Looking again at the Ashcan school, then, we recognize similar strategies of classification and hierarchization at play. These paintings are not reflections of everyday, urban life; they are carefully constructed expressions of gendered and racialized beliefs.

The over commitment of art historians to views of Bellows, Henri, and the other painters of early twentieth-century New York as realists overlooks their investment in shoring up white heteronormative patriarchy. This requires that we leave behind narratives of Ashcan art that ignore the violence these artists enacted against non-white bodies through their very denial of their existence in turn-of-the-century New York. As Gwendolyn DuBois Shaw has argued in her study of John Sloan, "we must engage the challenging and purposely obfuscated materials of the archive" and "dismantle the hegemonic structures of power that dominate the construction of academic knowledge."[46] Many have already recognized the gendered dynamics at play in discourses of realism.[47] However, let us also consider Bellows's nearly exclusive focus on white figures, even in distinctively urban settings where we would expect (and, in fact, can historically prove) interracial and interethnic contact.

Although he initially lived at the West Side YMCA in a decidedly white area of Manhattan, Bellows frequently traveled to other racial and ethnic neighborhoods for his painting. Even Bellows's first home, just south of Gramercy Park, was in an ethnically and racially diverse area of the city. In fact, the Black population of New York City more than doubled from 1900 to 1920, roughly the time Bellows lived there, as a consequence of migration from the southern United States and the Caribbean. But despite the reality of Bellows's lived experience in New York and of more than six hundred paintings, drawings, and lithographs created throughout his career, less than two dozen contain representations of non-white figures. Bellows visually effaced any signs of interracial contact, choosing instead to sacrifice reality in the pursuit of a new national style that was aimed specifically at a white, elite, and male audience.[48] In other words, while Bellows has been often celebrated by art historians for an unvarnished view of early twentieth-century New York, these views were in fact deeply inflected by gender *and* by race.

Moreover, the Aschan school was by default invested in the abject—the discarded people and rejected spaces of urban life. "Abjection," taken from the Latin word *abicere*, meaning "to cast off, or out," is both a theoretical concept and a cultural system. An oft-cited understanding of abjection comes from theorist Julia Kristeva, who argued in 1982's *Powers of Horror: An Essay on Abjection* that this is an essential process in the formation of the subject. As explained by Rina Arya, "on a psychic level (in the sense of psychoanalysis), the experience of abjection both endangers and protects the individual: endangers in that it threatens the boundaries of the self and also reminds us of our animal origins, and protects us because we are able to expect the abject through various means."[49] Kristeva uses the model of the infant's rejection of the mother's body—that is, in its embrace and subsequent rejection of the mother's body the infant begins to establish its own boundaries and thus a breakdown of the mother-infant unit. In the simplest terms, abjection refers to the impulse to reject that which disturbs or threatens the boundaries of the self; it is "the 'other' that comes from within, that we have to reject and expel in order to protect our boundaries."[50] For the Ashcan school of painters, their realism was always already focused on those most repulsive elements of the city. The alleys, the open sewers, the immigrants of downtown New York were exactly those things that most endangered a refined, middle-class existence. As I will argue below, Bellows's selection of boxing fell in line with this wider impulse toward the abject—the blood, the bruising, and the violence we see on these canvases pushes us to reconsider both the boundaries of the self and the boundaries of the social body. When he first encountered the sport—in the dim, cramped space of a saloon on Broadway—Bellows must have felt right at home.

Boxing and Manhood in the Gilded Age

In the spring of 1907, Bellows watched his first fight at Tom Sharkey's saloon on Columbus Avenue near West Sixty-Seventh Street. At this moment prizefighting was still illegal, and to circumvent the prohibition many saloons and bars established themselves as "clubs," whose "members" (likely initiated just that evening) were the fighters and spectators. Bellows was immediately struck by the raw spectacle of the boxing match and returned frequently to Sharkey's for more. His first boxing composition, a drawing entitled *A Knockout* that Bellows completed in the summer of 1907, shows us the explosive action of the ring in a series of shooting, angular forms (indeed a triangular composition) enclosed in a claustrophobic space (fig. 4.6). We see one boxer, who has been knocked to the ground, as he struggles to peel his body up from the canvas. He

George Bellows, *A Knockout*, 1907. Pastel, ink, and graphite on paper, 21.75 × 28 inches (55.25 × 71.12 cm). Crystal Bridges Museum of American Art, Bentonville, Arkansas.

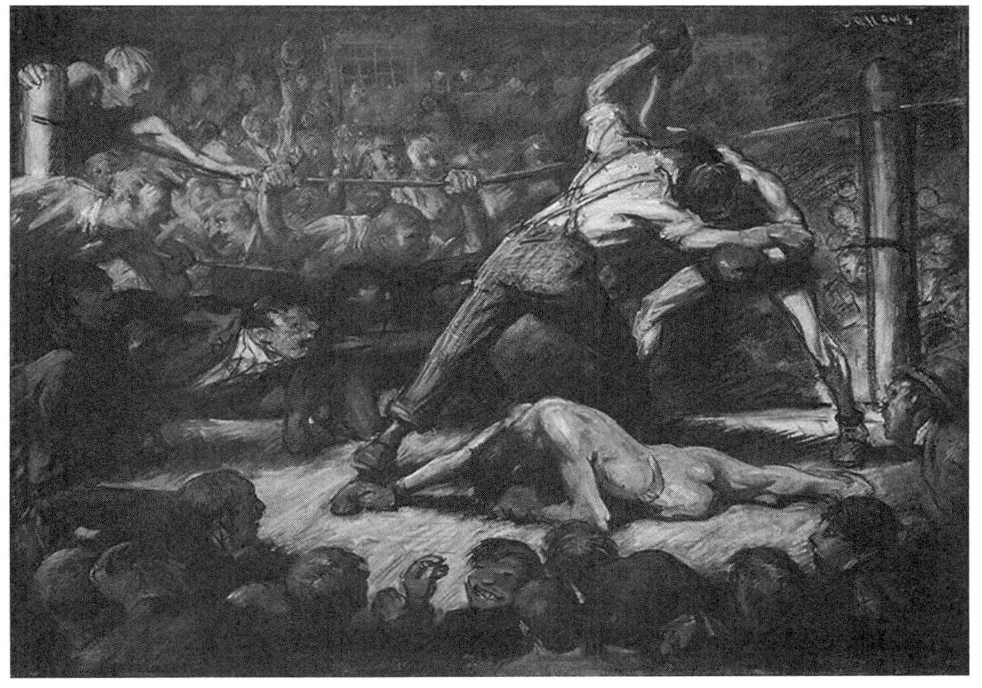

leans weakly against his folded left arm and attempts to push up with a right hand, as his head bows downward in defeat. Above him we see his opponent struggle against a referee, who uses his own arms and hands to pin down the fighter and prevent him from punching further. Surrounding it all is a frenzied crowd whose bodies and wild gestures take up almost all available pictorial space. As viewers we are put into the melee from our ringside position; Bellows has even omitted the two ropes that must have surrounded all four sides of the ring to allow us a more direct view of the violence—the primary attraction for viewers of these matches. As art historian Charles Morgan so vividly described such events, "no one [in the audience] wanted a decision, only a comatose body on the canvas and a blood-stained, hysterical victor standing above him in the ring."[51] These fights were brutal, dirty, and the complete antithesis of Bellows's own bourgeois origins in Ohio. And that was the point. In fact, among the crazed spectators in *A Knockout* we see a lone figure, highlighted in the darkness of the foreground, who grins back at us, taking pleasure in the action and inviting us to join in.[52]

Over the course of his career Bellows devoted six large canvases to the subject of boxing—a new sport of the moment that proved emblematic of the brutality of the city. The first group, painted between 1907 and 1909, includes *Club Night*, along with the more famous *Stag at Sharkey's* and *Both Members of This Club*. Bellows completed another three boxing canvases between 1923 and 1924; these included *Introducing John L. Sullivan* (1923), *Ringside Seats* (1924), and *Dempsey and Firpo* (1924).[53] Before and after these boxing paintings, Bellows also depicted matches and fighters in lithographs widely distributed in mainstream magazines—*Collier's*, *Metropolitan Magazine*, and *American Magazine*—as well as in smaller print publications like the socialist *The Masses* throughout the first decades of the twentieth century.[54] My choice to focus specifically on the earlier set of paintings in this chapter is grounded in the specificity of the cultural and political context of the first decade of the twentieth century. This was a period in which the culture of sports celebrity was firmly established via periodicals like New York's *National Police Gazette* and where the public embrace of boxing (although still illegal) indicated its larger interest in cultivating a specific brand of violent, corporeally dependent manhood that was always already racialized. Bellows's 1909 painting *Both Members of This Club* is of specific interest for its figuration of an interracial battle in this context, which I will argue reflects a wider anxiety about Blackness circulating in this moment.

By the end of the nineteenth century, American men were absolutely obsessed with health and athletics, as they sought to form muscled physiques that would communicate their inner virility and hopefully reclaim some of their lost social or personal power through an increase in sheer physical strength. These were losses experienced via increasing industrialization, which alienated workers from their labor, alongside the increasing popularity of suffragette discourse that threatened patriarchal control. This was the first generation of American men who did not experience the trials of war. Still under the influence of the Victorian obsession with hard work, during the last third of the nineteenth century many pointed to athletics in general to teach "Christian" values, to build moral character, and to instill lessons in leadership and cooperation. Even literature at this moment called for a new muscularity and physical action as the antidote to these urban ills. The novels of Jack London capitalized on the call for a virile masculinity based on physical strength. Books like Stephen Crane's *The Red Badge of Courage* (1895) and Herman Melville's *Moby-Dick* (1851) demonstrated manhood as a process, as something that had to be "earned."[55] Boxing—previously a sport associated with immigrant and working classes—became a fascination for middle- and upper-class men. In response to this sudden interest, the YMCA even began to offer instruction in amateur sparring. According to the historian Gail Bederman, "by the time Jack Johnson became champion in 1908, many middle-class men had come to accept boxing champions like Jim Jeffries as embodiments of their own sense of manhood."[56]

Bellows's 1913 drawing for *The Masses* titled *"Superior Brains": The Business Men's Class* illustrates the often comic consequences of this sudden adoption of boxing by the new, white middle-class (fig. 4.7).[57] Described by Bellows as an example of "brain workers taking their exercise," here we see satirical representations of physically unfit men as they attempt to follow the instruction of a boxing instructor, dressed in black and standing on a small stage on the left side of the composition.[58] The students of this class are variously chubby and scrawny; none fit the new physical type popularized by early bodybuilding culture—examples of which we see pictured in posters along the wall.[59] A balding man in the foreground has dropped one of his barbells, and others are visibly strained from holding the weights; a man on the left doubles over, clutching his stomach while another in the right corner of the composition waits out the session seated on a small chair. At the center of the image, the tallest figure in the group extends his right hip in an exaggerated pose but maintains his balance and thrusts his face upward with confidence. This man is presented to us as perhaps the most comic of them all—a reflection perhaps of the latent anxiety around feminization (and by extension homosexuality) that pervaded this moment. In fact, in the far left of the composition we see a room labeled as both a space of "massage" and as a "social parlor"; as we peer inside to observe the interlocking

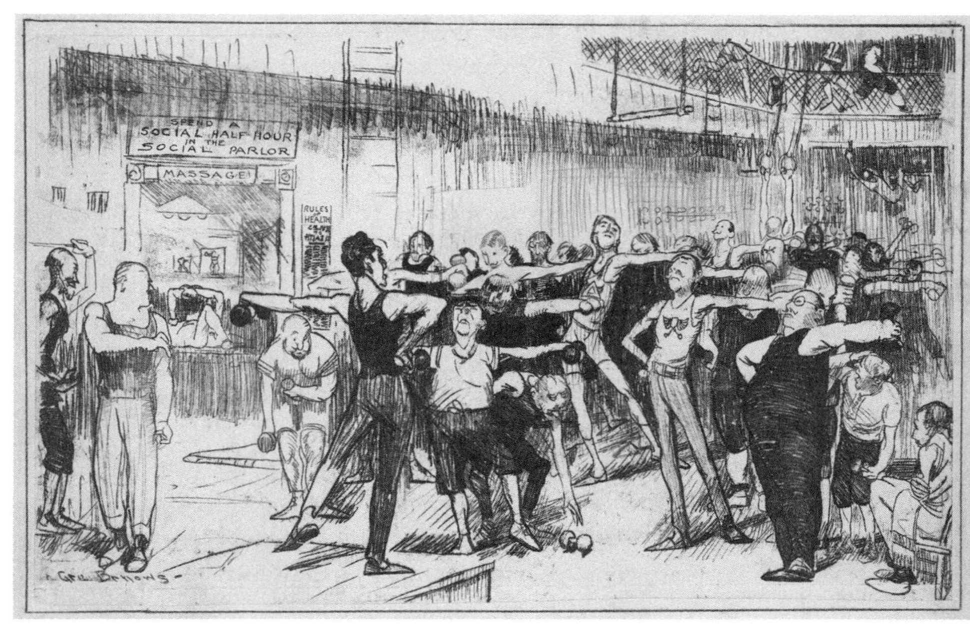

4.7

———

George Bellows, *"Superior Brains": The Business Men's Class*,
April 1913. Monoprint with graphite, crayon, pen and ink, and
scratchwork on the print and mount, 16½ × 25¾ inches (41.91 ×
65.4 cm). Wiggin Collection, Boston Public Library.

poses of two men—one prone on his back with knees raised and feet on the massage table, the other leaning over his groin—we glimpse a very queer scene.

Bellows's choice of featuring an outwardly feminized man at the center of his composition and his inclusion of references to massage parlors in the background reveal the layers of anxiety (shared by many middle-class men) around queer desire. During this period, homosexuality was subject to a disease model of interpretation—a case of something gone wrong within the male body, a consequence of disease or perhaps congenital deformity. The homosexual man, termed "invert," was investigated and medicalized in an attempt to contain the larger social or economic forces that comprised the real threat against middle-class manhood. The widespread anxiety among the public was that changes in the workplace (not to mention within the family) would lead to an overall "feminization" of society. This was amplified by the increasing predominance of women in the lives of young boys—both mothers left at home with their children as well as the teachers in the newly mandated elementary school. Many were alarmed by the perceived "psychic threat" to masculinity and feared the consequences of this feminization of boys.[60] The fears of feminization were so pronounced that the newly established department stores created separate entrances and elevators so that men could avoid the psychological threat to men engaged in the "feminine" activity of shopping.[61]

Boxing was part of a rough code of manliness, which celebrated the saloon and music halls as well as emphasized aggression and physical strength. Working-class men were drawn into the pleasures of downtown New York, which included going to the theater, drinking, gambling, and boxing. They frequented brothels, dance halls, minstrel shows, and circuses. Saloons were at the center of this new life, and saloon keepers offered various modes of recreation—dog fights, rat-baiting contests, and boxing matches. Men like Bellows found refuge in the saloons and taverns in major cities, where countless prize fighters established their headquarters. In the early twentieth century, even art criticism was obsessed with manliness— perhaps as an antidote to the perceived frivolity and decadence of European art. In one review of the National Academy of Design's winter exhibition—where *Club Night* appeared—the critic J. Nilsen Lauvrik used variations on "manly," "virile," and "healthy" five times.[62]

But tension within the sporting world existed as well. The middle-class fascination with athleticism was accompanied by morally sanctioned athletic spaces such as the YMCA, founded in London in 1844. That is, on the one hand the YMCA, where Bellows himself resided when first arriving in New York, promoted healthy bodies and physical exercise as necessary components of a balanced middle-class life. The YMCA was a place where Bellows may have felt a connection to the "Christian" values of his youth, reaching back to his own physical endeavors in baseball and basketball. On the other hand, clubs like Harry Hill's and Tom Sharkey's athletic clubs were places where the violent and vulgar elements of sport found their home. Bellows was caught between bourgeois expectations and the harsh environment of early twentieth-century New York. In the three boxing paintings he produced between 1907 and 1909, Bellows places his viewer in this precarious position, as we are invited into these scenes through the audience that not only revels in the brutality before them but often looks back at us as well. As art historian David Peters Corbett argues, "by inviting viewers into the picture to become participating members of the audience, Bellows engages them in the display of brutality, catharsis, and passion that the fight stages on their behalf."[63] Bellows's boxing pictures place us in the center of the action.

Upon Bellows's arrival to New York in 1904, the underground network of boxing was already well-established. His studio was conveniently located almost across the street from the saloon owned by the retired prizefighter Tom Sharkey, which by night transformed into a boxing club. Bellows had moved into a studio on the top floor of the Lincoln Arcade Building in September 1906 along with two roommates (Ed Keefe and Fred Cornell) and another four to five men, who regularly slept there. It was Mosey King (1884–1956)—an ex-classmate of one of Bellows's roommates and the lightweight champion of Connecticut—who suggested that Bellows come over to Sharkey's to watch a fight. The event took place in a small back room of the saloon, known as Sharkey's Athletic Club; the cramped, dark space fit the ring itself along with just a few people outside the ropes. As described by Charles Morgan, the space was "wreathed in blue cigar smoke and the aroma of cheap, stale beer, the hot concentration of light in the center, the hum of excitement rising to a roar." This was "the setting for the primitive violence of the bouts themselves and for the uninhibited reactions of the toughs and bums that were the charter and sustaining members of the club." Establishing his bar as a "club" allowed Sharkey to host these fights; the tickets sold were "dues" and the boxers were announced to the waiting audience "as both members of this club."[64]

Many historians have taken the description by Charles Morgan in his 1965 monograph, which explicitly linked the title of Bellows's 1909 canvas to this underground network, without question. They have argued that Bellows's boxing pictures provide a lens through which to view the violent and even grotesque elements of this new, urban spectacle. Analyses focus on the raucous crowds that populate these scenes or perhaps even the precarious links between anatomy, desire, and authority reflected in the ring. I would like to provide an alternative frame, one that considers more specifically the presence of race in these images. Doing so will require a focus on the fighter's body—both in Bellows's boxing paintings and in wider visual culture—in explicitly racial terms.

Boxers on Display

As discussed in the introduction, the culture of late Victorian America had already identified the body of the heavyweight boxer as the perfect example of manhood and power. The bodies of prizefighters were a model of physical superiority, and provided a necessary link between anatomy, identity, and power. The public fascination with these bodies and the corresponding rise of print media meant that images of these fighters moved to the foreground of public consciousness. As fights were promoted and advertised across national newspapers and magazines, the boxer's body was reproduced for public consumption. In the case of Jack Johnson, arguably the most notorious boxer of the early twentieth century, the publicity surrounding him in this period was inescapable. At the time of Bellows's choice to depict a Black fighter in *Both Members of This Club*, photographs of Jack Johnson were circulated widely in the popular press. Images of Johnson also appeared on tobacco trading cards, poster, cabinet cards, and in cartoons. Like many other Black boxers of the time, Johnson found success in Europe in prizefighting, sparring exhibitions, and even vaudeville performances.[65] In the summer of 1913, after Johnson had fled the United States for good, he was reportedly contracted for twice-nightly performances at Euston and South London music halls, where he would dance, sing, play the bass viol, and spar for $5,000 per week.[66] Audiences could not get enough of Johnson—inside or outside the ring.

A series of photographs of Jack Johnson, who had become heavyweight champion of the world the year before, and his training partner Joe Choynski, commissioned by the *Chicago Daily News* in 1909, illustrates the public appetite for Johnson's image.[67] In these examples we see Johnson and Choynski sparring in front of a white studio backdrop. Choynski appears in white boxing tights, while Johnson reveals more of his body in black boxing trunks that go down only to his upper thigh. In one photograph, the men stand opposite one another; Choynski lunges toward Johnson, who ducks to the right, while preparing a left hook (fig 4.8). In another image, we see Johnson deliver a jab to Choynski's mid-section, while Choynski's right cross moves past Johnson's head

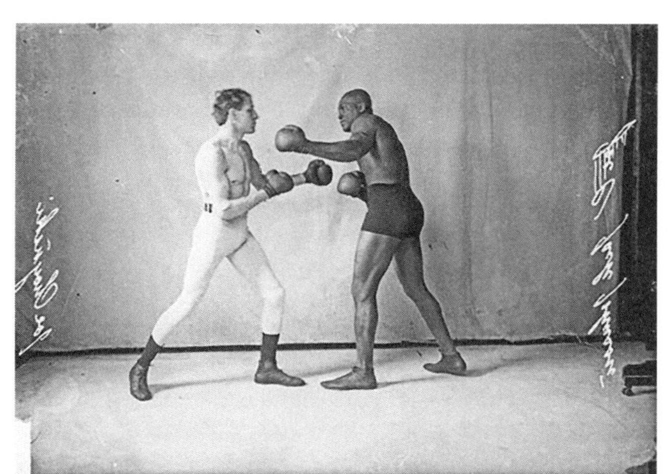

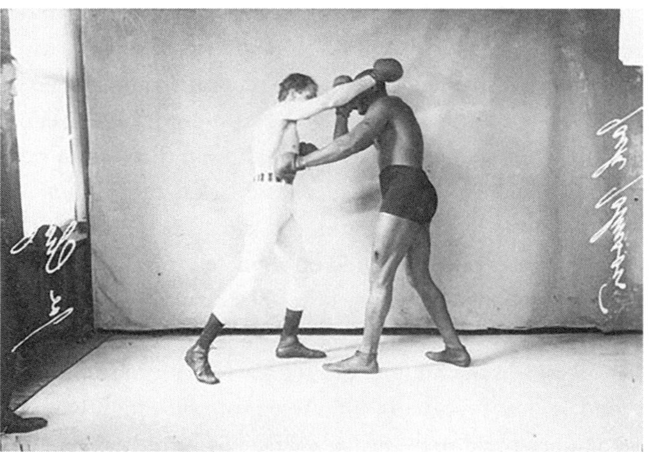

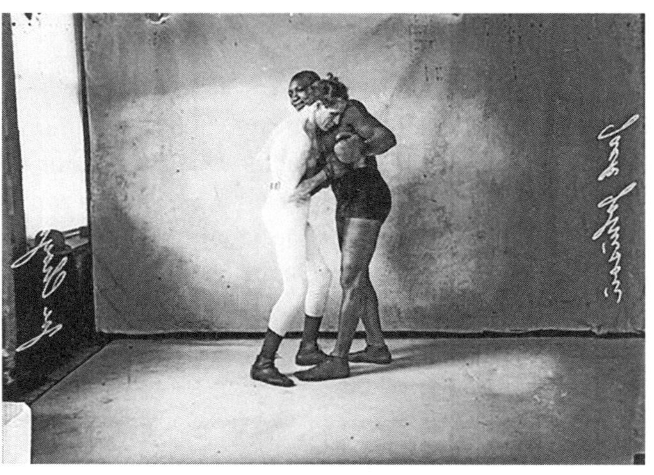

Jack Johnson and Joe Choynski, 1909. Digital file from
original glass negative, 30 × 42.5 inches (76.2 × 107.95 cm) each.
Chicago Daily News Inc. Chicago History Museum.

(fig 4.9). In a third sparring image, the two "opponents" appear in a modified
clinch—a pose in which one boxer clinches his arms over those of his opponent and places his forehead on his opponent's shoulder while simultaneously
pressing down with as much weight as possible (fig 4.10). Here, the proximity
of the two bodies allows us to see that Johnson is the taller of the two. Knowing
that this is a publicity shot, rather than an actual fight, Johnson does not put
his head down onto Choynski's shoulder as would be required for a true clinch;
instead, he places his chin there so that we are granted the full view of his face
and Johnson's subtle smile. Collectively, these small modifications to the posed
sparring routine create a playful scene for a popular audience.[68] Johnson's light
punches and sly smile underplay the potential damage and pain he would likely
inflict upon an opponent in the ring. And this is exactly the point. Following
his defeat of Tommy Burns in Australia in 1908, Johnson represented a threat
to not only other heavyweight fighters, but to white supremacy as he made a
move toward Jim Jeffries.

Johnson's threat was carefully and consistently managed through visual representation. Many of the images of Johnson that we see in the popular press
seem to reinforce the dominance of his white opponents. Among the staged
shots with Choynski, for example, we find a curious example where the boxers
are not sparring but instead stand statically in front of the camera (fig 4.11).
Choynski appears in front of Johnson, almost blocking him from the camera's view with his outstretched arm. Johnson raises his own arms in parallel,
looking out at us from over Choynski's right shoulder with a passive gaze. The
arrangement of their bodies within the frame invites us to compare the two
fighters—one Black, one white. We see that Johnson appears slightly taller than
Choynski; his arms and shoulders peek out above. However, the tilt of Johnson's head so that the top lines up with the top of Choynski's hairline creates an
illusion that the men are equal in height (Johnson was at least three and a half

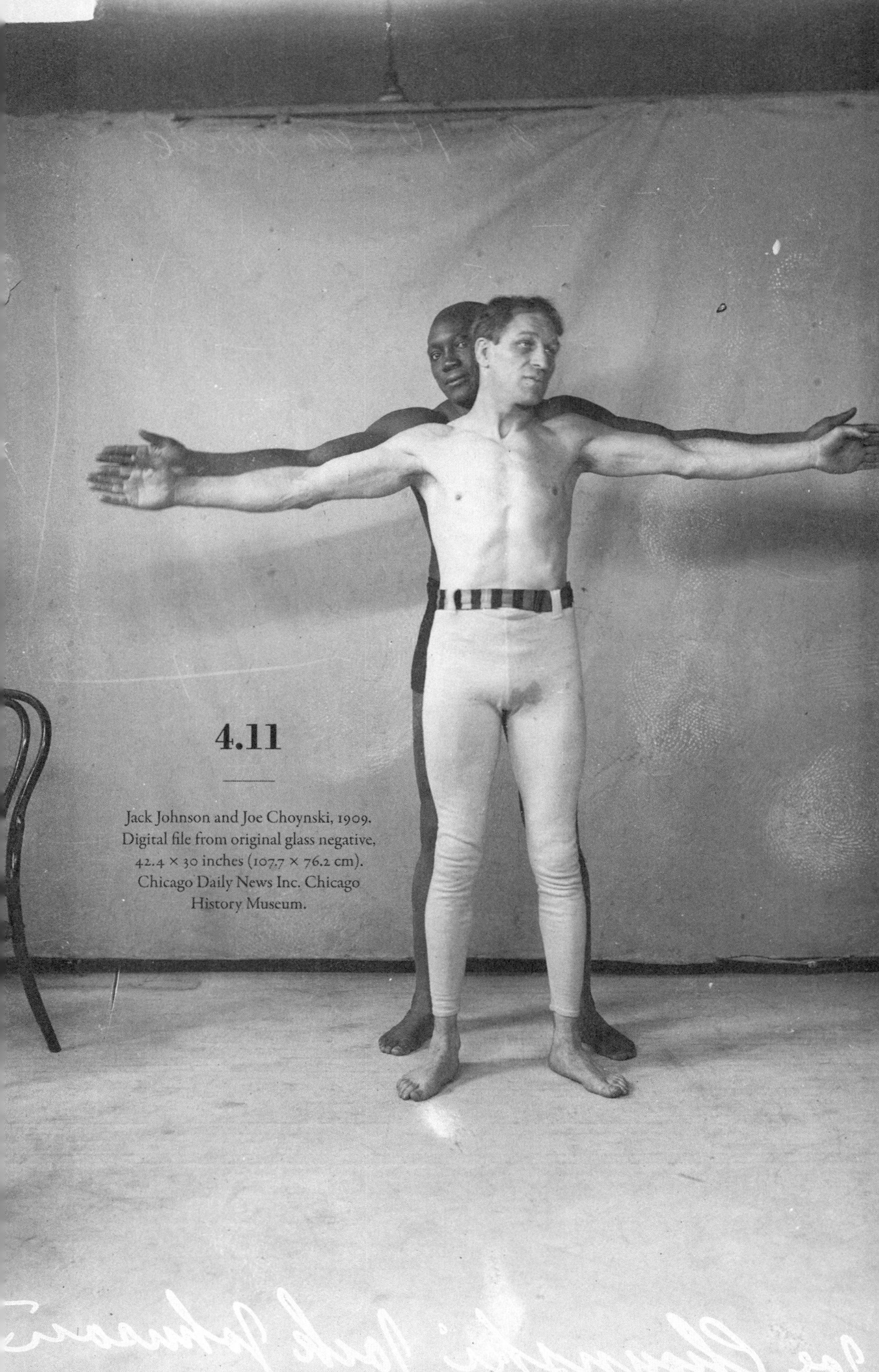

4.11

Jack Johnson and Joe Choynski, 1909.
Digital file from original glass negative,
42.4 × 30 inches (107.7 × 76.2 cm).
Chicago Daily News Inc. Chicago
History Museum.

inches taller). Placing Johnson behind Choynski also camouflages the larger size of the so-called Galveston Giant, who at this point weighed close to thirty pounds more than his sparring partner. Such inconsistencies are overshadowed by the pseudoscientific nature of their poses and hidden by the manipulation of the camera—facing frontally to position them as physical specimens rather than as men. We are meant to focus here on the equivalent reach of these fighters (i.e., seventy-four inches) as further proof of the supremacy of whiteness.[69]

Other images of Johnson during the period leading up to his fight against Jeffries similarly attempt to neutralize him as a physical threat. Previous fight photographs in the popular press were committed to capturing Johnson in passive or neutral positions—that is, falling backward from the impact of an opponent or standing at a great distance away between punches (fig 4.12). A series of boxing postcards circa 1908 that circulated in Australia before the Johnson-Burns match shows Johnson dressed in full three-piece suit with a cane, posed as if delivering a friendly right uppercut. Notice that his fists remain partially open rather than clenched. In one image, inaccurately captioned "after delivering left hook to the stomach," we even see Johnson smiling gamely at the camera (fig 4.13).[70] How could such a friendly, sophisticated man pose any threat?

The Black fighter as a threat to whiteness was first made manifest in the days of Peter Jackson, the St. Croix–born boxer who became the Australian heavyweight champion in 1886 but never had the opportunity to fight the American champion John L. Sullivan (1858–1918) for the world title.[71] This was likely due to the reaction to the brutal defeat of Jack Skelly by Black Canadian George Dixon in New Orleans in 1892, which effectively ended interracial fights for nearly two decades. Like Johnson, Jackson struggled for decades to define himself as a champion in a system that resisted interracial matches.

But unlike Jackson and Johnson, Black fighters in other divisions (lightweight and bantamweight) did hold championship titles in this same period. George Dixon (1870–1908), mentioned above, held the bantamweight title from 1890 to 1892, followed by the featherweight title until 1900. Joe Walcott (1873–1935) held the welterweight title from 1901 to 1906, and Joe Gans (1874–1910) won the lightweight title in 1902 and held it for six years. A key difference between these fighters and Johnson was their size; they posed less of a threat at 132 pounds (i.e., the maximum weight threshold for the lightweight division) than Johnson, weighing 205 pounds and standing six feet two. But there was something else different in Johnson as well he is the only fighter in this group born in the American South, and he is the darkest.[72] The firstborn

4.12

———

"Stanley Ketchell vs. Jack Johnson, October 16, 1909."
Photographer unknown, Digital file from original glass negative, 10 ×
11.62 inches (25.4 × 29.5 cm). Courtesy of Bettmann/CORBIS Archives.

4.13

———

"Mr. Jack Johnson of Galveston, Texas USA" / "Ready for
Tahmmy," ca. 1908. Postcard, 5.3 × 3.54 inches (13.5 × 9 cm).
National Archives of Australia.

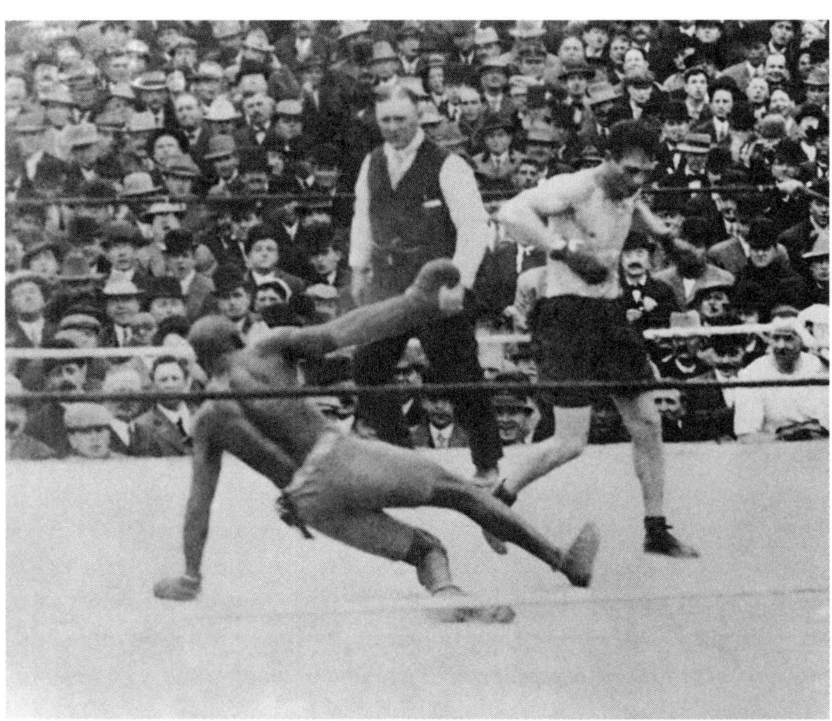

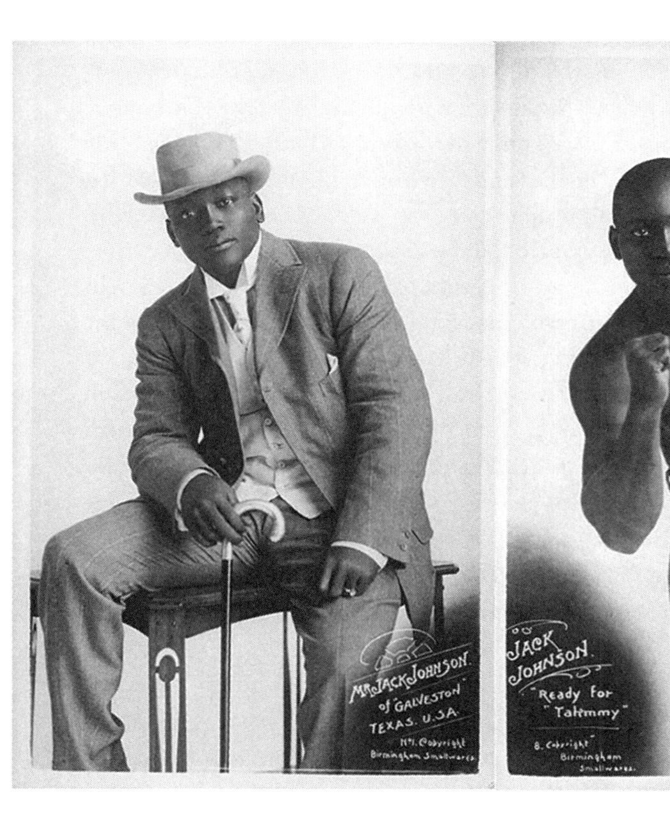

MR. JACK JOHNSON
of "GALVESTON"
TEXAS, U.S.A
Nº1. Copyright
Birmingham Smallwares

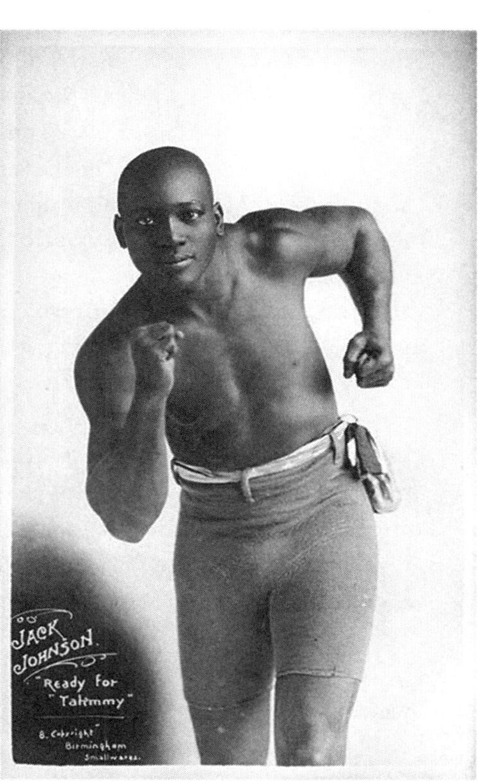

JACK
JOHNSON.
"Ready for
"Tammy"
8. Copyright
Birmingham
Smallwares.

son of former slaves, Henry and Tina Johnson, every single one of Jack Johnson's victories was a direct blow to Jim Crow.

From Johnson onward, the Black boxer's performance in the ring was as
much a performance of masculinity and Black power as one of athleticism.
According to historian Gail Bederman, at the turn of the twentieth century,
the body of the heavyweight prizefighter was "so equated with male identity
and power that American whites rigidly prevented all men they deemed unable to wield political and social power from asserting any claim to the heavyweight championship."[73] This was certainly the case for Johnson, whose threat
to white masculine identity was limited by restrictions on interracial fighting
in the United States as well as through the careful manipulation of his public
image. And, in fact, Johnson played upon the fears of a white public by publicly
laying claim to three of the "metonymic facets of manhood—body, identity,
and authority."[74] During public matches, Johnson wrapped his penis in gauze to
make it appear larger and strutted around the boxing ring wearing only his boxing shorts, so as to highlight his genitals. As a private citizen, the heavyweight
also made great efforts to assert a middle-class manly identity by taking on the
persona of a self-made, successful man. For example, he tried to move into exclusive, all-white suburbs and dressed himself and his blonde, white wives in
the finest furs and jewels. Johnson tried to align himself with members of high
society to establish his authority, writing in his autobiography that he had "min-
gled . . . with kings and queens; monarchs and rulers of nations have been my
associates."[75] In most cases, Johnson worked to establish his manhood in a race-
neutral context—as a self-made man, a champion. But in others, he exploited
his Blackness (and more specifically his status as a highly sexed Black body) to
reinforce a claim to manhood.

In the final section of this chapter, I turn back to Bellows's boxing paintings,
which intersect with these attempts to limit and constrain the excessive bodies
of Black fighters. Both popular visual culture and fine art attempt to manage
white anxieties around the Black body through the constraint of its perceived
physical and sexual excess.

Bellows's Boxers: Blackness and the Abject

Bellows painted *Stag at Sharkey's* in August 1909 and *Both Members of This
Club* two months later, in October. Both were exhibited at the 105th annual
exhibition at the Pennsylvania Academy of Fine Arts, which opened on January 23, 1910. Early reviews of the works cited their technical flaws in execution.
For example, one critic from the *New York World* noted that if the larger figure

in *Stag at Sharkey's* were ever to stand upright, he world measure eight feet tall.[76] Such criticisms led Bellows to proclaim that his intention was not an accurate depiction of a boxing match but "to make a picture of two athletes in intense action."[77] Unlike the earlier *Club Night*, with these paintings Bellows chose to place the fighters closer to the picture plane; the paint has been aggressively applied and the strong triangular shapes dominate the brightly lit figures (plate 5). The brushwork ranges from heavy impasto to thin washes, and Bellows prioritizes expressive effect over accuracy. In fact, the pronounced lack of definition suggests the action and speed of the fight depicted.

Art historian Rebecca Zurier has argued for reading Bellows's boxing pictures from the perspective of humor, focusing on the artist's manipulations and distortions of the visual tradition of cartoons. She also argues that Bellows took the examples of "the dramatic grotesques of Goya and Daumier" to create the audience in 1909's *Stag at Sharkey's*, the "flushed faces with indistinct features . . . indicated with blotches and smears of red and brown paint rather than being neatly defined by a stylized line" make them more caricatures than men.[78] Bellows, according to Zurier, shows the violence of the scene in the grotesque faces of the spectators, rather than in the confrontation of the two fighters at its center. She asks us to focus on the spectacle of the fight itself as Bellows's main subject, drawing perhaps from his own experience of watching live fights in similar clubs. Smears of red paint both form the faces of the crowd and highlight the injuries of the fighters above them, creating a connection between the spectator and the spectacle. "This and later prizefight images," she claims, "address the transforming effects of spectacle upon both fight fans and the paintings' viewers, as well as the artist. They proceed through a process of attraction and repulsion, as the viewer is drawn by the beauty of the bodies into the terror of the crowd."[79] As we look at the distorted faces in the crowd we also notice Bellows's insertion of his own visage into this scene; he appears in the lower right corner of the composition, crouching down and looking out at us, the viewer, so that we can see just one of his eyes and the bald top of his head. The artist, like us, is a voyeur of this scene. In Zurier's estimation, Bellows's boxing paintings center on the act of looking and reveal the underlying ambivalence of the Ashcan school artists, who are simultaneously engaged in and removed from the scenes they depict.

But Bellows's choice of boxing also illustrates the corporeal dependence of masculinity. According to art historian Robert Haywood, the artist's focus on the sport connected to a wider interest in the expressive potential of the fighter's body and even the "tensions and private desires between men."[80] His famous *Stag at Sharkey's* shows us two fighters mid-fight, bodies clenched together in the center of the ring. In Bellows's depiction, the entangled bodies of these two boxers push against each other, while remaining simultaneously wrapped together in an awkward embrace. We see the heads and opposing fists of the two fighters come together in a blur of dynamic force near the top center of the composition. The referee of the match stands in contrast, as he tries (unsuccessfully) to break up the fight; the cool colors of his uniform and the downward motion suggested by his left hand, which reaches out to grip one of the ropes, separates him from the scene. The focus in Bellows's painting remains the fighters and the few observers seated in the first rows of the arena, whose faces are painted in more detail and in fuller light than the remainder of the crowd.

As those around him blur into the darkness of the smoky arena, one figure, dressed in white, turns around and beckons us closer. His right hand points us toward the action in the center of the ring, where we see the raised knee of one boxer nearly land in the exposed groin of his opponent. The focus on the groin of each fighter at the center of *Stag at Sharkey's*, Haywood argues, provokes feelings of both anxiety and pleasure in the viewer. In fact, he argues for an interpretation of the boxing match itself as "a sadomasochistic fantasy made real" where "the body is subjected to the enactment and the determination of power, but signs of sexual desire and fear are also coded onto the boxer's body."[81] Bellows's focus on the phallus and its potential injury, argues Haywood, is a cycle of desire and repulsion that other historians have located in Bellows's canvases.

Taking a position on the erotic potential of Bellows's canvas, art historian David Peters Corbett has offered an interpretation of Bellows's paintings from the perspective of abjection, arguing that this concept allows us to reconcile Bellows's interest in the repulsive aspects of boxing. From Corbett's perspective, the fighters' beating of one another's bodies, drawing blood and threatening injury, is the central theme of these works.[82] In works like *Stag at Sharkey's*, for example, the fighter's degradation is highlighted through Bellows's treatment of the faces of each man, which dissolve into fluid strokes of paint. We struggle to differentiate between flesh and blood, as faces are beaten into an unrecognizable pulp. A similar distortion is at play in the faces of the audience members, who border on the grotesque. Corbett argues, following Kristeva, that the concept of abjection provides a path to understanding Bellows's focus on the negative or repulsive elements of boxing—that is, his apparent fascination with those elements that operate outside social norms. Corbett writes that the abject in Bellows's scene works to "evoke a part of ourselves with which we are uncomfortable."[83] Our fear drives us away from the violence, but our desire also attracts us.

According to Corbett, Bellows draws our attention to scenes in which the "victims are bound and constrained in ways that force them into situations of utter abjection."[84] For example, he reads the passive and submissive position of the boxers in the examples of Bellows's *Counted Out, No. 2* and *The White Hope*, where the fighters appear defeated and vulnerable, as abject. Corbett's argument then considers the erotic elements of the boxing pictures (here relying on the work of Robert Haywood, mentioned above). That is, the boxers' careful negotiation of which parts of the exposed body are open to or restricted from blows, the action of the match, and the pleasure we derive from watching it, center on the boxer's ability to resist or endure pain. Corbett reads Bellows's concurrent engagement with sexuality as subject in works such as the 1917 drawing *The Shower Bath*, where we see a flirtatious encounter between two men at the center of this scene, or later works showing scenes of brutal violence such as *The Cigarette* (1918) or *The Law Is Too Slow* (1922–23). He connects the abjected victims of these scenes to an overall concern with masculinity in an age of increasing industrialization. Boxing is, once again, a way to emphasize the power and agency of the human body in a time of constraint. While all this is certainly true, however, Corbett fails to consider race within his schema.

As discussed in the introduction, race played a key role in the fashioning of manhood, as those who attempted to renegotiate and reshape gender in the face of extensive social, economic, and cultural changes drew specific connections between male authority and white supremacy. Based on surviving records, it is unknown whether Bellows directly witnessed an interracial match and there is no evidence of a match like this taking place at Sharkey's in the fall of 1909. Nevertheless, Bellows did choose to insert the subject of race into this picture. What happens, then, when the white opponent becomes Black? I argue that the inclusion of a Black fighter complicates the reading of Bellows's boxing paintings as simply a rumination on manhood, or even sexuality.

The abject is not simply a way to reconcile the violence of Bellows's boxers. Corbett's analysis proves useful in our exploration of the complex relationship individual viewers have to these paintings; the spectators of Bellows's scenes reflect our own simultaneous fascination and repulsion with the fights depicted. Yet, the Black boxer in *Both Members of This Club* introduces a further complication. I would like to contend with the fear of the Other that materializes in this period and that we see reflected in Bellows's inclusion of a Black boxer in *Both Members of This Club*. To do so we must consider the social dimension of abjection—that is, to consider the consequences of the discovery that the "object of the Other" does not come from within the self but from an external force.

In the 1996 book *Bodies That Matter: On the Discursive Limits of "Sex,"* Judith Butler focuses on the processes by which subjects are constructed through strategies of exclusion. In Butler's example, normative sexuality (i.e., heterosexuality) is constructed via its abject inversion (i.e., homosexuality). "This exclusionary matrix by which subjects are formed," writes Butler, "thus requires the simultaneous production of a domain of abject beings, those who are not yet 'subjects,' but who form the constitutive outside of the domain of the subject."[85] In this view "homosexuality and heterosexuality are mutually exclusive phenomena that . . . can only be made to coincide through rendering the one culturally viable and the other a transient and imaginary affair."[86] In other words, there is nothing explicitly abject about homosexuality, but it is nevertheless *made* abject in order to reduce its threat. This process has ethical and political ends. In this light, some bodies matter and others do not. Some bodies are granted autonomy and dignity, while others must fight for these things. Although Butler is focused here on sexuality, we can certainly say the same for Blackness, which has been similarly pathologized to shore up whiteness.

Historians have previously connected the title of Bellows's *Both Members of This Club* to the histories of prizefighting clubs, even seeing it as an indication of equal standing between Black and white fighters in the buzzing metropolis of the early twentieth century. Following the example of Charles H. Morgan, the author of the first full-length biography of Bellows, many have claimed that the artist's title is drawn directly from the way a prizefight would have been announced. Boxing clubs—with members, both fighters and spectators, paying dues—were strategically used by many organizers and bar owners to evade the laws against prizefighting. Thus, the two fighters we see in Bellows's painting are "both members of this club." Some have pushed this reading even further to suggest that Bellows's title is indicative of racial progressiveness in such settings (and perhaps in Bellows himself)—that is, "in this club, African Americans were undifferentiated from whites in their membership status."[87] But there is also a less optimistic view of Bellows's relationship to Blackness.

I argue against the tendency to read Bellows's depiction of this Black boxer as a commentary on equality in the sports world and link it instead to the reality of the artist's own racism. This seems particularly convincing when considered alongside the fact that Bellows's *Both Members of This Club* was originally titled *A Nigger and a White Man*—a change that was recorded in Bellows's record book, which listed artworks by title alongside information about their dimensions and exhibition history. According to art historian Martin Berger, Bellows's racial views were very much in alignment with the mainstream. "His notebooks and correspondence," Berger writes, "document that [Bellows] used the terms 'Nigger' and 'Jap,' and the recollections of his daughter, Jean, suggest that he was comfortable dressing up in Blackface."[88] Bellows's relationship to Blackness, then, is one in which the artist does not simply efface racialized subjects in his paintings, but actively cultivates violence against them.

Minstrelsy—likely Bellows's inspiration for his own blackface performance—emerged in the 1830s, as white performers in blackface would deliver songs, group performances, narrative skits, and jokes to white audiences. The theatrics of minstrelsy were simultaneously rooted in the reality of white racialized anxiety and in the political development of a national identity. More than passive entertainment, these shows circulated ideologies of a primitive and pathological Blackness that must be kept in check by white authority. Most important for a study of boxers, minstrelsy reaffirmed the "Black buck" stereotype of a violent, rude, even lecherous Black man who refuses to submit to white authority and has a violent attraction to white women. This trope rested on the presumption of both the extreme physical power of the Black body (uniquely suited to the demands of agricultural labor) and a deviant sexual appetite.

Like many Black athletes, Johnson performed on stage (dancing, singing, sparring) on tours throughout Europe, lured outside of the United States by the promise of a life free from racism. While we might at first interpret Johnson's own success in vaudeville performances as evidence of his ability to overcome the color line, the historian Theresa Runstedtler has argued otherwise. "Just as growing numbers of Black performers, athletes, and workers began arriving to fill the nation's demand for cheap labor and entertainment," she writes, "Britain's policing of racial boundaries appeared to be tightening. The increasing visibility of African American men was causing white Britons to rethink the risks of living in an interracial society."[89] In so many ways, Johnson needed to conform to the image of the "happy darkie" to manage his threat to white supremacy—on both sides of the Atlantic.

As mentioned above, the early representations of Johnson positioned him as docile, a Sambo. Even as he prepared to meet Tommy Burns in 1908 for a nontitle fight, Burns took great pains to mount an argument for Johnson's inadequacy based on scientific racism.[90] He told the press of his plan to attack Johnson in the torso, believing that Black men had hard heads, but weak stomachs. "Take it from me," he claimed, "that if I ever make a man quit when I get him in the ring it will be that nigger."[91] The narrative of Johnson as a weak-minded simpleton continued even after his spectacular defeat of Burns. As he prepared to fight Jeffries, cartoons presented Johnson as an awkward caricature, complete with bulging eyes and impossibly wide lips.

As the fight against Jeffries came into closer view, however, news outlets could no longer ignore the physical prowess of Johnson. The press printed images of Johnson in training sessions—sparring, working with a medicine ball, and even cutting wood. Johnson flexed his taught muscles for rapt audiences, and even the physical culture expert Dr. Dudley Sargent concluded that Johnson's proportions were some of the finest ever observed. And in April—less than two months before the match—Dr. C. W. Piper, who had examined both Jeffries and Johnson, concluded that "If Jeffries is a Hercules, then Johnson is surely a Black Achilles . . . If the Caucasian is physically perfect it must be admitted in fairness that the Black is equally so."[92] Johnson's physical superiority, declared by experts no less, was a threat to white supremacy and virility. And the white press responded by reminding its readers of Johnson's Blackness, launching (yet again) a visual campaign that would illustrate Johnson as a lazy, chicken-eating darkie (fig. I.4).

After Johnson's public defeat of Jim Jeffries in 1910, his public behavior came under much closer scrutiny; scathing editorials and death threats became commonplace. Not only had Johnson defeated a white fighter, but he flaunted his relationships with white women. In a letter to Emmett Jay Scott, Booker T. Washington's secretary at Tuskegee Institute, the white army surgeon Major P. M. Ashburn gave the warning that Johnson should monitor his public behavior more carefully. This was especially important since he "will now for some years be the most talked of and in some respects the most eminent Black man in the world. It seems to us a matter of importance whether his eminence is to be that of the purely sporting, loud, dislike-exciting nigger, or that of a sober, sane, wise, and admirable Negro."[93] An editorial in the *Los Angeles Times* similarly cautioned the new champion: "Do not point your nose too high. Do not swell your chest too much. . . . Remember you have done nothing at all. You are just the same member of society you were last week."[94] Suddenly, Johnson's flaunting of his white girlfriends, his flashy clothing, and his sports cars all became cause for concern, and the fighter was under immense pressure to perform.

Johnson caught the attention of federal prosecutors, when in October 1912 the mother of Lucille Cameron accused Johnson of kidnapping her eighteen-year-old daughter and transporting her across state lines. Although Cameron and Johnson's relationship was consensual, the accusation alone was enough for prosecutors to pursue a charge under the Mann Act (also known as the "White Slavery Act"). Signed in 1910 to curb sex trafficking, the Mann Act was more commonly used to prosecute men who had sexual relationships with young girls.[95] Johnson was arrested by Chicago police, and a grand jury was called in to further investigate the fighter's relationships with white women.

Because Cameron refused to testify against Johnson, the case was temporarily dropped. Nevertheless, prosecutors brought a second charge again the fighter on November 7, using a prior relationship with the prostitute Belle Schreiber. As Johnson exited the court following his arraignment, a crowd of more than one hundred spectators hung a dummy of the champion with a note pinned to it that read "This is the last of Jack Johnson."[96] Unsurprisingly, Johnson was convicted of violating the Mann Act by an all-white jury and sentenced to one year and one day in prison. Refusing to serve his sentence, Johnson fled to Canada with Cameron (now his wife), and then to Europe.[97] The damage to Johnson's reputation was significant, and there was wide speculation about whether his title would be stripped from him. Even Black media outlets expressed their "humiliation," condemning his actions so as not to further damage the image of the race.[98] Cast out and publicly disavowed, Johnson would not return to the United States until 1920.

In 1915 Johnson traveled to Cuba to face the white boxer Jess Willard in Havana's Oriental Park on April 5. Willard, another "great white hope," was a large fighter, weighing in at 245 points and standing over six feet six . But despite Willard's size, many publicly doubted his chances at unseating the heavyweight champion. Spectators were therefore stunned when Johnson fell to the canvas in the final (forty-fifth) round, unresponsive as the referee counted him out (fig. 4.14). For most of the public, Johnson's fall from grace—losing a match against Jess Willard in 1915, and his arrest and eventual imprisonment for a violation of the Mann Act—was evidence not only of the superiority of whiteness in general, but the superiority of white *men* specifically. Matters of gender (masculinity) were inextricably tied to race (whiteness), as white men sought to develop further justification for their power and authority within public culture. Johnson was a threat to this view via his public defeat of white boxers, as well as through his generally flamboyant, sexual persona.

Returning once more to *Both Members of This Club*, we see two fighters—one white, one Black—surrounded by jeering spectators. The scene focuses on the two fighters in the ring, illuminated by a harsh spotlight and locked in a pose that creates a triangular shape at the center of the composition. In its pronounced aggression, the Black body threatens to overwhelm the white fighter, who strains against the downward pressure alongside the encouragement of the crowd below. The white boxer on the left squats down under the pressure of the Black boxer, who has locked arms with him at the top. We see the blood that obscures the white fighter's face, which is upturned and positioned behind the right arm so that it is partially hidden from view. The thick, red blood that covers his mouth and teeth runs down his neck and transforms the face into a pulpy

4.14

———

"Jack Johnson Is Counted Out by the Referee after Being
Knocked Out in the 26th Round by Jess Willard," 1915. Photographer
unknown, Digital file from original glass negative, 5.45 × 8.35 inches
(13.8 × 21.2 cm). Courtesy of Bettmann Archive.

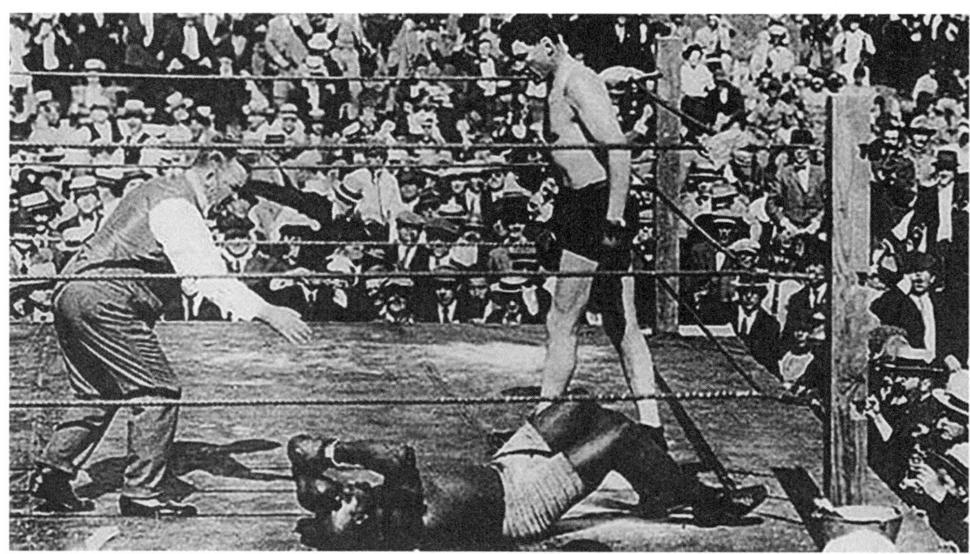

mass, leaving a partial view of the fighter's eye, nose, and mouth. The green shorts that this figure wears contrast with and highlight the bloodied head, while providing little protection from the impending blow of his opponents left knee. Here again we see the threat of emasculation as the central scene. The Black fighter on the right of Bellows's composition lunges so forcefully at the white opponent in front of him with his right leg extended behind him that he leans into his opponent to keep his balance.

Bellows has made a concerted effort here to highlight the Black boxer as an undifferentiated mass, rather than as an individual fighter. As we turn our gaze to where these bodies meet, things become more abstract. Discerning the space between the body of the Black fighter and the dark space that surrounds him is difficult. We see that the line between his gloves and skin is less discrete as well. Bellows seems to have laid a swath of brown paint *over* the Black glove at the very top so that it appears more as a twisted mass of flesh. Where we expect to see a face or head for the Black boxer, we see instead two dark masses; everything else is obliterated, even though this is the fighter that is turned toward the viewer. We can only differentiate the right fist from the head by the stroke of light brown highlight that suggests the Black figure's left ear. What we see here is a material expression of fear, a visual disintegration of the Black body as it is absorbed into the Black ground of the canvas.

As in *Stag at Sharkey's*, we can certainly locate the abject in the violence of this slightly later scene. In *Both Members of This Club*, we see a similar emphasis on blood and the most brutal drives of human nature—things that threaten the integrity of the self. We are witness to the opposing and interdependent forces of construction/destruction; we are simultaneously repulsed and attracted to this primal scene. But the introduction of the Black opponent in *Both Members of This Club* asks us to consider the abject on a social level. That is, its presence highlights whiteness by exclusionary means. Blackness is presented here as an abstract, aggressive threat that (like Jack Johnson himself) must be cast out of the social body.

Conclusion

Both Members of This Club currently hangs in a main-floor gallery of the National Gallery of Art in Washington, DC. As you enter the cavernous lobby, making your way to the central atrium, the canvas catches your eye. You are drawn into the small gallery at your left, noticing how the painting's installation on a front wall blocks the remainder of the gallery from your view. You sit on the bench in front of the canvas, taking note of the tactile application of paint—swirls of thick impasto applied by Bellows with what you imagine to be a sense of extreme urgency. And what do you feel sitting there in the cool, air-conditioned gallery, steps away from the National Mall? Do you notice that this is one of only a handful of Black bodies on display? Do you think about all the other Black bodies that escape our consideration, here in the capital of the nation that enslaved Africans built? Do you silently cheer for this Black fighter who presses against, who overwhelms, his straining white opponent? Perhaps it is all these things.

Bellows's boxing scenes provide a view into one of the more illicit activities of urban life, one which was under transformation in the decades surrounding the turn of the twentieth century. The artist's attraction to prizefighting connected to a widespread interest in defining (and reaffirming) manhood at a moment of great economic and political change. The visual spectacle of the boxer and his body was inescapable at this moment, as the rise of the sport's first celebrity coincided with the rise of mass media. These popular images of boxers asserted the body as the primary site of masculine identity and connected these fighters with intersecting discourses of nationalism *and* of race. Bellows signals his investment in the overall pathologization of Blackness in the (original) title, subject, and treatment of the fight at the center of *Both Members of This Club*.

I have argued that Bellows's boxing pictures, then, reveal to us not only the power of urban vision, but also operate on the level of affect. More specifically, we must look closely at the representation of the bodies in the center of the boxing ring, exploring their intersections with turn-of-the-century ideas about gender and race. Placing these scenes within the theoretical frame of the abject allows us to reconcile the oscillation between desire and repulsion that we experience as viewers of these violent matches as well as the fear of the Other that is realized in Bellows's depiction of a Black fighter in *Both Members of This Club*. Here we see that the boxer specifically provides a path toward both knowledge of the self as well as toward social critique.

Afterword

THE ART OF BOXING

For those of us who dare to desire differently, who seek to look away from the conventional ways of seeing blackness and ourselves, the issue of race and representation is not just a question of critiquing the status quo. It is also about transforming the image, creating alternatives, asking ourselves questions about what types of images subvert, pose critical alternatives, and transform our worldviews and move us away from dualistic thinking about good and bad.
—bell hooks, introduction to *Black Looks*

Throughout the 1960s the athletic prowess and global celebrity of the heavyweight champion Muhammad Ali continued to grow. During a cultural moment in which Black men increasingly exploited the threatening power of the Black male body to procure political agency, Ali, like many athletes before him, took up "macho" signifiers of masculinity—being tough, in control, independently minded—to compensate for a lack of political capital in the era of Jim Crow. This tradition continued into the 1960s and 1970s, as Black athletes made their bodies into political symbols. In 1968, for example, two track and field athletes from San Jose State University, John Carlos and Tommie Smith, stood on the podium at the Olympic Games in Mexico City, each with a single, gloved fists raised above their heads in a Black Power salute.

Ali exemplified the power and agency of the Black body, but we should also consider the potential for this specific body as a locus for desire. After all, alongside Ali's political protests and controversial political affiliations, we cannot ignore his wider reputation as a beautiful man. "Ain't I pretty?" Ali asked his viewers, repeatedly. Even on the canvas, Ali was praised for the elegance and grace of his movements. According to his biographer David Remnick, when Ali announced his affiliation with the Nation of Islam (the morning after his fight with Liston, discussed in the introduction; see fig. I.1), "he would never be more sexually magnetic."[1] Speaking with Alex Haley in 1964, Ali claimed: "Sometimes I've caught myself wishing I had found Islam about five years from now, maybe—with all the temptations I have to resist. But I don't even kiss none, before you get too close, it's almost impossible to stop. I'm a young man, you know, in the prime of life. . . . All types of women—white women, too—make passes at me."[2] It was clear that Ali's own desire often came into conflict with his new identity as a Black Muslim.

The press surrounding Ali likewise emphasized his sexuality, explicitly positioning him as the visual object of a spectator's desire. Consider, for example, the April 1968 cover photo of *Esquire* magazine, taken by Carl Fischer, after Ali was suspended by the New York Athletic Commission and stripped of his heavyweight champion title (plate 6). Here we see a very different Ali. Presented to us as the martyr Saint Sebastian, he is no longer the flexing aggressor, gloating over the body of a submissive opponent. Instead, Ali appears alone. We see the athlete in a classic contrapposto position; his straightened right leg bearing the weight of his body, while his left leg bends slightly so that the knee pushes forward into the frame. This boxer appears to turn away from our gaze, twisting in a somewhat languid pose, arrows piercing his body. The aesthetic divide of black versus white, echoed in the stark emptiness of the space surrounding Ali, as well as in the black and white silk trunks worn by Ali himself, seems to emphasize the dividing lines between Black and white bodies that became increasingly unstable in the spring of 1968. Although photographed in 1967, Ali's *Esquire* cover hit newsstands in April 1968—that is, just days before the assassination of Reverend Martin Luther King, Jr. in Memphis, which spurred violent protests in more than one hundred American cities. It was mere months before the demonstrations against the Johnson administration and the Vietnam War outside the Democratic National Convention in August and before Carlos and Smith raised their fists in Mexico City in the middle of October.

Fischer's photo metaphorically connects Ali's public disavowal to Christian martyrdom. However, I am not interested in this image for its clever use of visual history to place Ali in a continuum of undue persecution. I am interested in the instant transformation of Ali into a sexual object. We have seen in chapter 2 how the image of Saint Sebastian has historically stood in as a homosexual icon and an object of queer desire. In the example of Ali, he is penetrated right before our eyes, and his expression appears to be one of ecstasy. Like many other Black bodies, Ali, to cite Kobena Mercer, has been reduced to an "abstract visual thing, silenced in [his] own right as subject."[3] Ali, the man, risks becoming a passive object. But even more specifically, this image instantly complicates Ali's masculinity, positioning him as passive and penetrated in contrast to his dominant mode as aggressor. He becomes instantly homoerotic.

The sociologist Paul Gilroy has argued that "the question of sexuality has been the absolute sign for that rupture between a political sensibility from the movements of the 60s and 70s and those of the 80s and 90s."[4] Despite the many parallels between the Civil Rights and gay liberation movements, there was a distinct lack of reciprocity between them. In fact, while the Black Power and Civil Rights movements sought agency for the Black subject, we know that many gains were had at the expense of Black women and homosexuals. Scholars of this period often cite the example of the vicious attack on James Baldwin by the Black militant Eldridge Cleaver in his 1966 essay "Notes on a Native Son." In Cleaver's twisted review of Baldwin's literary contributions, he positions Richard Wright as the supreme African American novelist of his generation, claiming that Baldwin's own shortcomings derive from a lack of masculinity—a quality he claimed Wright, by comparison, possessed in excess. Leaving no doubt as to his position on the matter of homosexuality, Cleaver writes that it "is a sickness, just as much as baby-rape."[5] The model of hypermasculinity in the context of Civil Rights and Black Power was not only phallocentric, but staunchly homophobic.

Ali's homoerotic appearance as Saint Sebastian reflects this moment of rupture—between the assertion of a corporeal Black masculinity defined by physical prowess, patriarchy, and heterosexuality on one side, and the reality of a new, emergent sexual politics on the other. Ali exists, in fact, as a symbol of "rebellious masculinity," but the structures he works against are both white patriarchy *and* heterosexuality. Appearing on the cover of a popular men's magazine in this way, Ali simultaneously represents the potential of pleasure and of pain for the Black body. We might even imagine that for contemporary Black artists coming of age in the era of Ali, the boxer has performed as both an object of desire and a symbol of their own positions as Black queer men. Boxing, for these artists, offers an especially rich terrain for the larger project of thinking through such physical-corporeal-visual constructions of masculinity and ways to subvert them.

In the 1990s, boxing specifically emerged as a subject for several Black male artists. Glenn Ligon, for example, concentrated on the sport for his 1993 collaborative work with Byron Kim, *Rumble Young Man Rumble (Version #2)*—one of two works explicitly connected to the sport of boxing (the other being Keith Piper's installation *Step into the Arena*, 1991) that appeared in the exhibition *Black Male: Representations of Black Masculinity in Contemporary Art*, organized for the Whitney Museum by Thelma Golden in 1994. In *Rumble Young Man Rumble*, the artists covered the white canvas exterior of a hanging, punching bag with stenciled statements uttered by Muhammad Ali in the film *The Greatest*, a dramatized version of Ali's life starring the boxer himself.[6] In one version of *Rumble Young Man Rumble*, currently in the collection of the Walker Art Center, Minneapolis (plate 7), the quoted text reveals Ali's interpretation of his own public image—frequently positioned as inappropriately gloating—in the context of dominant white culture. Ali cites his relationship to Islam as a positive, uplifting one:

> So now that we have a man in America today, Elijah Muhammad, who teaches us that we are the greatest, and it is a fact that they cannot prove that we are not the greatest...so I don't see why the need for commotion and the trouble over people saying that they're the greatest, what's wrong with that? So, if you the greatest, you just the greatest, until proven wrong.[7]

Here we get a sample of Ali's racial politics, influenced by his membership in the Nation of Islam. As two non-white artists coming of age in the 1960s, Ligon (b. 1960) and Kim (b. 1961) certainly would have absorbed a complex appreciation for a figure such as Ali—one that included not only his earlier significance as a boxer, a dissident, and a successful Black man in the public eye, but also as embodying the potential to subvert the political, the racial, and the sexual identities assigned to him. In fact, for many artists emerging in the decades immediately following the Black Power movement and its radical politics, Ali represented a positive example of opposition.[8]

In a collection of seven photographs titled *Memoirs of Hadrian* (2002), the artist Lyle Ashton Harris (b. 1965) appears as a pugilist in various states of duress and undress. Bare-chested and wearing a jockstrap, the camera has captured his arms mid-swing or shortly thereafter, appearing to strain under the weight of the boxing gloves. His face twists into expressions of exhaustion, and his body glistens with sweat. In one image from the project, *Memoirs of Hadrian #17*, Harris's torso extends forward into the viewer's space (plate 8). Both arms bend at the elbow at an acute angle, leaving one gloved hand pointing upward as Harris's swollen and bloodied head recoils back. We cannot see an opponent and cannot help wondering if the wounds on Harris's face might be self-inflicted. The drips that run down the edges of the composition—a testament to the construction of the large-format Polaroid—emphasize the lines of blood that run down the figure's face.

According to the press release for the 2013 exhibition of Harris's *Memoirs of Hadrian* at CRG Gallery in New York, the photographs are a "meditation on conflict: both external (culture) and internal (momentary loss of self)."[9] Harris himself has argued that his goal as an artist is to challenge the idea of a unified (and arguably heterosexist) vision of the Black male experience. In a 1994 conversation with Holland Cotter, he explained: "I am deconstructing the hegemonic representation of black males through offering new vision and new possibilities. . . . I'm teasing at the multiplicities of black male experiences, exploring different subject positions, rather than just recycling the fantasy/projection of the available black stud."[10] Harris's self-performance as a boxer throughout *Memoirs of Hadrian* forces his viewers to contend with the paradox of the hypervisibility of Black men (specifically athletes) in American visual culture and their invisibility in political culture. We have seen throughout this book that the appearance of Black boxers in paintings, fine art photography, and popular media in the decades leading up to the twentieth century, was instrumental in giving visual form to fears (and fantasies) about Black bodies in the public sphere. *Memoirs of Hadrian*, and its representation of an anonymous Black boxer, has profound implications for our understanding of Black masculinity and its specific intersections with race and sexuality in our contemporary moment.

What initially struck me about *Memoirs of Hadrian*—a key motivation for this book—was how manipulating the tropes of Black athleticism, and specifically boxing, became a particularly effective way for Harris to negotiate the politics of race and masculinity. In these last pages of *Heavyweight*, I want to focus on how Harris mobilizes a visual history of athletes to illustrate the dynamism of the term "queer"—that is, its function both as an adjective to describe the artist's own nonnormative subject position and as a verb, an operation, a strategy to destabilize heteronormative patriarchy.[11]

Harris's project works across fine art and popular culture to unhinge the seemingly natural relationship between the Black athlete and the stereotypical

Black brute. Via the malleability of the image, Harris highlights the dynamic nature of both gender and sexuality. Identity here is constantly evolving. *Memoirs of Hadrian* confuses the tropes of gender and ultimately critiques the medium of photography along with its long-standing associations with the fetishization and pathologization of Black bodies. Perhaps most importantly, Harris's boxer invites us to reconsider the boundary between fear and fantasy, and the possibility of representation (in Harris's own words) to "provoke critique as well as arouse pleasure."[12] Like all the other examples in this book, *Memoirs of Hadrian* reveals to us the fragility of corporeal constructions of masculinity.

Lyle Ashton Harris is best known for his performative self-portraiture, in which he exploits and confuses normative cultural codes of gender, race, and sexuality via critical presentations of the body. The constructed nature of selfhood—that is, the degree to which one's identity is a social performance—is a prominent theme. He highlights the fragility, weakness, and, ultimately, inadequacy of vision in our construction of knowledge. As Harris explained in a 1994 interview, "I've found self-portraiture in particular to be a challenging way to interrogate the construction of my identity, as well as exploring the multifaceted relationship I have toward that construction."[13] Harris makes extensive use of disguises, which serve to highlight the artificial and constructed nature of identity. In some cases, he appears in drag as an unidentified female performer, as Josephine Baker, or even Billie Holiday. Meanwhile, in *Construct #10* (1989) he wears a ballerina's tutu and nothing else, leaving his genitalia in full view, and leaving the viewer to reconcile the oscillations between masculine and feminine. According to the art historian James Smalls, this ambivalence is at the critical core of Harris's practice. It functions as a sign "of a deconstruction of the codes of masculinity and femininity through focus on artificiality, performance gestures, and props."[14] In all his photographs, Harris reveals the constructed nature and the fragility of both race and masculinity.

The photographs that compose Harris's *Memoirs of Hadrian* series were first exhibited alongside other images under the title *Billie, Boxers, and Better Days*. The exhibition at CRG Gallery in 2002 included a total of eighteen works: the seven photographs of Harris as a boxer, two photomontages (*Memoirs of Hadrian #32* and *Memoirs of Hadrian #19*), six photographs of Harris as the mid-century songstress Billie Holiday, and two photographs (both titled *Je Ne Sais Quoi*) of the artist as a feminine-coded figure in motion. Harris appears in one additional photograph (*Better Days #7*) as a masked, seated figure with an exceedingly long phallus that extends between the legs and meets the floor in the foreground. In all these images, Harris plays with the boundary between the masculine and the feminine. When he appears as Holiday in *Billie #24*, for example, Harris seems to embody the jazz singer, mouth stretched open in mid-song. He dons a skirt, a bodice with fur collar, an ornate headpiece, earrings, a bracelet, and a necklace (all presumably made of pearls) and lipstick—as if these objects can somehow collectively transfer a female identity onto Harris's body. In this context, we might interpret Harris's appearance as a boxer as simply a masculine inversion of Holiday; boxing is, after all, an emphatically masculine enterprise. But in the boxing images, Harris fails to conform to the trope of the aggressive, dominating athlete. He appears before us weakened, battered. What then are we to make of the relationship between these images?

Across the series, Harris has concentrated specifically on Black performance and celebrity, or (as the artist puts it) "modernism's ambivalent negrophilia."[15] These photographs ask us to consider the contradictions within, or perhaps even the hidden cost of, American culture's embrace and commodification of Blackness—a tradition that we know began alongside the institution of slavery itself. That is, while these figures achieved widespread fame and, in some cases, fortune, they did so at considerable expense. Harris's evocation of these specific "types"—singer, dancer, athlete—highlights the fact that their success is almost always tempered by stereotype. For example, the famed "banana dance" of Josephine Baker—another subject for Harris during this period—drew its popularity from the widespread (and disturbing) fantasy of the inherently primitive nature of Black people. But we must also acknowledge the complexity embedded within this notorious act; Baker appropriated the primitive stereotype to subvert it. We can argue that Harris performs a similar subversion in his appearance across these photographs.

It seems no accident that Harris completed *Memoirs of Hadrian* shortly after his return from Rome. The American Academy in Rome sits in the quarter of Trastevere, just across the River Tiber from some of the most popular museums and historical sites in the city. Harris was living a short distance from the Colosseum, the Vatican, the Circus Maximus, and Palazzo Massimo alle Terme. That last institution—one of the four locations that make up the National Museum of Rome—houses a world-renowned collection of classical art. A Hellenistic bronze of a boxer, one of its most prized objects, sits on permanent display on the first floor. Known as the *Terme Boxer* or *Boxer at Rest*, this sculpture (late fourth to second century BCE) is a rare surviving example of ancient Greek sculpture. A compelling demonstration of mastery, the *Terme Boxer* stands apart for its realistic modeling of the boxer's face and body. We do not see the idealized body of the Greek athlete more typically represented by the earlier *Discobolus* of Myron (ca. 460–450 BCE)—a first-century CE Roman marble copy of an ancient Greek bronze discussed in chapter 3 that is also installed at the Palazzo Massimo alla Terme. Instead, the *Terme Boxer* does not appear to us in the midst of the action, but in a moment of repose after a match. He still wears the boxing gloves of leather straps with wool padding. Unlike *Discobolus*, the figure shows the strain and physical damage the athlete has endured. Instead of a serene expression, we are confronted with knitted and furrowed brows; the athlete bears the signs of his exertion and experience—a swollen, broken nose and cauliflower ears. Bruises and cuts cover the face, and his lips appear slightly recessed, as if the teeth behind them are missing. Drops of blood (represented by inlaid copper) have fallen from his face to land at his right arm and thigh.

With the *Terme Boxer*, we have a model for the athlete as vulnerable and in pain that relies on our reading of this body as "real." Yet, as discussed in chapter 4, on the work of the American artist George Bellows, the classification of "real" (meant to suggest a lack of artificiality) or "realism" (the French artistic movement that inspired Bellows and his contemporaries) remains particularly fraught in both fine art and visual culture contexts. In the images of the heavyweight champion Peter Jackson that informed chapter 3, we identified a similar disruption of the binary between "real" and "ideal" bodies. Jackson's awareness of the power of his own representation (as a boxer, as a gentleman, and as a specimen) relied in part on the assumptions we make about the relationship between the photographic medium and reality. The dominance of neoclassical aesthetic standards and the proliferation of bodybuilding in Jackson's moment and after were, in part, an obsessive attempt to make the ideal body a physical reality. And in the example of Eduard Muybridge's photographs of Ben Bailey—the subject of chapter 2—we have already seen that the boundaries inscribed by the conditions of the "real" have severely limited our understanding of the work those photographs do. We know now that Muybridge's photographs were not simply studies of movement. This project, and its overwhelming presentation of ideal white bodies (graceful women and powerful, athletic men) was an argument for the superiority of whiteness. I would further argue that Harris's use of photography, a medium directly associated with classification and pathologization, strengthens his larger critique of past artistic constructions of Black masculinity via the medium. Posing as Billie Holiday, Josephine Baker, or even a boxer, Harris purposely plays against the stereotype of corporeal, hegemonic masculinity while still leaving the desires embedded in those tropes exposed. He appropriates the trope of Black celebrity—a singer, a dancer, an athlete—while simultaneously queering them. We see the masculine become feminine, the stereotypical aggressor transformed into a weakened and passive victim. This allows the artist to establish a hybrid way of being both Black and queer.

Harris situates his Memoirs of Hadrian project within a specifically queer context with its title, taken from Marguerite Yourcenar's novel *Memoirs of Hadrian*, which the artist encountered during his fellowship in Rome.[16] Written in the form of a letter from the title character to his eventual successor, Marcus Aurelius, the novel details the life of the Roman emperor Hadrian (76–138 CE), who describes his experiences in love, family, and war. Throughout the text, the aging Hadrian expresses ambivalence around his marriage and addresses his homosexuality, specifically his relationship with Antinous (111–130 CE). Hadrian's political status, age, and wealth position him as the dominant figure, but he is also addicted to Antinous's exotic beauty. In Yourcenar's telling, the emperor's relationship with his young lover is a constant power struggle. Harris may have felt a personal connection to the story, as the artist's interest in *Memoirs of Hadrian* coincided with the untimely end of his own long-term romantic relationship.[17]

Aside from any personal connections that Harris may have had with the text, *Memoirs of Hadrian*, first published in 1951, was part of a larger, historical move toward a revival of the ancient world for homosexual audiences.[18] In the nineteenth century, for example, the works of John Addington Symonds and Oscar Wilde often centered on Greek imagery and history as a way to connect samesex orientation in the Victorian era to the model of a homosexual relationship between a man and a youth in ancient Greece. These interventions allowed queer readers not only to reconstruct a historical past from a nonnormative perspective, but also to use a classical model in their appeal for recognition. Just as Yourcenar engages the literary model of queering the history of the ancient world in *Memoirs of Hadrian*, Harris's project similarly intervenes in the history and iconography of masculinity.

Harris's representations of the boxer as a vulnerable, effeminate, and injured figure counter the popular, hypermasculine images of Black athletes most typically circulating in the public sphere. Here we see a counterexample to the eager, menacing boxer. The arms of Harris's boxer fall away from the body at wide angles, exposing the entirety of his slick, glistening torso to the viewer. This boxer does not meet the viewer with a menacing gaze, but instead closes his eyes, frequently with his head turned away from the camera. In Harris's presentation, we are forced to linger on the vulnerability of this figure. While the portraits of most Black athletes underscore the aggression and dominance of each athlete, the *Memoirs of Hadrian* series explores the fragility of that stereotype as well as the failure of some Black men to embody it. The figure is unable to perform as a successful athlete or to fulfill the definition of hegemonic, corporally based masculinity so often connected with these bodies.

In *Memoirs of Hadrian* Harris also works to destabilize the associations between masculinity and heterosexuality. For one, Harris's appearance alone in the composition makes a connection to pornography, where the convention of a single model within a solo frame allows the viewer to create a one-to-one fantasy with the photographic subject.[19] And certainly there is, as we know, an erotic element to the sport of boxing. The action of the match and the pleasure we derive from watching it center on the boxer's ability to resist or endure pain. Harris, for his part, emphasizes the homosocial complications of boxing via his incorporation of a jock strap—a standard piece of sporting equipment made sexual—throughout the *Memoirs of Hadrian* project. The rich, dark blacks of the composition offset the gleaming white fabric of the jockstrap (identified as "The Duke" with a vertical label that runs across three bands of thinly colored lines). Although the jockstrap is standard issue for many athletes, it is scarcely revealed to an audience outside the locker room. In boxing, the groin of a fighter is more typically both protected by a large, padded belt and covered with boxing trunks. In Harris's case, the groin is left vulnerable. In these images the jockstrap supersedes its protective function and highlights the genitals by way of the thin mesh fabric.

Harris's appearance in a jockstrap—a motif that also appears in Glenn Ligon's photo-text project *A Feast of Scraps* (1994–98)—alludes specifically to the aesthetic codes of gay male pornography as well. In the period before gay liberation, "muscle magazines" such as Bob Mizer's *Physique Pictorial* published intentionally homoerotic images while the publication was marketed nominally as a health and fitness resource. Published between 1951 and 1990, *Physique Pictorial* featured muscular men engaged in various leisure and sporting activities, such as wrestling, flexing, stretching, bathing, boxing, or perhaps even lounging in a cowboy hat and boots. Many times these men would wear little more than a jockstrap or similarly constructed "posing strap," made from jersey cloth. Such images were intended to project an image of a virile, athletic gay man. The men in *Physique Pictorial* bend their nude, fully muscled bodies into abstract shapes for the viewer's pleasure. And from the very first issue, readers could purchase the photographs for their own collections, as well as "posing straps" for the home photographer or fitness devotee.

Yet the appearance of the artist's suffering throughout the *Memoirs of Hadrian* project—evinced by his pained expression, squinting eyes, and bloodied face—moves these images past their erotic function. Literary scholar and cultural historian Saidiya Hartman has explored how depictions of suffering and violence derived from the spectacle of American slavery roused sentiment in nineteenth-century viewers.[20] I would argue that Harris's self-portrait of a bloodied and beaten boxer similarly exploits violence as a way of conjuring similar acts of aggression against queers of color in the early twenty-first century. Looking at these images calls to mind the historical and persistent violence against such bodies, such as the brutal murder of the twenty-six-year-old Arthur "J. R." Warren, an African American boy beaten to death in Grant Town, West Virginia, on July 3, 2000, by two teenage boys, who then ran over his body with a car, attempting to disguise the murder as a hit-and-run. We must recognize that images of the Black body often supersede the aesthetic function to act socially and politically as well.

In Harris's images we also see a boxer alone; no opponent appears within the frame. Harris's boxer faces the camera directly, and yet the body of the figure does not appear ready for the fight. Instead, his left leg crosses over his right (an arrangement that would put him immediately off balance when punched). His comically oversized gloves are raised not to shield the head, but instead to frame it so that we can see the makeup on the boxer's face. Both the awkwardness of the pose and the makeup suggest an effeminacy, or perhaps more specifically an ambivalence of gender, that Harris explores in other works—both before and after this series. The position of the boxer's body, however ill prepared for a fight, suggests that we—the viewers of this image—are the opponent. Harris places us in the position of aggressor. We are forced to linger on the vulnerability of the boxer, to consider his presence as an object in public space. Harris's images take a dominant, powerful image of Black masculinity and render it abject and passive. In doing so he resists the force of heterosexuality in Black culture through his disidentification with the corporeal codes of masculinity, drawn directly and purposely from the majoritarian sphere.

In Harris's case, the majoritarian sphere that he works on and against is multivalent. It includes a history of art, wherein Black bodies become abstract objects; the sphere of popular culture, wherein Black men are reduced to stereotypes; and Black popular culture, which promoted a deep connection between homophobia and Black nationalism in the era directly preceding the artist. Harris has spoken of his work as "a project of resuscitation—giving life back to the black male body."[21] Drawing from history, literature, and sports, Harris has built an artistic practice that simultaneously speaks to his unique position as a Black, queer artist as well as to more general perceptions of Black men in the public sphere. Harris deliberately attempts to undermine stereotypes by subverting and queering them, and in his choice of focusing explicitly on boxing in *Memoirs of Hadrian*, the artist necessarily puts pressure on both the sport and its specific implications for the ways in which we read Black men. His deployment of this athletic motif forces us to reconsider how issues of race and gender play out in the boxing ring. We have seen that in the nineteenth century the athlete—and more specifically the male boxer—emerged as the *ur*-example of masculinity. But I am most compelled, as the work of Harris demonstrates, by the specificity of boxing and its potential to complicate issues of race and sexuality as well.

I STARTED THIS BOOK in 2012, in the wake of the murder of Trayvon Martin. In the ten years that have passed between then and now we have all been witness to an explosion of anti-Black violence. We have been compelled to watch—via the somewhat chilling availability of video footage—the murders of unarmed Black boys and men by police, ad infinitum. We have seen Eric Garner (age 43), Michael Brown (age 18), Tamir Rice (age 12), Freddie Gray (age 25), Walter Scott (age 50), Philando Castile (age 32), George Floyd (age 46), and Rayshard Brooks (age 27) shot, choked, and beaten to their deaths.[22] Their collective crimes—selling loose cigarettes, walking on a public street, playing with a toy, holding a knife, driving with a nonfunctional brake light, paying for a pack of cigarettes with a counterfeit bill, sleeping in a car—quickly escalated by officers, who immediately and tragically identified them as a threat. And there are so, so many more. As I write this afterword, I am also reading about the death of the twenty-nine-year-old Tyre Nichols, who was pushed to the ground, kicked in the face, and relentlessly punched by five police officers for thirteen excruciating minutes during a traffic stop. I wonder: How do we continue to watch? How do *we* continue to breathe? As bell hooks reminds us, "changing representations of Black men must be a collective task."[23] While *Heavyweight* focuses on the late nineteenth century, I believe that its central concern—how Black men become the most threatening of all—has true, and often devastating, consequences in the present. It is by studying historical representations of Black boxers that we can expose the role that visual culture plays in the shaping of history *and* in the cultivation of anti-Blackness that organizes our world. It is by understanding the early production and reception of these racist and sexist stereotypes that we can get closer to understanding ourselves. And maybe it is by pushing back, by refusing to accept those stereotypes, and by fighting for other representations of Blackness that we can find a way to live.

Notes

———

PREFACE

1. Tony Pipitone, "Myths, Misstatements Surround Trayvon Martin's Death," *Click Orlando*, June 5, 2013, https://www.clickorlando.com/news/2013/06/05/myths -misstatements-surround-trayvon-martins-death/.

2. Marcus Christenson, "Euro 2012: Mario Balotelli Threatens to 'Kill' Banana-Throwing Fans," *Guardian*, May 30, 2012, https://www.theguardian.com/football/2012 /may/30/euro-2012-mario-balotelli-italy.

3. See Hartman, *Scenes of Subjection*.

4. James was only the third man (and the first Black man) to appear on the cover at the time.

5. See "Critics Go Ape over Lebron James Magazine Cover," Sportsfilter (weblog), March 27, 2008, https://sportsfilter.com/news/9733/critics-go-ape-over-lebron-james -magazine.

6. Steve Wyche, "Colin Kaepernick Explains Why He Sat During National Anthem," *NFL News*, August 27, 2016, https://www.nfl.com/news/colin-kaepernick-explains-why-he -sat-during-national-anthem-0ap3000000691077. Kaepernick's protests escalated the next week, when he decided to kneel during the anthem—a modification he made after a conversation with former Seahawks player and Green Beret Nate Boyer, who had written an open letter to Kaepernick suggesting a kneeling posture was a way to "show respect." Nate Boyer, "An Open Letter to Colin Kaepernick, from a Green Beret Turned Long-Snapper," *Army Times*, August 30, 2016, https://www.armytimes.com/opinion /2016/08/30/an-open-letter-to-colin-kaepernick-from-a-green-beret-turned-long -snapper/.

7. See Ben Jacobs, "Kim Jong-un, the NFL and 'Screaming at Senators,'" *Guardian*, September 23, 2017, https://www.theguardian.com/us-news/2017/sep/23/kim-jong-un -the-nfl-and-screaming-at-senators-donald-trumps-strange-night-in-alabama.

8. Bryan Armen Graham, "Donald Trump Blasts NFL Anthem Protesters: 'Get That Son of a Bitch off the Field,'" *Guardian*, September 23, 2017, https://www.theguardian .com/sport/2017/sep/22/donald-trump-nfl-national-anthem-protests.

9. Leonard and King, "Celebrities, Commodities, and Criminals," 3.

10. Hall, *Representation and the Media.*

INTRODUCTION

1. The 1965 match between Ali and Liston was a fight for the World Boxing Council (WBC) heavyweight championship. The WBC is one of four major organizations that sanctions professional boxing; the others are the World Boxing Association (WBA), the International Boxing Federation (IBF), and the World Boxing Organization (WBO). Ali won both the WBC and WBA heavyweight titles in 1964, but as explained below, his 1965 match was sanctioned only by the WBC. Wherever possible, birth and death dates for prizefighters are given at their first mention in each chapter.

2. See "1965 Photo Contest, Sports, 1st Prize," World Press Photo, https://www .worldpressphoto.org/collection/photo-contest/1965/john-rooney/1. Nearly fifty years later, readers of *Sports Illustrated* voted a similar image, taken by photographer Neil Leifer, as one of the hundred greatest sports photos of all time. A second image of Ali also appeared on the *Sports Illustrated* list—from the November 1966 match against Cleveland "Big Cat" Williams. "100 Greatest Sports Photos of All Time," *Sports Illustrated,* December 17, 2012, https://www.si.com/more-sports/2012/12/17/100 -greatest-sports-photos-all-time-final.

3. See also Fleetwood, *On Racial Icons*; Hariman and Lucaites, *No Caption Needed.*

4. Rooney's use of the 35 mm SLR camera indeed creates a rectangular composition, as opposed to the square image produced by Neil Leifer's Rolleiflex camera.

5. Robert Lipsyte, "Muhammad Ali Dies at 74: Titan of Boxing and the 20th Century," *New York Times*, June 4, 2016.

6. Bass, "State of the Field," 150.

7. Brooks and Blackman, "African Americans," 442.

8. For further discussion of the complex debates around the primacy of race in sports studies and its critics, see Davis, "New Directions," 17–18.

9. Davis, "New Directions," 184.

10. Bass, "State of the Field," 148–72; Carrington and MacDonald, *"Race," Sport and British Society*; Leonard, "Real Color of Money," 158–79.

11. See also Ferber, "Construction of Black Masculinity," 11–24. I have also benefited greatly from the works of Mike O'Mahony and Lynda Nead. See, e.g., Nead, "Stilling the Punch"; O'Mahony, "Art and Artifice."

12. Liston was arrested on March 10, 1964, in Denver for speeding (76 miles per hour in a 30-mph zone). The patrolman reported that Liston had no valid license and was in possession of a .22-caliber revolver. "Liston Draws Fine of $600 on Weapon, Driving Charge," *New York Times*, May 30, 1964.

13. Although biographers of Ali typically refer to him by the name Cassius Clay when describing events prior to his announcement of his Muslim name in March 1964, I have chosen here to call him by the name given to him by Elijah Muhammad throughout this text.

14. See Kindred, *Sound and Fury*, 38.

15. This is an excerpt of a poem written by Ali in 1960 on the flight home from the Olympics in Rome. See Maraniss, *Rome 1960*, 352.

16. In interviews Ali claimed that the model for his provocative behavior inside and outside the ring was the professional wrestler "Gorgeous George" Wagner. See John Burrows, dir., *Parkinson*, season 1, episode 14, BBC, 1971.

17. Chris Johnston, "Muhammad Ali's Greatest Quotes," *Guardian*, June 4, 2016, https://www.theguardian.com/sport/2016/jun/04/muhammad-ali-greatest-quotes -sting-butterfly-louisville-lip.

18. Roberts, *Joe Louis*, 51, emphasis added.

19. Johnson became champion in 1908 (with a fight against the Canadian fighter Tommy Burns) and held the title until 1915, when he was defeated by Jess Willard. Between 1915 and 1937 no heavyweight title fights were held between Black and white fighters. This changed in 1937 with the Black boxer Joe Louis's defeat of James Braddock on June 22. The first heavyweight title fight between two Black boxers did not happen until December 5, 1947, when Joe Walcott unsuccessfully challenged Louis. Title fights between two Black boxers became increasingly common in the second half of the twentieth century.

20. Arthur Daley, "Boy on a Man's Errand," *New York Times*, February 23, 1964.

21. Larry Merchant, "Sonny: Boy!!" *Philadelphia Daily News*, September 26, 1962.

22. Liston failed to return to the ring after the end of the sixth round.

23. Robert Lipsyte, "Clay Discusses His Future, Liston, and Black Muslims," *New York Times*, February 27, 1964.

24. Ali would get into a much more public fight with Ernie Terrell in the lead up to their match on February 6, 1967, for the WBA and WBC heavyweight championship, when Terrell repeatedly refused to call Ali by his Muslim name. Over fifteen punishing rounds, Ali famously taunted Terrell in the ring, asking him after several punches, "What's my name?"

25. Mercer, *Welcome to the Jungle*, 166. Mercer is discussing here a work by the artist Keith Piper, which takes the Ali-Patterson match of 1965 as its subject.

26. Jimmy Cannon, cited in Remnick, *King of the World*, 120. This is a reference to two boxing matches between the American Joe Louis (a.k.a. "the Brown Bomber") and the German Max Schmeling in 1936 and 1938. Positioning each fighter as a national representative—that is, Louis for the United States and Schmeling for Nazi Germany— the bouts came to symbolize the fight between democracy and fascism during the period leading up to World War II.

27. Eig, *Ali*, 220.

28. Ali very publicly refused induction on April 28, 1967, citing religious reasons. Almost immediately—before the official conviction of draft evasion—he was stripped of his WBA heavyweight champion title.

29. Walker introduces this term in a discussion about his own personal experience of multiculturalism, which he describes as "the sound of a door closing rather than opening." See Walker, "Renigged," 16–17.

30. See also hooks, "Representing the Black Male Body," 206–7. hooks discusses the hypermasculine image of the Black boxer in particular, using the examples of Jack Johnson in the early twentieth century and Joe Louis during the interwar period.

31. See Mitchell, *Seeing through Race*, 41.

32. Berger, *Man Made*, 1, emphasis in original.

33. Doezema, *George Bellows and Urban America*.

34. Mercer, "Endangered Species," 75.

35. hooks, "Representing the Black Male Body," 202.

36. Du Bois, "Of Our Spiritual Strivings," 3.

37. Du Bois first used this term in "The Strivings of the Negro People," published in *Atlantic Monthly* in August 1897.

38. Mitchell, *Seeing through Race*, 43.

39. In using the term *spectator*, I am referring simultaneously to a member of the viewing audience (or in this case a boxing match), as well as to the connections of this viewing experience to feelings of pleasure.

40. Benjamin, "Work of Art," 114.

41. Oates, *On Boxing*, 32.

42. Bederman, *Manliness and Civilization*, 5.

43. While this book is primarily focused on the United States, the sport of boxing in the late nineteenth century was indeed an Anglo-American phenomenon. For more on the sport within the United Kingdom and its territories, see Pointon, "Pugilism, Painters and National Identity"; Hyde, "Noble Art." Sports historians have explored the specific connection between the sport and the rise of imperialism in this period. See Stoddart, "Sport, Cultural Imperialism, and Colonial Response."

44. Ward, *Unforgivable Blackness*, 121.

45. "Sporting Notions," *Bulletin*, December 31, 1908, 28.

46. Jack Johnson, quoted in Ward, *Unforgivable Blackness*, 111.

47. Ward, *Unforgivable Blackness*, 114.

48. "Sporting Notions," *Bulletin*, December 31, 1908, 28. In the same issue, a poem entitled "Our Colored Brethren" succinctly made an argument for the segregation of Asians as a natural condition, claiming:

> they're nicely isolated in their islands overseas.
> And, as God has segregated
> Them with care from you and me,
> Let us keep them as they're rated
> By Eternity's decree.

49. According to Johnson's own reports, such epithets and taunts were repeated inside the ring by his opponent as well, writing "If I had killed Burns for the language he used to me I would have been fully justified." Johnson, cited in Ward, *Unforgivable Blackness*, 123.

50. The fight took place in Sydney on September 25, 1886.

51. "Sullivan Makes a Speech," *San Francisco Examiner*, June 1, 1891, cited in Petersen, *Peter Jackson*, 151.

52. See chapter 1 for a more detailed history of this publication.

53. John L. Sullivan, "Jolts from John L.," *San Francisco Sunday Call*, May 28, 1905, 7.

54. Fitzpatrick, quoted in Hornibrook, *Lure of the Ring*.

55. Rotundo, *American Manhood*, 222.

56. White, *First Sexual Revolution*, 9.

57. Henry George, cited in Trachtenberg, *Incorporation of America*, 43.

58. Gorn, *Manly Art*, 137–38.

59. Beard, "Neurasthenia," 217–21.

60. Lutz, *American Nervousness*, 6.

61. Reiss, "Sport."

62. Bederman, *Manliness and Civilization*, 14.

63. See also Roediger, *Working Toward Whiteness*. I note, however, that Roediger does not consider the role of sports in the ideological project of whiteness at the end of the nineteenth century.

64. For example, the introduction of Queensbury rules, which required a standardized boxing ring along with timed, specific intervals for rounds within the match, was one step toward legitimizing the sport for the white middle class.

65. Bederman, *Manliness and Civilization*, 17.

66. Zirin, *People's History*, 18.

67. Kimmel, *Manhood in America*, 120.

68. Bederman, *Manliness and Civilization*, 17.

69. Theodore Roosevelt, "The Value of Athletic Training," *Harper's Weekly*, December 23, 1893, cited in Reiss, "Sport," 186. For other essays by Roosevelt on this topic, see "Professionalism in American Sports," *North American Review* 151 (1890): 187; and Roosevelt, "American Boy." Roosevelt was also a vocal fan of boxing; he fought with gloves in college at Harvard, and when serving as the twenty-sixth president of the United States he even visited Jim Jeffries's training camp as he prepared to fight Jack Johnson. See Gorn, *Manly Art*, 197.

70. Gorn and Goldstein, *Brief History*, 178–79.

71. Gorn, *Manly Art*, 145.

72. Gorn, *Manly Art*, 189.

73. Gorn, "Meaning of Prizefighting," 227–28.

74. Kimmel, *Manhood in America*, 103, emphasis in original.

75. Kasson, *Houdini, Tarzan, and the Perfect Man*.

76. See chapter 3 for an extended examination of Sandow's images.

77. Hackenschmidt, *Way to Live*, 14.

78. A particularly fascinating and influential example is Kellogg, *Plain Facts*.

79. Bederman, *Manliness and Civilization*, 20.

80. See also Susan Goldberg, "For Decades, Our Coverage Was Racist. To Rise Above Our Past, We Must Acknowledge It," *National Geographic*, March 12, 2018.

81. *Chicago Daily Inter-Ocean*, April 26, 1893, supplement. Cited in Bederman, "'Civilization,' the Decline of Middle-Class Manliness, and Ida B. Wells's Antilynching Campaign (1892–94)," 10. The male emphasis of the exhibition was duly underscored by the exposition's exclusion of women in both its organization and its displays. In response to this exclusion, over one hundred prominent women, including Susan B. Anthony, petitioned Congress to appoint women to the exposition's governing commission. Denying their request, Congress instead established the patronizing "Board of Lady Managers." Despite the ridiculous name, this group of women organized the Women's Building,

a well-attended exhibit, inside the White City, and also attempted to post placards throughout the exposition to inform attendees about the role of women's labor. In reaction to the exclusion of African Americans from the Exposition, Frederick Douglass and Ida B. Wells distributed a pamphlet (in English, French, German, and Spanish) entitled *The Reason Why the Colored American Is Not in the World's Columbian Exposition.*

82. Lawrie, *Forging a Laboring Race*, 1.

83. Gorn and Goldstein, *Brief History*, 113.

84. Ashe, *Hard Road to Glory*, 23, cited in Zirin, *People's History*, 28.

85. Cited in Zirin, *People's History*, 28–29.

86. Fusco, "Racial Times," 16, emphasis in original.

87. Raiford, *Imprisoned in a Luminous Glare*, 12.

88. Campt, *Listening to Images*; Hartman, *Scenes of Subjection*; Lott, *Love and Theft*; Smith, *American Archives*; Smith, *At the Edge of Sight*; Willis, *Picturing Us*.

89. Sekula, "Body and the Archive."

CHAPTER ONE. THE BARE-KNUCKLE BREED

1. Heenan and Sayers fought bare-knuckle, as was common practice at the time. Throughout this chapter I differentiate between "boxing" and "prizefighting" when describing historical events.

2. Whether individual fighters were able to profit off such merchandise remains unknown.

3. *Cartes de visite* were sold in multiples, for a dollar a dozen or a dime each. Broadway theaters began to sell them, and they quickly became a staple in advertising for productions. Popular figures could have several thousands of cards made of them based on one image. By 1861, *cartes de visite* had replaced daguerreotypes as the most widely available and sought-after portrait photography.

4. Bederman, *Manliness and Civilization*, 8.

5. Burgos, *Playing America's Game*, 3.

6. Burgos, *Playing America's Game*, 4.

7. Burgos, *Playing America's Game*, 3, emphasis added.

8. Burgos, *Playing America's Game*, 3.

9. Hariman and Lucaites, *No Caption Needed*, 7. Thanks to Irene Cheng for pointing me to this reference.

10. Roediger, *Working Toward Whiteness*, xvii–xviii.

11. I am working from the example of David Roediger here in maintaining the language of race (rather than ethnicity) in relationships to new immigrants, which is more aligned with the past usage of the term. That is, "race" was a concept in industrializing America that applied to Black as well as European ethnic difference. See Roediger, *Working Toward Whiteness*, 31.

12. *Boston Gazette*, March 5, 1733, cited in Gorn, *Manly Art*, 36.

13. Moreau de St. Méry, *Moreau de St. Méry's American Journey*, 328–29, cited in Gorn, *Manly Art*, 37.

14. Obi, "Black Terror," 101.

15. Betts, "Technological Revolution."

16. Anderson, "Brief Legal History," 33.

17. Wiggins, "Good Times."

18. Douglass, *My Bondage and My Freedom*, 252, cited in Wiggins, "Good Times," 272–73.

19. Wiggins, "Good Times," 273.

20. See Abrahams, *Singing the Master*, 23, cited in Obi, "Black Terror," 104.

21. Obi, "Black Terror," 100.

22. As noted by Obi, Richmond's challenge to the social hierarchy also extended to his education and professional position within British society.

23. James J. Corbett, "Molineaux First American Fighter to Invade England and Achieve Success," *Syracuse Herald*, September 18, 1918.

24. Although outside the scope of this particular chapter, of further interest here is the movement of Black figures into domestic spaces—via figurines like those of Molineaux, as well as via lithographic prints. The way in which the desire white audiences had for Black bodies was expressed in the collection and consumption of images of Black heavyweight fighters in the US a century after Molineaux, a subject discussed in chapter 3.

25. Birth and death dates for many early prizefighters remain unverified.

26. James, *Life and Battles of Yankee Sullivan*, 14.

27. *American Fistiana*, 10–13, cited in Anderson, "Brief Legal History," 35. The fight against Bell took place on August 29, 1842.

28. *New York Morning Herald*, November 28, 1842, cited in Anderson, "Brief Legal History," 36.

29. The Queensbury rules were drafted in London in 1865 and published in 1867 by a Welsh sportsman named John Graham Chambers. They were named *Queensbury Rules* after John Douglas, 9th Marquess of Queensberry, who publicly endorsed the code. Other stipulations included a ten-second count for any fallen fighter, who would be declared the loser of the match in the event that they were unable to resume fighting within the ten seconds.

30. Commonwealth v. Welsh and Mitchell (1865) and Commonwealth v. Barrett (1871). See Anderson, "Brief Legal History," 45.

31. Isenberg, *John L. Sullivan*, 81, cited in Anderson, "Brief Legal History," 46.

32. James, *Life and Battles of Yankee Sullivan*, 24, cited in Gorn, *Manly Art*, 72.

33. *New York Express*, August 30, 1842, cited in Gorn, *Manly Art*, 73.

34. "On Pugilism," 468–69, cited in Gorn, *Manly Art*, 60.

35. Jacobson, *Barbarian Virtues*.

36. The original name was changed in January 1845.

37. Washington's address did include several references to the ill effects of immigration, including, "Against the insidious wiles of foreign influence (I conjure you to believe me, fellow-citizens) the jealousy of a free people ought to be constantly awake, since history and experience prove that foreign influence is one of the most baneful foes of republican government."

38. Gorn, *Manly Art*, 39.

39. Gorn, *Manly Art*, 39.

40. Gorn, *Manly Art*, 46, emphasis in original.

41. Sullivan and Hyer also engaged in a series of scuffles and challenges before the official fight, including a bar fight in April 1848.

42. Gorn, *Manly Art*, 81.

43. The formal contract for the fighters was signed on August 7, 1848.

44. "Excitement Relating to the Fancy Prize Fight," *New York Herald*, February 6, 1849. Cited in Gorn, *Manly Art*, 83.

45. *National Police Gazette*, February 10, 1849, cited in Gorn, *Manly Art*, 83.

46. *National Police Gazette*, February 10, 1849, cited in Gorn, *Manly Art*, 83.

47. *National Police Gazette*, February 10, 1849, cited in Gorn, *Manly Art*, 92.

48. This broadside ballad appeared in "The Pleasant Ballad of Tomme Hyer and Ye Sullivan," *Spirit of the Times*, March 10, 1849, 27.

49. Original quote: "The way the Raines law divides the different classes of licenses is also an outrage. The sumptuous hotel saloons, with $10,000 paintin's and bricky-brac and Oriental splendors gets off easier than a shanty on the rocks, by the water's edge in my district where boat-men drink their grog, and the only ornaments is a three-cornered mirror nailed to the wall, and a chromo of the fight between Tom Hyer and Yankee Sullivan. Besides, a premium is put on places that sell liquor not to be drunk on the premises, but to be taken home." Riordan, *Plunkitt of Tammany Hall*, 85.

50. In the image, numbers are marked beside the people, and at the bottom of the image there is a list of spectators' names. 1. Tom Hyer (boxer); 2. Yankee Sullivan (boxer); 3. Johnny Ling; 4. McCluskey; 5. Joe Murphy; 6. John Way; 7. John Colton; 8. Van Nostrand; 9. Mike Walsh; 10. Wm Hoyt; 11. Awful Gardner; 12. Si Shay; 14. G. B. Over; 15. Tom Burns; 16. Joe Winroe.

51. It would be an error to oversimplify the tensions around race as a sole binary between African Americans and immigrant whiteness. However, for the purposes of this book, the history of other racial identities in the United States (e.g., Asian Americans and Latinos) has not been analyzed due to the lack of these groups' participation in national boxing matches in the nineteenth century.

52. Holliman, *American Sports*, 141.

53. A discussion of neo-classicism—a reference in the commemorative coins as well—appears in later chapters.

54. My reading of early American newspapers is informed by the research and scholarship of K. G. Barnhurst and J. C. Nerone. See Barnhurst and Nerone, *Form of News*.

55. The exception here would have been Henry Chadwick, who worked for both the *Times* and the *Brooklyn Eagle* as a dedicated correspondent on cricket and baseball during the 1850s. See Betts, "Sporting Journalism."

56. For a compelling analysis of horse racing and its intersections with race in the nineteenth century, see Mooney, *Race Horse Men*.

57. *George P. Rowell and Company's American Newspaper Directory*, 1869, 274.

58. Hallock, "To Correspondents," *Forest and Stream*, August 14, 1873, 24, cited in Betts, "Technological Revolution," 47–48.

59. The list includes, e.g., *Fur, Fin, and Feather* (1868), *American Sportsman* (1871), *American Field* (1874), *New York Sportsman* (1875), *American Angler and Nature's Realm*

(1881), *Sportsman's Review* (1890), *Field and Stream* (1896), *Outdoor Life* (1897), and *Outdoorsman* (1900). For a complete list, see Betts, "Technological Revolution," 48.

60. *Outing* magazine reached an average circulation of 88,148. Building on the cycling craze of the late 1870s, the League of American Wheelmen's *Bulletin* peaked at an average of 94,000 subscribers in 1898.

61. Reel, *National Police Gazette*, 4.

62. The 1870s were remarkable in the history of publication. In this decade, the total number of American newspapers doubled, reaching seven thousand by 1880. See Stephens, *History of News*, 98–99.

63. Isenberg, *John L. Sullivan*, 94.

64. Cited in Reel, *National Police Gazette*, 29.

65. Betts, "Sporting Journalism," 51.

66. Reel, *National Police Gazette*, 45.

67. Gorn, "Wicked World," 12.

68. Reel, *National Police Gazette*, 115.

69. "A Valuable Gift," *National Police Gazette*, November 27, 1880, 2. Cited in Reel, *National Police Gazette*, 104.

70. Cited in Gorn, *Manly Art*, 210.

71. Gorn, *Manly Art*, 210.

72. Queensbury rules came into effect later in the United States than in Britain, and Sullivan fought under the older London Prize Ring rules through 1889. Boddy, *Boxing*, 91–92.

73. Gorn, *Manly Art*, 222.

74. Gorn, *Manly Art*, 225.

75. According to boxing historian Kasia Boddy, "the *Police Gazette* devoted itself to slandering Sullivan, and Fox set about finding a fighter who could defeat him." Boddy, *Boxing*, 111.

76. For an analysis of women boxers in the *Gazette*, see Park, "Contesting the Norm."

77. Gorn, "Wicked World," 8.

78. Isenberg, *John L. Sullivan*, 81.

79. Gorn, *Manly Art*, 247.

80. Horsman, *Race and Manifest Destiny*, 131; Croly and Wakeman, *Miscegenation*, 29–31.

81. Roediger, *Wages of Whiteness*, 134.

82. Roediger, *Wages of Whiteness*, 136–37, emphasis added.

83. Sargent's evaluation was published in Sullivan's autobiography, *The Life and Reminisces of a 19th Century Gladiator*. Cited in Gorn, *Manly Art*, 207. The prevalence of scientific measurements of fighters is discussed further in chapter 3.

84. Moore, *I Fight for a Living*, 119.

85. Moore, *I Fight for a Living*, 119–20.

86. Moore, *I Fight for a Living*, 117.

87. "Science," *Chicago Tribune*, November 17, 1883, cited in Moore, *I Fight for a Living*, 118.

88. Lippert, *Consuming Identities*, 315.

89. Lippert, *Consuming Identities*, 316.

90. Kasson, *Houdini, Tarzan, and the Perfect Man*, 19.

91. Bhabha, *Location of Culture*, 86.

92. Bhabha, *Location of Culture*, 88.

93. Bhabha, *Location of Culture*, 88.

94. See Bederman, *Manliness and Civilization*, 8.

CHAPTER TWO. BOXING IN THE FRAME

1. One battery would have been parallel to the subject for a "lateral view," and the other two positioned at sixty or ninety degrees to produce either a "front" or "rear foreshortening." As explained by Marta Braun, "Each photograph was made by a different camera (in tandem with the subject) against the same background as the one before it and after it but from a subsequent vantage point." See Braun, "Muybridge's Scientific Fictions," 4.

2. Solnit, *River of Shadows*, 187.

3. The *Animal Locomotion* project also included five images of a Black jockey riding a thoroughbred horse at the racing oval in Narbeth. However, I choose to focus here on Bailey due to his specific isolation within the frame as the subject of the motion study (i.e., as opposed to the horse being studied in Muybridge's plate 626).

4. In using the word "manhood" here I mean to refer to a particular Victorian construction of gender (both ideological and cultural) that had a moral dimension. As the historian Gail Bederman explains, the Victorian concept of "manliness" or "manhood" was likewise associated with specific traits, such as "sexual self-restraint, a powerful will, a strong character." Manhood was by default associated with whiteness. The shift to "masculinity" in the last decade of the nineteenth century occurred alongside an increased emphasis on the physical or mental power thought to be unique to men. "Masculine" was an adjective applied to *all* men, regardless of race or class. As Bederman has argued, the very fluidity of "masculine" meant that an extraordinary amount of attention was devoted to describing and explaining the specific nature of male power in this period. See Bederman, *Manliness and Civilization*, 17–19.

5. Sekula, "Body and the Archive," 7.

6. See Foucault, "Nietzsche, Genealogy, History."

7. See Braun, *Eadweard Muybridge*, 182.

8. I am working here from the model of Saidiya Hartman, who in her 2019 book *Wayward Lives, Beautiful Experiments* sets out to recreate the history and landscape of Black social life, working outside the confined boundaries of the archive and within the powers of the creative imagination. "Every historian of the multitude, the dispossessed, the subaltern, and the enslaved," Hartman writes, "is forced to grapple with the power and authority of the archive and the limits it sets on what can be known, whose perspective matters, and who is endowed with the gravity and authority of historical actor." See Hartman, *Wayward Lives*, xiii.

9. According to the 1900 census, two men matching Ben Bailey's age and race can be found in Philadelphia: Bengamen Bailey (born c. 1860) and Benjamin Bailey (born c. 1860). I believe the former to be the most likely option, as the second appears to have

been misrecorded in either the 1900 or an earlier census. Bengamen Bailey could read and write and was a day laborer. In 1900 he lived in a lodging house in the Philadelphia Tenth Ward at 1025 Spring Street, a twenty-minute walk from the University of Pennsylvania. On July 18, 1886, the *Philadelphia Times* records Bailey as being "of the eighth ward"—which was only a few blocks south from the Tenth Ward, and is located in central Philadelphia. The easternmost edge of the Eighth Ward is only a seven-minute walk from the University of Pennsylvania. Given that no one appearing to be Ben Bailey lived in Philadelphia in 1880, it is likely that our Ben Bailey was still residing in Virginia at that time. I have found two possible candidates whose records in Virginia stop after 1880 (suggesting they moved). The first is a Ben Bailey working as a laborer in Eastville, Northampton (born in 1860–61, age 19, listed as "mulatto"), in the household of Preston Trawer, a white merchant. His parents are listed as being from Virginia. Another black servant, Leah Mattheus, also worked in the house. The other candidate, Benjamin Bailey (born around 1864, age 16, listed as "black"), worked as a laborer in Zion, Greensville, in the household of Richard Phayson, a farmer. Benjamin and his brother, Jackson (age 18), have their parents listed as being from North Carolina. I would like to thank Claire Rasmussen for her help with this research.

10. "Saturday Night Fights," *Philadelphia Times*, July 18, 1886.

11. "The Black Diamond" was also the moniker of the Cincinnati-based fighter Harry Woodson (1858–1887). Woodson was one subject of a trading card series issued by the P. Lorillard Company to promote Mechanics Delight Longcut Tobacco in 1887. The "Prizefighter" series was produced by Bellin & Liebler Lithography (New York) and also included a card of the boxer Jack McAuliffe, currently in the Jefferson R. Burdick Collection of the Metropolitan Museum of Art, New York.

12. "Hart Hitting with Gloves," *Philadelphia Record*, March 7, 1885.

13. "A Desperate Set-To," *Philadelphia Times*, March 24, 1885.

14. "Sporting Notes," *Philadelphia Record*, April 14, 1885.

15. "A Plucky 'Coon,'" *Morning Oregonian*, April 11, 1890.

16. "Quaker City Athletic Club," *Philadelphia Inquirer*, October 13, 1891.

17. See also Lawrie, *Forging a Laboring Race*.

18. Among the potential rationales for Muybridge's choice of Bailey as a subject may have been his designation as "mulatto," which afforded the fighter both lighter skin and a slightly higher social status. See Creswell and Ott, *Muybridge and Mobility*, 75–76.

19. O'Mahony, *Photography and Sport*, 39–40.

20. *Pennsylvanian*, November 13, 1886, 106. Cited in O'Mahony, *Photography and Sport*, 40. Muybridge also produced images of women engaged in lawn tennis (*Animal Locomotion*, plates 297 and 299, for example).

21. O'Mahony, *Photography and Sport*, 39.

22. Cited in Solnit, *River of Shadows*, 199–200.

23. Solnit, *River of Shadows*, 16.

24. See also Nead, "Stilling the Punch."

25. Models in the boxing photographs were numbered 52, 53, 64, and 65. Bailey was model number 22. See "Muybridge's Animal Locomotion Study," Penn Libraries, University of Pennsylvania, n.d., accessed August 18, 2023, https://archives.upenn.edu

/exhibits/penn-history/muybridge#Origins%20of%20Muybridges%20Interest%20in%20Animal%20Locomotion.

26. Sullivan, "Boxing," 5. I rely throughout this chapter on this 1893 manual, which details the required body positions for bare-knuckle and gloved fighting.

27. For comparison, see Sullivan, "Boxing," 14–15.

28. In the late nineteenth century, the conventions of the sport of boxing and the technology of photography were developing in parallel. While we do not have many details regarding nineteenth-century boxing techniques, the readings that I provide here are based upon the rudimentary principles regarding the protection of one's face and head in the ring (a natural impulse) as well as the power of cross-lateral movements.

29. The original cyanotypes (#527) from this session, which would have been used to produce the final collotype prints in plate 343, reveal not just the reversal of the sequence for these images, but also that the second plate in the cyanotypes was horizontally flipped in the collotype.

30. Comparing plate 343, where he punches with his right hand, and plate 344, where he punches with his right, it does appear possible that Bailey may have been a left-handed fighter (or southpaw). However, these technicalities are neither verifiable nor particularly relevant to the arguments I am making about these photographs.

31. Higgins, *Grid Book*, 6.

32. Throughout this chapter I use the term *gaze* to mean the condition of becoming the object of another's look, and by extension aware of the self as the object. I am also interested in the intersubjective relationship between the viewer or spectator and the object, wherein the spectator also becomes part of the spectacle and the boundary between the object and the subject of the gaze becomes unstable. In Foucault's words: the "observer and the observed take part in a ceaseless exchange. No gaze is stable . . . subject and object, spectator and model, reverse their roles into infinity." Foucault, "Las Meninas," 5.

33. Prodger, *Time Stands Still*, 122.

34. Cited in Solnit, *River of Shadows*, 191.

35. Letter from Delaroche to François Arao. Quoted in Gernsheim, *Creative Photography*, 24.

36. Cited in Mosley, "Introduction to the Dover Edition," xviii.

37. Mosley, "Introduction to the Dover Edition," xxiii.

38. See Braun, "Muybridge's Scientific Fictions," 4.

39. According to Marta Braun, Muybridge and Eakins had been communicating since 1878. See Braun, "Muybridge's Scientific Fictions," 20n9. Rebecca Solnit also mentions that "upon first seeing the motion studies, [Eakins] immediately wrote Muybridge, incorporated them in to his class, and began a picture of four carriage horses whose positions were based on information gleaned from Muybridge." Solnit, *River of Shadows*, 197.

40. The supervisory commission may have also been charged to Muybridge as a consequence of suspicions regarding his character. He had been tried in February 1875 for the murder of wife's lover, for example, though found not guilty.

41. Maxwell, *Picture Imperfect*, 111.

42. Brown, "Racialising the Virile Body."

43. In the early nineteenth century, Irish immigrants were reviled right alongside Af-

rican Americans. The process of transformation from immigrant to "white" is discussed briefly in chapter 1. She also Pittenger, "World of Difference."

44. Cited in Maxwell, *Picture Imperfect*, 34.

45. Lamprey, "On a Method of Measuring the Human Form," 84–85; Braun, "Leaving Traces."

46. Galton, "Composite Portraits," 97.

47. See also Maxwell, *Picture Imperfect*, 21–47.

48. Cited in Maxwell, *Picture Imperfect*, 29.

49. Maxwell notes that despite these strict criteria, most photographs did not follow Huxley's exact instructions and instead used a more generalized approach, including the production of ethnographic portraits that would have been distributed as postcards. See Maxwell, *Picture Imperfect*, 33.

50. Mirzoeff, "Shadow," 111.

51. Gordon, *Indecent Exposures*, 69.

52. Gordon, *Indecent Exposures*, 69.

53. Brown, "Racialising the Virile Body," 631. The quoted text in Brown's passage comes from Omi and Winant, *Racial Formation*, 55–56.

54. Brown, "Racialising the Virile Body," 637.

55. Smith, *At the Edge of Sight*, 84.

56. Sekula, "Body and the Archive."

57. Shawn Michelle Smith further reminds us that when Muybridge photographed a white body, the emphasis remains on the body itself; the white body is neutral. Moreover, the scientific gaze is always presumed to be white. See Smith, *Photography on the Color Line*.

58. Costantino, "Seeing without Feeling," 73.

59. More recently, art historian John Ott has read these images of Bailey in terms of their impact on mobility—in both physical and social terms—for the Black photographic subject. He also argues that Muybridge's presentation of Bailey in the final volumes of *Animal Locomotion* (i.e., interspersed with white men in similar sporting sequences) attests to Muybridge's lack of segregation. See Creswell and Ott, *Muybridge and Mobility*, 53–66. However, I am arguing here that several aspects of Bailey's presentation (e.g., introduction of the anthropometric grid, the "shadow boxing" performed by Bailey, his nakedness, his race, and his status as a heavyweight) do in fact separate him from the other models. While Ott analyzes Bailey's presence in visual culture and in the wider social scene of the Gilded Age alongside the boxer George Dixon (a featherweight), he does not pay sufficient attention to Bailey's unique position as a heavyweight. As discussed in my introduction to this book, Black heavyweight fighters were perceived by the white middle-class public as a particular threat to the social order.

60. "The Record, 1887," Penn Libraries, University Archives and Records Center, p. 8. https://archives.upenn.edu/digitized-resources/docs-pubs/the-record/record-1887.

61. Homer and Eakins, *Thomas Eakins*, 13, 23.

62. Frank Fitzpatrick, "'Between Rounds': An Eakins Classic." *Philadelphia Inquirer*, July 22, 2007.

63. Walter, "Fine Art," 270.

64. "Between Rounds, 1898–1899: Thomas Eakins (American, 1844–1916)," Philadelphia Museum of Art, n.d., accessed September 28, 2022, https://www.philamuseum.org/collections/permanent/42496.html.

65. Walter, "Fine Art," 144.

66. Walter, "Fine Art," 214.

67. Homer, "Group of Photographs," 68.

68. Eakins's technique was apparently more precise than that used by Muybridge. For example, Muybridge's system took photographs from different viewpoints, rendering scientific comparisons difficult as the cameras could not exactly follow the speed of the object, and the intervals between exposures were irregular. Eakins photographed from a single camera with exact intervals; this camera had a disk with several openings that revolved in front of the lens. Eakins calculated the exact refraction for the camera lens himself. See Homer, "Group of Photographs," 67–68; Hendricks and Eakins, *Life and Work of Thomas Eakins*, 217.

69. "The Fight Between Deaf Burke and O'Connell," *New York Morning Herald*, August 21, 1837, 2.

70. Gorn, *Manly Art*, 142.

71. Gorn, *Manly Art*, 142.

72. "Seven Rounds a Draw," *Wilkes-Barre Times Leader, the Evening News*, March 18, 1889.

73. The first sociological study of a Black community in the United States, by W. E. B. Du Bois, was undertaken in Philadelphia. See Du Bois, *Philadelphia Negro*.

74. Walter, "Fine Art," 275.

75. Berger, *Man Made*, 32.

76. "Fine Arts. Eleventh Exhibition of the Water-Color Society. II," *The Nation*, 157. Cited in Berger, *Man Made*, 32.

77. Berger, *Man Made,* 32. See also Braddock, "Eakins."

78. There is also the tradition of the "battle royal," in which multiple fighters would be placed inside a ring to fight one another (sometimes blindfolded) to the last man standing.

79. Oates, *On Boxing*, 93.

80. Oates, *On Boxing*, 105–6.

81. Douglass, *Life and Times of Frederick Douglass*, 119.

82. Hartman, *Scenes of Subjection*, 19.

83. Hartman, *Scenes of Subjection*, 19.

84. Cited in Zirin, *People's History*, 28–29.

85. Roderick A. Ferguson presents a critical framework he terms "queer of color analysis" as a mode of addressing the intersections of racial, gendered, and sexual subjectivities. See Ferguson, *Aberrations in Black*.

86. Sekula, "Body and the Archive," 7.

87. Fusco, "Racial Times," 60.

88. Faulkner, *Absalom, Absalom!*, 20–21. Cited in Young, *Embodying Black Experience*, 221.

89. Young, *Embodying Black Experience*, 82.

90. Litwack, "Hellhounds," 12.

91. Equal Justice Initiative, *Lynching in America*, 46.

92. Linder, "Lynchings."

93. "One Year Imprisonment," *Philadelphia Inquirer*, January 30, 1884.

94. Cook was accused of the assault and rape of Mrs. Carrie V. Knott of Mount Airy. Another of the victims that year was Howard Cooper, a fifteen-year-old Black boy convicted by an all-white jury in Baltimore County, Maryland, for the rape of Katie Gray. He was hanged outside the Towson jail by a mob of seventy-five white men on July 13, 1885, just three weeks after Bailey posed for the English photographer. "Howard Cooper Hanged," *Baltimore Sun*, July 13, 1885.

95. Litwack, "Hellhounds," 11.

96. See also Raiford, *Imprisoned in a Luminous Glare*.

97. "Waited Weeks for the Victim," *St. Louis Dispatch*, July 23, 1899.

98. "Flayed and Lynched," *West Australian Sunday Times*, 3.

99. Raiford, *Imprisoned in a Luminous Glare*, 18.

100. Raiford, *Imprisoned in a Luminous Glare*, 18.

101. For a further discussion of abjection in relation to Blackness, see chapter 4.

102. Litwack, "Hellhounds," 22.

103. For more on the adoption of patriarchal values (e.g., physical strength, sexual prowess) by Black men as a direct response to their subordination in the white majority public sphere, see Staples, *Black Masculinity*.

104. See Mercer, *Welcome to the Jungle*, 133.

105. See Ferguson, *Aberrations in Black*.

106. Most of the walking models (37 of 58) in Muybridge's *Animal Locomotion* project are shown naked. All but one of the twenty-three ascending incline models appear naked, as well as seventeen of the twenty-six descending incline models.

107. Mercer, *Welcome to the Jungle*, 174.

108. Smith, *At the Edge of Sight*, 46–47.

109. Smith, *At the Edge of Sight*, 49.

110. While Shawn Michelle Smith addresses images of lynching as a counter-visual narrative to Day's homoerotic presentations of Black men, she does not explicitly connect that same history to Muybridge.

111. For more on the role of these images within debates around the Ethiopian roots of Greek (and thereby Western) civilization, see Smith, *At the Edge of Sight*, 55–62. It is also worth noting that the pose of the sculpture being held in the model's hand bears a similarity to the Greek-inspired photographs of Eugen Sandow discussed in chapter 3.

112. Cherise Smith has compared Day's *Ebony and Ivory* to the earlier example of Day's *Evening*, which shows a white model seated in a similar pose amid a bucolic landscape scene. She argues that the adjustments made in the later photograph (e.g., the emphasis on the tight frame and removal of any background) uniquely highlights the male body, constraining it within the claustrophobic frame and proffering it for the pleasure of the viewer "as an object to be devoured scopically." See Smith, "White on Black," 35.

113. Fanon, *Black Skin, White Masks*, 170.

114. Mercer, *Welcome to the Jungle*, 191. Here Mercer draws on the work of Laura Mulvey to rethink visual representation in terms of the power and privilege of the viewer.

115. Mercer, *Welcome to the Jungle*, 176.

116. Hall, "New Ethnicities," 445.

117. Mercer, *Welcome to the Jungle*, 194.

118. Fanon, *Black Skin, White Masks*, 109.

CHAPTER THREE. THE BLACK PRINCE

1. Although Jackson was known to cite Christiansted as his birthplace, this is unverified. According to his biographer Bob Petersen, the 1860 census recorded the Jackson family as inhabitants of Frederiksted. Peter also appears (along with all of his siblings) in the baptismal records in Frederiksted, rather than Christiansted. Petersen has also noted that during his lifetime Jackson's birthdate was variously recorded as July 6 or July 16, 1891. However, the baptismal register notes Jackson's birthdate as September 23, 1860. It was not uncommon during this period for Black people to remain unaware of their exact date of birth. To further confuse matters, Peter Jackson was also known to describe himself as Jamaican and to invent other biographical details. See Petersen, *Peter Jackson*, 5–6.

2. Petersen, "Peter Jackson," 40. According to Petersen, a portrait of Jackson by the artist Alfred Dickman Bastin hung at the National Sporting Club for several years.

3. "Peter Jackson versus Jem Smith," *Australian Town and Country Journal*, December 28, 1889.

4. Miller, *Slaves to Fashion*, 11.

5. Powell, "Sartor Africanus."

6. Powell, "Sartor Africanus," 222.

7. An example of a boxer of the Black diaspora who exceeded traditional representations of Blackness through the strategies of self-presentation would be the Panamanian bantamweight, Alfonso Teofilo Brown. However, the example of Jackson precedes Brown by nearly half a century. Brown was also part of celebrity culture in Paris, rather than the United States. See Williams, "Glamorous One-Two Punch."

8. *New York Herald*, April 17, 1894, cited by Petersen, *Peter Jackson*, 177.

9. *The Freeman*, February 15, 1890.

10. See Sontag, *On Photography*, 2.

11. Barthes, *Camera Lucida*, 13–14.

12. This is a perspective that has been influenced by Broderick D. V. Chow's research on Stanley Rothwell. See Chow, "Sculpting Masculinities," 39.

13. Muñoz, *Disidentification*, 31.

14. See also Chow, "Sculpting Masculinities."

15. See also Cassils, "Body as Social Sculpture."

16. Michel Foucault also examines the body and its inscription (i.e., its construction via social and historical conditions). See Foucault, "Nietzsche, la généalogie, l'historie."

17. The biographical details of Jackson provided throughout this chapter are sourced from the only known published biographies of the boxer, by Bob Petersen. See Petersen, *Gentleman Bruiser*; and Petersen, *Peter Jackson*. Unfortunately, attempts to reach Petersen to confirm exact dates and sources were unsuccessful. Where available, additional details have been taken from a series of essays on Jackson's biography titled "From Orange

Groves to the World's Pugilistic Championship: The Life and Reminisces of Peter Jackson," which appeared in the *Referee* across seven issues between March and December 1901.

18. In this chapter I refer to my subject by his first name, "Peter," in cases where I discuss the personal and strictly biographical dimensions of his life. I use "Jackson" to signify elements of his public life. Petersen, *Peter Jackson*, 15.

19. "From Orange Groves," *Referee*, July 10, 1901.

20. "From Orange Groves," *Referee*, July 10, 1901.

21. Ingram, *Australian World Boxing Champions*, 15.

22. The *Referee* identifies only John Waterhouse.

23. Donnelly, *Self-Defense*.

24. Donnelly, *Self-Defense*.

25. "From Orange Groves," *Referee*, April 10, 1901.

26. Although Petersen claims that Jackson's relationship with Sallars ended in conflict, further evidence to substantiate this has not been found.

27. Frederick Egerton Diamond (1840–1915), also known as Fred Diamond, was also Sydney correspondent of the *Boston Police News*.

28. During his career as a heavyweight boxer, Farnan was the first champion of Australia. According to the American records for this fight, Farnan was five foot nine, thirty-two years old, and 165 pounds.

29. "From Orange Groves," *Referee*, August 21, 1901.

30. During this time, "Professor Jackson" also taught boxing. Bob Fitzsimmons (1863–1917) was his most famous student.

31. "Fatal Prize Fight," *Evening News*, April 18, 1884.

32. "Professor Jackson," *Referee*, March 24, 1887.

33. Louis Moore has written of the opportunities afforded to Black men in the United States, who opened gymnasiums and other training facilities in the nineteenth century. See Moore, "Fit for Citizenship."

34. "Jackson, The Silent," *Herald-Despatch*, March 24, 1894.

35. Petersen, *Peter Jackson*, 43.

36. "The Australian Pugilistic Championship," *Bulletin*, October 2, 1886. Cited in Petersen, *Peter Jackson*, 43.

37. Petersen, *Peter Jackson*, 53.

38. Petersen, *Peter Jackson*, 55.

39. As discussed below, the city of San Francisco was perceived by many in the nineteenth century as an environment of newcomers, which was in turn more receptive to difference. This does not, however, account for the reality of historical discrimination experienced by Asians in the diaspora, particularly those of Chinese descent. For further reading, see Choy et al., *Coming Man*; Wu, *"Chink!"*; and Lee, *Picturing Chinatown*.

40. Lippert, *Consuming Identities*, 12.

41. Lippert, *Consuming Identities*, 13.

42. Andrews, "Carnival of Muscle," 33–34.

43. Andrews, "Carnival of Muscle," 40.

44. Burgos, *Playing America's Game*, 23–26.

45. *Boston Sunday Globe*, May 6, 1894.

46. Taine, *Notes on England*.

47. "Facts about Fighters," *Philadelphia Times*, June 30, 1889, emphasis added. See also "Sporting Notes," *St. Louis Globe-Democrat*, July 3, 1889.

48. Ward, *Unforgivable Blackness*, 18.

49. "Our Victory in the City," *Newark Advocate*, April 4, 1893; *Commercial Gazette*, September 4, 1893.

50. Cited in Petersen, "Peter Jackson," 40.

51. Petersen, "Peter Jackson," 40.

52. "The Race Question in the Arena," *Washington Post*, April 1, 1894. See also Ward, *Unforgivable Blackness*, 18.

53. "George Godfrey," Box Rec, n.d., accessed February 17, 2023, https://boxrec.com /en/proboxer/46632.

54. Petersen, "Peter Jackson," 40.

55. Burgos, *Playing America's Game*, 4. See chapter 1.

56. "'Parson' Davies, Peter Jackson and Joe Choynski in Town Today," *Leavenworth Standard*, April 18, 1893.

57. The white American fighter James John Corbett (1866–1933) was marketed as "Gentleman Jack" for his performance in a play of the same name. The play opened in New Jersey in 1892 and toured both nationally and internationally (with at least one performance at the Theatre Royal in London) through 1894.

58. As discussed in chapter 1, the last decades of the nineteenth century in the United States saw a rapid increase in the coverage of sports (and specifically boxing) across a wide range of news media. This included both sports coverage in existing mainstream periodicals, which recounted recent boxing matches or reported on the activities and lifestyles of the fighters via dedicated sports correspondents, as well as the emergence of several dedicated sporting journals in the decade after the Civil War such as *Turf, Field, and Farm* (1865), *American Sportsman* (1871), *Forest and Stream* (1873), *American Field* (1874), and *New York Sportsman* (1875). Although these new publications initially centered on reputable, middle-class sports—for example, cycling, yachting, and tennis—their coverage of prizefighting (previously considered a lower-class, immigrant bloodsport) increased exponentially in the 1880s to increase circulation, and thereby profit margins. The readership of these publications subsequently expanded to include the lower classes, which were increasingly dependent on visual imagery given their limited literacy. Engravings and illustrations, such as those produced by the *National Police Gazette*, were a critical component in the development of a gendered (and racist) looking practice.

59. Kurutz, "Introduction."

60. Although we do not have many records of Jackson's time in San Francisco, he most likely lived alongside the other Black residents of the Barbary Coast—a nine-block section of the city that was formed during the Gold Rush and was home to dance halls, saloons, bars, jazz clubs, and theaters. Although frequently maligned as a "red light district," this area was a city within a city for its residents. There were three churches (including the Union Bethel AME Church), Masonic lodges, barber shops, and bathhouses.

61. Bonnet, *Isaiah West Taber*, 2004.

62. "Isaiah W. Taber Dies across Bay," *Oakland Tribune*, February 23, 1912.

63. According to public records, Dr. William H. Mays was assistant to the chair of the Department of Obstetrics and Gynecology at the University of California starting in the late 1870s. In the 1880s, Dr. W. H. Mays was a superintendent and assistant physician at the Stockton Asylum for the insane at Stockton, the State Medical Society, at least from 1884 to 1888, as well as a professor of mental diseases and medical jurisprudence at the University of California, San Francisco, between 1887 and 1890 (or 1891). He also published his lecture on insane asylums: Mays, *Modern Distrust of Insane Asylums*.

64. The photographer Frank Davey also published photographs of acrobats and athletes (pugilists) for the *San Francisco Examiner* in May 13, 1888, and June 17, 1889.

65. See the introduction for a discussion of the rise of physical culture and bodybuilding in this period.

66. Macfadden published more than one hundred books in his lifetime.

67. Sandow, *Sandow's System*, 170.

68. Sargent, "The Physical Characteristics of the Athlete," *Scribner's Magazine*, July 1887. Sargent had devised, published, and even copyrighted his own measurement system in 1886.

69. When a decade later Scribner published *Athletic Sports* as one book in its "Out of Door" library series, "Physical Proportions of the Typical Man" and "Physical Characteristics of the Athlete" were reprinted to accompany chapters on golf, tennis, bicycling (including a section for women which included "a Gibson bicycle girl"), surf bathing and hunt clubs.

70. "Peter Jackson Measured for the Benefit of Science," *San Francisco Examiner*, May 26, 1889.

71. "Peter Jackson Measured," *San Francisco Examiner*, May 26, 1889.

72. An article in 1894 also compares Jackson's physique to that of boxer James Corbett and includes an illustration labeled "Peter Jackson's Powerful Back." See "Corbett and Jackson: Dr. John Wilson Gibbs Compares the Great Gladiators," *Kansas City Gazette*, March 27, 1894.

73. The history of this traditional game is somewhat murky, but official rules for the game first appear in the April 1881 edition of the *Field*.

74. "From Orange Groves," *Referee*, July 10, 1901.

75. "How Peter Jackson Missed an Opportunity to Benefit His Race; But He Is Not Cast in Martyr Mold," *Cincinnati Enquirer*, August 20, 1894.

76. Hatt, "Thoughts and Things."

77. Orcutt, *Pictures and Posterity*, 10. The art program at the Centennial was particularly fraught, entangled within larger debates about what the direction of American art should be. Lewis's work is now housed at the Smithsonian American Art Museum in Washington, DC; both Story's *Cleopatra* and Connelly's *Thetis and Achilles* are in the collection of the Metropolitan Museum of Art in New York.

78. Nelson, *Color of Stone*, 162.

79. Nelson, *Color of Stone*, xxx.

80. Hatt, "Thoughts and Things," 46.

81. The statue, likely a copy of a bronze statue attributed to the Greek sculptor Lysip-

pos (fourth century BCE), was discovered in the Baths of Caracalla in Rome in the sixteenth century. There are at least eighty known copies of Lysippos's example.

82. Wyke, "Herculean Muscle," 52.

83. Sandow, cited in Lindsay, "Mirror of All Perfection," 25.

84. See Reid, "Athletic Beauty."

85. Chow, "Sculpting Masculinities," 37.

86. Mullins, "Nudes, Prudes, and Pigmies," 28.

87. "Sandow, the Imperfect Man," *San Francisco Examiner*, May 20, 1894.

88. "Where Is the Perfect Man? Sandow, Peter Jackson, and Professor Wood of Stanford Give Their Opinions," *San Francisco Examiner*, May 27 1894.

89. "Where Is the Perfect Man? Sandow, Peter Jackson, and Professor Wood of Stanford Give Their Opinions," *San Francisco Examiner*, May 27 1894.

90. This image of Sandow has been sourced from a portrait by the New York photographer B. J. Falk. It is worth noting here that the arrangement of the figures also alludes to representations of "The Three Graces" (the daughters of Zeus in Greek mythology) in painting and sculpture during and after the classical period.

91. This pose appears to be a common trope, as we have similar images of Eugen Sandow from July 1893 in a collection of cabinet cards published by the New York photographer Napoleon Sarony.

92. This photograph also appeared in the salacious sporting newspaper the *Dead Bird* in Sydney on July 20, 1889.

93. *Dead Bird*, July 20, 1889. Unlike the illustration in the *San Francisco Examiner*, the Australian publication featured the photograph printed in half-tone, meaning that the dark skin of Jackson was preserved.

94. Winckelmann, *History of the Art of Antiquity*, 333.

95. "Champion Peter Jackson," *Dead Bird*, July 20, 1889. Cited in Petersen, *Peter Jackson*, 77.

96. Smalls, *Homoerotic Photography*.

97. The *tableau vivant* was one part of a larger variety show—a program that also included musical comedy and sketches—designed to attract bourgeois audiences to a venue more traditionally associated with a raucous middle class. Many of the interiors of these theaters and halls were decorated with wallpaper, electric lights, marble fixtures, and plush furniture. See Barrow, "Toga Plays," 211.

98. "The Strong Man Appears," *New York Times*, June 12, 1893.

99. Budd, *Sculpture Machine*, 73.

100. Budd, *Sculpture Machine*, 59. Sandow's magazine competitors, such as *Health and Vim*, also staged similar competitions in order to find the reader with the best developed male physique. Although occasionally invited to submit photographs, women never appeared within these publications.

101. Kasson, *Houdini, Tarzan, and the Perfect Man*, 84.

102. Langley, *Life of Peter Jackson*, cited in Clark, "Up against the Ropes," 161.

103. Mercer, "Endangered Species," 74.

104. Mitchell, *Picture Theory*, 76.

105. Bhabha, *Location of Culture*, 57–93.

106. Clark, "Up against the Ropes." The San Francisco debut of the play on February 27, 1893, was preceded by two weeks of previews in smaller Bay Area towns.

107. Clark, "Up against the Ropes," 174.

108. Several other contemporary fighters similarly took to the stage, including Jim Corbett and John L. Sullivan. Sullivan even featured as Simon Legree in his own version of *Uncle Tom's Cabin*.

109. Clark, "Up against the Ropes," 170.

110. Jackson died on July 13, 1901.

111. Johnson, *Black Manhattan*, 73, cited in Clark, "Up against the Ropes," 181.

112. The monument was designed by Mr. L. L. Page of Rockwood, New South Wales, who was awarded the commission through open competition. It was funded through public donations after Jackson's death. I am indebted to Susan Clark, whose article brought this monument to my attention. See Clark, "Up against the Ropes."

113. It was reported in 1901 that Jackson also possessed a heart-shaped locket with the inscription "To Peter Jackson, a Man." See "From Orange Groves," *Referee*, March 27, 1901.

CHAPTER FOUR. BELLOWS'S BOXERS

1. Seidel, "Jan van Eyck's Arnolfini Portrait," 55.

2. Huneker, "Academy Exhibition—Second Notice," *New York Sun*, December 23, 1907, 4.

3. Bare-knuckle prizefighting was popularized among immigrant communities, while the type of fighting practiced by most American men in the nineteenth century was markedly different. See chapter 1 for a brief history of these sports in the United States.

4. See Carmean, "Bellows," 27; "Both Members of This Club," *Harper's Weekly*, August 16, 1913.

5. Records of Johnson's early fighting career are spotty, but we do know that he first stepped into the ring in 1897. The *Ring Record Book* lists five fights for Johnson between 1897 and 1898, though there were likely more. See Roberts, *Papa Jack*, 12.

6. Roberts, *Papa Jack*, 15–16.

7. Roberts, *Papa Jack*, 19.

8. Roberts, *Papa Jack*, 21.

9. Roberts, *Papa Jack*, 39.

10. James L. Jeffries became world heavyweight champion in June 1899, when he defeated Bob Fitzsimmons by knockout in the eleventh round.

11. "Our Inquiry Department in Which Are Answered Many Intricate Questions," *National Police Gazette*, January 23, 1904, 11.

12. "Johnson, Negro Champion, Camps on Jeffries' Trail," *National Police Gazette*, November 5, 1904.

13. "Fighters Draw Color Line," *National Police Gazette*, December 3, 1904, 10.

14. Cited in Ward, *Unforgivable Blackness*, 63.

15. Ward, *Unforgivable Blackness*, 115–16.

16. Moore, *I Fight for a Living*, 113–14.

17. This single loss (versus Danny Duane on June 26, 1903) has been attributed to an unfair call made by the fight's referee. Moore, *I Fight for a Living*, 114.

18. Dana, cited in Zirin, *People's History*, 28–29.

19. See Runstedtler, *Jack Johnson*, 68–100.

20. "Even Athletes against Them," *San Francisco Examiner*, July 9, 1910.

21. Ward, *Unforgivable Blackness*, 56.

22. The historian Theresa Runstedtler has argued that the suppression of Johnson's history after his death was undone by the growing public awareness of his story following the petition for a presidential pardon by a committee led by the filmmaker Ken Burns in July 2004 and the premiere of Burns's PBS documentary *Unforgivable Blackness: The Rise and Fall of Jack Johnson* on Martin Luther King Jr. Day the following January. See Runstedtler, *Jack Johnson*, 3–4.

23. "Jack Johnson in His Latest and Gladdest Rags," *Los Angeles Times*, February 11, 1903. Cited in Ward, *Unforgiveable Blackness*, 56–57.

24. Theresa Runstedtler convincingly argues for the significance of Johnson outside the geographic borders of the United States as well. See Runstedtler, *Jack Johnson*. However, this falls outside the scope of my study and will not be taken up here.

25. Mike Murphy, "His Courage Is as White as His Skin Is Black," *Times Dispatch*, July 5, 1910.

26. The historian Louis Moore has convincingly argued for the persistence of such stereotypes in press coverage of the Canadian boxer Sam Langford (1886–1956), also known as the "Boston Tar Baby," who became the "colored" heavyweight champion five times between 1910 and 1918. See Moore, *I Fight for a Living*, 113–17.

27. Moore, *I Fight for a Living*, 124.

28. "Johnson, Sah Remains It," *Los Angeles Times*, February 27, 1903.

29. "Tip Wright's Column," *Tacoma Times*, May 1, 1909. Cited in Moore, *I Fight for a Living*, 126.

30. Doezema, *George Bellows and Urban America*, 74.

31. Morgan, "Foreword," 9–10.

32. Moore, *I Fight for a Living*, 10.

33. Keny, "Brief Garland," 10.

34. Cited in Slayton, *Beauty in the City*, 2.

35. Samuel Swift, "Revolutionary Figures in American Art," *Harper's Weekly*, April 13, 1907.

36. James Huneker, "That Tragic Wall," *New York Sun*, March 16, 1907.

37. The group included Arthur B. Davies, William J. Glackens, Robert Henri, Ernest Lawson, George Luks, Maurice B. Pendegrast, Everett Shin, and John Sloan.

38. Doezema, *George Bellows and Urban America*, 75.

39. Doezema, *George Bellows and Urban America*, 75.

40. See Moore, *I Fight for a Living*, 52.

41. See Zurier, *Picturing the City*.

42. Charles Morgan notes that Bellows likely did not see the painting by Eakins, who was working in Philadelphia. Nevertheless, he may have heard about the work through

either Robert Henri or Bellows's own contacts in Philadelphia. Morgan, *George Bellows: Painter of America*, 58.

43. For a history of the Pittsburgh Survey, see Greenwald and Anderson, *Pittsburgh Surveyed*.

44. Bender, *American Abyss*, 133–34.

45. See also Jacobson, *Barbarian Virtues*; Pittenger, "World of Difference."

46. Shaw, "Decolonization of John Sloan."

47. See Nochlin, "Issues of Gender."

48. Berger, "George Bellows."

49. Arya, *Abjection and Representation*, 2.

50. Arya, *Abjection and Representation*, 4.

51. Morgan, *Drawings of George Bellows*, 76.

52. Some historians have noted the influence of Daumier and Goya in Bellows's predilection for these types of caricatures. See Ayres, "Bellows," 51; Carmean, "Bellows," 34.

53. This second group of paintings is dramatically different in its treatment of the matches. The fighters depicted are more stylized in comparison with those produced between 1907 and 1909.

54. Schreiber, "George Bellows's Boxers."

55. While we must be wary of the degree to which the creation of Bellows's persona is self-conscious, these two novels (in addition to Mark Twain's *Adventures of Huckleberry Finn* [1885]) were claimed by Bellows to be personal favorites.

56. Bederman, *Manliness and Civilization*, 17.

57. This drawing was reversed and printed as an editioned lithograph in 1916 under the title *Business-Men's Class (Business-Men's Class YMCA)*. One example is held by the Brooklyn Museum.

58. Bellows quoted in Oakley, *Catalogue.*, n.p.

59. See the introduction for further discussion of the relationship between emerging physical culture and the establishment of a masculine body ideal.

60. Filene, *Him/Her/Self*.

61. Kimmel, *Manhood in America*, 106–7.

62. Lauvrik, "Winter Exhibition." Cited in Doezema, *George Bellows and Urban America*, 89.

63. Corbett, "Life in the Ring," 74.

64. Morgan, *George Bellow*, 69.

65. See also Runstedtler, *Jack Johnson*, 136–41.

66. Runstedtler, *Jack Johnson*, 151. For more on Johnson's vaudeville career, see "Jack Has Music Hall Engagements Galore," *The Freeman*, September 2, 1911; "Johnson Is a Big Hit," *Washington Post*, July 9, 1911.

67. Johnson first met boxer Joe Choynski in 1901 when Choynski was in Galveston, Texas, to fight Johnson. He knocked Johnson out in the third round, and both boxers were arrested for engaging in an illegal contest. They spent twenty-three days in jail together, during which time Choynski taught Johnson some of his tricks.

68. The technical limitations of the camera at this time meant that it was not possible to capture the high-speed movement of bodies with a single exposure.

69. For further discussion of the intersection of race and photography in other representations of boxers, see chapter 2.

70. According to one biographer, Johnson earned most of his income between 1908 and 1912 from vaudeville performances. The particularly performative nature of these cabinet-card images may have been directly tied to Johnson's stage career. See Ward, *Unforgivable Blackness*, 103.

71. See chapter 3 for further discussion of Peter Jackson.

72. George Dixon was Canadian and Joe Walcott was born in Barbados in 1873. Joe Gans was born in Baltimore, Maryland, in 1874. Gans's threat was also minimized by constant references to his presumed "exotic" heritage—more Arab than African—and his slight, slender frame.

73. Bederman, *Manliness and Civilization*, 8.

74. Bederman, *Manliness and Civilization*, 8.

75. Johnson, *Jack Johnson Is a Dandy*, 22.

76. Cited in Doezema, *George Bellows and Urban America*, 217.

77. Cited in Doezema, *George Bellows and Urban America*, 97.

78. Zurier, *Picturing the City*, 240.

79. Zurier, *Picturing the City*, 244.

80. Haywood, "George Bellows's *Stag at Sharkey's*," 12.

81. Haywood, "George Bellows's *Stag at Sharkey's*," 12.

82. Corbett, "Life in the Ring," 71–79.

83. Corbett, "Life in the Ring," 75.

84. Corbett, "Life in the Ring," 77.

85. Butler, *Bodies That Matter*, 3.

86. Butler, *Bodies That Matter*, 111–12.

87. For example, historian Rachel Schreiber reads depictions of fights between Jess Willard (*The Savior of His Race*, May 1915) and Jim Jeffries (*The White Hope*, 1921) as critical of the ideology of white supremacy, calling our attention to the depiction of both "heroes" in these interracial matches as humbled and defeated by their shared Black opponent, Jack Johnson. See Schreiber, "George Bellows's Boxers." For similar optimism regarding Bellows's conception of race, see also Adams, "Win, Lose."

88. Berger, "George Bellows," 79.

89. Runstedtler, *Jack Johnson*, 152.

90. This was not a title fight; Burns sold his championship prior to the match for $30,000.

91. "Burns Tells of Plans after Australian Fights," *Anaconda Times*, June 30, 1908. Cited in Moore, *I Fight for a Living*, 128.

92. "Physical Culture Expert Declares Johnson an Athletic Marvel," *Salt Lake Telegram*, April 30, 1910. Cited in Moore, *I Fight for a Living*, 131.

93. Cited in Roberts, *Papa Jack*, 225.

94. "The Fight and Its Consequences," *Los Angeles Times*, July 6, 1910.

95. Charlie Chaplin was prosecuted (and acquitted) under the Mann Act in 1944. Fifteen years later, Black musician Chuck Berry was accused (and convicted) for violat-

ing the Mann Act for his relationship with a fourteen-year-old white girl named Janice Escalanti.

96. "US Holds Girl in Johnson Case," *Chicago Daily Tribune*, October 19, 1912.

97. Cameron accompanied Johnson when he was sailing to Europe and Mexico until July 20, 1920, when he surrendered. By the time he was released from US custody on July 9, 1921, Cameron was waiting for Johnson. Their marriage ended in divorce in 1924 because of infidelity.

98. See Gilmore, "Jack Johnson and White Women."

AFTERWORD

1. Remnick, *King of the World*, 229–30.

2. "Haley, "Alex Haley Interviews Cassius Clay," 72.

3. Mercer, "Looking for Trouble," 351.

4. Paul Gilroy, "Roundtable Discussion," in Jones and Sokolowski, *Interrogating Identity*, 59.

5. Eldridge Cleaver, "Notes on a Native Son," *Ramparts Magazine*, June 1966.

6. *The Greatest*, directed by Tom Gries (USA/UK, 1977), 101 min.

7. Quotation transcribed from the punching bag, ellipsis in original.

8. See Ezra, *Muhammad Ali*. For other heroic representations of Ali, see the photographs made by Gordon Parks for *Life* magazine in 1966 and 1970.

9. "Lyle Ashton Harris: Memoirs of Hadrian," press release, CRG Gallery, New York, 2003, accessed July 13, 2017, http://crggallery.com/exhibitions/lyle-ashton-harris-memoirs-of-hadrian/#.

10. Cotter, "Art after Stonewall," 64.

11. My use of "queer" in this instance is intended to place an emphasis on the relational, social, and intersectional quality of all sexual identity, including heterosexuality. This is a way to avoid a binary of heterosexuality as the normative, privileged position, while thinking of homosexuality as the aberration. "Queer" is a way to think about the intersections of social boundaries—race, gender, and sexuality—rather than their singular dimensions.

12. Coblentz, *Lyle Ashton Harris*, 144.

13. Vince Aletti, "It's a Family Affair: Photographer Lyle Ashton Harris Scores a Strategic Hit," *Village Voice*, September 27, 1994.

14. Smalls, "African-American Self-Portraiture," 59.

15. Lyle Ashton Harris, "Billie, Boxers, Better Days," accessed February 28, 2020, https://www.lyleashtonharris.com/series/billie-boxers-better-days/.

16. "Lyle Ashton Harris: Memoirs of Hadrian," press release, CRG Gallery, New York, 2003, accessed July 13, 2017, http://crggallery.com/exhibitions/lyle-ashton-harris-memoirs-of-hadrian/#.

17. Harris, interview with the author, San Francisco, February 15, 2018.

18. Yourcenar's novel does not reference boxing, but my interest in the text is provoked by Harris's citation of it. I will note here that the book was for sale in the bookstore of the Palazzo Massimo alle Terme on the day of my visit there in the summer of 2018.

19. Mercer, *Welcome to the Jungle*, 136.

20. Hartman, *Scenes of Subjection*.

21. Harris, cited in hooks, "Feminism Inside," 140.

22. See also the list compiled by Renée Ater, "In Memoriam: I Can't Breathe," blogpost, May 29, 2020, https://www.reneeater.com/on-monuments-blog/tag/list+of+unarmed+black+people+killed+by+police.

23. hooks, "Reconstructing Black Masculinity," 113.

Bibliography

NEWSPAPERS AND MAGAZINES

American Art News (New York)
Anaconda (MT) Times
Army Times (Springfield, VA)
Australian Town and Country Journal
Baltimore (MD) Sun
Bird O'Freedom (Sydney, Australia)
Boston Gazette
Boston Sunday Globe
Bulletin (Sydney, Australia)
Chicago Daily Inter-Ocean
Chicago Daily News
Chicago Daily Tribune
Chicago Tribune
Cincinnati Enquirer
Commercial Gazette (Baltimore, MD)
Dead Bird (Sydney, Australia)
Evening News (Sydney, Australia)
Forest and Stream (New York)
The Freeman (Indianapolis, IN)
Guardian (London)

Harper's Weekly
Herald-Despatch (Decatur, IL)
Kansas City (KS) Gazette
Lancaster (PA) Intelligencer
Leavenworth (KS) Standard
Literary Magazine and American Register (Philadelphia)
Los Angeles Times
Morning Journal (New York)
Morning Oregonian
The Nation (New York)
National Geographic
National Police Gazette (New York)
Nature
New York Evening Post
New York Express
New York Herald
New York Morning Express
New York Morning Herald
New York Sun

New York Times
New York World
Newark (NJ) Advocate
NFL *News*
Oakland (CA) Tribune
Pennsylvanian
Philadelphia Daily News
Philadelphia Inquirer
Philadelphia Record
Philadelphia Times
Referee (Sydney, Australia)
Salt Lake Telegram (Salt Lake City, UT)
San Francisco Chronicle
San Francisco Examiner
San Francisco Sunday Call
Scientific American

Scribner's Magazine
Spirit of the Times (New York)
Sports Illustrated
St. Louis Dispatch
St. Louis Globe-Democrat
Sydney Bulletin
Sydney Morning Herald
Syracuse (NY) Herald
Tacoma (WA) Times
Times Dispatch (Richmond, VA)
Turf, Field, and Farm (New York)
Vanity Fair
Washington Post
West Australian Sunday Times
Wilkes-Barre (PA) Times Leader, the Evening News

OTHER SOURCES

Abrahams, Roger D. *Singing the Master: The Emergence of African American Culture in the Plantation South*. New York: Pantheon Books, 1992.

Adams, Peter A. "Win, Lose, and Drawing Conclusions: Bellows, Boxing, and Progressivism." OAH *Magazine of History* 7, no. 1 (Summer 1992): 34–38.

The American Fistiana. New York: Franklin Classics, 1860.

Anderson, Jack. "A Brief Legal History of Prize Fighting in Nineteenth Century America." *Sport in History* 24, no. 1 (Summer 2004): 32–62.

Andrews, M. P. "A Carnival of Muscle: Popular Amusements and Public Culture in Turn-of-the-Century San Francisco, 1880–1920." PhD diss., University of North Carolina at Chapel Hill, 2008.

Arya, Rina. *Abjection and Representation: An Exploration of Abjection in the Visual Arts, Film, and Literature*. London: Palgrave Macmillan, 2014.

Ashe, Arthur. *A Hard Road to Glory: A History of the African American Athlete, 1619–1918*. New York: Amistad, 1993.

Ayres, Linda. "Bellows: The Boxing Drawings." In *Bellows: The Boxing Pictures*, edited by E. A. Carmean Jr., John Wilmerding, Linda Ayres, and Deborah Chotner, 49–66. Washington, DC: National Gallery of Art, 1982. Exhibition catalog.

Barnhurst, Kevin G., and John Nerone. *The Form of News: A History*. New York: Guilford Press, 2001.

Barrow, Rosemary. "Toga Plays and Tableaux Vivants: Theatre and Painting on London's Late-Victorian and Edwardian Popular Stage." *Theatre Journal* 62, no. 2 (May 2010): 209–26.

Barthes, Roland. *Camera Lucida: Reflections on Photography*. Translated by Richard Howard. New York: Hill and Wang, 1981.

Bass, Amy. "State of the Field: Sports History and the 'Cultural Turn.'" *Journal of American History* 101, no. 1 (June 2014): 148–72.

Beard, George Miller. "Neurasthenia or Nervous Exhaustion." *Boston Medical and Surgical Journal* 80, no. 13 (1869): 217–21.

Bederman, Gail. "'Civilization,' the Decline of Middle-Class Manliness, and Ida B. Wells's Antilynching Campaign (1892–94)." *Radical History Review* 52 (Winter 1992): 5–30.

Bederman, Gail. *Manliness and Civilization: A Cultural History of Gender and Race in the United States, 1880–1917*. Chicago: University of Chicago Press, 1995.

Bender, Daniel E. *American Abyss: Savagery and Civilization in the Age of Industry*. Ithaca, NY: Cornell University Press, 2009.

Benjamin, Walter. "The Work of Art in the Age of Mechanical Reproduction." In *Walter Benjamin: Selected Writings, Volume 3: 1935–38*, edited by Michael W. Jennings, Howard Eiland, and Gary Smith, 101–33. Cambridge, MA: Belknap Press of Harvard University Press, 2002.

Berger, Martin A. "George Bellows and the Complication of Race." In *George Bellows Revisited: New Considerations of the Painter's Oeuvre*, edited by M. Melissa Wolfe, 71–86. Newcastle-upon-Tyne: Cambridge Scholars Publishing, 2016.

Berger, Martin A. *Man Made: Thomas Eakins and the Construction of Gilded Age Manhood*. Berkeley: University of California Press, 2000.

Betts, John Rickards. "Sporting Journalism in Nineteenth-Century America." *American Quarterly* 5, no. 1 (1953): 39–56.

Betts, John Rickards. "The Technological Revolution and the Rise of Sport, 1850–1900." *Mississippi Valley Historical Review* 40 (September 1953): 231–56.

Bhabha, Homi K.. *The Location of Culture*. New York: Routledge, 1994.

Boddy, Kasia. *Boxing: A Cultural History*. London: Reaktion Books, 2008.

Bonnet, Linda. *Isaiah West Taber: A Photographic Legacy*. Sausalito, CA: Windgate Press, 2004.

Braddock, Alan C. "Eakins, Race, and Ethnographic Ambivalence." *Winterthur Portfolio* 33 (Summer/Autumn 1998): 135–61.

Braun, Marta. "Chronophotography: Leaving Traces." In *Moving Pictures: American Art and Early Film 1880–1910*, edited by Nancy Mowll Mathews, 95–99. New York: Hudson Hills Press, 2005. Exhibition catalog.

Braun, Marta. *Eadweard Muybridge*. London: Reaktion Books, 2010.

Braun, Marta. "Muybridge's Scientific Fictions." *Studies in Visual Communication* 10, no. 3 (Summer 1984): 2–21.

Brooks, Scott N., and Dexter Blackman. "African Americans and the History of Sport: New Perspectives." *Journal of African American History* 96, no. 4 (Fall 2011): 441–47.

Brown, Elspeth H. "Racialising the Virile Body: Eadweard Muybridge's Locomotion Studies 1883–1887." *Gender and History* 17, no. 3 (November 2005): 627–56.

Budd, Michael Anton. *The Sculpture Machine*. New York: New York University Press, 1997.

Burgos, Adrian. *Playing America's Game: Baseball, Latinos, and the Color Line*. Berkeley: University of California Press, 2007.

Butler, Judith. *Bodies That Matter: On the Discursive Limits of "Sex."* London: Routledge, 2014.

Campt, Tina M. *Listening to Images*. Durham, NC: Duke University Press, 2017.

Carmean, E. A., Jr. "Bellows: The Boxing Paintings." In *Bellows: The Boxing Pictures*, edited by E. A. Carmean Jr., John Wilmerding, Linda Ayres, and Deborah Chotner, 27–47. Washington, DC: National Gallery of Art, 1982. Exhibition catalog.

Carrington, Ben, and Ian MacDonald. *"Race," Sport and British Society*. New York: Routledge, 2001.

Cassils. "The Body as Social Sculpture." Lecture, Goldsmiths College, University of London, November 10, 2015. http://www.gold.ac.uk/calendar/?id=9243.

Chow, Broderick D. V. "Sculpting Masculinities in Nineteenth- and Twentieth-Century Physical Culture: The Practiced Life of Stanley Rothwell." *TDR: The Drama Review* 63, no. 2 (Summer 2019): 34–56.

Choy, Philip P., Marlon K. Hom, and Lorraine Dong. *Coming Man: Nineteenth-Century American Perceptions of the Chinese*. Seattle: University of Washington Press, 1995.

Clark, Susan F. "Up against the Ropes: Peter Jackson as 'Uncle Tom' in America." *TDR: The Drama Review* 44, no. 1 (Spring 2000): 157–82.

Coblentz, Cassandra, ed. *Lyle Ashton Harris: Blow Up*. Scottsdale, AZ: Scottsdale Museum of Contemporary Art, 2008. Exhibition catalog.

Corbett, David Peters. "Life in the Ring: Boxing, 1907–1909." In *George Bellows*, edited by Charles Brock, 71–79. Washington, DC: National Gallery of Art, 2012. Exhibition catalog.

Costantino, Jesús. "Seeing without Feeling: Muybridge's Boxing Pictures and the Rise of the Bourgeois Film Spectator." *Film and History* 44, no. 2 (Fall 2014): 66–81.

Cotter, Holland. "Art After Stonewall (Part 1)." *Art in America* 82, no. 6 (June 1994): 56.

Creswell, Tim, and John Ott. *Muybridge and Mobility*. Berkeley: University of California Press, 2022.

Croly, David Goodman, and George Wakeman. *Miscegenation: The Theory of the Blending of the Races, Applied to the American White Man and Negro*. New York: Dexter, Hamilton & Company, 1863.

Davis, Amira Rose. "New Directions in African American Sports History: A Field of One's Own." *Journal of African American History* 106, no. 2 (Spring 2021): 182–95.

Doezema, Marianne. *George Bellows and Urban America*. New Haven, CT: Yale University Press, 1992.

Donnelly, Ned. *Self-Defense; or, The Art of Boxing*. Scotts Valley, CA: CreateSpace, 2017.

Douglass, Frederick. *My Bondage and My Freedom*. Auckland, NZ: Floating Press, 2009.

Douglass, Frederick. *The Life and Times of Frederick Douglass: From 1817–1882*. London: Christian Age Office, 1882.

Du Bois, W. E. B. "Of Our Spiritual Strivings." In *The Souls of Black Folk*, 1–12. Chicago: McClurg & Co., 1909.

Du Bois, W. E. B. *The Philadelphia Negro: A Social Study*. New York: Schocken Books, 1967.

Eig, Jonathan. *Ali: A Life*. New York: Houghton Mifflin Harcourt, 2017.

Equal Justice Initiative. *Lynching in America: Confronting the Legacy of Racial Terror*. Third edition. Montgomery, AL: Equal Justice Initiative, 2017. https://eji.org/wp-content/uploads/2019/10/lynching-in-america-3d-ed-080219.pdf.

Ezra, Michael. *Muhammad Ali: The Making of an Icon*. Philadelphia: Temple University Press, 2009.

Fanon, Frantz. *Black Skin, White Masks*. Translated by Charles Lam Markmann. London: Pluto Press, 1986.

Faulkner, William. *Absalom, Absalom!* New York: Vintage, 1991.

Ferber, Abby L. "The Construction of Black Masculinity: White Supremacy Now and Then." *Journal of Sport and Social Issues* 31, no. 1 (2007): 11–24.

Ferguson, Roderick A. *Aberrations in Black: Toward a Queer of Color Critique*. Minneapolis: University of Minnesota Press, 2004.

Filene, Peter G. *Him/Her/Self: Gender Identities in Modern America*. Baltimore: Johns Hopkins University Press, 1998.

Fleetwood, Nicole. *On Racial Icons: Blackness and the Public Imagination*. New Brunswick, NJ: Rutgers University Press, 2015.

Foucault, Michel. "Las Meninas." In *The Order of Things: An Archaeology of the Human Sciences*, 3–16. New York: Vintage Books, 1994.

Foucault, Michel. "Nietzsche, Genealogy, History." In *The Foucault Reader*, edited by Paul Rabinow, 76–100. Harmondsworth, UK: Penguin, 1986.

Foucault, Michel. "Nietzsche, la généalogie, l'histoire." In *Hommage a Jean Hyppolite*, edited by Suzanne Bachelard et.al., 145–72. Paris: Presses Universitaires de France, 2001.

Fusco, Coco. "Racial Times, Racial Marks, Racial Metaphors." In *Only Skin Deep*, edited by Coco Fusco and Brian Wallis, 13–50. New York: Abrams, 2003.

Galton, Francis. "Composite Portraits." *Nature* 18 (1878): 97–100.

George P. Rowell and Company's American Newspaper Directory, vol. 1. New York: George P. Rowell and Co., 1869.

Gernsheim, Helmut. *Creative Photography*. New York: Bonanza Books, 1962.

Gilmore, Al-Tony. "Jack Johnson and White Women: The National Impact." *Journal of Negro History* 58, no. 1 (January 1973): 18–38.

Golden, Thelma, ed. *Black Male: Representations of Masculinity in Contemporary American Art*. New York: Whitney Museum of American Art, 1994. Exhibition catalog.

Gordon, Sarah Anne. *Indecent Exposures: Eadweard Muybridge's Animal Locomotion Nudes*. New Haven, CT: Yale University Press, 2015.

Gorn, Elliott J. *The Manly Art: Bare-Knuckle Prizefighting in America*. Ithaca, NY: Cornell University Press, 2010.

Gorn, Elliott J. "The Meaning of Prizefighting." In *The New American Sport History: Recent Approaches and Perspectives*, edited by S. W. Pope, 225–50. Urbana: University of Illinois Press, 1997.

Gorn, Elliott J. "The Wicked World: *The National Police Gazette* and Gilded-Age America." *Media Studies Journal* 6 (Winter 1992): 1–16.

Gorn, Elliott J., and Warren Goldstein. *A Brief History of American Sports*. Urbana: University of Illinois Press, 2004.

Greenwald, Maurine W., and Margo Anderson. *Pittsburgh Surveyed: Social Science and Social Reform in the Early Twentieth Century*. Pittsburgh: University of Pittsburgh Press, 1996.

Hackenschmidt, Georg. *The Way to Live in Health and Physical Fitness*. London: Athletic Publications, 1908.

Haley, Alex. "Alex Haley Interviews Cassius Clay." In *Alex Haley: The Playboy Interviews*, 46–79. New York: Ballantine, 1993. First published in *Playboy*, October 1964.

Hall, Stuart. "New Ethnicities." In *Stuart Hall: Critical Dialogues in Cultural Studies*, edited by David Morley and Kuan-Hsing Chen, 442–51. New York: Routledge, 1996.

Hall, Stuart. *Representation and the Media*. Northampton, MA: Media Education Foundation, 1997. https://www.mediaed.org/transcripts/Stuart-Hall-Representation-and-the-Media-Transcript.pdf.

Hariman, Robert, and John Louis Lucaites. *No Caption Needed: Iconic Photographs, Public Culture, and Liberal Democracy*. Chicago: University of Chicago Press, 2007.

Hartman, Saidiya. *Scenes of Subjection: Terror, Slavery, and Self-Making in Nineteenth Century America*. Oxford: Oxford University Press, 1997.

Hartman, Saidiya. *Wayward Lives, Beautiful Experiments: Intimate Histories of Social Upheaval*. New York: W. W. Norton, 2019.

Hatt, Michael. "Thoughts and Things: Sculpture and the Victorian Nude." In *Exposed: The Victorian Nude*, edited by Alison Smith, 37–49. London: Tate Publishing, 2001. Exhibition catalog.

Haywood, Robert. "George Bellows's *Stag at Sharkey's*: Boxing, Violence, and Male Identity." *Smithsonian Studies in American Art* 2, no. 2 (1988): 2–15.

Hendricks, Gordon, and Thomas Eakins. *The Life and Work of Thomas Eakins*. New York: Grossman, 1974.

Higgins, Hannah B. *The Grid Book*. Cambridge, MA: MIT Press, 2009.

Holliman, Jennie. *American Sports, 1785–1935*. Durham, NC: Seeward Press, 1931.

Homer, William Innes. "A Group of Photographs by Thomas Eakins." *J. Paul Getty Museum Journal* 13 (1985): 151–56.

Homer, William Innes, and Thomas Eakins. *Thomas Eakins: His Life and Art*, 2nd ed. New York: Abbeville Press, 2002.

hooks, bell. "Feminism Inside: Toward a Black Body Politic." In *Black Male Representations of Masculinity in Contemporary American Art*, 127–40. New York: Whitney Museum of American Art, 1994. Exhibition catalog.

hooks, bell. "Reconstructing Black Masculinity." In *Black Looks: Race and Representation*, 87–113. Boston: South End Press, 1992.

hooks, bell. "Representing the Black Male Body." In *Art on My Mind: Visual Politics*, 202–12. New York: New Press, 1995.

Hornibrook, Frederick. *The Lure of the Ring*. London: Pendulum, 1946.

Horsman, Reginald. *Race and Manifest Destiny: The Origins of American Racial Anglo-Saxonism*. Cambridge, MA: Harvard University Press, 1981.

Hyde, Sarah. "The Noble Art: Boxing and Visual Culture in Early Eighteenth-Century Britain." In *Boxer: An Anthology of Writings on Boxing and Visual Culture*, edited by David Chandler, John Gill, Tania Guha, and Gilane Tawadros, 93–98. Cambridge, MA: MIT Press, 1996.

Ingram, Brian S. *Australian World Boxing Champions*. Bloomington, IN: Xlibris, 2012.

Isenberg, Michael. *John L. Sullivan and His America*. Chicago: University of Illinois Press, 1994.

Jacobson, Matthew Frye. *Barbarian Virtues: The United States Encounters Foreign Peoples at Home and Abroad.* New York: Hill and Wang, 2000.

James, Ed. *Life and Battles of Yankee Sullivan.* New York: E. James, 1880.

Johnson, Jack. *Jack Johnson Is a Dandy.* New York: Chelsea House, 1969.

Johnson, James Weldon. *Black Manhattan.* New York: DaCapo Press, 1991.

Jones, Kellie, and Thomas W. Sokolowski. *Interrogating Identity.* New York: Grey Art Gallery and Study Center, New York University, 1991. Exhibition catalog.

Kasson, John F. *Houdini, Tarzan, and the Perfect Man: The White Male Body and the Challenge of Modernity in America.* New York: Hill and Wang, 2001.

Kellogg, John Harvey. *Plain Facts for the Old and Young: Embracing the Natural History and Hygiene of Organic Life.* Burlington, IA: I. F. Signer, 1887.

Keny, James M. "A Brief Garland: A Life of George Bellows." *Timeline: A Publication of the Ohio Historical Society* 9, nos. 5/6 (October–December 1992): 2–39.

Kimmel, Michael. *Manhood in America: A Cultural History,* 4th ed. New York: Oxford University Press, 2018.

Kindred, Dave. *Sound and Fury: Two Powerful Lives, One Fateful Friendship.* New York: Free Press, 2007.

Kurutz, Gary F. "Introduction." In *Isaiah West Taber: A Photographic Legacy 1870–1900,* by Linda Bonnett and Wayne Bonnett, 7–16. Sausalito, CA: Windgate Press, 2004.

Lamprey, J. H. "On a Method of Measuring the Human Form, for the Use of Students in Ethnology." *Journal of the Ethnological Society of London* 1 (1869): 84–85.

Langley, Tom. *The Life of Peter Jackson: Champion of Australia.* Leicester, UK: Vance Harvey, 1974.

Lauvrik, J. Nilsen. "The Winter Exhibition of the National Academy of Design." *International Studio* 33 (February 1908): cxxxix–cxlii.

Lawrie, Paul R. D. *Forging a Laboring Race: The African American Worker in the Progressive Imagination.* New York: New York University Press, 2017.

Lee, Anthony W. *Picturing Chinatown: Art and Orientalism in San Francisco.* Berkeley: University of California Press, 2001.

Leonard, David J. "The Real Color of Money: Controlling Black Bodies in the NBA." *Journal of Sport and Social Issues* 30, no. 2 (May 2006): 158–79.

Leonard, David J., and C. Richard King. "Celebrities, Commodities, and Criminals: African American Athletes and the Racial Politics of Culture." In *Commodified and Criminalized: New Racism and African Americans in Contemporary Sports,* edited by David J. Leonard and C. Richard King, 1–22. Lanham, MD: Rowman and Littlefield, 2011.

Linder, Douglas O. "Lynchings: By Year and Race." Famous Trials, n.d. Accessed August 15, 2023. https://www.famous-trials.com/sheriffshipp/1084-lynchingsyear.

Lindsay, Rachel McBride. "'The Mirror of All Perfection': Jesus and the Strongman in America, 1893–1920." *American Quarterly* 68, no. 1 (March 2016): 23–47.

Lippert, Amy DeFalco. *Consuming Identities: Visual Culture in Nineteenth-Century San Francisco.* Oxford: Oxford University Press, 2018.

Litwack, Leon F. "Hellhounds." In *Without Sanctuary: Lynching Photography in America,* edited by James Allen, Jack Woody, and Arlyn Nathan, 8–37. Santa Fe, NM: Twin Palms, 2000.

Lott, Eric. *Love and Theft: Blackface Minstrelsy and the American Working Class*. New York: Oxford University Press, 2013.

Lutz, Tom. *American Nervousness, 1903: An Anecdotal History*. Ithaca, NY: Cornell University Press, 1991.

Maraniss, David. *Rome 1960: The Olympics that Changed the World*. New York: Simon and Schuster, 2008.

Maxwell, Anne. *Picture Imperfect: Photography and Eugenics 1870–1940*. Eastbourne, UK: Sussex Academic Press, 2008.

Mays, William H. *The Modern Distrust of Insane Asylums: Address Delivered at the Graduating Exercises of the Medical Department of the University of California, November 15, 1887*. London: Forgotten Books, 2018.

Mercer, Kobena. "Endangered Species: Danny Tisdale and Keith Piper." *Artforum* 30 (Summer 1992): 74–77.

Mercer, Kobena. "Looking for Trouble." In *The Lesbian and Gay Studies Reader*, edited by Henry Abelove, Michéle Aina Barale, and David M. Halperin, 350–59. London: Routledge, 1993.

Mercer, Kobena. *Welcome to the Jungle: New Positions in Black Cultural Studies*. London: Routledge, 1994.

Miller, Monica L. *Slaves to Fashion: Black Dandyism and the Styling of Black Diasporic Identity*. Durham, NC: Duke University Press, 2009.

Mirzoeff, Nicholas. "The Shadow and the Substance: Race, Photography, and the Index." In *Only Skin Deep: Changing Visions of the American Self*, edited by Coco Fusco and Brian Wallis, 111–28. New York: Abrams, 2003.

Mitchell, W. J. T. *Picture Theory: Essays on Verbal and Visual Representation*. Chicago: University of Chicago Press, 1994.

Mitchell, W. J. T. "Representation." In *Critical Terms for Literary Study*. 2nd ed., edited by Frank Lentricchia and Thomas McLaughlin, 11–22. Chicago: University of Chicago Press, 1995.

Mitchell, W. J. T. *Seeing through Race*. Cambridge, MA: Harvard University Press, 2012.

Mooney, Katherine C. *Race Horse Men: How Slavery and Freedom Were Made at the Racetrack*. Cambridge, MA: Harvard University Press, 2014.

Moore, Louis. "Fit for Citizenship: Black Sparring Masters, Gymnasium Owners, and the White Body, 1825–1886." *Journal of African American History* 96, no. 4 (2011): 448–73.

Moore, Louis. *I Fight for a Living: Boxing and the Battle for Black Manhood 1880–1915*. Urbana: University of Illinois Press, 2017.

Moreau de St. Méry, Médéric Louis Élie. *Moreau de St. Méry's American Journey, 1793–1798*. Translated and edited by Kenneth and Anna Roberts. Garden City, NY: Doubleday, 1947.

Morgan, Charles H. *The Drawings of George Bellows*. Alhambra, CA: Borden Publishing, 1973.

Morgan, Charles H. "Foreword." In *The Lithographs of George Bellows: A Catalogue Raisonné*, edited by Lauris Mason and Joan Ludman, 9–10. Millwood, NY: KTO Press, 1977.

Morgan, Charles H. *George Bellows: Painter of America*. New York: Reynal and Company, 1965.

Mosley, Anita Ventura. "Introduction to the Dover Edition." In *Muybridge's Complete Human and Animal Locomotion*, xii–xxii. New York: Dover Publications, 1979.

Mullins, Greg. "Nudes, Prudes, and Pigmies: The Desirability of Disavowal in 'Physical Culture.'" *Discourse* 15, no. 1 (1992): 27–48.

Muñoz, José Esteban. *Disidentification: Queers of Color and the Performance of Politics*. Minneapolis: University of Minnesota Press, 1999.

Muybridge, Eadweard. *Animal Locomotion. An Electro-Photographic Investigation of Consecutive Phases of Animal Movements 1872–1885*. Philadelphia: University of Pennsylvania, 1887.

Nead, Lynda. 2011. "Stilling the Punch: Boxing, Violence and the Photographic Image." *Journal of Visual Culture* 10, no. 3 (2011): 305–23.

Nelson, Charmaine A. *The Color of Stone: Sculpting the Black Female Subject in Nineteenth-Century America*. Minneapolis: University of Minnesota Press, 2007.

Nochlin, Linda. "Issues of Gender in Cassatt and Eakins." In *Nineteenth Century Art: A Critical History*, edited by Stephen Eisenman, 349–67. New York: Thames and Hudson, 2007.

Oakley, George. *Catalogue of an Exhibition of Original Lithographs by George Bellows, N.A.* Chicago: Albert Roullier Art Galleries, 1919.

Oates, Joyce Carol. *On Boxing*. Hopewell, NJ: Ecco Press, 1994.

Obi, T. J. Desch. "Black Terror: Bill Richmond's Revolutionary Boxing." *Journal of Sport History* 36, no. 1 (Spring 2009): 99–114.

O'Mahony, Mike. "The Art and Artifice of Early Sports Photography." *Sport in Society: Cultures, Commerce, Media, Politics* 22, no. 5 (2019): 785–802.

O'Mahony, Mike. *Photography and Sport*. London: Reaktion Books, 2018.

Omi, Michael, and Howard Winant. *Racial Formation in the United States: From the 1960s to the 1990s*. London: Routledge, 1994.

Orcutt, Kimberly. *Pictures and Posterity: American Art at Philadelphia's 1876 Centennial Exhibition*. University Park: Penn State University Press, 2017.

Park, Roberta J. "Contesting the Norm: Women and Professional Sports in Late Nineteenth-Century America." *International Journal of the History of Sport* 29, no. 5 (2012): 730–49.

Petersen, Bob (Robert Charles). *Gentleman Bruiser: A Life of the Boxer Peter Jackson 1860–1901*. Sydney: Croydon Publishing Company, 2005.

Petersen, Bob (Robert Charles). *Peter Jackson: A Biography of the Australian Heavyweight Champion, 1860–1901*. Jefferson, NC: McFarland and Company, 2011.

Peterson, Bob (Robert Charles). "Peter Jackson: Heavyweight Champion of Australia." In *The First Black Boxing Champions: Essays on Fighters of the 1880s to the 1920s*, edited by Colleen Aycock and Mark Scott, 32–47. Jefferson, NC: McFarland and Company, 2011.

Pittenger, Mark. "A World of Difference: Constructing the 'Underclass' in Progressive America," *American Quarterly* 49, no. 1 (March 1997): 26–65.

Pointon, Marcia. "Pugilism, Painters and National Identity in Early Nineteenth-Century England." In *Boxer: An Anthology of Writings on Boxing and Visual Culture*, edited by David Chandler, John Gill, Tania Guha, and Gilane Tawadros, 35–42. Cambridge, MA: MIT Press, 1996.

Potts, Alex. "Winckelmann, Johann Joachim." Grove Art Online, 2003. https://doi.org
/10.1093/gao/9781884446054.article.T091800.

Powell, Richard J. "Sartor Africanus." In *Dandies: Fashion and Finesse in Art and Culture*,
edited by Susan Fillin-Yeh, 217–42. New York: New York University Press, 2001.

Prodger, Phillip. *Time Stands Still: Muybridge and the Instantaneous Photography Movement*. Oxford: Oxford University Press, 2003.

Raiford, Leigh. *Imprisoned in a Luminous Glare: Photography and the African American
Freedom Struggle*. Chapel Hill: University of North Carolina Press, 2011.

Reel, Guy. *The National Police Gazette and the Making of the Modern American Man,
1879–1906*. New York: Palgrave Macmillan, 2006.

Reid, Heather. "Athletic Beauty in Classical Greece: A Philosophical View." *Journal of the
Philosophy of Sport* 39, no. 2 (2012): 281–97.

Reiss, Steven A. "Sport and the Redefinition of American Middle-Class Masculinity." In
The New American Sport History: Recent Approaches and Perspectives, edited by S. W.
Pope, 173–97. Urbana: University of Illinois Press, 1997.

Remnick, David. *King of the World: Muhammad Ali and the Rise of an American Hero*.
New York: Vintage Books, 1998.

Riordan, William L. *Plunkitt of Tammany Hall: Very Plain Talks on Very Practical Politics*. New York: Knopf, 1948.

Roberts, Randy. *Joe Louis: Hard Times Man*. New Haven, CT: Yale University Press, 2010.

Roberts, Randy. *Papa Jack: Jack Johnson and the Era of White Hopes*. New York: Free
Press, 1983.

Robinson, Cedric J. *Black Marxism: The Making of the Black Radical Tradition*, 3rd ed.
Chapel Hill: University of North Carolina Press, 2020.

Roediger, David R. *The Wages of Whiteness: Race and the Making of the American Working Class*. London: Verso, 2007.

Roediger, David R. *Working Toward Whiteness: How America's Immigrants Became
White—The Strange Journey from Ellis Island to the Suburbs*, rev. ed. New York: Basic
Books, 2018.

Roosevelt, Theodore. "The American Boy." In *The Strenuous Life and Other Essays*,
147–58. New York: Scribner, 1956.

Roosevelt, Theodore. "The Strenuous Life." In *The Strenuous Life: Essays and Addresses
by Theodore Roosevelt*, 1–21. New York: Century, 1902.

Rotundo, E. Anthony. *American Manhood: Transformations of Masculinity from the Revolution to the Modern Era*. New York: Basic Books, 1993.

Runstedtler, Theresa. *Jack Johnson, Rebel Sojourner: Boxing in the Shadow of the Global
Color Line*. Berkeley: University of California Press, 2012.

Sandow, Eugen. *Sandow's System of Physical Training*. London: Gale and Polden, 1894.

Sargent, Dudley A. "Report of Dr. D. A. Sargent's Examination," In *The Life and Reminisces of a Nineteenth Century Gladiator*, 283–94. Boston: Alfred Mudge & Son, 1892.

Schreiber, Rachel. "George Bellows's Boxers in Print." *Journal of Modern Periodical Studies* 1, no.2 (2010): 159–81.

Seidel, Linda. "'Jan van Eyck's Arnolfini Portrait': Business as Usual?" *Critical Inquiry* 16,
no. 1 (Autumn, 1989): 54–86.

Sekula, Allan. "The Body and the Archive." *October* 39 (Winter 1986): 3–64.

Shaw, Gwendolyn DuBois. "The Decolonization of John Sloan." *Panorama* 7, no. 2 (Fall 2021). https://journalpanorama.org/article/does-colonial-america-end/decolonization -of-john-sloan/.

Slayton, Robert A. *Beauty in the City: The Ashcan School.* Albany: State University of New York Press, 2017.

Smalls, James. "African-American Self Portraiture." *Third Text* 15, no. 54 (Spring 2001): 47–62.

Smalls, James. *The Homoerotic Photography of Carl Van Vechten: Public Face, Private Thoughts.* Philadelphia: Temple University Press, 2006.

Smith, Cherise. "White on Black: Power Relations in F. Holland Day's *Ebony and Ivory.*" *Exposure* 42, no. 1 (Spring 2009): 33–42.

Smith, Shawn Michelle. *American Archives: Gender, Race, and Class in Visual Culture.* Princeton, NJ: Princeton University Press, 2000.

Smith, Shawn Michelle. *At the Edge of Sight: Photography and the Unseen.* Durham, NC: Duke University Press, 2013.

Smith, Shawn Michelle. *Photography on the Color Line: W. E. B. Du Bois, Race, and Visual Culture.* Durham, NC: Duke University Press, 2004.

Solnit, Rebecca. *River of Shadows: Eadweard Muybridge and the Technological Wild West.* New York: Penguin, 2004.

Sontag, Susan. *On Photography.* New York: Farrar, Straus and Giroux, 1977.

Staples, Robert. *Black Masculinity: The Black Male's Role in American Society.* San Francisco: Black Scholar Press, 1982.

Stephens, Mitchell. *A History of News: From the Drum to the Satellite.* New York: Viking, 1988.

Stoddart, Brian. "Sport, Cultural Imperialism, and Colonial Response in the British Empire." *Comparative Studies in Society and History* 30, no. 4 (October 1988): 649–73.

Sullivan, James E. "Boxing." *Spalding's Athletic Library* 1, no. 4 (1893): 3–33.

Taine, Hippolyte. *Notes on England.* Translated by W. F. Rae. London: W. Isbister and Co., 1872.

Trachtenberg, Alan. *The Incorporation of America: Culture and Society in the Gilded Age.* New York: Hill and Wang, 2007.

Walker, Hamza. "Renigged." In *Freestyle*, edited by Hamza Walker, Thelma Golden, Christine Y Kim, and Franklin Sirmans, 16–17. New York: Studio Museum in Harlem, 2001. Exhibition catalog.

Walter, Marjorie A. "Fine Art and the Sweet Science: On Thomas Eakins, His Boxing Paintings, and Turn-of-the-Century Philadelphia." PhD diss., University of California, Berkeley, 2008.

Ward, Geoffrey C. *Unforgivable Blackness: The Rise and Fall of Jack Johnson.* New York: Knopf, 2005.

White, Kevin. *The First Sexual Revolution: The Emergence of Male Heterosexuality in Modern America.* New York: New York University Press, 1993.

Wiggins, David K. "Good Times on the Old Plantation: Popular Recreations of the Black Slave in the Antebellum South, 1810–1860." *Journal of Sport History* 4, no. 3 (Fall 1997): 260–84.

Williams, Lyneise. "The Glamorous One-Two Punch: Visualizing Celebrity, Masculinity, and Boxer Alfonso Teofilo Brown in Early-Twentieth-Century Paris." In *Migrating the Black Body: The African Diaspora and Visual Culture*, edited by Leigh Raiford and Heike Raphael-Hernandez, 116–33. Seattle: University of Washington Press, 2017.

Willis, Deborah. *Picturing Us: African American Identity in Photography*. New York: New Press, 1996.

Winckelmann, Johann Joachim. *History of the Art of Antiquity*. Translated by Harry Francis Mallgrave. Los Angeles: Getty Publications, 2006.

Wu, Cheng-Tsu. *"Chink!": A Documentary History of Anti-Chinese Prejudice in America*. Cleveland: World Publishing Company, 1972.

Wyke, Maria. "Herculean Muscle! The Classicizing Rhetoric of Bodybuilding." *Arion: A Journal of Humanities and the Classics* 4, no. 3 (Winter 1997): 51–79.

Young, Harvey. *Embodying Black Experience: Stillness, Critical Memory, and the Black Body*. Ann Arbor: University of Michigan Press, 2010.

Zirin, Dave. *A People's History of Sports in the United States: 250 Years of Politics, Protest, People, and Play*. New York: New Press, 2009.

Zurier, Rebecca. *Picturing the City: Urban Vision and the Ashcan School*. Berkeley: University of California Press, 2006.

Index

championship of Australia, 143–44

Chase, William Merritt, 195

Chicago Daily Inter-Ocean, 25

Chicago Daily News, 207

"Chicken versus the Championship" (cartoon), 26, *27*, 28

Chinese Male (Lamprey), 92, *93*, 94

Chow, Broderick D. V., 169

Choynski, Joe, 149, 187, 207, *208*, 209, *210*, 211, 259n67

The Cigarette (Bellows), 217

Cincinnati Enquirer, 58, 166

Civil Rights movement, gay liberation movement and, 227

Clark, Susan F., 180–81

class politics: boxing and, 20–21, 108, 203; British immigration policies and, 90–91; capitalism and, 19–20; early boxing and, 39–40; prize-fighting and, 46–47; realist painting and, 197, 199–200

Cleaver, Eldridge, 227

Cleopatra (Story sculpture), 166

Cliff Dwellers (Bellows), 184

Club Night (Bellows), 185, 197, 202, 205, 215, *plate 5*

Coburn, Joe, 46

Collier's (magazine), 202

colonialism: anthropological photography and, 94–97; anti-immigrant politics and, 49; Black boxers and legacy of, 152; boxing and, 39; mimicry as tool of, 69; racism and, 129–30

The Color of Stone (Nelson), 167

commemorative boxing medals, 53

Commercial Gazette, 151

Connelly, Pierce Francis, 166

convicts, boxers as, 43

Cook, Townsend, 112–13, 251n94

Cooper, Howard, 251n94

Corbett, David Peters, 207, 216–17

Corbett, James John (Gentleman Jack), 17, 64, 149, 254n57, 255n72; theater career of, 257n108

Cornell, Fred, 206

Costantino, Jesús, 102

Cotter, Holland, 229

Counted Out, No. 2 (Bellows), 217

Crane, Stephen, 203

Crania Aegyptiaca (Morton), 96

Crania Americana (Morton), 96

CRG Gallery, 229–30

Cribb, Tom, 42, *plate 1*

critical culture, popular culture and, 3–4

cultural imagination, Blackness in, 9

Currier & Ives, 53, 150; boxing prints by, 34

"Cutting a Watermelon" (Minor), 191, *192*

Daguerre, Louis-Jacques-Mandé, 88

Daley, Arthur, 6

Daly, Daisy, 60

Dana, Charles A., 26

dancing jab, Ali's use of, 5

The Dancing Lesson (Eakins), 107

Danish West Indies, 141

Davey, Frank, 158, 176, 255n64

Davies, Parson, 180–81

Davis, Amira Rose, 4

Day, F. Holland, 74–75, 111, 120, *122*, 123, *124–25*, 126, *127*, 128, 251n110

Dead Bird (Australian sporting newspaper), 142, 176, *178*, 256nn92–93

death, boxing and, 108–9

The Death of Cleopatra (Lewis), 166–67

Delaroche, Paul, 88–89

Dempsey, Jack ("Nonpareil"), 149

Dempsey and Firpo (Bellows), 202

desire: Ali as object of, 226; Jackson's photographs and aesthetics of, 176–77, 179–80; photography and, 74

Detaille, Édouard, 89

Diamond, Frederick Egerton, 142–43

difference, photography as demarcation of, 90–92, 94–97, 101–3

Discobolus of Myron, 161, *165*, 166, 168, 231–32

Dixon, George, 26, 152, 211, 260n72

Doberty, Hughey, 46

Doezema, Marianne, 9, 196

domestic space, Black figures in, 243n24

Donahue, Clipper, 75

Donaldson, John, 58

Donnelly, Ned, 142

Donovan, Mike, 58

Douglas, John (Marquess of Queensberry), 243n29

Douglass, Frederick, 40, 110, 152, 241n81

Duane, Danny, 258n17

Du Bois, W. E. B., 11

Dudley Street Opera House, 58

Swarzas, George, 141
Sydney Morning Herald, 142
Symonds, John Addington, 234

Taber, Isaiah West, 154–56, 158
Taber Gallery, 154, 176
tableaux vivant, male body in, 177, 256n97
Tacoma Times, 193
Taine, Hippolyte, 151
Tarzan, 22
Terme Boxer (Boxer at Rest), 231–32
Terrell, Ernie, 239n24
"Texas Watermelon Pickaninny Makes Big
    Dents" (*Los Angeles Times*), 189
Thetis and Achilles (Connelly), 166
Thiesson, E., 96
Time (magazine), xii
Tissandier, Gaston, 89
trading cards, 207
Trump, Donald, xii
Turf, Field, and Farm, 55
Twisting Somersault (Muybridge), *78–79*

UEFA European Football Championship, x
Uncle Tom, Jackson's theatrical portrayal of,
    180–81
Uncle Tom's Cabin (Stowe), 132
"United Americans of the State of New York"
    (lithograph), 47, *48*, 49
United Kingdom, boxing in, 240n43
United States: early boxing in, 38–47; immigra-
    tion policies in, 90–91; prizefighting in, 52–53
United States Hotel (Sydney, Australia), Jackson
    as manager of, 143–44
Untimely Meditations (Nietzsche), 75

Vanity Fair, boxing coverage in, 34
veil of racism, Du Bois's concept of, 11
Vietnam War protests, 226
violence: anti-Black violence, 236; Blackness and,
    74, 234–35; boxing and, 21–22, 31; in early
    prizefighting, 39, 45–46; images of non-white
    bodies and, 199; race and representation and,
    108–17
visual media: of Black sexuality, 117, 120, *121, 122,
    123, 124–25*, 126, *127*, 128; body measurement
    craze and, 160–61, 165, 167, 169; boxing cover-

age and, 34, 51, 53–57, 65–70; fetishization of
Black men in, 111–12; sports and athletic culture and growth of, 53, 145, 149–50; technical
innovations in, 64–65; white masculinity and
Blackness in, 28–29. *See also* media; paintings;
photography; print media
Vogue (magazine), x–xi
voyeurism, in media coverage of boxing, 106–8

Wagner, Gorgeous George, 239n16
Walcott, Joe, 17, 211, 239n19, 260n72
Walker, Hamza, 8–9, 239n29
Walker Art Center, 228
Walter, Marjorie, 105, 107
Ward, Geoffrey C., 16, 151
Warren, Arthur J. R., 235
Washington, George, 47, 243n37
Waterhouse, Bill, 141
Waterhouse, Tom, 141
Waterhouse Hall (Australia), 141
Watkins, Carleton, 154–55
The Way to Live in Health and Physical Fitness
    (Hackenschmidt), 23
Wayward Lives, Beautiful Experiments (Hart-
    man), 246n8
Wells, Ida B., 241n81
White, Derrick E., 4
white boxers: heroic image of, 49–50, 64;
    nineteenth-century predominance of, 70
The White Hope (Bellows), 217
white masculinity: body as reflection of, 25–26,
    105–8, 232, 246n64; boxing and, 33–34, 36,
    64–65; class politics and, 19–20; sports cul-
    ture and, 102; visual media influence on, 66,
    69–70, 149–50
whiteness and white supremacy: athletic images
    as reinforcement of, 66, 69–70; in Bellows's
    paintings, 199–200; Black boxers as threat
    to, 189–92; Black masculinity as threat to,
    10–11, 110–17, 214; boxing and, 14, 36, 64;
    immigration fears and, 49–50; inclusion and
    exclusion and, 37; integrated boxing matches
    as challenge to, 190, 211; Johnson as threat to,
    207, *208*, 209, *210*, 211, *212–13*, 214, 220–21;
    masculinity and, 25–26; photographic rein-
    forcement of, 86; prizefighting and power of,
    47–53
Wiggins, David, 40